# RICHARD HEATH

# Charles V
# Duty and Dynasty

*The Emperor and his Changing World 1500-1558*

Charles V: Duty and Dynasty

First published in 2018 by Milford Publishing

Copyright © Richard Heath 2018

This book is sold subject to the condition that no part of it may be reproduced, stored in a retrieval system or transmitted in any form or by any means without the author's prior consent nor be circulated in any form of binding or cover other than that in which it is published and without a similar condition being imposed on the subsequent purchaser.

The moral right of the author has been asserted.

See **www.emperorcharlesv.com**
for additional information, photographs and ideas about places to visit connected to Charles V.

Charles V: Duty and Dynasty

*To Deborah, for all her help and encouragement without which this book would never have been written.*

*Also to Rachel, David, Isabelle and Sophia, with love*

*Photographs and design by Deborah Heath.*

Charles V: Duty and Dynasty

Charles V: Duty and Dynasty

# CONTENTS

Introduction     1

## Part One – Youthful Endeavours

1. 'You, fortunate Austria, marry' – Birth-right     7
2. 'More in his head than appears on his face' – Education     20
3. Duke of Burgundy – Apprenticeship     32
4. 'Managed by M. de Chièvres' – King in Spain     46
5. 'There is nothing in this world we want more' – Emperor     58

## Part Two – Discovering the Realities of Power

6. 'Scandal and Disturbance' – Revolt in Spain     73
7. 'My Body and Soul' – Reformation     84
8. 'He wants Milan and so do I' – Conflict with France     97
9. 'Peace cannot be had without the enemy's consent' – Pavia and Madrid     107
10. 'Bedrock' – Settling Spain     117
11. 'He should look to his honour' – Renewed War with France     131

## Part Three – Chasing Ambitions

12. 'I have come where I have long desired to be' Coronation     145
13. 'Make the best of things' – Florence, Machiavelli and Warfare     156
14. 'Good Viceroys' – Meeting his Family     167
15. 'Most important is the Religious Question' - Seeking Unity     179
16. 'Trouble, Danger and Expense' - 16$^{th}$ century finances     189

17. 'Two Suns in the Sky'- The Ottoman Menace    198
18. 'Great Deeds' – The Struggle for the
    Mediterranean                               207

## Part Four – Confronting Challenges

19. 'Anguish and Sorrow' – Conflict and
    Family Death                                221
20. 'We also come from Ghent' – Imposing
    his Authority                               231
21. 'We must thank God for all – Failure and
    Defeat                                      240
22. 'You will be troubled enough for money' –
    Family and Finances                         250
23. 'The Greed of some of our subjects' –
    Faith and Bullion                           264
24. 'The Netherlands were never in so much
    Danger – Final Conflict with Francis        274

## Part Five – Highs and Lows – Imperial and Dynastic

25. 'Arrogance and Obstinacy' – Muhlberg      289
26. 'Unfraternal and false' – The future of the
    Dynasty                                     301
27. 'No cage big enough' – Innsbruck and Metz  311
28. 'I can no longer participate' – Relinquishing
    Power                                       319

## Part Six – Retreat from the World Stage

29. 'We shall not be asked what we have read but
    what we have done' – Reflections            333
30. 'No other pass shall I cross' – Final Rest  348

| | |
|---|---|
| Principal Characters | 358 |
| Family Tree | 363 |
| Chronology | 364 |
| Acknowledgements | 370 |
| References | 371 |
| Bibliography | 382 |
| Index | 389 |

Charles V: Duty and Dynasty

## Introduction

On his arrival in Bologna for his coronation as Holy Roman Emperor by Pope Clement VII, Charles declared: 'I have come where I have long desired to be ... that we may take measures together to relieve the needs of afflicted Christendom'. Less than three years earlier troops acting in his name had brutally sacked Rome and forced Clement to pay a ransom for his freedom. This is one of many apparent inconsistences in the life of Emperor Charles V, the major figure in Europe during the first half of the 16th century. He ruled by right, as opposed to conquest, more lands than anyone since the days of the Roman Empire. He was a key figure at the time of the Reformation and Renaissance, in the dynastic conflict between Habsburg and Valois, in the conquest of the Americas, and in efforts to hold back Ottoman expansion from the east. He met with many whose names resound through history – Titian, Erasmus, Luther, de' Medici popes, Henry VIII, the conquistadores Cortes and Pizarro. Yet against such men Charles remains a rather opaque figure, difficult to get into focus in a world that was undergoing profound changes.

Charles has rarely received the attention that is lavished upon his contemporaries Henry VIII and Francis I, with their starring role in the histories of England and France (just as they would have wished). This is because Charles' influence was so widespread that it has been difficult for any one nation to take him to their hearts. Nevertheless, as political, social, economic, religious, scientific and technological changes were underway at an ever increasing pace – to the great excitement of some and to the horror of others – his decisions were of fundamental importance to the lives of his subjects in Spain, Germany, the Low Countries, Italy, and the Americas.

## Charles V: Duty and Dynasty

He is frequently remembered only for his unprepossessing lower jaw, as being a religious bigot who aimed to eradicate Protestantism, for his lack of imagination and originality, and (in England) as the father of Philip II who sent the Armada. This does not do justice to a man of such responsibilities, who inherited his various lands and was elected Holy Roman Emperor before the age of twenty and then ruled them for almost forty years. His devotion to duty is unquestionable. He was the most travelled monarch of his time, as he reminisced in his abdication speech. He had journeyed to Germany nine times, to Spain six, to Italy seven, to the Low Countries ten, four times to France, to England twice and to Africa twice. He had sailed on the Atlantic Ocean three times and on the Mediterranean eight times. After his marriage to Isabella of Portugal in 1526 and the birth of an heir, Philip, the following year, he became directly involved in military campaigns, seeking 'honour and reputation'.

Hard work alone, though, could not overcome the difficulties that confronted him. Charles' life was in many ways a mass of contradictions, ones that still have relevance in today's world. He was brought up with the values of dynasty, chivalry and duty, held in high esteem at the Burgundian court of his youth. His instincts were essentially conservative - to preserve his inheritance and existing institutions - yet he lived at a time when old social structures and long held beliefs were under threat as never before. As the 'superpower' of his age the very extent of his territories aroused fear and jealousy. He was accused of seeking to dominate Europe whereas in his own mind he only wished for universal peace in Christendom and to pass on his lands to his successors. He faced continual hostility from France, a very uneasy relationship with the papacy, and uncertain loyalty from the princes in Germany, while Sultan Suleiman would refer to him only as 'king of Spain'. Charles wished for Christian unity but his reign saw the rapid growth of religious dissent. His faith was deep but he was accused of hypocritically using religion as a cover for extending his own power.

He ruled a multitude of lands just as the wish for more local or national sovereignty was developing.

His frequent travels dismayed many of his subjects and put considerable pressures on his wife, Isabella. After 1515 it has been estimated that he spent one day in every four travelling. Even when in Spain or the Low Countries his court shifted constantly between various cities. He had capable family members who acted as regents. He was skilled at identifying the strengths and weaknesses of his advisors and had the ability to inspire loyalty in them. But most of his territories were unhappy about the time that he spent elsewhere. They wanted their king to be present. In his absence decisions might be delayed, appointments not made, grievances not deal with, rewards not given. On occasions this could lead to rebellion, as in Spain in the early 1520s and in Ghent, the city of his birth, in the late 1530s.

There are many different interpretations of Charles' life and policies. Each nation, and often each period of time, has its own perspective of this ruler whose lands were so widespread and problems so diverse. Whether he was seen as a lover of peace or an aggressor, religious bigot or seeker of reconciliation, national hero or destroyer of nations' hopes, major player or marginal figure, historians have expressed a wide range of opinions about his character and his reign. 'As a ruler Charles was a figure with the power to decide the fate of nations. As a historical figure, however, he is subject to their whim'.[*] A study of the reign of Charles V provides an insight into the world of 16th century Europe and has the essential quality which brings history alive – an individual that we can relate to. In this case it was someone who, by chance of birth and the incidental death of others, had immense power but who also revealed a characteristic range of human virtues and frailties. Few, if any, rulers had received such a rich inheritance, but the problems that he faced were immense. How he dealt with them, and with what success, is the subject of this book.

---

[*] C. Scott-Dixon and M. Fuchs: 2005

Charles V: Duty and Dynasty

# Part One
# Youthful Endeavours
# 1500-1520

The courtyard of Margaret of Austria's palace in Mechelen (Malines) where Charles spent much of his youth.

Charles V: Duty and Dynasty

# 1
# 'You, fortunate Austria, marry' – Birth-right

Early in the new century, on the night of 24$^{th}$ / 25$^{th}$ February 1500, Juana, known to history as Juana 'the mad', gave birth to her first son. The boy's father, Duke Philip, was naturally delighted. The celebrations befitted the arrival of a future ruler of Burgundy. Two weeks later the citizens of Ghent witnessed a procession the like of which few would see again. A raised wooden walkway had been constructed, stretching some seven hundred metres from the Prinsenhof palace to St John's church. It was decorated with numerous colourful gateways, representing Justice, Peace, and Wisdom, covered with coats of arms, and lit by thousands of torches. Along it walked the leaders of the various guilds, the town magistrates, members of the court and the Council of Flanders, knights of the Order of the Golden Fleece, and lastly relatives of the infant[1]. Foremost were Margaret of Austria, the child's aunt, and Margaret of York, the surviving wife of his great-grandfather, Charles the Bold of Burgundy, after whom the boy was to be named. As the senior female member of the family Margaret of York carried the child to the font, just as she had in Bruges at Philip's own baptism back in 1478.

This was no ordinary family baptism. The marriage of Philip and Juana had brought together many of Europe's ruling families and the infant Charles' birth was a culmination of the policy of 'matrimonial imperialism'[2] pursued by his grandfathers. Charles' father, Philip, was the son of Emperor Maximilian I, whose Habsburg family held considerable lands in southern Germany and Austria as well as being elected to the Imperial throne since 1438. Maximilian had married Mary of Burgundy, the daughter of Archduke Charles the Bold. That marriage had joined the families of Habsburg with the junior (Burgundian) branch of the Valois.

Through his father the young Charles was heir to large and diverse territories.

His mother, Juana, was the third child of Ferdinand of Aragon and Isabella of Castile. These rulers had completed the 'Reconquista', driving the last Muslim rulers (based in Granada) out of Spain in 1492, thus earning the epithet 'the Catholic Monarchs' from Pope Alexander VI[*], though they had not united their two kingdoms in any other than a personal sense. Juana was soon to be heir to all the kingdoms of Spain and their lands overseas, the Balearics, Sardinia, Sicily, Naples and growing lands in the New World. Her only brother, Juan, had died childless only six months after his wedding to Charles' aunt, Margaret, in 1497, and was followed to the grave by her eldest sister, Isabella, in 1498. The subsequent death of Isabella's young son, Miguel, left Juana with this vast inheritance.

That Charles might inherit all of these territories was the unintended result of various marriages, births and deaths in the years before or shortly after his own birth. 'Let others wage wars, (but) you fortunate Austria, marry'. It is easy to see that what Matthias Corvinus, King of Hungary, wrote about the Habsburgs in the late fifteenth century was still accurate in the early sixteenth century. But little was certain at a time of high infant mortality, ruthless political manoeuvring and ever changing alliances. Given that both his parents were in their early twenties it could well be several decades before Charles would come into his birth-right. The wheel of fortune could quite possibly turn, and turn again, before then.

Most of the Low Countries had come under the control of the Dukes of Burgundy by the late 14th century. They ruled numerous counties, provinces and dukedoms in what is now the Netherlands, Belgium and Luxembourg, as well as Burgundy and Franche Comte. These were prosperous areas with fertile agricultural land, and their cities had become wealthy through the cloth industry and extensive

---

[*] The Spaniard, Rodrigo Borgia.

trading links, with the Baltic, across the Channel and via the Atlantic to Spain and the Mediterranean. A greater proportion of the population lived in cities, such as Ghent, Bruges and Antwerp, than anywhere else in Europe, and these citizens jealously guarded their rights and privileges.

Though born in Ghent, Charles spent much of his childhood in Mechelen (or Malines, its French name that was commonly used at the time) located between Brussels and Antwerp. The city had been part of the dower settlement of Margaret of York (1446-1503), the younger sister of both Edward IV and Richard III of England, when she married Archduke Charles (known as 'the Bold' or more accurately 'the Rash') of Burgundy in 1468. Margaret was known for her energy, intelligence and piety, as well as her looks. She and Charles had no children, though Margaret became close to her step daughter, Mary, only eleven years her junior. Mary had spent some of her early years in Ghent at Hof Ten Waele, later to be renamed 'Prinsenhof', the ducal residence outside the forbidding Gravensteen[*]. Known as Mary the Rich, the most sought after heiress in Europe, she inherited the Burgundian lands on the death of her father, Duke Charles. He had aimed to create a more unified state, administratively and geographically, particularly seeking to link the Low Counties with Burgundy and the Franche Comte through control of Lorraine. This was to cost him his life in January 1477 at the battle of Nancy when his army was defeated by René II of Lorraine assisted by Swiss mercenaries. With his death, Lorraine and Gelderland in the north of the Low Countries were lost and Burgundy itself reverted to French control.

At the time there was widespread anger in the cities of the Low Countries at the waste of men and money caused by the wars of Charles the Rash, and his death was seen as an opportunity to redress their grievances and restore privileges undermined over the previous fifty years. A virtual prisoner in Ghent, his daughter and heir Mary was forced to sign the Great Privilege, which re-

---

[*] Its location now only revealed by a street-name.

established the rights of the cities of Flanders, Brabant, Hainault and Holland. She promised to rule with advice from the estates (delegates of the provinces and cities), and submit matters of war and peace and the issue of her marriage to them. The estates could meet whenever they saw fit to do so, and the powers of the central court at Malines over regional courts were removed. Ducal officials were executed, though a threatened French invasion encouraged the provinces to agree to Mary's marriage to Maximilian, son of Frederick, the Holy Roman Emperor, which was celebrated in Ghent in August 1477.

The couple had three children, Philip (b. 1478), Margaret (b. 1480) (later known as Margaret of Austria or the Duchess of Savoy), and Francis (who died in infancy). The fragile political stability was shattered by Mary's untimely death in Bruges after an accident while out hunting with falcons in the marshes of Wijnendaele in March 1482[3]. The cities objected to the regency of Maximilian, who as an outsider was regarded as a threat to their liberties. The children, the heir, Philip, aged four, and his sister Margaret, aged two, were held in Ghent and the city refused to release them to their father. Philip remained their pawn until November 1484, when Maximilian's position had strengthened and he was able to be reunited with his son. Even then there were riots as Maximilian's troops entered the city and a number of executions took place, even though Maximilian generally honoured the amnesty he had granted the city on the request of Margaret of York[4]. Maximilian's rule was plagued by ongoing problems especially with Ghent, Bruges (where he was held captive for 3 months early in 1488) and Ypres. The situation only really improved with the signing of the Treaty of Cadzand (1492) which to some extent nullified the Great Privilege of 1477, the Treaty of Senlis (1493) which ended French interference, and Philip's coming of age in 1494. Young Duke Philip, Burgundian by birth, was more acceptable to the citizens.

Margaret of York would have had a major influence in the upbringing of her step grand-daughter, Philip's sister Margaret, if not for the Treaty of Arras in 1482 between Maximilian and Louis

XI of France. This arranged for the future marriage of Margaret to Louis' son and heir, Charles, who later became Charles VIII. As a result the three year old Margaret went to live in France, where she remained for ten years, educated at the French court. In 1491, however, Charles repudiated this betrothal and instead married the fourteen year old Anne of Brittany (who had already married Maximilian by proxy the previous year) in order to gain Brittany for the French crown. Anne was an unwilling bride; it is said that she brought two beds to her wedding as a sign that she was unwilling to share her own with Charles. The marriage alienated both Maximilian and his daughter Margaret and increased the tensions that already existed between the French monarchy and the Habsburgs. Margaret was eventually returned to the Low Countries after the Treaty of Senlis and went to live with her step grandmother in Malines.

The older Margaret had selected Malines for her court for a number of reasons. It was the largest of the dower towns; her husband Charles had made it the judicial centre of the Low Countries; it was regarded as more loyal to the ruling family than Ghent or Bruges; it was well protected with walls and moats; it was relatively prosperous, and regarded as healthier than many other towns because it had more paved streets since the rebuilding after a major fire in the 14th century. Malines benefitted from her presence, through the trading privileges granted by England (Margaret's royal brothers) and by her husband's successors as rulers of the Low Countries, as well as from the visits of high ranking noblemen and foreign ambassadors.

She purchased a large property in what is now Keizerstraat, bought up adjoining houses, organised rebuilding and added extensions. Behind fine reception rooms and a council chamber (now a theatre) there were gardens, a tennis court, and baths.[5] Over the next twenty-five years Margaret of York established an impressive library of manuscripts, and collected paintings, tapestries and plate. She is known to have had a meeting (probably in Bruges) with William Caxton before he returned to England to establish the first printing press there. Margaret furthered the pattern of the Burgundian court in the Low Countries – learned, cultured, patron to some of the best artists, with a keen interest in the new ideas of the time. It was also at this time a centre of Yorkist plots and intrigue against Henry Tudor (Henry VII) who had ousted Margaret's brother, Richard III, from the throne of England.

After her return from France the young Margaret was not to remain in the Low Countries for long. She was still an important pawn in the dynastic considerations of her father, Maximilian, who had become Holy Roman Emperor on the death of his father in 1493. In 1496 he arranged a double marriage that would closely link his family with that of the Spanish monarchs. Margaret would marry Juan, Prince of Asturias, son and heir to Ferdinand and Isabella of Spain, while her brother Philip, now Duke of Burgundy, would wed Juana, Juan's sister. Since all the participants were of age things moved swiftly. Juana arrived in the Low Countries with a fleet of 130 ships in 1496. Having been married by proxy in November 1496, Margaret, now aged 17, travelled back to Spain with the returning fleet, arriving in March 1497. En route, fearing for her life in a violent storm, Margaret wrote her own epitaph: 'Here lies Margot, the willing bride, Twice married – but a virgin when she died'. It is said that Margaret and Juan, only two years her senior, fell for one another and had a very active love life, which some blamed for his premature death, only seven months later. This explanation was certainly recounted by Charles to his son Philip as a cautionary tale over 40 years later. Margaret was pregnant but the baby girl was stillborn in December 1497. She remained in Spain until 1499, eventually leaving Granada in September, arriving back in the Low Countries in March 1500, just in time for the christening of her nephew, Charles, where she joined Margaret of York in pride of place in the baptismal procession.

Charles lived his first 17 years in the Low Countries. His upbringing there, as a Burgundian prince, was undoubtedly influential in shaping the later monarch. This was clearly the intention of his father Philip, who determinedly resisted all attempts of Juana's parents, Ferdinand and Isabella, to have him brought to Spain. Charles was Philip and Juana's second child; his elder sister, Eleanor, had been born in November 1498. Soon another child was added to the growing family when Juana gave birth to Isabella in July 1501. This was a real success – a son and two daughters born within five years of marriage, with every reason to expect more children soon. But Charles saw little of his parents. The dynastic concerns that encouraged rulers to have numerous children, particularly an heir, a spare and several girls for marriage alliances, also took his parents from him at an early age. It was usual for leading members of a ruling family to have their own households established at a young age, overseen by an appointee of the head of the family. Duties in the various provinces that made up the Low Countries were always going to make Philip and Juana's absences frequent, but it was events on the Iberian peninsula that resulted in the couple being even more distant.

Emperor Maximilian and King Ferdinand of Aragon had regarded the double marriage they had arranged as a way to counter French aggression, particularly Charles VIII's invasion of Italy in 1494. They had not intended a coming together of all the widespread lands that they controlled. In Spain the unification of the kingdoms of Aragon and Castile under one ruler was expected to come about with the accession of Isabella and Ferdinand's son Juan. His death in 1497 and the still birth of his daughter three months later meant that his eldest sister Isabella, married to King Manuel I of Portugal, would now inherit, with the benefit that their young son, Don Miguel, would eventually become ruler of the whole of Iberia. The deaths of Isabella and Miguel completely changed the dynastic landscape. Only five months after Charles' birth Juana became heir to her mother in Castile and her husband Philip saw that he could add the title King of Castile to that of Archduke of Burgundy.

In late 1501 Philip and Juana left their young family and travelled through France to Castile so that they could be acknowledged as heirs to the throne. That achieved, Philip left for Austria and then the Low Countries leaving his pregnant wife in Spain. Juana gave birth to another son, christened Ferdinand, in March 1503. It was at this stage that Juana's unpredictable behaviour first emerged. Philip, known as 'the Handsome', cut a fine figure, steeped in the chivalry and sophistication of the Burgundian court, in contrast to the more austere Spanish traditions. Juana was intensely jealous of all who had her husband's attention. She had not wished to be separated from him and she now violently insisted that they be reunited. Lodged in the castle of La Mota, near Medina del Campo, she had to be forcibly restrained as she made frenzied attempts to leave and make her own way to the coast, much to the despair of her mother. When at last she was considered fit to travel she was escorted back to the Low Countries. Here she gave birth to another daughter, Mary, in September 1505.

The combination of Philip's widely known infidelities and Juana's violent reaction to his betrayals, many real and even more imagined, meant their relationship all but collapsed. But Philip needed her if he was to further his ambitions. In November 1504 her mother Isabella died leaving Juana as queen of Castile. She refused Philip's demands that she sign away her inheritance and his response was to undermine her position. Philip put the word around that she was insane, her independent funds were withdrawn and she was kept out of the public eye, although it should be remembered that her pregnancy and the birth of Mary would have meant that she would have withdrawn from public appearances for several months in any case.

As soon as possible after her confinement, they left their children once again and set sail from the Low Countries, this time to claim the throne of Castile. Accompanied by forty ships and several thousand troops, at first they made good progress along the Channel. However this was mid-winter and on the night of 15th January 1506 the fleet was hit by a violent storm coming in from the Atlantic. There was no chance of the fleet holding together; each captain had to seek his own survival. As the sun rose Philip's ship anchored off the Dorset coast at Melcombe Regis and the full extent of the damage became clear. Gone was the mainsail; the ship's cannons had been abandoned and fires had destroyed some of the superstructure. Few other ships were with them; his fleet had been scattered.

Philip had no choice but to go ashore where the local worthy offered him hospitality while immediately sending news to Henry VII at Richmond about his unexpected visitor. To Henry this was a godsend, his opportunity to dictate terms to Philip. Although treated as an honoured guest the Archduke realised that he would not be leaving until he had agreed to a number of demands. Henry decided that he would formally welcome Philip at Windsor Castle. As the Archduke was escorted from the south-west, the king sent Prince Henry, now aged 14, to greet him in his fluent French at Winchester – the young prince's first venture onto the international stage. By all accounts he acquitted himself well.[6] He was also greatly impressed by Philip, just as a young Charles was to be impressed by Henry several years later.

Once at Windsor, Philip was subjected to Henry's charm offensive: ceremonial reception, fine apartments, banquets, dancing, hunting, a trip along the Thames to London. Henry wished to show that Tudor England could put on a show to match any in Europe. In St. George's chapel Philip was invested with the Order of the Garter by Prince Henry and he in turn was received into the Order of the Golden Fleece, the highest honour in the gift of the Burgundian ruler. The business side of the ceremony was the signing of the treaty. Along with a mutual defence alliance, Philip was to hand over Edmund de la Pole, Duke of Suffolk, held in his territories, who, as nephew of Edward IV and potential claimant to the English throne, had been a thorn in Henry's side for many years. In addition, a trade agreement gave English merchants the right to import cloth without payment of taxes into Philip's lands. This was so unpopular in the Low Countries that the treaty soon became known as the 'Intercursus malus' (the wicked treaty)[7]. Plans for Henry's marriage to Philip's sister, Margaret, were moved forward and there was talk of the betrothal of Henry's eleven year old daughter Mary to Philip's young son, Charles. This had not been the first marriage planned for Charles. As early as 1501, negotiations had been held for his marriage to Claude, the daughter of Louis XII of France, only three months his senior. This arrangement had been dropped in 1505 when Louis betrothed Claude to his heir, Francis, Duke of Angouleme, whose career, as Francis I, was to be so closely linked with that of Charles.

Philip had prevented Juana from travelling to Windsor with him. He continued to talk of her unpredictable behaviour and mental instability. She eventually arrived on 10th February, a day after the ceremonies at St George's chapel, and was welcomed by Henry, his daughter Mary, and Juana's sister, Catherine of Aragon, much against Philip's wishes. Catherine had been in England since 1501, when she had married Prince Arthur, only for him to die within six months. Kept in England, partly by her father's failure to pay her dowry, and isolated from her family, she was keen to be reunited with her older sister. Catherine had already experienced Philip's hostility when he snubbed her attempts to dance with him. The sisters met for only one day and even that meeting was cut short. Catherine was left depressed by Juana's appearance and mood. She later wrote to her, concerned about her 'hasty departure', explaining that if Henry 'had acted as he secretly wished, he would, by every possible means, have prevented your journey', but he was advised not 'to interfere between husband and wife'.[8] Henry himself later commented that Philip's accounts of Juana's insanity did not match the behaviour of the queen that he had met.

Philip and Juana eventually re-joined their reassembled fleet and soldiers, sailed from Falmouth, and arrived on the north coast of Spain at Corunna in late April after a ten day voyage. Events in Spain had moved on rapidly. Juana's father Ferdinand of Aragon had done all in his power to prevent Philip and Juana's arrival and to bolster his own support in Castile. Isabella's will had removed his title as King of Castile, though named him 'governor and administrator' of the country 'in consideration of his great experience' until Juana took up the reins of power. Neither

Ferdinand nor Philip had any intention of allowing that to happen, and both wished to take her place. Ferdinand had coins minted in his own and Juana's name 'King and Queen of Castile, Leon and Aragon'. His problem was that he would never gain the support of the Castilian nobility who disliked him as a 'foreigner' from Aragon and feared his power. They believed that they would have much greater freedom of action under Philip and on his arrival almost the whole of the nobility sided with him.

Ferdinand could not hope to win by force and had to negotiate. But he was to be highly regarded in Machiavelli's 'The Prince' as 'the fox' for good reason. At meetings with Philip between 20th and 27th June, mediated by Cardinal Cisneros, Archbishop of Toledo, the senior churchman in Spain, he accepted that his 'most beloved children'[*] should take over control of Castile[9]. The two kings then agreed that Juana was neither inclined nor fit to rule 'considering her infirmities and sufferings, which for the sake of honour are not expressed' and further that if 'the said most serene Queen, either from her own choice or from being persuaded by other persons should attempt to meddle in the government' both would prevent it[10]. It suited both her father and her husband that she be regarded as incapable - hence Juana 'la Loca' ('the Mad'). Yet on the same day, 27th June, Ferdinand drew up secret documents renouncing both treaties on the grounds of coercion, claiming that he would never otherwise have signed treaties that did 'such enormous damage to the said most serene Queen, my daughter and me'.[11] Having left his options for the future open, he departed for Aragon.

Ferdinand had realised early on that just this situation could arise and had already made his plans. A treaty with his erstwhile enemy Louis XII of France in October 1505 included his betrothal to the French king's niece, Germaine de Foix. While unpopular in Castile, it had the merit for Ferdinand that if the marriage produced a child, particularly a son, he would have another heir to all his territories on the Spanish mainland as well as Naples, Sicily,

---

[*] Meaning Juana and Philip.

Sardinia and the Balearics. It might even throw open the whole succession issue in Castile. This was soon to take on an even greater importance. While in Burgos, lodging at the Casa del Cordón, Philip was suddenly taken ill and died on 25th September 1506. The actual cause of his death is unknown. Many suspected Ferdinand's involvement, poison perhaps, since Philip's illness was put down to 'something he ate'. A fever developing from 'a chill' has also been suggested, as has typhoid fever.

Despite his treatment of her, Philip's death left the pregnant Juana distraught. She refused to leave his body for months and as she moved around the country she took it with her in torch-lit processions, opening the coffin at regular intervals to check that his corpse was still there. As Ferdinand wrote to de Puebla, his ambassador in England, in 1507, 'the said Queen, my daughter, still carries about with her the corpse of King Philip... they could never persuade her to bury him'[12]. During this time, in January 1507, she gave birth to their sixth child, Catherine. In light of her condition Ferdinand explained that he was not yet willing to raise the issue of her re-marriage with her, even though negotiations were being held about the possibility of her marrying Henry VII of England. Ferdinand assured Henry that this was very much his wish, and her sister Catherine was writing about her father-in-law in favourable terms.

Although, in the words of Ferdinand, Juana 'does not occupy herself with affairs of state', she consistently refused to sign away her powers even though she was now clearly unable to take on the responsibilities of government. A regency council was set up under Cardinal Cisneros. Ferdinand, having waited for the crisis to develop to a state in which his presence might be welcomed, returned in late 1507. He eventually became 'administrator' of Castile, though he largely left the running of the country to Cisneros while he focused on foreign policy, particularly in Italy. In 1509 Juana was eventually persuaded to settle, with her young daughter Catherine, in the convent of Santa Clara overlooking the river Duero at Tordesillas where she was to remain, effectively a prisoner, until her death forty six years later.

Charles' personal contact with his parents was thus almost non-existent. By the time he was six his father was dead and his mother, isolated in Spain, was no longer in communication with her four children in the Low Countries. As her 'guardian', the Marquis of Denia, later recorded, Juana's response when he suggested that she write to Charles in 1519 was that 'she had never written to him since the death of the King her lord (Philip)'.[13] Philip had been seen by many as providing a model for the early 16th century prince, but his unlimited ambition and his treatment of his wife, while certainly not unique at the time, suggest another side to his character.

There was little doubt that Charles would become ruler in the Burgundian lands, but his position in Spain was not as secure. Through his mother he was the acknowledged heir to Castile, but the situation there was difficult. She was the legitimate monarch and the degree of her mental instability has been the subject of heated debate over the centuries. Could she have been capable of ruling with the support that she might have hoped for from her father or her husband? Had Philip's death pushed her over the edge into insanity or was she suffering from grief and depression from which she might, with time, have recovered? She had never been given the chance to prove her abilities, and her son was to continue a similar approach in later years. Also, in Castile, there were rivalries between the local nobility and the Burgundian nobles who had travelled there with Philip hoping for advancement. After Philip's death some Castilians who had supported him, with an eye to the future, travelled to the Low Countries to seek favour at court there. In Aragon, Charles was the heir, but that could still change if Ferdinand and Germaine de Foix were to have a child. Although his parents had provided him with a rich birth-right they had also left a problematic one.

# 2
# 'More in his head than appears on his face' – Education

With his father dead and his mother confined 'for her own safety', Charles' upbringing was now more than ever in the hands of others. Along with sisters Eleanor (Alienor), Isabella (Ysabeau) and Mary (Marie), Charles remained in the Low Countries. His brother Ferdinand and the new born Catherine were in Spain, the latter with her mother. Their guardians, grandfathers Maximilian and Ferdinand, continued to be involved in complex political and dynastic machinations. There was a danger that the young Charles and his sisters might have been left subject to the ambitions of the nobility or held by the cities of the Low Countries for their own political ends. However Maximilian was to ensure that the children received a good education and that Charles was trained for his future role as monarch. He appointed his daughter, their aunt Margaret, as regent in the Low Countries and gave her the 'governorship of our very dear and much beloved children, Charles, Archduke of Austria and his ... sisters ... with full and entire power and authority'.

Margaret had been betrothed to Charles of France for ten years but then cast aside. She had married Juan of Spain only for him to die within a year. By the time of Charles' birth she was once again the focus of numerous marriage plans – Ludovico Sforza of Milan, Prince Arthur of England (until he married Catherine of Aragon) and Vladislav, King of Hungary, were all possible matches. In 1501 her brother Philip, with the agreement of the Emperor Maximilian and Louis XII of France, selected Philibert II, Duke of Savoy. By November Margaret had travelled to Geneva, married and established herself in a new role. She came to care deeply for

Philibert; he was lively and fun to be with. Both aged 21, the couple were well suited and contented. If Philibert did not always apply himself to the governance of his lands, Margaret soon proved herself to be more than capable of making good the deficit, probably expecting this to be her life's work. Again ill-health destroyed her happiness. Philibert died in September 1504. The couple were childless. With an heir she would have acted as regent in Savoy, but the accession of Philibert's half-brother, Charles III, left her with no significant role. In the future she was rarely, if ever, seen in anything but the white widow's cap and black clothing as portrayed in portraits by Bernard van Orley and later Lucas Cranach. As dowager duchess she set about planning the construction of a magnificent tomb for her husband at the monastery of Brou, outside Bourg-en-Bresse. Margaret was determined that she would not marry again and was able to withstand the pressure of both her father and her brother, refusing to countenance a match with the widowed Henry VII of England. As it turned out her talents were to be much better used in the Low Countries. She was to be one of the greatest influences in Charles upbringing from 1507 and later a loyal and astute adviser.

The centre of Charles' early life was the Burgundian court. Many of its traditions had been developed under Philip 'the Good', duke from 1419 until 1467. He is best known for his political manoeuvrings, alternating between English and French alliances*, and for his 'personal' life. Married three times, with three children from his third marriage, he also had at least eighteen illegitimate children by numerous of his twenty-four known mistresses. His court in the early and mid-fifteenth century was extravagant. Medieval notions of chivalry, gallantry and honour were highly regarded; membership of the Order of the Golden Fleece, established in 1430, was the highest honour that could be bestowed upon a nobleman. Banquets, balls and pageantry played an

---

* He took advantage of the rivalry between the two countries during the later stages of the Hundred Years War. It was Philip who captured Joan of Arc and then handed her over to the English in 1430 for a substantial sum.

important role in the life of the court, which became the leader in fashion throughout Europe. Lavish patronage of the arts resulted in commissions for tapestries, jewellery and painting from artists such as Jan van Eyck and Roger van der Weyden and six hundred illustrated manuscripts were added to the ducal collection. This approach was continued, though perhaps on a less grand scale, by Charles 'the Bold' (died 1477), his widow Margaret of York, his grandson Archduke Philip, and his grand-daughter Margaret of Austria.

It was into this world that Charles and his sisters were born, spending much of their early years at the palace of Margaret of York. After her death in 1503, the household was under the control of Anna de Beaumont, a former lady-in-waiting of Juana[1], who had accompanied her from Spain for her marriage to Philip. After returning from Savoy in early 1507, Margaret established her 'Court of Savoy' in a palace near-by. A new gatehouse, one of the earliest Renaissance-style buildings in northern Europe, was added to existing Gothic buildings reflecting her enthusiasm for the new ideas that were flourishing at the time. It was here that Charles gradually became acquainted with the business of government evidenced by the regular reports Margaret sent of his progress to Maximilian.

The palace was not on a monumental scale, with both administrative and living quarters based around a small courtyard. About 150 people worked there, under Margaret, her chancellor Gattinara (who had come with Margaret from Savoy and would later be Charles' chancellor in the 1520s) and the Privy Council, but few lived there. In the 'Chambre de Madame', Margaret's private quarters, she assembled portraits and other works by Memling, Bosch, and van Orley to add to the existing collection. She also bought tapestries, miniatures, dining services and a substantial library, with writings from the classics, philosophers, and recent Renaissance humanists. This was a cultural centre as well as a place of government. Margaret's court welcomed the presence of the finest thinkers and artists, such as Erasmus and Albrecht Durer.

The court became known for its taste, refinement, comfort and, on a small scale, splendour; a northern renaissance court that others would seek to emulate. Many noblemen sought to send their daughters to Malines as ladies-in-waiting; they regarded it as Europe's finest finishing school. There they would mix with Europe's future leaders, and have access to the music, poetry, ideas, art and courtly behaviour thought to be so desirable. It was in this court, as well as in Paris, that the young Anne Boleyn, daughter of the English diplomat Thomas Boleyn, spent a year developing the courtly charms that were eventually to gain the serious attentions of Henry VIII. Over a decade later this was to have a lasting impact upon the history of England and the relations between England and Spain, Henry VIII and Charles.

Charles became a member of the Order of the Golden Fleece in infancy. The order emphasised the ideals of the medieval knight and the desire for Christian unity to fight against the infidel. He was in constant contact with those who had a similar background. Young men at court, such as Henry of Nassau (1483-1536), Frederick, Count Palatine (1482-1556) and Charles de Lannoy (1487-1527), often fine exponents of horsemanship and jousting, influenced the young duke, and many were later to become his trusted advisers and commanders. The pages of honour who were educated alongside Charles were the children of nobility from Germany, the Low Countries and Italy, such as John of Saxony and Maximilian Sforza. It was clear early on that Charles' interests lay in horses, hunting, tournaments and fencing rather than in more scholarly pursuits. These activities were what stimulated and excited those around him. The skills that he developed in these fields were to stand him in good stead. He was, after all, to spend a remarkable amount of his life after the age of fifteen on the move, travelling through his territories and later with his armies on campaign. This was still an age in which monarchs and their heirs sought to gain honour on the battlefield and participated in dangerous activities such as jousting, as witnessed by the injuries to Henry VIII of England, which some believe resulted in a significant character change, and the later death of Henry II of France in 1559 at the age of 40.

Charles would not have cut a particularly striking figure if one were to rely on physical features alone. In his early years he was regarded as delicate. He had a pale complexion and developed a large protruding lower jaw, which meant that his mouth was often hanging open and caused difficulty chewing food. This unprepossessing genetic characteristic of the Habsburgs, which was to become even more marked in some of his descendants, may well have been what caused people to assume at first glance that the young Charles was not promising material, either physically or mentally. An element of self-consciousness may account for Charles' preference to eat alone, something that he was often able to insist upon in later life. It might also explain his reputed shyness in youth, which to the superficial observer suggested a dull, unresponsive and apathetic character.

This was misleading. Charles developed a well-proportioned body and although he lacked the reputed good looks of England's young Henry VIII and Francis I of France, his near contemporaries, he was more than able to take an active part in court life and absorb the values of knightly behaviour. One of his favourite books was 'Le Chevalier délibéré', by Olivier de la Marche, who had been in charge of ceremonies at the Burgundian court in the fifteenth century. The poem told of the chivalry of the Burgundian rulers, Philip the Good, Charles the Bold and Mary the Rich, in the form of a fable, providing a model for others to emulate. Bravery, honour and loyalty were seen as characteristics to be much admired and Charles imbibed them from an early age. His delight in the hunt was pleasing to his family. When Margaret wrote to Maximilian in 1509 telling him 'our son Charles takes such pleasure hunting', the Emperor replied that this was to be expected, and that if Charles had not done so 'people would think he was a bastard'.

All this did not mean that his broader education and his introduction to affairs of state were ignored or indeed that Charles did not see their value, even though his interests clearly lay in the practical and pragmatic rather than the theoretical. Margaret's cultural interests influenced the young prince as she introduced him to his wider responsibilities. Early on he was signing letters to his parents in Spain and to his betrothed, Mary Tudor, the youngest daughter of Henry VII. At the age of seven, in the company of Margaret, he was required to make a speech to the estates of Louvain. French was his first language and he also became fluent in Flemish, but was never strong in Latin, though he believed it important. He later learned Spanish, German and Italian to varying degrees of competence. The saying that he spoke French to his friends, Spanish to his confessors, Italian to his women and German to his horses, which he loved most, may have some wit but is probably wide of the mark.

Charles' religious and philosophical education was put in the hands of some of the best minds of the time. One of his teachers was Adrian of Utrecht, later to become Pope Adrian VI, along with Luis de Vaca and Robert of Ghent. Adrian Floriszoon Boeyens was from humble origins but he rose to become vice-chancellor of the University of Louvain before being appointed as tutor to Charles soon after Margaret took up her responsibilities. The son of a ship's carpenter, he had studied at Zwolle and then Louvain on a scholarship funded by Margaret of York, becoming a doctor of theology in 1491. As a member of the Brethren of the Common Life he came to believe in the need to lead a simple religious life, in contrast to the great wealth often displayed by the Church. He wished to see the end of the growing abuses of Church power, while opposing any doctrinal change. The impact of these ideas on Charles was considerable.

He was also influenced by the famous humanist philosopher Erasmus of Rotterdam (1466-1536), who introduced him to ideas about the nature of government and the relationship between the ruler and his subjects. Erasmus had already written 'Handbook for a Christian Knight' (Enchridion militis Christiani) in 1503, in which he stressed the importance of personal spiritual disciplines, such as reading the scriptures, as against institutional forms of religion.

Erasmus wished to see a change of emphasis and he continued to work for such reforms from within the church. In 1516 he dedicated his 'Education of a Christian Prince' (Institutio principis Christiani) to Charles. In it he argued that while monarchy was the preferred form of government, the sovereign must not forget that 'a large part of authority depends on the consent of the people', and that it was important to avoid tyranny. He also advised: 'Conduct your own rule as if you were striving to ensure that no successor could be your equal, but at the same time prepare your children for their future as if to ensure that a better man would indeed succeed you'. Charles certainly came to believe that study and learning, especially of history, were essential preparation for government. Whether he was able to put into practice some of Erasmus' other advice, such as on the virtues of peace, not to be a slave to one's deficiencies and passions, and to strive to avoid exceptional inequalities of wealth, must be open to question, though he might have claimed that he did so more than most rulers of the time.

Through such influences Charles developed a sincere, generally conventional, religious belief which lasted throughout his life. His faith was deep but he was not someone who wished to dwell overlong on the finer theological points. He had a good knowledge of the scriptures, attended frequent masses, and had a belief in divine control that provided a degree of fatalism. Nothing was to shake this faith in God which he retained through successes and failures alike. He did see the need for some reform of the clergy but he never grasped the depth or the spiritual nature of the challenge to the Catholic Church which developed during his reign after the impetus provided by Martin Luther in 1517.

Another mentor central to Charles' political development was Guillaume de Croy, Lord of Chièvres. Born in 1458, elected a knight of the Golden Fleece in 1491 and becoming a member of Philip the Handsome's court in 1494, he was well regarded by both Philip and Maximilian. He was for a time ambassador to France and had been sent on various diplomatic missions. By 1506 he was the leading nobleman of the Low Countries, left in charge by Philip when he sailed for Spain, and later confirmed as commander-in-chief by Maximilian. In 1509 he was appointed Charles' governor and Grand Chamberlain, replacing his cousin, Charles' godfather, Charles de Croy, Prince of Chimay. In his new role he was constantly with Charles, day and night, an opportunity to strongly influence the young man's ideas and beliefs. Like Margaret, Chièvres ensured that Charles was introduced to both the skills and rigours of leadership. He made Charles work hard; 'I am the defender and guardian of his youth. I do not want him to be incapable because he has not understood affairs nor been trained to work'[2]. In this he was undoubtedly successful; there can be no question that Charles took his future role seriously, even though there were times when some around him believed that he was prone to spells of indolence.

Such diverse influences helped to develop Charles' awareness of the problems and subtleties of the political world. Even though there can be little doubt that both Margaret and Chièvres had Charles' best interests at heart, they had different priorities. Chièvres saw Charles as a Duke of Burgundy and intended to use all means to further Burgundian interests, while Margaret thought of him as a future head of the much wider Habsburg dynasty. This clash eventually had the effect of bringing forward Charles' formal assumption of power in the Low Countries.

Chièvres spoke French and in common with the Burgundian nobility was culturally close to their powerful western neighbour, understanding that they had little to gain and much to lose from conflict with France. This was at odds with the pro-English leanings of Margaret who recognised the importance of the English trade to the Low Countries, especially the thriving cities of Brabant[3]. She was not likely to easily forgive her earlier treatment by Charles VIII and was bound to be supportive of the Habsburg Emperor's wish to further extend his family's power, often in conflict with French interests. Although in 1508 the situation in Italy had persuaded Maximilian, with Margaret's help, to negotiate with Louis XII of France, bringing about the League of Cambrai, it was unlikely that this state of affairs would last. By 1511 an anti-French alliance, the

## Charles V: Duty and Dynasty

Holy League, was formed and Maximilian joined it the following year. The Empire and France were once again in conflict, though the Low Countries, through Margaret's insistence, remained officially neutral and were able to benefit financially by supplying both armies.[4]

When in the summer of 1513 Henry VIII entered the European military scene for the first time, seeking glory on the battlefield against France, Maximilian joined him. At the battle of Guinegate (known in England as the 'battle of the Spurs') outside Therouanne on 16th August, they inflicted a defeat on a French relieving force, captured the town on the 22nd and took Tournai a month later. English success was completed by the rout of the Scottish army at Flodden, in Northumberland, on 9th September by forces under Thomas Howard, Earl of Surrey. James IV of Scotland, many noblemen and possibly ten thousand Scottish troops died. The seventy year old Howard had been disappointed not to be leading Henry's army in France. He realised that defeat by the Scots would almost certainly cost his life, either in battle or as punishment. Success meant advancement: he was created Duke of Norfolk the following year.

Margaret, threatened by Chièvres and his French links, was keen to further Charles' regard for the English court. She arranged for him to visit the English king, who was by now married to his other aunt, Catherine of Aragon, and if all went to plan would be his future brother-in-law. It appears that both sides were suitably impressed – Charles by the confident, recently victorious, Henry, and the English by the thirteen year old Charles' 'quiet dignity'.[5] Emboldened by this success Margaret sought to press home her advantage. The Ordinance of Lille on 19th October appointed Maximilian, Ferdinand of Aragon and Henry VIII as Charles' 'governors', each to act through a representative in the Low Countries. These events are the first to be recorded by Charles in his 'Memoirs', dictated to William van Male thirty-seven years later. In the third person, and with the understated style that he adopted throughout the document, he recalled that 'the Archduke Charles, grandson of the Emperor, proceeded to Tournay, which was then in the hands of King Henry, and to Lille, where he had his first interview with the same king, and where, amongst other things, his emancipation was discussed and resolved upon'.[6]

The antagonism between Margaret and the Burgundian nobility was exacerbated by the involvement of two factions of Spaniards. Those whose allegiance had been to Philip rather than Ferdinand, led by Don Juan Manuel, were now close to the pro-French Burgundian nobles. They opposed those sent by Ferdinand to bolster his position at the Burgundian court, in particular his ambassador Juan de Lanuza. Ferdinand gave instructions to de Lanuza to thank 'the Emperor and Madame Margaret for what they have done' (nominating him as one of Charles' 'governors'). He continued that 'It would be a good thing if Monsieur de Chièvres could be removed from his place; but the most important thing to be done is to get rid of Don Juan Manuel, who is the worst and most dangerous person near the Prince'[7]. Margaret, with Maximilian's approval, ordered the arrest of Don Juan Manuel.

The following twelve months were difficult for both Charles and Margaret. Margaret saw her adoptive family begin to break up as Charles came increasingly under the sway of Chièvres, and two of his sisters left Malines. As Manuel was a member of the Order of the Golden Fleece, the protests of the Burgundian nobility over his arrest were channelled through the Order, and it was Charles himself who led the delegation to confront Margaret. He was already showing just how important the chivalric code was to him. Although she refused to back down, it was clear that her position was weakening. Maximilian meanwhile was busy continuing his policy of 'matrimonial imperialism' by arranging betrothals for his young grandchildren. In May 1514 eight year old Princess Mary left Malines for Austria and was placed under the direct supervision of Maximilian, to be married in the future to a son of the Hungarian king. In June, Princess Isabella, days before her thirteenth birthday, was married by proxy to King Christian II of Denmark and left the next year to begin married life. Margaret's situation was made worse by Maximilian's negotiations for another possible marriage, this time of Charles to a French or Hungarian princess, without her knowledge.[8] On hearing of these plans Henry VIII promptly arranged the marriage of his eighteen year old sister, Mary, to whom Charles had been betrothed for nearly ten years (though never met) to the elderly and recently widowed Louis XII of France. Marriage to the fifty-two year old king horrified Mary, though the king was dead within three months. Henry's favourite Charles Brandon, Duke of Suffolk was then sent to escort her back to England. More to Mary's liking, the two secretly married in France before their return, much to Henry's anger when the union became known.

Of more importance to Charles was that Henry's actions were seen in the Low Countries as a betrayal, thus weakening the 'English' party. It was also believed that Maximilian was acting purely for the benefit of his dynasty and not in the interests of his subjects. Chièvres had favoured more local marriages for the two princesses which would secure the borders of the provinces. With Margaret's position thus undermined, the nobility successfully pressed for Charles' formal coming of age to be brought forward. Maximilian was offered 140,000 florins by the States-General (the representative body of the provinces of the Low Countries) to agree.[9] Whether he was motivated by the belief that Charles was now ready to take on much greater responsibilities, or the calculation that he would be able to control Charles' decisions, or by a simple need for money, is uncertain. Many contemporary observers did not have a particularly high opinion of the Emperor. An Augsburg merchant, Wilhelm Wem, wrote of him: 'He was pious, not of great wit, and always poor. He always wanted to make war, but he never had any money. In his lands he had mortgaged many cities, castles, rents and rights'. He was known to be brave, warm-hearted and caring towards his family, but was certainly an unreliable ally, likely to swap sides with alacrity if he saw an opportunity for gain or if he was paid enough.

## Charles V: Duty and Dynasty

In the ceremony which took place on 5th January 1515 in the Great Hall of Coudenberg Palace* in Brussels, shortly before his fifteenth birthday, Charles was declared to be of age. Margaret's role as both guardian and regent, undermined by both her father's unreliability and the hostility of the nobility, ended. Although it was agreed that Ferdinand would continue to act for him in Castile until his twenty-fifth birthday, Charles was now able to begin his personal rule in the Low Countries. Surrounded by those in whom he placed much trust but who were also intensely ambitious, it remained to be seen how independent he could be.

He had been educated for a life of leadership and government. He had developed an understanding of the value of tradition and ceremony, the importance of impressing others with culture and style, while at the same time acquiring a devout faith, and a serious approach to his responsibilities. But Charles was not always easy to read. Rarely did he show signs of emotion in his dealings with others or in his letters. To what extent this was his 'public face', behind which the real Charles could shelter, or how much it was his real character, is difficult to determine. Perhaps the two merged, both in Charles' mind and in the view of those who met him. Certainly his later advice to his son and heir, Philip, indicate that this may well be the case: 'In your bearing be calm and reserved. Say nothing in anger'. Given reports of his reticence and even slowness in his youth, what most contemporaries saw in Charles from the time of his taking up real power were his reserve, dignity and courtesy. He was known to be committed, careful and self-controlled. The papal envoy to the Diet of Worms in 1521 reported that 'this prince is gifted with good sense and prudence, far beyond his years; and indeed has, I believe, much more in his head than appears on his face'.

---

* On the hill of Coudenberg in Brussels. Originally an 11th century castle, it had been gradually transformed into a more comfortable place of residence for the Dukes of Brabant. It was destroyed by fire in 1731. The cellars can be visited from the Bellevue Museum, where displays reveal its history. The States-General of the Low Countries met in the Great Hall.

# 3
## Duke of Burgundy – Apprenticeship

Brought up as ruler of the Burgundian territories, there was the possibility of a much greater role on the European stage for Charles if, and it was a significant if, all went according to the plans of those around him. But for the moment he was Duke of Burgundy. As he travelled through his lands in the Low Countries he was formally welcomed to the major cities, and promised, as tradition demanded, to protect their privileges. He received diplomats carrying greetings sent by rulers from across Europe. Back in the palace at Brussels, where his elder sister, Eleanor, also had a household, court life was all that was expected – processions, formal dances, feasts, tournaments and lavish expenditure on clothes and decor – with the Order of the Golden Fleece at its heart. It is said that the dinner at the first Chapter held after Charles' coming of age was so extensive that many knights missed the evening church service either because they had over-indulged or were still at the feast. However, even if the court was extravagant and flamboyant it was one in which formalities and protocol were carefully followed and religious conviction regarded as important. It was not known for loose living or dereliction of duty; it had a good reputation[1]. This matches what we know of Charles, both then and in his later life.

In this environment Charles was surrounded by the nobility, mostly Burgundian, but some Spaniards with their eyes on the future. Each had their official roles and sinecures, taking charge of the table, of the cellars, of the stables, of the bedchamber. By 1517 his household consisted of 473 members. Led by the Lord Chamberlain, Henry of Nassau, there were 208 nobles (including seven stewards, fifty-four counsellor-chamberlains, over one hundred and twenty squires), together with 265 servants.[2] Most of the nobility were not permanently in attendance; a roster meant that between a quarter and a half were on duty at any given time. Each had their own place in the daily running of the court, especially at meal times, with clear rules and expectations of behaviour.

Charles was fortunate that he was in a position to be able to turn to those who had been around him since his early years and whom he trusted. The camaraderie and loyalty associated with the Order of the Golden Fleece gave him a link to these nobles that transcended mere personal interest. Some, such as Henry of Nassau, had been knights of the order for a decade; others, such as Charles de Lannoy and Frederick, Count Palatine, were invested in 1516. They were ten or so years older than Charles, the dashing young knights at court when Charles was a boy; they were now valuable supporters, useful on diplomatic missions, and military commanders when required. The role that the Order played in providing Charles with a degree of continuity and a sense of belonging can be seen from the fact that in paintings or on commemorative medallions throughout his life he is invariably wearing its gold symbol.

In his formative years Charles had witnessed the shifting and often antagonistic relations between Margaret of Austria and Chièvres. With Margaret's formal position as Regent ended, his inner circle became Adrian of Utrecht, Jean de Sauvage, a member of the council of Flanders since 1490 and appointed Grand Chancellor of Burgundy in 1515, and Chievres. All were to play a significant role in Charles' life over the next few years, but Chièvres in particular guided him through the early years of his personal rule. However this did not mean that Margaret's influence was completely removed. She still maintained her court in Malines, and had many local and foreign visitors. If Chièvres was the dominating force over Charles in domestic affairs, then Margaret was able to exert some control over foreign policy; she retained her family's contacts and influence with European courts. For Charles it was important that some accord between Chièvres and Margaret was reached. Peace with France and working to ensure Charles' inheritance of the thrones in Spain met the requirements of both

## Charles V: Duty and Dynasty

groups.[3] Margaret and Maximilian's dynastic interests would be furthered and the nobility would be secure in their homeland and have hopes of future advancement in Spain.

The internal politics of Charles' Burgundian lands were complex. Charles the Bold had lost Burgundy, Picardy, and part of Artois (and Lorraine which he had claimed) to France after the battle of Nancy in 1477. The rest of his lands were only preserved by the marriage of Mary the Rich to Maximilian who had the power of the Habsburgs and the Holy Roman Empire behind him. Thus the Burgundian inheritance that his great-grandson Charles came into in 1515 consisted of Franche Comte and various lands in the Low Countries. These were in no way a united entity but rather a group of provinces which recognised Charles as either their Duke (e.g. Brabant, Limburg and Luxembourg), Count (e.g. Flanders, Artois, Hainaut, Zeeland, Namur) or Lord (e.g. Friesland – in name only until 1523 when the inhabitants accepted his rule). Each had a tradition of independence that they sought to retain, their own assembly (Estates), legal system and administration, though a stadholder in each province was appointed by their overlord. Delegates from all the provinces met together in the States-General. It was here that their divisions became obvious.

The States-General had voting powers on taxes, customs duties and issues of war and peace, but each province wished to defend their own interests against both central coercion and the needs of other provinces. They rejected majority voting in the States-General and decisions, especially financial ones, had to be confirmed by each province. Often economic and political interests differed; unanimity was rare. The extent of the powers given to delegates sent to the 'national' assembly was an issue that troubled many countries at the time. If the delegates had complete freedom to decide as they saw fit, power was taken from the local Estates and the delegates could be subject to coercion or bribery by the central government. Rulers therefore often wished the delegates to have such freedom to facilitate speedy decision making, even though such freedom could give delegates the option of working together to block a government measure. If, on the other hand, their instructions forced them to follow detailed decisions made by their own local assembly they had no room for manoeuvre, thus reducing the chance of compromise, requiring them to return to their provinces to report back and receive new instructions.[4] In larger countries this was very difficult in the sixteenth century, but one advantage in the Low Countries was that distances were small and communications were generally better than elsewhere.

History, language and church also failed to bring about much unity. Some provinces, such as Luxembourg and Hainault, were traditionally part of the Holy Roman Empire, but Artois and Flanders owed allegiance to France, though the rights of the French monarchy had long been ignored and in 1435 the Treaty of Arras exempted Dukes of Burgundy from doing homage for any of the lands held from France. On his accession, though, Charles was still regarded as the foremost vassal of the French king. Linguistically the provinces were divided, the southern provinces spoke French, the northern ones Dutch. Church organisation pre-dated the growth of the cities and therefore bore no relation to the 16th century population distribution. The provinces had only two bishoprics Utrecht and Tournai, other areas being under the jurisdiction of bishops from outside - Liege, Arras, Cambrai, and Therouanne. Thus major cities had no resident bishops and in the eyes of many, Charles included, lacked proper ecclesiastical control.

Charles' control of every province was not disputed. In the north the province of Guelders had seized the opportunity offered by the defeat of Charles the Bold to assert their independence. In 1492 Charles of Egmond became Duke and he resisted all attempts by Maximilian to reassert control. From 1515, supported by France, he was a constant thorn in Charles' side, seeking to extend his control to the provinces of Zutphen, Overijssel, Drenthe and Groningen, and posing a threat to neighbouring Holland and Utrecht. Charles, who had been brought up in the belief that these areas were his ancestral right, was determined to remove this threat and restore the lost provinces to his family, just as he regarded regaining Burgundy from France as his duty. Thus the scene was set for future conflicts and possible additions to his lands.

As the most urbanised area of Europe, in which perhaps 40% of the three million people lived in towns and cities (in England it was 15%), there were twenty cities with a population of over 10,000 (in England there were three). Their wealth was based on commerce, the cloth industry, other manufactured goods, and for some, herring fishing. The largest of them, Antwerp, Ghent, Bruges and Brussels matched any in Europe. Their rights and privileges, granted by charter and confirmed by Charles on his accession, gave them a considerable degree of self-government. Each city had its own council, dominated by the families made wealthy by trade and manufacturing. Within the larger cities the guild organisations were also a powerful force, protecting the interests of their skilled artisan members and often being able to exert considerable influence on the council, though their specific demands were often different. Charles needed to be able to retain the support of the ruling burghers if he was to have a relatively untroubled reign. The councils, however, fiercely opposed interference by a central power or the challenge of neighbouring cities.

Nowhere was this more evident than over taxation. Charles' 'ordinary' revenues, derived from sources such as land ownership, customs duties and traditional taxes on certain goods, did not meet all the costs of government. Therefore it was necessary for Charles to request taxes from the provincial estates or the States-General. The usual 'aides' were not particularly onerous and were often voted for several years at a time, usually without too much opposition, but in times of exceptional expenditure, especially war, Charles' requirements could be high. In both cases the assemblies would draw up a list of conditions to be signed by Charles before the money was voted. Problems inevitably arose. It was a slow process and sometimes Charles needed the money urgently. If the 'aides' were not automatically renewable he was unable to borrow against future income since it was not guaranteed. There was always resentment of the non-tax paying nobles by those in the cities and countryside who did pay. Some provinces might not contribute if they believed that the money was to be spent in the interests of another – perhaps a distant province under attack - and others sometimes placed restrictions on how the money could be spent.

All of this made funding his government difficult, a problem that was to loom large throughout Charles' life, in the Low Countries and elsewhere. In times of war taxation was undoubtedly high. When war on their doorstep, endangering their lives or livelihoods, the cities and provinces paid up, but if the war was further afield and they came to believe that it was more in the interests of the dynasty and its other lands, then opposition could be stubborn. Rotterdam born Erasmus wrote: 'Taxation beyond measure is something everyone has to bear, but for us it is far worse because the money is carried off to Germany or Spain'. But the cost of defending the Low Countries was high given their proximity to France and the lack of any natural defences. The Low Countries were also a relatively wealthy area which had the resources to raise significant taxation revenue, though declining economic circumstances, particularly in Flanders, had a significant impact later in Charles' reign. Despite the fears of the inhabitants, who like most societies throughout history believed that they were paying too much taxation, it is unlikely that a high proportion of the revenues raised there were used to further Charles' ambitions elsewhere.

Such constraints meant that Charles' power in 1515 was more restricted than might at first be thought. Some centralisation was necessary if he was to establish effective government to support his authority. He inherited a Privy Council, a Council of Finance and a central law court based in Malines, which had been removed after death of Charles the Bold but restored by Charles' father Philip in 1504, although several states did not accept its right to overrule locally made decisions. The major social group that Charles was able to rely on in his government of the Low Countries was the nobility. Their political power rested on ownership of large estates, which provided them with wealth, control of local courts and appointment to many local positions of power. This might have resulted in them being very protective of provincial privileges, but Charles continued the tradition which enabled the nobles to see themselves in partnership with the Duke. It was the nobles who sat in Charles' councils, held major offices of state, senior military commands and were appointed as the Stadholder, his personal representative, in the various provinces. Life at court, with its formal ceremonies and personal contacts, tended to create mutual interests, a shared ethos and loyalty to their Duke. Charles also used his great powers of patronage to reward those committed to his cause, and the nobility gained in terms of both wealth and prestige from the offices so awarded, with the highest honour becoming a knight in the Order of the Golden Fleece.

Many of the problems in ruling the Low Countries became all too clear during the next forty years, but in 1515 Charles' accession was widely welcomed. The new reign was greeted, as is often the case, with a sense of optimism both for the region as a whole and for individual ambitions. The various estates, which had supported Chièvres in petitioning Maximilian for Charles' coming of age to be brought forward, made little protest before voting 'aides'. Numerous new appointments were made at court and in the provinces. Domestic affairs, with the exception of hostility from Charles of Egmond in Guelders, were relatively trouble free. Elsewhere in Europe there was considerably more activity, much of which was relevant to both Charles' immediate and longer term future. Even though he was not yet in the position to be the major initiator of policy, his advisors ensured that he was involved in the whole process of discussion, debate and decision making.

Unrelated but contemporaneous events often produce situations that have a long-lasting impact on history. On 1st January 1515, just days before the declaration of Charles' majority in Brussels, King Louis XII of France died. With no sons, his successor was his cousin once removed, Francis, Duke of Angouleme, who as his heir had married Louis' daughter, Claude, the previous year. At his birth in 1494 there seemed little likelihood of Francis inheriting the French throne; his third cousin, King Charles VIII was only twenty-four, and the next in line was his father's cousin, Louis, Duke of Orleans. This was the same Charles who had ended his betrothal to Margaret of Austria in order to marry Anne of Brittany. His early death in 1498, with no surviving children meant that the older Louis inherited the throne and Francis became heir presumptive. Having come into their inheritances within days of each other, Charles' relationship with Francis, five years his senior, was to be one of the major influences on the next thirty years of European history, with Henry VIII of England a third, albeit rather lesser, player at the table.

The Burgundian dynasty had originated from Philip, the fourth son of King John II of France, in the late fourteenth century. Later, the rivalry between the two branches of the Valois family had frequently erupted into war and assassinations. In 1407, Louis, Duke of Orleans, had been murdered on the streets of Paris with the full knowledge of John (the Fearless) of Burgundy, and in 1419 the same John had been murdered at what he believed to be a diplomatic meeting with the dauphin of France, who was to become King Charles VII. These events had been one hundred years earlier, but there had been more recent wars. Charles the Bold had expanded his lands until his defeat and death in 1477 gave the French the opportunity to seize back Burgundy itself, and the French had been regularly in conflict with Charles' grandfathers Maximilian and Ferdinand, even if the Low Countries had not always been directly involved. There was no particular reason why Francis should be well disposed towards Charles or his Habsburg and Spanish families.

Francis invited Charles, as Duke of Burgundy, to his coronation on 25th January. Charles did not attend; it is likely that his advisors did not wish to see Charles put in a position of subservience to the new French king. Henry of Nassau and Michel de Sempy were sent in his place. They were able to negotiate an agreement with Francis over some disputed northern border areas, promised to help put pressure on Ferdinand of Aragon to return Navarre to France, and planned that Charles might marry Renee, second daughter of the former king, Louis XII, Francis' sister-in-law[5]. As it removed the threat of war, thus protecting trade and landholdings, the agreement proved extremely popular in the Low Countries. Henry of Nassau was rewarded with the stadholderships of Holland, Zeeland and Friesland when the current office holder died the following year.

Safety from French invasion had been achieved but there was still work to be done in securing Charles' undisputed succession in Spain. In Castile there was no question that he would be the next monarch, accepting that his mother remained incapable of fulfilling the role. This was the clear intention in Isabella's will when 'my grandson, the Infante Don Carlos, first born son and heir of the said Princess and her husband Prince Philip, has attained the age required by law for governing and reigning in these kingdoms, and has at least accomplished his twentieth year'[6]. In Aragon things were not so straightforward. Ferdinand's marriage to Germaine de Foix had indeed produced the much desired son, but he had died within hours of his birth in May 1509. This left the way open for Charles to inherit not just Castile but all the Aragonese lands as well. However, Ferdinand had been largely responsible for the upbringing of Charles' younger brother, named after him, in Spain. He had involved Emperor Maximilian in talks about the future role of the young Ferdinand, and had a strong inclination to name him as his heir. The two brothers had never met, but such an action had the potential to provoke a crisis both in Spain and within the family. In the Low Countries it was decided to send an ambassador to Spain, whose tasks would be to prevail upon Ferdinand, who was now in his sixties, to unequivocally name Charles as his successor and, in the event of Ferdinand's death to act as regent in Charles' name.

The selection of the ambassador was to be critical to the success of the venture and Adrian of Utrecht initially proved to be an effective choice. He knew Charles' mind as well as anyone, and had the intellect to be able to argue his case with logic and passion. He travelled to Spain in 1515 and accomplished his first mission. We do not know what the twelve year old Ferdinand thought about it at the time, but the eventual relationship between the brothers was to be a major factor in both Charles' life, and the history of Europe. By the time Ferdinand of Aragon died on 23rd January 1516 an earlier will naming young Ferdinand had been rescinded and Charles was set to be the ruler of all the kingdoms of Spain, although it was to be two years before he was able to be formally recognised as such in the various Spanish kingdoms. On 13th March, however, he was acclaimed in the cathedral of St. Michael and St Gudule in Brussels. Following a requiem for the dead king, the herald of the Golden Fleece called 'Long live their Catholic Majesties, Queen Juana and King Charles', and, raising a consecrated dagger handed to him by the bishop of Badajoz, Charles was met with the cry of 'Long live the King' from the two thousand invited guests.

At some time in the not too distant future Charles would have to travel to Spain if he was to be acknowledged as king. When a request for a formal proclamation of his accession in Spain was made, Cardinal Cisneros reminded Charles' representatives that Queen Juana had never renounced her rights and pointed out that Charles had to be present in order to carry out the traditional ceremonies and receive the acclamation of the Cortes, the representative body in each of the kingdoms of Spain. Isabella's will had stated that if 'he comes to these kingdoms with the intention to govern, he may reign and govern'[7]. Cisneros did not question Charles' rights but insisted that only if the proper procedures were followed could Charles be the undisputed ruler.

Charles' letter of 30th April 1516[8], though probably drafted for him, provides an insight into the sixteen year old Charles' role in government. He wrote that 'I clearly see what great pains you take in all that concerns my service and the welfare and pacification of those kingdoms. For all this I am much obliged to you.' Cisneros would work to maintain much of what had been achieved in Spain over the previous thirty years and this suited the new king. Charles continued: 'I have had long conferences on all these subjects with the Count and with some of my Privy Councillors, but as the subjects are many and of different kinds, and as we have been much occupied in other great affairs which cannot well and ought not to be delayed, we have come to a conclusion on only three points'. Charles was learning early that his wide responsibilities meant that he could not deal with everything at once, and, as a result, his representatives would have to wait a considerable time to get instructions, with priority often being given to other issues.

In order for Charles to go to Spain, it was regarded as advisable that a general peace should prevail, certainly between France and Spain, but ideally between France and the Emperor Maximilian as well. There had been intermittent war in Italy involving the major powers – France, Spain (Aragon) and the Emperor – since the French invasion of 1494. Aragon's rule of Naples and Sicily had been reasonably secure from French challenge ever since the victories at Cerignola (near Bari) and Garigliano (between Naples and Rome) in 1503. Further north, however, Francis' decisive victory at Marignano in September 1515, re-taking Milan lost by Louis XII in 1512, had been a major blow to Maximilian, since he wished to assert Imperial authority over Milan, a rich source of revenue, to which end he had married into the Sforza ducal family.

Francis for the moment was in a position of strength. Having made an advantageous peace with Pope Leo X, he then concluded the Treaty of Noyon with Charles and his advisors, led by Chièvres, in August 1516. This recognised Charles' rights (as king of Aragon) in Naples and Francis' in Milan. The treaty also made mention of a marriage between Charles and Francis' new-born daughter, Louise. Charles wrote in friendly terms to his possible future father-in-law and later they exchanged honours – Charles receiving the Order of St. Michael and Francis the Golden Fleece. How sincere these agreements were is highly questionable. Did Charles, now nearly seventeen, really intend to wait to marry a bride who was not yet one year old? Was confirmation of control in Naples, which Aragon already held, sufficient dowry for such a marriage? In Spain Cisneros regarded the treaty as too generous to France and warned of the risks of trusting their neighbour. As far as he was concerned the French were jealous of 'a greater ruler and mightier King than their own', and might well be planning to deceive Charles[9]. In this he was reiterating what the experienced King Ferdinand had believed: 'The nature of the French is never to keep any part of the promises they make, except to the extent that they are forced to'[10].

But it was in the interests of Charles, Chièvres and the Burgundians that a settlement be reached and they were clearly as adept at dissimulation as were the French. With Maximilian's renewed invasion of northern Italy a failure, by late 1516 he was also ready to join the general peace. In December he signed the Treaty of Brussels, by which he accepted French occupation of Milan and confirmed Venetian control of territories in Lombardy. He, too, showed what seemed to be the prevailing attitude to treaties, hardly honourable or chivalrous, when speaking to his grandson early in 1517 by suggesting that Charles was about to cheat the French just as he was about to cheat the English, or at least do his best to do so[11].

It was still over six months before Charles and his retinue set out for Spain. With him he would take a large number of nobles from the Low Countries, who would provide him with the comfort of familiarity. They, in turn, were keen to support Charles' new position with the expectation of advancement under their king in a new land. Having worked alongside Spanish nobles for a decade and accepted their introduction into the Order of the Golden Fleece, they were now reassured that the peace with France would protect their lands. Charles could not travel until all was ready. He needed to have ships assembled, a full complement of crew, properly equipped soldiers, and supplies for this considerable company. This was expensive. Money that he would have liked to have used on these preparations had to be spent on military action against raiders from Guelders who were threatening Amsterdam. Not for the last time were Charles' travel plans to be delayed and sometimes even abandoned because of financial or military pressures. Chièvres requested 400,000 florins from the States-General, to which they eventually agreed, payable over four years, though the money was to be used for defence if war broke out. Erasmus wrote to Thomas More complaining that the nobles and prelates agreed to large sums in taxes that would have to be paid by the common people.[12] But Charles' representatives were able to negotiate a loan from Henry VIII which would go a long way to pay for the cost of the voyage to Spain. They had pointed out that with Charles and Francis now at peace, it would be in the king's interest if he too had friendly relations with Charles. Henry calculated that with Charles in Spain, France's position could be significantly weakened if he was in alliance with its new ruler.

A fellow traveller on his voyage to Spain was to be his eldest sister, Eleanor. As a potential marriage partner she was a valuable asset to the dynasty. Now eighteen, while her younger sisters had already been betrothed or married, Eleanor had been reserved for a worthy match. The concern was considerable when it was discovered that she had apparently received and encouraged the attentions of Count Palatine Frederick, a well-established figure at court. When love letters written by him to Eleanor were discovered, Charles acted immediately in his capacity as head of the family. This was not the marriage that he intended for his sister; there was to be no 'love-match'. Both had to swear under oath that they had not been secretly married and that they would never renew their relationship. Frederick was banished from court, although he was later to regain favour with Charles. Perhaps these events pushed Charles into making definite plans for Eleanor. With an eye to the situation in Iberia, it was soon agreed that she would marry Manuel I of Portugal. King since 1495, his reign had seen the successful exploration and establishment of overseas settlements from Brazil to the East Indies. He had previously been married to Spanish princesses, sisters of Eleanor and Charles' mother – first Isabella, whose two children had died in infancy, and then Maria, by whom he had ten children of whom eight reached adulthood. Charles had for the first time acted decisively in the disposition of his family; he was to do so on numerous occasions in the future.

Having established a regency council to govern in the Low Countries, in which Margaret of Austria was once again to play an important role, by July 1517 all was ready. Raised as a Burgundian prince, Charles was imbued with the importance of tradition, notions of honour, chivalry and defending his deeply held Christian beliefs, ideas that were essentially medieval in outlook. The wider world into which he was now launching, the one he would have to deal with over the next forty years, was one in which political, social, economic, religious, scientific and technological changes were taking place at a faster pace than ever before. This was the time of the Renaissance, of Leonardo, Michelangelo, Raphael, Bosch and Durer in art, of Erasmus, Thomas More and Machiavelli in political philosophy, of Magellan, Cortes, and Pizarro in exploration and conquest, of Copernicus and Vesalius in science and medicine, and of Luther and Calvin in religion. This was a changing world, in which new ideas and new approaches challenged, and in some cases, changed the established order. It was these issues, as well as the older political problems, that awaited Charles. Success would depend upon his ability to respond to new challenges while retaining the principles that had become part of his very being.

## 4
### 'Managed by M. de Chièvres' - King in Spain

As he set sail from Flushing (Vlissingen) on 8th September 1517 Charles must have experienced a cauldron of emotions. He was leaving his homeland for the first time heading towards a new land whose language he did not speak, and most of whose customs were unfamiliar. He knew that there would be many difficulties ahead, but he had been brought up for a life full of these very responsibilities and he had with him many of those who had shaped him since his early years. The voyage itself, with the danger of fires, shipwrecks and the ever present risk of disease, held fears for everyone. But he would also have been keen for new experiences and he knew that his future almost certainly held many more such journeys.

Charles was at first sea-sick, and then saw two of his ships destroyed by fire with over one hundred deaths. These had included some men known to him, though most of those lost were crew, along with some courtesans and stable boys who went down with their horses. The threat posed by privateers, though not as serious as in the Mediterranean, was one which could not be ignored, especially if a ship were to be isolated. Storms could easily break up a fleet and force an unplanned, unwelcome landing, as had happened to his parents eleven years before. The Channel was negotiated successfully but Charles' worries increased as the fleet of 40 ships hit storms in the Bay of Biscay. The fleet was indeed scattered and his vessel, the *Real*, its sails decorated with religious and dynastic emblems, was blown off course, far to the west of Santander, their intended destination, landing at Villaviciosa on 18th September.

## Charles V: Duty and Dynasty

This was not the well planned arrival that one might expect for a new king. Charles and his immediate company had to undergo an arduous journey along the difficult northern coastline of Spain in order to reassemble his court. Many of the local inhabitants took these foreigners for pirates and ran to the hills for safety. This, together with the lack of suitable lodgings and the apparent reluctance of the party to make immediately for a city such as Leon or Burgos, deterred by rumours of epidemics, made for an inauspicious start in Spain. They made slow progress over the mountains and it was nearly six weeks before Charles reached his first destination, Tordesillas.

Now that Charles was in Spain, he needed to gain a better understanding of these lands. Some sense of unity had only been achieved in Spain with the marriage of his maternal grandparents, the 'Catholic Monarchs', Ferdinand of Aragon and Isabella of Castile, in 1469, but regional antagonism and jealousies still loomed large. The preceding two hundred years had been anything but tranquil. The defeat of the Moorish rulers of Cordoba and Seville by Ferdinand III of Castile in the first half of the 13th century (leaving Granada as the only remaining Muslim state in Iberia) might have been expected to lead to a golden age. Instead the period could be characterised as one of internal rivalries (especially in Castile, both within the ruling family and between the monarchy and the nobility), growing religious intolerance, economic weaknesses and social unrest[1]. There had, however, been considerable cultural achievements and some external success with Aragon's expansion in the Mediterranean. Ferdinand and Isabella had been able to establish royal power more effectively, complete the 'Reconquista', and start the work of the Inquisition towards greater religious uniformity.

However, there remained significant social, economic and political problems. There were great inequalities of wealth. Land was mainly held by large landowners, leaving the majority of the rural population to pay high rents, for what was often unproductive land, and high taxes. The power of the nobility, who paid little tax, was increasingly resented by the urban middle class. The years after the death of Isabella in 1504 saw a resurgence of political instability. It had never been the intention of Isabella and Ferdinand's marriage alliances, aimed against France, to hand Spain to a foreign dynasty[2]. There had been rivalry between Ferdinand and Philip, as Juana's husband, and after Philip's death antagonism between Ferdinand and the Castilian nobility who, disliking the idea of rule by Aragon, had thrown in their lot with the Burgundians. It had been Cardinal Jimenez de Cisneros who had managed to control the situation in Castile after 1506, with Ferdinand continuing his reign in Aragon and taking the lead in foreign policy.

On his death bed, in the village of Madrigalejo in Extremadura, Ferdinand had appointed Cardinal Cisneros as regent in Castile and his natural son, Alfonso de Aragon, the Archbishop of Zaragoza, as regent in Aragon. There was the risk of conflict between Cisneros and Adrian of Utrecht, sent from Brussels as Charles' ambassador. Any lack of clear leadership would allow various groups, particularly the nobility and the cities, to try to exploit the power vacuum. Adrian showed good sense and carried out a watching brief, looking after Charles' interests but allowing Cisneros to use his experience and authority to run the country. This was needed. Charles' eighteen month delay in coming to Spain, despite many appeals for urgency, did nothing to allay the natural fears that a 'foreign' ruler would give precedence to the affairs of his other countries. In Castile there were concerns that the many courtiers from Aragon who had travelled to the Low Countries after King Ferdinand's death had gained too much influence with Charles and his advisers. Many Castilian nobles wished to increase their power in relation to the crown and achieve a position from which they could control the young king when he arrived, or even establish his younger brother, Ferdinand, in his place. A planned attempt to oust the authoritarian Cisneros was thwarted by his prompt actions, raising a militia and removing Prince Ferdinand from their influence.

Charles had arrived none too soon, but his first years in Spain were not to be easy. As the eighty year old Cisneros set out to greet him, word circulated that Chièvres was keen to avoid such a meeting. Mistrust was already growing between the Burgundians and the Spanish. Charles could have benefitted from the advice of one who had played a leading role in Castile for thirty years. It is possible to imagine the pleasure that Cisneros might have gained from meeting his young king and handing over his responsibilities with words of guidance. It was not to be. At Roa, between Valladolid and Burgos, Cisneros fell ill and was unable to continue. He died on 8th November, before a meeting could take place. On the same day a letter from Chievres arrived commanding him to meet Charles, thanking him for his services and letting him know that they would be required no longer[3].

Charles' priority was to visit his mother, legally his co-monarch, who had already been in the Convent of Santa Clara at Tordesillas for nearly a decade. Before his arrival he had written to Cisneros that, 'whilst she is to be treated well, she be so well guarded and watched that if any persons should endeavour to counteract my good intentions, they shall be prevented from doing so. Since it belongs to nobody more than to myself to take care of the honour, contentment, and consolation of the Queen my lady, those who endeavour to meddle [in this affair] cannot have any good intention.'[4] His claim to the throne would be greatly strengthened by obtaining her blessing and he was alert to the danger that others might seek to use Juana's position to undermine his own. Together with his sister Eleanor, he arrived at Tordesillas on 4th November. It was their first meeting since her departure from the Low Countries nearly twelve years earlier. He mentioned this first visit in his memoirs: 'he went to kiss the hands of the Queen his mother'.[5] Ever after he made it his custom to pay her a visit whenever he returned to Spain from a journey outside the country. He was kept fully informed as to her health and demeanour by the Marquis of Denia and his wife who were appointed to oversee Juana's confinement in March 1518. It is clear from this correspondence that Juana was not allowed contact with anyone outside her apartment or allowed money to spend as she wished. Like his grandfather and father before him, Charles had no intention of allowing Juana to rule. It did, however, suit his purpose if it were known that he had brought about an amelioration in her situation. Also, with Eleanor's assistance, he ensured that the circumstances of their sister Catherine were improved, though they did not at this stage feel able to remove her completely from her mother.

Family considerations continued to dominate. Charles met his fourteen year old brother Ferdinand for the first time, at Mojados just south of Valladolid, and gave assurances that he would always be a true brother. Charles' memoirs recorded that 'he met the Infant Don Ferdinand, his brother, whom he welcomed with great fraternal love'[6]. Ferdinand had been born in Alcala de Henares in 1503, brought up at court, spoke the language and was familiar with Spanish affairs. Many Spaniards believed that Charles would prefer the Low Countries of his birth, regard Spanish interests and concerns as secondary, and divert Spanish money to other areas of his empire. In their eyes Ferdinand would at least be a Spanish ruler.

This could have been a very awkward meeting. The brothers had no common language to help make the encounter less formal. Charles and his advisors had no intention of backing down, these were his kingdoms by right; he was determined to establish himself on the thrones of Castile and Aragon as Carlos I. Ferdinand could have made things difficult had he insisted on challenging his brother, but Adrian of Utrecht, sent from Brussels in 1515, had done his job well. It had been agreed that Ferdinand, having waited to meet his brother, would shortly afterwards leave Spain and travel to the Low Countries to continue his upbringing in the care of his aunt, Margaret, and grandfather, Maximilian. This would avoid the ever present threat of the development of a rival, anti-Charles, faction around him. Ferdinand was given expectations of Habsburg lands in Austria in the future, but as he had never left Spain before, he must have regarded his future as uncertain. Even so, he accepted the settlement without apparent protest. Ferdinand had an outgoing and appealing personality. He had been a centre of attention in Spain, and was to find a warm welcome in the Low Countries.

Before his departure he was presented with the chain of the Order of the Golden Fleece and given a place of honour in Charles' ceremonial 'entry' to Valladolid. Castile did not have an official capital city until Philip II settled on Madrid half a century later. It was customary for monarchs and their court to travel around the country, to Toledo, Segovia, Seville and other major cities, a tradition followed by Ferdinand and Isabella. People expected to be able to see their rulers, and needed to believe that they had access to them for the redress of grievances. However, as the administrative machinery of government became more complex, certain functions had become centralised in Valladolid. Thus the city had many palaces belonging to noble families, impressive squares, fine churches and a university.

Astride a charger and dressed in splendid armour, accompanied by both Burgundians and those Spaniards who had travelled from the Low Countries with him, Charles' entry procession was intended to impress. It was followed by a series of spectacular tournaments held in the market place of Valladolid during December, January and February, which again aimed to display the valour of the Burgundian lords to the Spaniards. Such tournaments were an essential part of a royal entry and also used to celebrate marriages and births in the ruling family. As well as providing entertainment they served the important social and political function of enabling the ruler to display skills and interact with the nobility. They consisted of a combination of jousts (in which armoured horsemen attempted to unseat their opponent or shatter a lance against his shield), a melee (in which teams of horsemen or armoured knights on foot would attack each other, fighting for several hours), and 'juegar de canas' (in which teams of horsemen, often dressed in Moorish costume, repeatedly threw blunt cane spears at each other and then wheeled in retreat, demonstrating their skills in horsemanship)[7]. In one tournament an enormous effigy of a 'Turk' was burned[8], a symbolic way to demonstrate Charles' devotion to the idea of 'crusade'.

Shortly after his arrival Charles passed under the fine facade of the church of San Pablo with the leading nobles of Spain – archbishops, bishops, dukes, marquises, viscounts and counts – who had assembled to swear allegiance to their new king.[9] Charles was comfortable in Burgundian court life but it is possible that he was finding that in Spain rather too austere. He was missing the company of some of his earlier companions who had not travelled with him. He wrote to Henry of Nassau that he was in danger of becoming too serious and that he found few of the ladies appealing, except one, and she 'paints herself atrociously'[10].

Charles may well have given Henry less than the whole truth. Present in Valladolid on his arrival was the 29 year old widow of Ferdinand of Aragon, Germaine de Foix. The chronicler Laurent Vital records that Charles had an infatuation and that he made frequent use of a wooden bridge to visit his lover. Though Vital does not name this lover, Germaine's apartments were located opposite the royal palace, to which they were linked by a covered bridge. Sometime in 1518 Germaine gave birth to a daughter. Years later, in her will, she refers to the 'dona Isabella, Infanta of Castile, daughter of his majesty the Emperor' to whom she leaves her 'best necklace with 133 fat pearls'[11]. This can only make sense if this Isabella is the daughter of Germaine and Charles. There is no doubt that Germaine later travelled with Charles to Barcelona, to provide him with advice on the running of Aragon and Catalonia, together with more personal services. Germaine was to be married twice more, and a sign of Charles' regard for her was that she was made joint viceroy of Valencia (along with her new husband) in 1523.

Charles had plenty of official business to occupy the rest of his time. He had to appear before the cortes of Castile and Leon to take the oath promising to defend their privileges and to accept their homage. This was not achieved without difficulty. Charles had no experience of Spanish affairs and had yet to learn the language. He relied heavily on the familiar Burgundians, particularly Chièvres, who had travelled from the Low Countries with him. They saw the possibilities of power, wealth and influence, and their behaviour did little to placate local unease. Many Spaniards had been outraged by two recent appointments. William of Croy, Chièvres' twenty year old nephew, already bishop of Soria, was promoted to fill the vacancy caused by the death of Cisneros as Archbishop of Toledo, the most lucrative see in Spain, even though he was not even in Spain. Jean le Sauvage, Charles' Burgundian Chancellor, was made president of the cortes. The serious reservations of many were made clear to Charles by a delegate from Burgos, who argued that there was an unwritten but clear contract between king and subjects, at the heart of which was justice[12], which many believed was not apparent in these appointments.

Extensive negotiations with leading members of the cortes were still required. These were carried out by Charles' advisors. It was customary practice on the accession of a new king that a substantial 'servicio', or subsidy, was agreed by the cortes, while they put forward a list of complaints and demands. The cortes of Castile was an assembly consisting of representatives of the clergy, nobility and major cities. As the clergy and nobility had other means of access to the monarch and they contributed little, if anything, to the payment of the 'servicio', it was those from the cities who attended and played the leading role in formulating demands. Their list of eighty-eight demands included that appointees to court and to government and religious posts should be Spanish; that the new Archbishop of Toledo travel to Spain immediately; that Queen Juana be treated with kindness; that Charles should learn their language, stay in Spain until he had an heir, and allow Ferdinand to remain until then. Charles was able to agree many of these, but would not alter plans for Ferdinand's departure. In foreign policy the cortes emphasised the importance of retaining control of the disputed kingdom of Navarre, a point on which Charles and his advisors fully agreed. The generous 'servicio' of 600,000 ducats that the cortes granted to cover a three year period was not without strings attached. They requested that the towns take a greater responsibility in raising the money as opposed to the old system of selling the right to collect the taxes to 'tax farmers', demanded that it not be spent elsewhere in Charles' lands, and made the provocative statement that 'Most powerful lord, you are in our service'.

Given the divided nature of Spain this was just the first of a series of such negotiations. Having settled with Castile he now needed to move on to Aragon. Ferdinand's kingdom had consisted of three parts in Spain, Aragon itself, Catalonia and Valencia, each with a separate cortes, as well as the territories of the Balearics, Sardinia, Sicily and Naples, with their own governors, appointed by the king, and representative assemblies. Each of the Spanish areas expected Charles to visit, to follow the formalities required of a new monarch, to take his oath, to receive their demands and accept their homage. In May 1518 Charles arrived in Zaragoza to meet the cortes of Aragon. While there his Grand Chancellor, the unpopular Jean le Sauvage, died and was replaced by Mercurino Gattanara, formerly the Chancellor to his aunt, Margaret of Austria. Over the next eleven years he was to have a major influence on Charles' thinking, giving it a broader international, even universal, rather than regional, perspective. While Charles was in Zaragoza, his sister Eleanor married Manuel I of Portugal as planned, in a move that Charles hoped would remove any danger of Portugal intervening in the affairs of Castile.

By January 1519 Charles was in Barcelona for a meeting of the cortes of Catalonia. This was every bit as contentious as that in Valladolid. Indeed in Aragon the talks were longer, the cortes less willing to compromise, and more bound by formalities. However they eventually granted a 'servicio' of 200,000 ducats and in Catalonia they granted 100,000 ducats, both quite generous given their size. It was not surprising that he and his court had no desire to repeat the experience yet again in Valencia, a decision that was later to produce further difficulties.

Charles had spent seven months in Zaragoza and then the best part of 1519 in Barcelona. So long spent in Aragon and Catalonia generated wide-spread anger in Castile where he had only remained for five months and visited no major city other than Valladolid. If these matters weren't difficult enough, early in his stay in Barcelona Charles heard news that would bring him even wider responsibilities. On 12th January 1519 Emperor Maximilian had died. As his heir Charles inherited all the Habsburg lands in central Europe. In addition, as head of the family which had held the imperial throne since 1438, Charles felt honour bound to continue this tradition and become the next Holy Roman Emperor. He immediately announced his intention of seeking election, increasing suspicions that Spain would only be of secondary concern to Charles.

Once that election had been achieved in June 1519 (see Chapter 5), at great cost, with money borrowed in Germany partly guaranteed by his Spanish income, it became necessary for Charles to travel to Germany for his enthronement at Aix-la-Chapelle (Aachen). In Spain the fear of an absentee monarch was genuinely and widely felt, especially in light of their recent experiences. But the elevation gave Charles a new prestige. There was a sense of pride that their king was emperor and some recognised that this could open up new opportunities for them, on a stage broader than just Castile or Aragon. Nevertheless it was the negative aspects that came to the fore, especially in Castile. Factions formed, for and against Charles, in the towns and amongst the nobility. Some, often motivated by personal grievances, called for representatives to meet, and repeated demands that Charles should not leave Spain, that no money should be taken out of the country and that there must be no more foreign appointments.

As preparations for Charles' departure continued, Chièvres and Gattinara realised that more funds were required to pay the costs of the voyage and Charles' onward journey to Aix in a style appropriate to his new status. Gattinara was aware of the dangers of calling a cortes, but was over-ruled by Chièvres.[13] The new cortes was summoned, this time to Santiago in the remote north-west, suitable only because of Charles' planned departure from Corunna. Since the aim was to raise money and avoid lengthy wrangling about complaints, it was demanded that those attending the cortes, the 'procuradores', should have full powers and not be bound by decisions already made by their cities. This was so that pressure could be exerted on them by the royal representatives, with threats, bribes and promises of advancement for co-operation. This had happened on occasions before but, with the tensions growing, it resulted in widespread opposition. Only three towns, Burgos, Granada and Seville, fully acceded to these demands.[14] In April, an opening statement on behalf of the king emphasised that although his responsibilities elsewhere meant that his departure was essential, Spain would be the bedrock of the empire, and that Charles would return within three years. Despite this the cortes refused to grant a subsidy until their grievances had been discussed. They were especially aggrieved that this new 'servicio' was being requested even before the previous one had expired. The cortes was moved to Corunna where, presumably after much arm twisting, the subsidy was agreed (even though it was never collected). Virtually Charles' last act before embarkation was to appoint Adrian of Utrecht as regent, thus breaking his earlier commitment not to appoint foreigners[15]. This was hardly calculated to calm the situation.

As he was to write nine years later, 'then I was managed and governed by M. de Chièvres, and I was not old enough to know these kingdoms or experienced enough to govern them.' Charles' first two and a half years in Spain had brought the country to the brink of revolt. Many of his subjects had been offended by the attitude of his Burgundian followers. There is no doubt that they saw Spain as an opportunity to enrich themselves and their families. Some considered that they behaved 'as though they were in a conquered country'.[16] It is not surprising that those in Spain who lost out would complain vehemently; they had good grounds. Many appointments rewarded those who had arrived with Charles and the subsequent sale of these offices to others for vast sums caused anger. Getting around the promise not to appoint foreigners by issuing them with letters of naturalisation, only increased the fury. Chièvres himself sold the position of 'contador major' of Castile to the Duke of Bejar for 30,000 ducats. Chièvres' wife and that of Charles de Lannoy were permitted to remove clothes, bullion and jewels from Spain in such quantity that they needed three hundred horses and eighty pack-mules. The licence to transport African slaves to the Indies was sold by its Burgundian recipient to the Genoese for 25,000 ducats[17]. Even if only a small proportion of bishoprics and other offices were handed to outsiders, it was obvious to many Spaniards that they were being over-looked. All this was sufficient to inflame an already volatile situation, and to turn long standing rivalries and divisions into open conflict.

Nor did Charles particularly impress his new subjects. Still not fully mature on arrival and not blessed with natural good looks, he was yet to attain the stature of one who could dominate by his presence or charm by his wit and good cheer. His youthfulness was both a hindrance and an advantage. He could take a leading role at court, in its social life and conventions, but in the political world he was still a novice, largely controlled by Sauvage, until his death, and Chièvres. Under their influence for so long, and then thrust into a completely new environment, he relied on their decisions. Therefore the blame for much that went wrong could fall upon his councillors and advisers, not on the king himself. At the time this was not a calculated manoeuvre by Charles, but in the future he was ready to use it to reduce his own responsibility. Perhaps he should have challenged them more, but he was still not quite ready for that. In his favour there was a belief in Spain that his person, as the rightful heir, was the only guarantee of stability. Most did not wish for the feuds and conflicts which might occur with his death or removal. Hence the demand for him to remain in the country; but the call of other duties was too strong for him to remain.

# 5
## 'There is nothing in this world we want more' – Emperor

Charles was already experiencing the conflicting demands of ruling widespread territories. Just as he had travelled to Spain in order to claim his kingdoms there, now he had to risk departure so that he could be acknowledged in Germany as the newly elected Emperor. By 1520 the Holy Roman Empire was already an ancient institution, in existence since 800 when Charlemagne was crowned by the Pope.[*] In the early 16th century it consisted of over 300 separate principalities, duchies, free imperial cities and other territories ruled by dukes, counts, princes, archbishops, bishops, city councils, imperial knights and others. These covered a large area of central Europe, and all owed allegiance to the elected Emperor. At its greatest extent it included most of the modern states of Germany, Austria, Switzerland, Liechtenstein, the Czech Republic, Slovakia, Slovenia, the Netherlands, Belgium, northern Italy (excluding Venice), western Poland, and eastern France (Alsace, Lorraine, Franche Comte, and Savoy).

Such were the divisions and complexity of the territories that many ruling princes had to cross their neighbour's land to visit outlying portions of their own. By the time of Charles' accession the effective power of the Emperor was in decline with on-going conflict about the degree of influence and access to the resources of the territories that the Emperor should have. Each territory aspired to as much independence as possible, and the more powerful princes were steadily gaining authority, but most were also keen to have the strength that association brought against external enemies.

---

[*] In all it lasted over 1000 years, until its dissolution after defeat by Napoleon in 1806.

## Charles V: Duty and Dynasty

The term 'Holy Roman Emperor' was used to signify the elected head of the Empire. There were 7 'electors': the Archbishops of Mainz, Trier, and Cologne; the King of Bohemia; and three secular 'princes', the electors of Brandenburg, Saxony, and the Palatinate. The title of Emperor remained in the Habsburg family from 1438 through to the end of the Empire – with one short exception in the mid-18th century. In earlier centuries those elected became 'King of the Romans', until such time they were crowned by the Pope, at which point they became 'Emperor of the Romans'. Charles' grandfather and predecessor, Maximilian, had been prevented from going to Rome for his coronation in 1508 and so Pope Julius II gave him the title 'Emperor-elect of the Romans'. From then on those elected were called Emperor and if during their lifetime a successor was chosen, that heir designate was given the title 'King of the Romans'.

The Emperor was acknowledged as the supreme judge in law, had the right to bestow titles and decide on issues for discussion at the Diets - formal meetings of the rulers within the Empire divided into the three 'estates' of the 'electors', other secular and ecclesiastical rulers (the 'princes'), and representatives of the imperial cities. He also had the obligation to uphold ancient rights and protect the Empire from foreign aggression. But this was in no way a modern state with a central government. As princes of the Empire themselves, the Habsburgs were at times in conflict over territory with other German princes. There was no permanent army, no established system of Imperial taxation, and no really effective means of enforcing decisions made at the Diets. Thus the task of the Emperor was always going to be difficult. When added to the problems in Charles' other lands it would make his burdens so immense that it has been questioned whether anyone could have tackled them successfully.

Charles had no doubt that it was his duty to take on the role. In his later years Emperor Maximilian had been working hard to have Charles elected as King of the Romans, his automatic successor. Maximilian well understood that this would be achieved not by promises alone but by hard cash, but he had not achieved his aim by the time of his death in January 1519. This meant that Charles would have to be elected in a more open contest, since any commitments made by the electors to Maximilian, however expensive to the ageing Emperor, were now null and void. Although he was the most likely successor, Charles' election was not a certainty. Earlier, Maximilian and Margaret had considered the young Louis of Hungary or Charles' brother, Ferdinand, as possible candidates. When early in 1519 it was gently suggested that perhaps with all his other responsibilities Charles should give way to his brother, he responded vigorously that a division of Habsburg lands was exactly what the French wanted. He went on to argue in a letter to Margaret of Austria: 'It seems to us that if the said election is conferred on our person...we will be able to accomplish many good and great things, and not only conserve and guard the possessions which God has given to us, but increase them greatly and, in this way, give peace, repose and tranquillity to Christendom.' '..we are resolved to spare nothing and to commit everything we have, since there is nothing in this world we want more and which lies closer to our heart'. Even if he was yet to impose himself in Spain, Charles was certainly able to make clear his wishes about this election.

It was so important to Charles because he recognised, as did others, that the Imperial throne brought with it the claim to the secular leadership of Christendom, as 'God's standard bearer'. Charles, undoubtedly influenced by the ideas of his new Chancellor, Gattinara, came to see this as his destiny; to defend Christian Europe against the threat posed by Ottoman expansion in the east and in the Mediterranean, and against the threat of heresy from within. He believed that he would be more effective with the resources of his other territories behind him than another ruler who lacked such support. The Habsburgs had held the Imperial throne since the mid-15$^{th}$ century and Charles considered that his reputation and honour depended on it. There was much more to it than mere territorial expansion; after all he must have recognised the difficulties that were inherent in the office.

The election itself took place while Charles was still in Barcelona and so his campaign was organised by his representatives in the Low Countries and Germany. Much of the work was coordinated by Margaret of Austria, now confirmed by Charles as his regent in the Low Countries, along with her advisers, especially Philip of Cleves, Henry of Nassau and Antoine de Lalaing. The other contenders for the Imperial throne were Francis I of France and, perhaps less of a threat, Henry VIII of England and Frederick of Saxony, himself one of the electors. Francis certainly had serious hopes, initially encouraged by the Pope and by some of the electors. They clearly had a vested interest in a contested election, since this provided an opportunity for the receipt of bribes and other inducements from the various candidates. During the campaign Charles used three main approaches to gain the support of the electors: bribery, propaganda and the threat of force. Maximilian had already spent considerable sums and these had to be renewed. Charles did not have sufficient ready money (nor did the other contenders) but he did have access to the German banking houses, particularly the Fugger and the Welser of Augsburg. Jacob Fugger's agent in Antwerp, Wolff Haller, already known to Charles from his days as Duke of Burgundy, travelled to Spain and negotiated the loan. It is estimated that of the 835,000 florins that Charles used to win the election, the Fugger family provided 65% (543,000 florins).

Francis could not match this level of funding. His campaign was based on the arguments that, if elected, Charles would become too powerful, something that the German princes would see as a threat; that it was undesirable for one family to continuously hold the title; that he had friendly relations with some electors and indications of support from the Pope. On the last point the contemporary Florentine diplomat and writer Francesco Guicciardini commented that Francis 'deceived himself more every day'. Pope Leo X was indeed concerned about Charles' potential power, but he was equally worried about the impact of a victory for the French king on Italy. But even the hint of an alliance between France and the Pope strengthened Charles' hand. According to Guicciardini the Pope then wished Francis to put his support behind a third candidate, elector Frederick the Wise of Saxony, whose election, however unlikely, would leave Leo X a much freer hand in Italy. In the end Frederick declined to become a candidate.

Charles' propaganda countered that the title should not go to a 'foreign' non- German ruler, since this was against custom and would not be tolerated by other rulers and free towns in the Empire. Francis was characterised as a foreign adventurer out for what he could get; Charles as the 'national candidate' (even though he had yet to learn German or visit Habsburg lands there). Only Charles, it was argued, could be relied upon to look after the interests of German lands and be powerful enough to defend the Empire against the growing external threat of the Ottoman Turks. To back up his case Charles was able to take advantage of the defeat of Francis' ally Duke Ulrich of Wurttemberg by troops of the Swabian League to establish a military presence by funding those troops to remain mobilised, as well as by buying the support of Swiss soldiers for 30,000 florins and of the German mercenary Franz von Sickingen for 40,000 florins. Von Sickingen positioned himself just outside Frankfurt where the electors met on 28th June 1519.

The details of the negotiations, financial dealings, manoeuvrings and promises made were complex. Suffice to say that the self-interest of the electors, whether motivated by greed, ambition, fear or genuine belief in his cause, eventually resulted in the unanimous choice of Charles and a consequent deepening of the enmity between the new emperor and Francis I. Henry VIII sent a message of congratulation to the new emperor and reminded Charles of the long friendship between England and both the Low Countries and Spain. So too did Francis. However, as the Venetian ambassador to France, Antonio Giustinian, wrote; 'These sovereigns are not at peace; they adapt themselves to circumstance, but they hate each other very cordially'. If Charles claimed it as his duty to become Emperor, others saw it as ambition to further his own power and that of his dynasty. These perceptions were to remain unchanged and had a major influence on European affairs for the rest of their lives and beyond.

Soon after the election Gattinara wrote to Charles: 'God has by His grace elevated you above all other Christian kings and princes, making you the greatest Emperor since Charlemagne..... You are on the road to Universal Monarchy and on the point of uniting Christendom under a single shepherd' He argued that it was Charles' duty 'to arrive at world peace which cannot be achieved without world-monarchy'. What should be understood from this is that Charles was being encouraged to think in terms of a universal Christian peace which would then enable him to lead the defence of Christianity against the threats posed by the Turks and by those who challenged its unity from inside. Given this idea of world-monarchy it is tempting to imagine that Charles had grandiose ideas of somehow taking over all existing states and creating a European wide empire, a re-creation of the Roman Empire.

Even if some of his advisors sometimes thought along those lines, this was not an idea embraced by Charles. Even in the lands that he inherited, in Spain, the Low Countries, Germany and Italy, there was never a real effort to create a uniform, central administrative, legal or financial structure. Moves by administrators like Gattinara, until his death in 1530, helped in some ways to make the systems more efficient, but many pre-existing customs and institutions were maintained. Charles ruled as the king of each. He did fervently wish for a universal Christian peace and, as Emperor, recognised his own unique position and responsibility to bring it about. This can be seen as a constant theme in many of his words and actions. However it never meant that he envisaged, for example, the full scale invasion, conquest and control of France or the overthrow of other existing monarchies. His aims were never simple domination or aggressive expansion in the modern sense, but a more complex set of beliefs, gradually developed, influenced by dynastic, religious and even chivalric, considerations. Dynastic marriages were a force for unity, ideally developing into a network that would provide the desired peace. Charles himself later suggested to his son Philip that plenty of children could provide 'the best way of holding kingdoms together'.

However, the impact of talk of world-monarchy or 'monarchia universal' at the time was considerable. Whereas his supporters saw this as a positive move for peace, unity, and the defence of the Christian faith, opponents were ready to portray it as a sinister quest for domination and to claim that Charles was a destroyer of ancient liberties. In Italy in the 1520s each time Charles gained the upper hand, others would begin to see this as a major threat and gather together to undo the successes that he had achieved. In Germany in the 1530s and 1540s his wish for a united church and the end of the divisions between Catholic and Protestant was often portrayed as a cynical, hypocritical use of religion to mask what some claimed were his true aims, complete political control and the reduction of local powers. In fact Charles did not have one single guiding principal, and understood his task to be a range of complex commitments and duties.

Once his election had been achieved, arrangements had to be made for Charles' voyage to northern Europe for his enthronement. Even though he left Spain in turmoil, he had much to do elsewhere. En-route to the Low Countries he disembarked in England for a few days. He was greeted at Dover by Cardinal Wolsey, Archbishop of York and Henry VIII's chancellor. He travelled to Canterbury on 27th May 1520 with numerous nobles from Spain and the Low Countries together with their ladies, where he met Henry, his wife, Charles' aunt, Catherine of Aragon, and the king's sister, Mary, now Duchess of Suffolk, to whom Charles had once been betrothed. A new trading treaty was signed between England and the Low Countries and it was agreed that the two monarchs would meet again the following month. Five days later Charles returned to his native Low Countries, sailing into Flushing, and immediately travelled, by way of Bruges and Ghent, to Brussels.

On the same day Henry crossed the Channel with a vast company ready to meet Francis I at the 'Field of the Cloth of Gold', just south of Calais. Here the kings of England and France made declarations of mutual friendship, but these fair words could do little to disguise the underlying distrust. Henry, guided by Wolsey, saw the opportunity to play the power broker between the Emperor and the king of France, extracting as much as he could from both while seeming to act as arbiter. Wolsey himself hoped to be able to further his ambitions to become Pope, although both Charles and Francis, whatever they might promise, had more compliant candidates in mind. Soon after, Charles and Henry met again, this time at Gravelines on the coast between Calais and Dunkirk. Discussions centred on friendship between the two monarchs and the possible future marriage of Charles to Henry's young daughter Mary. This would break the obligations that Charles had to marry a French princess undertaken in the Treaty of Noyon, and Henry promptly sought advantage by revealing the discussions in a confidential note to Francis[1]. The likelihood of Charles waiting almost a decade to marry Mary, who was only four, was in any case remote.

After time in Brussels, renewing old friendships and acquaintances, Charles travelled to Aachen (Aix-la-Chapelle) and on 22nd October his lengthy procession, packed with the electors, princes, counts and lords from throughout his realms, with accompanying horsemen and foot soldiers, entered the city. That evening he took the coronation oath. By this he swore to guarantee the electors and rulers of the multitude of territories in their rights and possessions, to use only Germans in official posts, use German or Latin in official documents, to call no Diet outside the frontiers of the Empire and to permit no foreign troops in the Empire. The next morning he was crowned by the Archbishop of Cologne in Aachen cathedral, where having sworn to rule justly, protect ancient imperial rights, defend the church and revere the Pope, he was acclaimed by the congregation who promised to obey their new lord. The coronation banquet followed at midday and another was held that evening in the rathaus. Three days later the blessing of the Medici Pope Leo X arrived enabling Charles to use the title 'elected Roman Emperor'[2].

At the age of twenty he was now the monarch of vast swathes of Europe, controlling the destiny of nearly 40% of its population, the largest empire ruled by right, as opposed to conquered by might, for five hundred years either before or after his time. This, of course, did not mean that he could control events and achieve his goals with ease. If anything the reverse was true. As his territories expanded so his ambitions broadened. From ruling a number of provinces in the Low Countries and hoping to restore former Burgundian lands, he now had to think in terms of holding together all his Spanish lands, as well as those in the Holy Roman Empire, being a unifying force within Christendom and defending Christian Europe from outside assault. His widespread domains brought an enormous number of problems, ones that he would find difficult to resolve simultaneously.

To Charles, his inheritance was of great importance. His grandfathers had both considered whether it was wise to have all these lands under one ruler – yet this had been the logical, though unintended, result of their marriage policies. There was certainly a concern as to whether any one ruler would be able to meet the demands of such a vast, diverse, empire. Each land wanted the ruler to be present in their territory, especially as the presence of the monarch could result in patronage, privileges, and promotions which would otherwise not be available. The personal presence of a leader has always been regarded as important for the settlement of a stubborn internal or international issue. Spade work can be done by ambassadors, diplomats and ministers, but the final push for a resolution, involving either concessions or the strength to face down opponents, needs the ultimate decision makers to be there. This was something that would be a constant issue for Charles. When he was in Spain he was wanted in the Netherlands and Germany. When in the Low Countries he was required in Spain and needed in Italy. When in Italy he was urged to help combat the Ottoman threat in Austria and Hungary. In addition he had to be 'a lord of many states: a Burgundian among the Burgundians; a Spaniard in Castile and Aragon; an Italian among the Italians.'[3]

What made these tensions harder to resolve was the fact that sixteenth century communications were slow. News, letters requesting advice or instructions, appeals for support or money from viceroys and regents, as well as Charles' orders and responses to such requests, all took a considerable time to reach their destinations. Charles required a reliable postal service. An agreement negotiated with the Taxis family involved guaranteed delivery times and an understanding with Francis I in 1518 gave his couriers and their post security on the journey across France in times of peace. This route involved one hundred and six stages, each with two horses. Even with this system for efficient and safe delivery, letters from Valladolid took on average three weeks to reach northern Italy, four weeks to reach Brussels and six weeks to be delivered in Vienna.[4] Times varied considerably. A study of letters arriving in Venice between 1497 and 1522 reveals that those from Brussels took between nine and thirty-five days, from Valladolid between twelve and sixty-three days, and from Vienna between eight and thirty-two days[5]. With the widespread nature of Charles' territories and with France blocking land routes from Spain in times of war, links to Italy and northern Europe often had to rely on sea transport. This was slower still and not totally safe as ships could be intercepted, blown off course, or wrecked by storms as they sailed across the Mediterranean or around France.

When Charles himself had to travel things were even slower. The routes that he followed were determined by the constraints of geography, as well as the diplomatic situation at any given time. To and from Spain he had to go by sea, except on one occasion when he went north through France as the guest of Francis I. If travelling between the Low Countries and Spain he would sail along the Channel and across the Bay of Biscay (Flushing to Laredo or Santander). If going to Italy he would usually leave from Barcelona, crossing the Mediterranean for Genoa. From Italy northwards his route would often be via Milan, Innsbruck and into southern Germany. From here if he wished to travel east he would frequently go via Augsburg, Regensburg and the Danube; if moving to the Low

Countries he would frequently travel up the Rhine. If we add to these journeys the military campaigns in which he was directly involved, especially after 1535, and his attendance at various Imperial Diets, Spanish Cortes and other representative bodies in his domains, it is difficult to believe that anyone was so well travelled as Charles in the first half of the 16th century.

Nevertheless his personal security had to be the first priority. If travelling by sea, a fleet of sufficient size to deter any aggressor, be it enemy state or privateers, had to be assembled, with suitable troops supplied and crew recruited. When all was ready they would set sail and hope to avoid the dangers posed by storms, fire, as well as disease resulting from poor food, lack of fresh water and overcrowded conditions. Everyone was aware of these dangers and surviving a voyage did not always make travellers keen to repeat the experience. Thus in December 1522, Dantiscus, the Polish ambassador to Charles V's court, wrote after his voyage from England to Spain: 'If I were to gain the empire of the world for the price of that voyage, I should never again enter upon such a perilous venture'.[6]

Travel overland (when not on a military campaign) was safer, but still had its problems. Charles would rarely have travelled without a large retinue of councillors, courtiers, soldiers, servants, cooks, and grooms. The larger the company the slower the progress. Even if the high ranking individuals travelled on horseback, many others walked. All the possessions and supplies that needed to be moved would be in carts or on pack animals. Charles, until age took its toll, would certainly be able to ride ahead with a few courtiers, but most just plodded on. The 'roads' were often one metre wide tracks for horses to be ridden along, with a wider space on either side flattened out by the passage of pedestrians, carts and flocks of sheep.[7] It could take hours to dismantle an encampment and hours to reassemble it later the same day. Naturally travelling in summer was easier than in winter, especially in northern Europe. If one adds in the ceremonies at towns and negotiations with local rulers (a necessary part of such royal 'progresses') then the pace was slowed down even further. The speed of the court when moving around Spain or travelling through Europe was something like 6-8 miles per day, very similar to the speed of a large army at the time.[8] It is difficult to imagine a journey from say Bologna to Innsbruck, now completed by motorway in a few hours, taking two months, or the journey from Vienna back to Spain, a couple of hours on a modern flight, occupying Charles for 6 months. More rapid movement was possible occasionally, in military emergencies or over relatively short distances, but this was rare.

Despite the obvious pressures that his ever widening responsibilities would place on Charles, it must have been particularly pleasing for Margaret of Austria to see her nephew take on the imperial mantle and fulfil the extensive ambitions of her family. Charles now wished to be regarded as the leading Christian monarch of his day. He was starting to rise above being a mere ceremonial figurehead, albeit an essential one, or an inexperienced youth controlled by others. He was taking on a more active role in discussions with his councillors and showing a greater independence of spirit in policy making. He was beginning to have that dignified presence of one in authority, for which he was to become widely respected over the next thirty-five years. He was to need all these evolving skills. The next few years were to test him to the full and in many ways set the pattern for the rest of his reign, in the Empire, Spain, Italy, and in his relations with France.

Charles V: Duty and Dynasty

# Part Two
# Discovering the Realities of Power 1520 – 1529

The Court of the Lions in the Alhambra Palace where Charles and Isabella spent several months after their marriage.

Charles V: Duty and Dynasty

# 6
## 'Scandal and Disturbance' – Revolt in Spain

The tensions that Charles had left behind on his departure from Spain erupted into open revolt well before his coronation in Aachen. Between 1519 and 1522 there was widespread violence and considerable loss of life in many parts of Spain. He later wrote that because of his youth, inexperience and over-reliance on Chievres, 'as I left for Flanders, having spent very little time here (Spain) and what is more, being unmarried and without an heir, it is not surprising that there was scandal and disturbance'. There is much truth in this statement, written in 1529, showing that by then he had gained a much firmer grasp of Spanish affairs and was willing to take a measure of responsibility for the earlier problems. This analysis, however, fails to give sufficient emphasis to the deep-rooted problems which had existed within Spanish society for many decades if not centuries. Charles had to deal with the uprisings from afar. Information and requests to him from Spain, appointments and instructions by Charles to Spain, each took weeks to be received. It was impossible for him to respond to events quickly and he often had to rely on his representatives in Spain to take independent decisions. Given the extent of the lands that he now ruled this was to become a common feature of his reign.

In Valencia, on the Mediterranean coast, serious difficulties had started as early as May 1519. As in the rest of Aragon, the nobility dominated land ownership, wealth and political power in both town and countryside. The revolt was caused by a complex combination of social discontent, political grievances and the outbreak of plague. One immediate issue was the failure of Charles and his court to come to Valencia to attend the cortes, partly because of the plague and partly because of the wish not to delay his return to the Empire even further. This, together with the exodus of the nobility and other wealthier citizens to what they believed to be places that were safer from the plague, meant that the traditional authority figures were removed from the cities. The resultant power vacuum gave an opportunity for strong anti-feudal feelings to be unleashed, especially as many believed that the plague was punishment for immoral behaviour, most closely associated with the nobility who had been able to avoid its greatest impact. A messianic element was also revealed in hostility to Muslims who still made up over 25% of the population in the Valencia region. They played an important part in the rural economy, mostly working on the estates of the noble landowners, who were seen as their protectors, but they were always regarded as 'outsiders' by many Spaniards. Also, those who had succumbed to pressure to convert to Christianity were often accused of covertly continuing their old religious practices.

The start of the revolt centred on the numerous guilds or brotherhoods (Germanias) which had been given royal permission to build up their own militias as a defence against the depredations of Muslim corsairs along the coast – yet another reason for the mistrust of their co-religionists. Led by Juan Llorenc, a weaver, and other urban artisans, the 'Germanias' set up a Council of Thirteen (after Christ and the 12 Apostles). Some had the idea that Valencia could become a republic, like Venice, though most were more fervently against the nobility and their privileges than anti-monarchist. After a refusal to give the guilds a greater influence on the city council, riots in Valencia forced the unpopular Castilian viceroy, Mendoza, to flee from the city in 1520. Llorenc's death following a heart attack soon after enabled more radical elements of the Council of Thirteen, led by Vicenc Peris, to take control as the movement spread across the province. The rebels took over most Valencian towns and captured the castle of Xativa before defeating a royalist force at the battle of Gandia in July 1521. The rebellion caused much devastation on the rural estates of the aristocracy and the church. Some Muslims had joined the royal forces through fear of persecution whipped up by the violent rhetoric of the rebels, and these were most harshly treated, but even the majority who had not joined the fighting were subject to forced conversion to Christianity on pain of death. Even so thousands died.

However, divisions within the rebel forces caused by a lack of agreed aims, the wish of many to return to their homes, together with the realisation among the nobility that they faced economic and political disaster unless they united, enabled royal forces to regroup. Marching from the south, they defeated Peris' forces at the battle of Oriola in August 1521. Valencia itself was recaptured in November. Peris, after sheltering for six months at Xativa, was captured when he returned to the city in February 1522 to make a final attempt to reignite the revolt. He was executed the following month.

Meanwhile in Castile the summoning of the cortes in April 1520 to demand more taxes and the appointment of Adrian of Utrecht as Charles' regent proved the final straw. Toledo and Salamanca had both refused to send representatives to the cortes and Toledo, led by Juan de Padilla and Pero Laso de la Vega, then expelled its corregidor, the royal representative in the city[1]. After Charles' departure the revolt of the comuneros - known in Spanish as 'Guerra de las Comunidades de Castilla' (the War of the Communities of Castile) - spread. Major Castilian cities began to resist royal authority, refusing to pay taxes, expelling royal officials and then turning to respected local families for leadership.[2] In Segovia the corregidor was lynched and in other cities they fled for their lives. However, at a meeting in Avila in July 1520 called to set up a junta to co-ordinate their plans, the leaders from only five cities attended (Toledo, Segovia, Salamanca, Toro and Avila). With the traditional rivalries between the cities and perhaps a natural conservatism of the relatively wealthy burgesses, it seemed that the momentum had been lost. And so it might if it had not been for the heavy handed response of the regent.

He ordered loyal troops to take Segovia by force, but with aid from Toledo the city successfully repulsed the assault.[3] Then, on 21st August, Adrian's troops sought to take control of Medina del

## Charles V: Duty and Dynasty

Campo, a major financial and trading centre which also had a substantial arsenal with much needed artillery. The attack was fiercely resisted, resulting in considerable loss of life amongst the inhabitants and the destruction of much of the city by fire. In the atmosphere of anger thus generated, other cities sent representatives to join the Junta in Avila. Only the cities of Andalucía did not join; Jaen, Ubeda and Baeza briefly set up 'comunidades', though they had no lasting authority. Charles was informed that 'the Junta is very indignant with Sevilla, Cordova, Granada, and other townships of Andalusia, because they are willing to remain in the obedience of your Majesty and your governor'.[4]

The enlarged Junta requested that Charles return to Spain, marry soon and exclude foreigners from his advisers[5]. These were not new demands. They also managed to draw up more radical plans for reform of taxation (to be reduced and collected by the towns) and of the constitution, with the cortes having a greater role in the government of the country and meeting every three years[6]. Many also wished to restrict raw wool exports to protect the domestic textile industries of cities like Segovia and Cuenca, although the merchants of Burgos and other northern cities involved in the wool trade objected to this[7]. Such divisions were ominous for the future.

It was agreed that several of the leaders would approach Queen Juana to gain her support. She was undoubtedly a higher authority and commanded more respect than the regent and if they gained consent to govern in her name, thus legitimising the revolt, they would be immeasurably strengthened.[8] As the regent pointed out to Charles: 'The worst of all this is, that for everything they make use of the name of the Queen our lady, as of a person who is perfectly sane and able to govern, thus taking all authority from your Highness, in order that they may not be called rebels, but appear only to obey her royal commands'.[9]

Juana's situation may have improved slightly in the years since 1516. Her 'guardian', Denia, had provided Charles with many reports of his conversations with her and the requests that she made. What comes over strongly in 1518 and 1519 was her desire to be allowed to go out, to have a meeting with the grandees (high ranking noblemen), to have money on her own account, and to leave Tordesillas, perhaps for Valladolid. It seemed that at least she was eating more regularly; her previous 'guardian', in a letter defending his position to Charles in 1516, had made a disturbing claim that in the time of Ferdinand 'to prevent her from destroying herself by abstinence from food…. he had to order that she was to be put to the rack to preserve her life'.[10] Also her reluctance to hear mass had been partly overcome by September 1518, though she insisted that it was held in the corridor where she had met Charles in November 1517. Denia was concerned that many believed that she was held as a prisoner as opposed to being confined for her own good, as Charles would have it, and that her attendants went into the town and talked about her condition and treatment to local friends and relatives.[11] It is clear that other than these attendants, her daughter Catherine, Denia, his wife, her confessor and the physician Dr Soto, she saw no-one. She was not kept informed about current events; even the death of her father, Ferdinand, was kept from her.

Having secured Tordesillas, representatives of the Junta had an audience with the Queen. Documents produced by the Junta and letters sent to Charles informing him of the events that followed provide a clear picture of the aims of the 'comuneros', and the concerns of Charles' regent at this stage of the revolt. Since Juana was unwilling to sign anything, 'they (the Junta) have an instrument drawn up by notaries of all she says, and receive it as her commands, as though her Highness were perfectly sane.'[12] At an initial meeting on 1st September, Juan de Padilla for Toledo, Juan Bravo for Segovia, Luis Quintanilla for Medina, and Juan Zapata for Madrid treated her with the respect that would be expected towards a monarch and put the case that the Junta was acting for the good of the country. In their attestation it was recorded that 'Her Highness answered and said that the Junta was good, and she considered that she was well served by it', and that 'they may come here, and I shall

## Charles V: Duty and Dynasty

be glad to concert with them what is serviceable for my kingdoms.'[13] The Junta moved to Tordesillas and thereafter had regular audiences with the Queen between September and December 1520.

Adrian wrote to Charles and made clear the seriousness of the situation. He recognised the problems that the Junta's contact with Juana would cause. 'It is to be supposed they will procure other mandates of a similar kind, that is to say, to dismiss the members of the Privy Council, and to order that no foreigner be permitted to be governor, that no money be exported, and other things which may occur to them. If that is done—and it is believed that it will soon be done—the whole kingdom will renounce obedience to your Highness and obey the mandates of the Queen our lady.' He then pointed out that the rebels were making the case that since Charles was absent from the country he was not personally ruling and therefore they were entitled to regard Juana as the sovereign queen. 'They already say that she cannot do less than your Highness.... as all that your Majesty is doing is through others, and you approve and sign only what they have decided upon. That, they say, the Queen can do also.' He continued that Charles' demands for funds could not be met as anyone attempting to collect taxes was attacked. Adrian then advocated the need to pardon the actions of the cities' representatives: 'send as quickly as possible a power to pardon. This is the only medicine for this incurable malady. It is no longer the question of suffering pecuniary losses, but of a total and everlasting downfall, as though your Highness had usurped the royal name and imprisoned the Queen, pretending that she was insane'. He concluded that 'the assembly at Avila goes forward, that all the other cities join it, and that it is their intention to declare that your Majesty has usurped the title of King of these kingdoms against all right.'[14]

In a letter written on the same day to Mendoza, Adrian repeated his concerns and mentioned another possible solution. 'The officers and servants of the Queen say publicly that her father and her son have tyrannically detained her, and that she is as able to govern as she was when 15 years old.' 'The most prudent think that a great part of these evils could be remedied, if his imperial Majesty would immediately contract marriage with the Señora Infanta of Portugal, or promise to marry her', together with a general pardon.

By 14th September Adrian was in despair. The rumour that Juana was 'perfectly sane' was sweeping the country, and the council were no longer satisfied with his letters to Charles, wanting to send their own. Even more tellingly he continued: 'They (members of the council) say in their instruction that I ought to share my office of governor with some native of these kingdoms. I, however, am of opinion that it would be best for your Highness entirely to release me from my duties, and give the office to some Spaniard. The complaints of the commons that it is against the laws of the country that a foreigner should be governor would thereby be entirely satisfied. I certainly do not wish this office, and could not satisfactorily serve your Highness for any length of time, nor perform what is due to your authority and honour.'[15]

On the 18th September Charles appointed two of the most senior grandees in the country, Inigo Fernandez de Velasco, Constable of Castile, and Admiral Fadrique Enriquez, as two co-regents to work with Adrian. He also abandoned any idea of collecting the 'servicio' agreed under duress by the cortes in Corunna. He had thus removed two of the major complaints of the 'comuneros'. This was the vital first step in pulling Castile back from the brink, but it would be a slow process to fully re-establish Charles' authority. For a while the setbacks continued. From Tordesillas Denia reported to Charles that he did all he could to remain at his post, supervising the queen, until he was removed on 20th September. He met Adrian the next day in Valladolid and then travelled on to his estates in Lerma. Soon after this, the royal council was forced to leave Valladolid and moved to Medina de Rioseco, in Admiral Enriquez' lands, between Valladolid and Leon.

The junta continued to repeat their grievances in their meetings with Juana and on 24th September documented that she had heard their argument that 'the son of her Highness, our prince, accompanied by foreigners, whom your Highness knows better than anyone else, have entered these kingdoms of your Highness, they have treated them so badly that, in addition to many other great evils which they did, and which it would be too long to state here at length, they left them almost without money.' She replied that 'When I learnt that the foreigners had come to us they were already in the kingdom, and I was very sorry for it, but thought that they had come to do something that was in the interest of my children.' She continued, according to this report, that she would attend to state business when she could but 'As long as I am not in a disposition to do it, you must despatch all business.'[16] As predicted by Adrian the junta had in effect claimed the power to rule. Two days later they announced that the royal council no longer had any authority. 'Those who until this time have been members of the Royal Council do not repent what they have done, but, imitating the devil, try again with all their strength to enlist soldiers, to gain over the grandees, and to carry out their diabolical intentions. We have, therefore, during many days discussed and deliberated on this subject, and finally decided that it is necessary to suspend them from their offices.'[17]

As the rebellion had taken hold it provided the opportunity for all sorts of grievances to be aired. They gradually concentrated on the abuses of power by the nobility and wealthy rather than the original causes of the uprising; after all, many of the 'foreigners' had left with Charles and it was now clear that the additional taxes were not going to be collected. The card that those loyal to the crown were now able to play was the hostility of the nobility towards social upheaval, especially as it spread into their estates in the countryside[18]. While many nobles had shared some of the initial concerns expressed by the Junta about foreign appointments and an absent king, the increasingly radical tone of some of the Junta's supporters alarmed them.[19] Their acquiescence, if not whole hearted support, was essential to the eventual success of the comuneros movement. The events in Valencia had already warned the nobles of what could go wrong and they would act to defend their own interests if not those of an absent king. Just as the new regents were attempting to build up support based on such fears, the junta was beginning to lose its unity of purpose. On 23rd September, even before their usurpation of power from the royal council, Adrian wrote to Charles that: 'I hear that in the Junta they are deliberating and disputing whether the orders shall be given in the name of the Queen and your Highness conjointly, or only in the name of the Queen. Toledo, Madrid, Segovia, and I know not what other towns, say that the name of your Majesty on the orders ought to be suppressed and cancelled, and only the names of the Queen and commons placed on them. Valladolid, Burgos, Soria, Toro, and other places insist that the said orders ought to be given in the name of her Highness and of your Majesty. It is doubtful which party will prevail.'[20]

The royal council immediately made use of these divisions. Timely concessions persuaded the leaders of Burgos to leave the Junta in October 1520. A few other towns followed this lead, but both sides began to build up their forces in expectation of a military conflict. Moderates in the leadership of the junta were now losing ground to those with more radical views, such as Gonzalo de Guzman of Leon. The junta also gained the support of Don Pedro Giron, a discontented nobleman whose claim to the Duchy of Medina-Sidonia Charles had refused, and Antonio de Acuna, Bishop of Zamora. Both were ambitious individuals seeking to use the political chaos to further their own ends. Giron commanded the Junta's army, taking them towards Medina de Rioseco, blocking the route to Tordesillas, but royal forces were able to seize Tordesillas in December when Giron left the town temporarily undefended as he took smaller settlements further west. The loss of Tordesillas, along with the capture of several of its leaders, was a major blow to the Junta since it deprived them of being able to claim that they were acting on behalf of the queen. Having failed to recapture the city Giron resigned his post and withdrew from the conflict. It is possible that he betrayed the junta; he was a cousin of the Constable, Inigo Fernandez de Velasco, and in 1524 he received a pardon from Charles for his involvement in the rebellion.

Antonio de Acuna, from one of the most influential families in Castile, already had a chequered career. Starting as the agent of the Catholic Monarchs in Rome, he had supported Philip against Ferdinand and on Philip's death persuaded Pope Julius II to appoint him as bishop of Zamora on condition that he would defend the interests of the papacy in Spain. Never fully accepted, he was expelled by a rival faction at the start of the revolt, and then became leader of the rebels in Zamora and joined the Junta with two thousand troops. After raids against the property of the nobility and a failed siege of Burgos in January 1521, Acuna's troops marched south to Toledo where he proclaimed himself archbishop, filling the vacancy caused by the death of William de Croy, the absentee incumbent. Meanwhile in February junta forces under Juan de Padilla were successful in capturing Torrelabaton, north of Tordesillas, but failed to press home their advantage.

On 17th December 1520 Charles had issued an edict which declared that those who supported the Comunidades were 'traitors, disloyal, rebels, and infidels', and condemned 249 prominent Comunidad members. Secular rebels were to be put to death, clergy were to receive lighter penalties. Attempts by moderates to negotiate a peaceful settlement failed, hampered by more intransigent elements on both sides, and the stage was set for a decisive military showdown. In April 1521 the armies met at Villalar, to the north-west of Tordesillas. Although the infantry were of comparable size (7,000 comuneros and 6,000 royalists), the massive royalist advantage in cavalry, outnumbering their opponents by six to one (400 comuneros, 2,400 royalist), was critical to the outcome. Padilla's army was cut down as it sought safer ground; its leaders Juan de Padilla, Juan Bravo and Francisco Maldonado were captured and executed the following day[21]. Many involved with the revolt, recognising their defeat, rapidly moved to Navarre, joining the army formed against the French invasion, hoping to show their allegiance to the king. Most towns soon surrendered to royal control, although resistance continued in Toledo under Padilla's widow, Maria Pacheco. Only in February

1522 did royal troops enter the city. Her execution was ordered but subsequent protest riots provided the distraction which enabled her to escape in disguise to Portugal. Acuna had already left the city, only to be captured and imprisoned at Simancas, where he was eventually executed in 1526 after murdering a guard in an attempted escape.

    The rebellions that had seriously threatened Charles' position in Spain were over, defeated by the nobility, more in their own interest rather than out of any great loyalty to their king. There would still be widespread discontent when Charles returned later in the year. He would have to learn from the experience of the revolts, both in Castile and Valencia, if he was ever to consolidate his power and become readily accepted or even welcomed as king. This would be his task when he had completed his duties in the Low Countries and the Holy Roman Empire.

# 7
## 'My body and my soul' – Reformation

On 31st October 1517, shortly after Charles had first arrived in Spain, Martin Luther is said to have posted his 95 theses on the door of the Castle Church in Wittenberg, where Frederick III (the Wise) Elector of Saxony had amassed many thousands of holy relics. In fact he probably sent the "Disputation of Martin Luther on the Power and Efficacy of Indulgences," to Archbishop Albert of Mainz, though he may also have pinned it to the church door. This detail is of little significance when compared with the eventual consequences of his action. The problems of the Holy Roman Empire were about to become intertwined with religious divisions sparked by Luther's protest and it was to fall to Charles to deal with the on-going upheaval thus caused. By the time Charles was elected and then crowned as Emperor this challenge had become an open wound that was threatening to poison the religious framework which for centuries had been fundamental to the structure of society. As Emperor, one of the 'twin pillars' of the Church together with the Papacy, Charles believed that it was his duty to deal with this danger.

Born in Saxony in November 1483, Luther's parents, Hans Luther (Luder), a copper mine leaseholder, and his wife Margarethe, had ambitions for him to become a lawyer. Educated in Mansfeld, Magdeburg, Eisenach and then entering university at Erfurt in 1501, he initially studied law but soon changed to religion. Having obtained his degree in 1505, he was ordained as an Augustinian priest in 1507 and the following year obtained a post as lecturer in theology and moral philosophy at Wittenberg University, an institution supported by the elector Frederick. In 1512 he was awarded a doctorate in theology.

On a visit to Rome in 1510 he had been appalled by the luxury of the papal court and by the abuses he witnessed there. He was later troubled by the idea that indulgencies could be sold (with penance being a financial transaction rather than genuine contrition) as well as by the destination of the money raised in this way. The sale of indulgencies was not new. In 1300 Pope Boniface VIII had issued a 'jubilee indulgence' and in 1476 Pope Sixtus IV had extended the scope of indulgencies to include souls in Purgatory (i.e. for those who had already died). In 1506 Pope Julius II started the construction of the new basilica of St. Peter, in Rome, and new indulgencies were granted to contribute towards the enormous cost of the undertaking. Those being sold in Germany in the late 1510's were promoted by Albert of Brandenburg, the younger brother of the elector of Brandenburg. He had purchased the archbishopric of Magdeburg (1513) and then the archbishopric of Mainz (1514) and paid 30,000 ducats for his posts to be confirmed. Needing to recoup his costs he then purchased the right to sell indulgencies in Germany for another 10,000 ducats. Of the money raised 50% went to the rebuilding of St Peter's in Rome, while the other 50% went to Albert, or more specifically his bankers. Johann Tetzel, the Dominican priest who travelled around Germany selling the indulgencies, was accompanied by an agent of the Fugger banking house of Augsburg, who had lent Albert 21,000 ducats. Add to this the fact that Frederick of Saxony and other rulers were concerned about the amount of currency that was leaving their territory (Frederick had banned the indulgence from his lands)[1], and it is easy to see why the church authorities were concerned about Luther's arguments. They were being challenged on theological, moral and financial grounds.

Luther had intended his '95 theses' to be a document for discussion, not a full blooded challenge to the Church, but the nature of his questions caused confrontation. In Thesis 86 he asked: "Why does the pope, whose wealth today is greater than the wealth of the richest Crassus, build the basilica of St. Peter with the money of poor believers rather than with his own money?" Luther at this stage stated that 'I submit all things to the judgement of the Holy Church'. He soon found himself under attack and as he defended his position he began to put forward other beliefs that clashed with the Roman Church. In his view 'good works', such as penance, buying indulgencies, sacraments and Mass, pilgrimage and fasting, could not alone bring about 'justification' – God's act of freeing an individual from the consequences of sin and making the sinner righteous. For Luther the most precious of all good works was faith in God. The idea that salvation depended on faith, and therefore that the individual's relationship with God was central, undermined the position of the Pope and the Church, who emphasised the importance of the priest as an intermediary between God and the individual.

His views spread quickly. Some could see strength in his theological arguments and it was now difficult to prevent its dissemination. The advent of printing meant that the era of almost complete control of the written word was over. In January 1518 the original Latin document was translated into German, printed and distributed widely. In 1519 copies reached Italy, France and England. By 1521 it is estimated that perhaps half a million copies of Luther's various books and pamphlets were in circulation.[2] With the literacy rate in German towns rising to perhaps 30% (compared with 5% in rural areas) the audience for his views was growing. There was also widespread concern about the domination of the Church from Rome and the abuses of power that were all too obvious. Many objected to the outflow of finances to Rome. Political divisions meant that Luther was not opposed by all German rulers, especially as he was a social conservative. Even if, as yet, none of the electors or other leading princes fully supported his religious views, few attempted to prevent the spread of his ideas.

The authorities in Rome were slow to react, perhaps because the perils of heresy were subordinated to papal/Italian political interests, especially after the death of Emperor Maximilian and the run up to the Imperial election. This, it has been claimed, proved the very point that Luther was making about nature of the papacy![3]

Luther was summoned to Augsburg in October 1518 to have a disputation with the Pope's representative, Cardinal Cajetan. He stayed in the monastery of St Anna, where the original 14th century church of the monastery had seen the construction of a new chapel over the previous ten years (1508-1518), the first Renaissance sacred building north of the Alps. With the involvement of artists and sculptors such as Albrecht Durer, Hans Burgkmair and Adolf Daucher, the enormous cost was funded by Jacob Fugger, head of the very family which had facilitated Charles' election and were recipients of money produced by the sale of indulgencies to which Luther so strongly objected. The chapel and the Lutherstiege, a plain wooden staircase, are still much visited in the church. Luther had four 'interviews' with Cajetan at the cardinal's lodgings in the Fuggerpalast, the Fugger family residence on Maximilianstrasse. The cardinal demanded that he repent, revoke his errors, agree not to teach them again and make no future challenges – in other words capitulate completely. Luther, unable to do this, was wisely encouraged by his supporters to leave secretly at night for his own safety.

Pope Leo X (Giovanni di Lorenzo de'Medici), who had been elected pope in 1513 on the death of Julius II, eventually issued a rebuttal of Luther's beliefs in a papal bull of June 1520. Forty-one lines from Luther's writings were condemned; he was ordered to recant or face excommunication. His writings were to be burnt. This did little to stem the growth of interest in his ideas. When a symbolic book burning was carried out in Mainz, students substituted other religious texts for Luther's works and the papal nuncio, Hieronymous Aleander, unwittingly threw these into the flames to the amusement of many.[4] Luther continued to criticise abuses of power and call for reforms, refusing to be silenced. 'I prefer the wrath of the world to the Wrath of God; they can do no more than take my life', he wrote, adding that 'a prince is a rare bird in heaven'. When in January 1521 he was finally excommunicated Luther's followers reacted by publicly burning the order. Once the Church had decided upon excommunication the responsibility for his arrest and punishment fell to the secular authorities, ultimately the Emperor.

During the autumn Charles and his councillors had been preparing for the imperial diet summoned to meet at Worms in January 1521. The promises made by Charles in order to secure his election would now be put to the test, and even though such pronouncements were usually kept deliberately imprecise, some of them could threaten the basis of the emperor's power in the Empire. These included a commitment to renew a programme of reform and to re-establish an Imperial Governing Council. The governance of the Empire was to be the main subject for debate at Worms. There was a clear hierarchy in the three estates (elector, princes and cities) of the Diet. It was summoned by the emperor, with the consent of the electors, and various proposals were tabled to be discussed by each estate separately. When the electors managed to come to an agreement, they passed their views on the princes, and if they could accept what was proposed the cities could be asked for their opinion. The final decision or statement on the subject would have to be agreed with the emperor.

The Empire was a complex entity and there was an on-going power struggle between the different parties involved. In the century before Charles' reign the position of the princes, always protective of their independence, had been enhanced. An Imperial court set up by Maximilian had most of its judges named by the Diet not by the emperor; if it did not suit them the princes would not allow the court to over-rule their own courts. The only Empire-wide tax, the 'common penny', had to be agreed by the Diet, though many cities and principalities frequently refused to pay it. The system of regional groupings or 'imperial circles' favoured by Maximilian, the most effective example of which was the Swabian Circle, became largely controlled by the princes. On the other hand there were still ways in which the emperor could effectively influence events. Old rivalries divided the princes, making it difficult for them to work together. The emperor could sometimes use the antagonism between the princes and the imperial cities to his advantage, and timely compromises could often bring about the decision that he desired.⁵

Charles recognised the limitations of his power and never attempted to completely change the constitutional arrangements of the Empire. What he hoped to achieve was to maintain or enhance the traditional powers of the emperor and to keep the post within the Habsburg family on his death. Charles wished to impose his authority, but not give the impression that he would attempt to rule without any consideration of the wishes of the Diet. He stated that 'our own honour and dignity is the honour and dignity of you all; it is not our desire and will that there be many lords, but one lord alone as is the tradition of the holy Empire'.⁶ Typically, though, he was prepared to negotiate, as when reaching an agreement in Worms about the Imperial Governing Council. It was to have twenty-two members, chaired by the representative or regent of the emperor. Seventeen of its members were to be chosen by the Diet. However it would only operate when the emperor was out of Germany (in effect making it a Regency Council), it would swear allegiance to Charles and not to the Diet, and its future would be reconsidered at the next Diet that Charles attended.⁷

Although never intended to be the main issue facing Charles and the German princes as they assembled in Worms*, the Diet is remembered as a major turning point in religious history. In the months leading up to this meeting Charles had to decide how to deal with the 'turbulent priest'. He was clearly in two minds. The papal nuncio, Aleander, argued that Luther should be outlawed immediately on the basis of his excommunication. Elector Frederick of Saxony, on the other hand, reminded Charles of his agreement not to outlaw subjects without giving them a hearing. Luther was required to attend the Diet and promised safe conduct to and from the meeting. Aleander responded by pointing out to Charles the danger of giving Luther such a prominent forum for his heretical

---

*Originally to have been in Nuremberg, but moved to Worms because of an outbreak of the plague.

views, with the risk of him gaining more support, and that only the pope could make judgement on such matters. Charles withdrew the invitation to Luther before the end of 1520. However, in February 1521, when Aleander put forward the motion to outlaw Luther, there was uproar in the Diet and it was demanded that he be given a hearing and the chance to recant. It was argued that there was the risk of widespread revolt if they failed to do so. Charles did not wish to over-rule the clear wish of the Diet and Luther was summoned to appear.

This is one of the most famous meetings in European history. Luther arrived in Worms on 16th April. Great excitement and expectation was reported in much of the town. His appearance before the assembled Diet with Charles at its head on the 17th was a disappointment to many: those who supported him had expected a forceful defence of his views; Charles had expected him to back down. Instead he asked for time to think, and was permitted to withdraw until the next day. It seemed that the grand setting or the seriousness of his position had overwhelmed him. It was on the 18th that he made his stand. Despite the fact that the questions put to him were intended to prevent him from providing a full explanation of his beliefs, he ignored them and put his case with knowledge, skill and vigour, concluding with the words: 'I am neither able nor willing to recant, since it is neither safe nor right to act against conscience. God help me. Amen'. In later propaganda, probably produced by Luther's supporter Philip Melanchthon, this was reported as being the memorable and resounding: 'Here I stand; I can do no other. God help me. Amen'.

Charles, perhaps angered by the temerity of the priest and the fact that he had not been able to force Luther to back down, made an equally compelling statement. Written in his own hand, this was an important demonstration of Charles' coming of age as a ruler, showing his ability to express his opinions clearly, guided by political, religious and dynastic beliefs which were to change little over the next thirty-five years. He stated that his ancestors as 'the Most Christian Emperors of the great German people, of the

Catholic Kings of Spain, of the Archdukes of Austria and the Dukes of Burgundy' were 'all to the death true sons of the Roman Church' and 'the defenders at all times of the Catholic faith'. He 'resolved to maintain everything which these my forebears have established'. He asked how 'the whole of Christendom' could have 'been in error for a thousand years?' It was therefore 'certain that a single monk must err if his opinion is contrary to that of all Christendom'. 'To settle this matter I have resolved to stake upon this course my dominions and my possessions, my body and my soul'. He then stated that to allow this heresy 'would be a disgrace to me and to you, the noble and illustrious German nation, since through privilege and special election we have been appointed defenders and protectors of the Catholic faith'. He regretted not having acted sooner and ordered that Luther 'be escorted home with due regard for the stipulation of his safe conduct,' and to stop preaching his 'evil doctrine and not incite (people) to rebellion'.

Charles honoured his promise; Luther was permitted to leave Worms. On his return journey he was taken in an arranged 'kidnap' to Wartburg Castle high above Eisenach and received the protection of Frederick of Saxony. Living incognito as 'Junker Jorg' (George the knight)*, he translated the New Testament into German, in the process creating for the first time a form of the written language that could be understood throughout Germany.[8] Almost twelve months later he returned to Wittenberg University and was to remain a powerful influence in the religious controversies until his death in 1546, protected by Frederick and his successors. The Edict of Worms finally issued on May 26th declared him a notorious heretic and an outlaw who should be apprehended and punished. Those helping in his capture would be rewarded. No-one should 'receive, defend, sustain, or favour' him. The reading or possession of his writings was banned and it was intended that these books would be burnt. But the time when this was possible to enforce had already passed.

---

* See portrait of 'Junker Jorg' by Lucas Cranach the elder.

Although the Diet of Worms is remembered for the appearance of Martin Luther, this was by no means the only religious issue, or indeed regarded as the main one at the time. The 'Complaints of the German Nation against the Holy See' was presented to the Diet. It was a list of 102 grievances, many of which had existed for decades, most of which were not so much theological as organisational and financial. They were raised repeatedly throughout the 1520s at each Diet. Later in the decade there was a demand for a National German Council to fully debate these issues and bring about reform, but by then Charles wished to settle Germany's religious problems through a general council which would bring about reform in the Church throughout Europe.[9]

With the conclusion of the Diet of Worms, Charles travelled north to the Low Countries, reaching Brussels by July, and then on to Ghent and Bruges. Margaret of Austria had already been confirmed as his regent, but Charles had other dynastic matters to settle before his return to Spain, in particular the position of his brother. Back in 1515 Maximilian had agreed with King Vladislas of Hungary and Bohemia that one of his grandsons would marry the king's daughter, Anne. Later in the year it was settled that it would be the younger brother, Ferdinand, on condition that he became ruler of substantial lands in his own right. At the same time it was decided that a long standing agreement would be honoured – Charles' sister, Mary, would marry Vladislas' son, Louis. This marriage took place in July 1515 in St. Stephen's Cathedral, Vienna, though given that both were only nine years old, it was decided that they should not live together for a few years yet. On Vladislas' death in 1516, both Louis and Anne were effectively adopted by Maximilian, making the ties between the two families even closer. The prospective sisters-in-law Anne and Mary were educated together in Innsbruck.

During 1521 and 1522 Charles, head of the family since Maximilian's death, finalised these arrangements. Ferdinand's situation had been difficult since his departure from his native Spain in 1517. Although he was welcomed in the Low Countries by his aunt Margaret, he had no official role, not an easy position for someone of his rank. The brothers met again when Charles arrived in the Low Countries and it was decided that Ferdinand's marriage to Anne should go ahead. Ferdinand was granted the five Austrian dukedoms (Upper and Lower Austria, Styria, Carinthia and Carniola) and created Archduke, thus meeting the earlier requirement. In May 1521 Ferdinand and Anne, aged eighteen and seventeen respectively, were married in Linz, Austria. The following month, Mary, now nearly sixteen, travelled to Hungary, to join her husband, now King Louis II, where she was crowned and their marriage formally blessed. Written into these marriage agreements was the understanding that if Louis was to die without issue, Ferdinand would succeed him as king of Hungary as the husband of Louis' sister. This was not to go unchallenged in the future.

Another question that Charles needed to resolve was who would take his place in the Empire in the event of his absence. The situation in Castile, though militarily resolved by April 1521, undoubtedly required his presence in the near future. Without a suitable and acceptable regent this could result in the weakening of imperial power in the Empire. To Charles, ever the dynast, the obvious answer was Ferdinand. As a Habsburg he could be seen by others as a proper substitute for the emperor, and as a brother, albeit one who scarcely knew Charles, he was perhaps less likely to attempt to abrogate Charles' authority. This latter point Charles sought to confirm in a secret addition to the published arrangements. Charles promised to work for Ferdinand's election as King of the Romans, his successor as emperor, as soon as he himself was crowned by the Pope. In addition Ferdinand was given full hereditary rights to the Habsburg lands granted to him.

The dynasty was central to Charles' view of the strategic and political landscape. The vast majority of his lands were inherited and thus represented the achievements of his ancestors in various areas of Europe. Charles believed that it was his sacred duty to pass this inheritance on to his successors. During his reign he added certain areas by conquest, both in Europe, such as Milan,

Guelderland and Friesland in the Netherlands, as well as in the vast lands of the New World following Cortes' victory over the Aztecs and Pizarro's conquest the Incas. Thirty years on the succession was to become a thorny issue for Charles, though in reality he had just taken some crucial decisions that would largely determine the outcome.

While the political issues were being sorted out the young, unmarried, Charles also had some time for leisure. He was still a young ruler who enjoyed fine clothes and the excitement of the tournament. He was known to over indulge in food and drink, both now and in later years. He was certainly sexually active. In the time after the Diet of Worms and before his departure to Spain he had a number of affairs. This was common practice for monarchs at the time, as we know from the much better documented activities of his contemporaries, Henry VIII and Francis I. One relationship in late 1521 and early 1522 was with Johanna Maria van der Gheyst, the daughter of a tapestry worker in Oudenaarde, between Ghent and Tournai, who had entered the service of Charles de Lalaing, seigneur of Montigny.[10] In December 1522 when Charles had already left the Low Countries to return to Spain, Johanna gave birth to a girl, Margaret. She was acknowledged as Charles' daughter in the late 1520s and brought up under the supervision of successive regents of the Low Countries, Margaret of Austria and Mary of Hungary. Charles was later to use this daughter for his political ends and she was married first into the de' Medici and then the Farnese families. Margaret and her son, Alexander, Duke of Parma, were subsequently to have a major role in the history of the Low Countries. Her mother was given a small pension and in 1525 married a local financial administrator.

It is probable that Charles had two other daughters in his early 20s, neither of whom was brought up at court. At what must have been about the same time as his affair with Johanna van der Gheyst, Charles met an Italian widow Orsolina de la Pena. Their liaison resulted in the birth of another daughter, Tadea, born in Bologna as Orsolina travelled back to Rome with her brothers. Tadea lived most of her life in a convent and when Charles was in Bologna in 1530 and 1532 he requested that she visit him. Much less is known about a third daughter. Dona Juana, probably born in 1522 or 1523, died in a convent at Avila in 1530, her mother having complained of Charles' lack of interest.[11]

Such activities did not mean that he was distant from the process of government. In fact his personal involvement was increasing. In late May 1521, while still in Worms, the governor of his youth and main political mentor for more than ten years, Chièvres, died. His influence had already been waning. Charles was listening more to his new Chancellor, Gattinara, as witnessed by a steady shift in his attitude towards France. Chièvres pro-French policy had not been sustainable in the light of Francis' hostility. During this period Charles was to develop the practices that continued for most of his life. He worked daily with his councillors and advisors, reading reports from his ambassadors, making notes and comments in the margins, discussing matters of the day, in short taking a greater control over the running of his territories and the formulation of policies. Chièvres' objectives of developing Charles as a monarch who was capable of grasping the issues and who was prepared to work hard had been achieved.

Neither leisure nor personal affairs were going to delay Charles' departure from the Low Countries once the arrangements for his absence had been finalised. What might have done so was the war that had broken out between Charles and Francis I in 1521 with conflict in Italy and in the Low Countries. Personal animosity was now added to the underlying dynastic and territorial disputes between France and the Habsburgs. In his 'Memoirs' Charles blames Francis for this conflict. 'He was continually making complaints and such unreasonable proposals'.[12]  This, Charles claimed, also prevented him from dealing effectively with the heresy in Germany: 'For this reason the Emperor was obliged to close the Diet at Worms. By so acting, he rather did what he could than what he wished and had resolved to do' (with regards Luther).[13] Henry VIII sent Cardinal Wolsey to act as mediator, meeting ambassadors from both sides at Calais in August 1521. Since both Henry and Wolsey aimed to secure as much as they could for themselves out of the conflict, he could hardly be regarded as an honest broker. Wolsey also held talks with Charles' advisers in Bruges and gradually the English position became more hostile to France. In November 1521 a secret agreement was signed between the Emperor, Henry VIII and the Pope. This confirmed that Charles would marry Princess Mary when she was 12 years old in 1528, that Charles would visit England on his return journey to Spain and that both countries would invade France in 1523. Wolsey would receive an imperial pension to replace his French one!

So it was that in June 1522 Charles left for Spain once again. This was a more self- confident Charles than the one who had left Flushing five years before, even though he drew up his first will 'having regard to our coming perilous journey'[14]. He landed at Dover, travelled to London where he was greeted with full ceremony, and then on to Windsor for a state visit. Charles had taken with him some of the superb treasures of Montezuma, the Aztec ruler, which had been sent to him by Hernando Cortes from Mexico. Articles such as gold shields and feathered cloaks had gone first to Spain and then on to Brussels before coming to London. They impressed all who saw them with their beauty, ingenuity and value. Albrecht Durer wrote: 'In all my life, I have seen nothing that rejoiced my heart so much as these things'. While the monarchs were involved in jousting, feasting and dancing, their advisers were putting the final touches to the negotiations for the Treaty of Windsor, signed on 16th June, with secret sections signed three days later.

# 8
## 'He wants Milan and so do I' - War with France: 1521-1525

The war with Francis I that started in 1521 could not have come as a surprise to Charles. It was part of the rivalry between the Habsburgs and the Valois (and subsequent ruling families) of France which started in the late 15th century, before Charles' reign, and was to continue for two hundred years. This was not just the antagonism of two monarchs but had a more profound causation, though Charles' personal rivalry with Francis (more than continued by Francis' son Henry II) added an extra dimension. Essentially this was about dynastic ambition and the fear of a strategic advantage being gained by a rival. Both claimed territories on the basis of dubious ancestry that went back to the 13th century; neither were able to take the advice of Erasmus, who wrote that if such ancient claims could be abandoned there would be a much more stable political system and fewer wars in Europe.

France was the largest and most populous country in Europe at the time. It had a unity that Charles' lands lacked, had expanded during the 15th century, and was still in the process of incorporating adjacent territories, such as Provence, Dauphine and Brittany, into the kingdom. France had also taken direct control of Burgundy in 1477. The House of Burgundy, now led by Charles, was committed to regaining it. However, the French feared encirclement by the dynastic ambitions of both Ferdinand of Aragon and Maximilian of Austria which had their outcome in the vast territories that Charles inherited. By 1520 he ruled the remaining Burgundian lands in the Low Countries and Franche Comte to the east of France, and was also Holy Roman Emperor. In the south he was king of Castile and Aragon, which meant that he also controlled Naples, and had a major interest in the north of Italy, claiming Milan as an Imperial fief. Northern Italy was an important line of communication between Spain (and its lands in southern Italy) and the Habsburg lands north of the Alps in Germany, Austria and the Low Countries.

The war, when it came, was fought in a number of different theatres - on the periphery of the Low Countries, along the Pyrenees, but most of all in Italy. Control of Italy was seen as vital by the major players in Europe at the time and it therefore suffered the misfortune of becoming a major battlefield in the conflict between foreign powers. French monarchs had ancient claims both to the kingdom of Naples in the south and to the duchy of Milan in the north. These claims were revived by Charles VIII (r. 1483 – 1498) and Louis XII (r. 1498 – 1515), and continued by Francis I. All were keen for territorial gain and military glory to make their mark on history. Charles commented: 'My cousin Francis and I are in complete accord; he wants Milan and so do I'.

Renaissance Italy was ripe for foreign interference. It was seriously divided. The most important states were the republic of Venice, with its maritime empire, the duchy of Milan, the republic of Florence, the Papal States and the kingdom of Naples. Also of significance were Savoy, Genoa, Ferrara and additional smaller city states. A delicate balance of power had been maintained by means of subtle diplomacy and wars in which the citizens stayed at home while mercenary soldiers fought each other in campaigns that often involved more manoeuvre and posturing than hard fought battles. This balance was all too easily destroyed by the intervention of foreign powers eager for gain. Indeed, on occasions, they were invited in to assist a local Italian ruler. The fact that the Papacy was based in Rome was another incentive, for control of or influence over the Papacy provided an additional diplomatic weapon. The lack of this support could be a problem as Henry VIII was to learn to his cost in the late 1520s.

The wealthy Italian states had little effective defence and offered rich pickings for foreign troops who had their own interests at heart. Italian rulers were therefore keen to side with whichever power might seem to offer the chance for gain and security. Growing instability encouraged existing ducal families and more recent condottiere (mercenary commanders) to attempt to carve out territories for themselves and their families. The Medici (Florence), the Borgia (the Papal States and Romagna), the Sforza (Milan), the Farnese (Parma), the Este (Ferrara), the Gonzaga (Mantua) - these are the names that frequently occur in any history of Italy in the 15th and 16th centuries, many of which are still familiar to us today. As well as being patrons of the famous artists of the Renaissance, they are usually associated with the rapidly shifting alliances, enmities, truces and double crosses that make a study of the period fascinating, but often complex. This was, of course, the world of Cesare Borgia and Machiavelli, as well as Leonardo, Raphael and Michelangelo.

There is, however, a pattern that emerges from a study of late 15th and early 16th century Italy. French claims to a territory, backed up with the support of some Italian rulers and substantial military force, would have initial success. The allies would then fall out, either over the spoils of war or over fear of French domination. This would allow France's rivals, initially Ferdinand of Aragon and Maximilian of Austria, and later Charles, to make local alliances, fight back and eventually defeat French forces. The Italian states and their ruling families would then be concerned about Habsburg control of Italy. This in turn enabled France to put together alliances and restart the cycle. As Pope Clement VII commented, most Italians did 'not wish the eagle to land in Italy or the cock to crow there'.

The damage done to Italy was immense. Although they had a part to play, the Italian states were no-longer in control of their own destiny, despite feelings of cultural and economic superiority, and however much they disliked foreign domination. They would switch sides frequently, fearful of first one foreign power and then another. They would aim to maximise their power at the expense of other local rulers, ever mindful of the need not to offend the monarch who held sway at the time, but ready to change allegiance if they judged circumstances to be right. The French, Spanish and Imperial armies, together with the feared Swiss and German mercenary troops, were much larger than anything previously seen. They frequently gave no quarter, either in battle or when looting a captured town, unlike some of the earlier choreographed campaigns which had much less material or personal cost. Long sieges and the devastation of the countryside had a major impact on food supplies. The lack of security, together with the cost of employing large mercenary armies, made further economic development difficult. The troops suffered from and spread diseases, whether it was cholera, the plague, or syphilis, of which the first major recorded outbreak in Europe was among the French soldiers at Naples in 1494, and which, known as the 'French disease', rapidly became widespread across Italy. By the second decade of the 16th century Machiavelli regarded Italy as 'leaderless, lawless, crushed, despoiled, torn, over-run'.

A brief summary of the events before Charles' time, events of which he would have been increasingly aware during his youth, will give a flavour of these wars. In 1494 Charles VIII of France claimed a hereditary right to Naples and backed this with an initially successful invasion which took his army through Florence, Rome and on to Naples, causing terror and political instability as it went. For instance, the Medici family were removed from Florence in 1494, only to return to power in 1513 in a later phase of the conflict. Once in Naples, Charles VIII's lines of supply and communication were so stretched that a sustained occupation was impossible in the face of a hostile coalition, and withdrawal was the only realistic option.

His successor, Louis XII, claimed Milan, used Italian hostility to its ruler Ludovico 'Il Moro' Sforza, and invaded in 1499. A deal with Ferdinand of Aragon also partitioned the kingdom of Naples, but the French were unable to retain their sector, being defeated by Ferdinand's general Gonzalo de Cordoba at the battle of Garigliano in December 1503. Louis remained a power in northern Italy in the first decade of the 16th century which saw first Cesare Borgia (son of

Pope Alexander VI – the Spaniard Roderigo Borgia) and then Pope Julius II (Giuliano della Rovere – deadly enemy of the Borgias) establish short lived control in the Romagna and central Italy. Further French intervention in 1509 was initially organised against Venice by Pope Julius II, who then turned on his ally having achieved his purpose, resulting in French withdrawal in 1512. The failure of an attempted comeback by Louis XII in 1513, with defeat at Novara by Swiss mercenaries, and the loss of all French held territories in Italy, did nothing to halt French ambitions.

On his accession in 1515 Francis I was keen to regain lost land, avenge defeats and pursue dynastic claims and military glory in his own right. Treaties with Henry VIII, and Charles, as the recently inaugurated Duke of Burgundy, and agreements with Venice and Genoa, paved the way. Francis' defeat of the Swiss defenders of Milan at the battle of Marignano in September 1515 established French control over the duchy. This position of strength was used to sign the Concordat of Bologna with the Medici Pope Leo X, which gave Francis more power over the church in France. The situation seemed stable, but the death of Ferdinand of Aragon in January 1516 changed the balance of power. Charles' new lands, when added to his existing territories, threatened to encircle France. However his immediate situation was not strong. At the age of 16, he had only been ruling the Burgundian lands in his own right for a year and his accession in Spain had to be secured. His energies were going to be directed elsewhere for some time. The Treaty of Noyon in August 1516 therefore confirmed French control of Milan and planned for Charles' marriage to Francis' daughter, Louise, with Naples as her dowry, until which time Charles promised to pay an annual tribute, validating French claims to the territory.

Charles' election as emperor increased the likelihood of renewed conflict, with the additional factor of Francis' personal animosity towards his rival. Both Charles and Francis wished to be able to portray their adversary as the aggressor. The idea of the 'just' war was important to them in their efforts take the moral high ground. It also mattered because their subjects would be more willing to pay the taxes required to meet the ever growing costs of war if they believed that their monarch was fighting in their interests and for what was justified. By 1521 Francis rightly feared that if the negotiations between Charles' representatives and those of both Pope Leo X and Henry VIII resulted in agreement his position would be precarious. He therefore encouraged Charles' enemies to begin military actions on several fronts, in Navarre, Luxembourg and Gelderland. Francis was probably not intending a full scale war but was hoping to distract Charles' attention from Italy. If this was indeed his plan it failed spectacularly. In 1519 Francis had said of Charles: 'He is young and has no practical experience of war'. He believed Charles' position was too weak for him to risk a full scale war. Charles, on the other hand, needed to end any perception of personal or political weakness.[1] He reacted more aggressively than Francis expected, a response made more likely by the death of his essentially pro-French advisors, Jean de Sauvage in 1518 and Chièvres in 1521. Charles' armies successfully defended the areas where his lands were attacked and then launched counter-attacks.

In 1512 Navarre had been seized by Ferdinand of Aragon, fearing the increase of French influence there, and Charles had continued to assert his rights as ruler. Henry d'Albret, the son of the previous monarchs, Catherine of Navarre and John III, invaded with French backing in 1521, seeking to take advantage of the disarray in Castile caused by the revolt of the Comuneros. Initially successful in occupying virtually the whole territory, the Spaniards hit back swiftly after the defeat of the Comuneros, crushing the invaders in late June. Elsewhere, Francis' ally Robert de la Marck, Lord of Sedan, invaded Luxembourg and was also repulsed, with Charles' general Henry of Nassau moving on to besiege Tournai, defeating the French attempt to relieve the town and then taking it in December 1521. Charles, though not directly involved in the fighting, moved to Oudenaarde to be in close contact with his commanders. Further north Charles had more difficulty with Charles of Egmond, Duke of Guelders, who, needing little encouragement from Francis, had extended the territory under his control until driven out of Friesland in 1522 by Charles' troops, enabling Charles to annex the province soon after.

Charles' major offensive, however, took place in Italy. A Habsburg-Papal army drove the French out of Milan in November 1521 and the Sforza family were re-instated with Francesco as the new Duke. The papacy gained Parma and Piacenza. Unlike the French, Charles, guided by Gattinara, preferred to control northern Italy through local alliances rather than directly. A French attempt to regain Milan was defeated at Biocca in April 1522 and they were removed from the whole of northern Italy. By the time Charles was signing the Treaty of Windsor with Henry VIII in June 1522 on his journey to Spain he looked to be in a strong position. However his recent ally Pope Leo X had died in December 1521, after a typically unrestrained banquet celebrating his victories. In the words of one historian 'As a Renaissance Prince he would have been superb; as a Pope he was a disaster'[2]. He had spent a fortune on wars, building works, banquets; corruption had continued unabated; Luther's challenge to the Church had been badly handled.

His successor was a surprise choice and one much to Charles' liking. The two cardinals with the most supporters were Leo X's cousin, Giulio de' Medici and Alessandro Farnese, but both had enough determined opponents to prevent their election. There was stalemate. A compromise candidate was proposed, perhaps first suggested in a letter by Charles,[3] and elected on 9th January 1522 - Adrian of Utrecht, Charles' former tutor and regent in Spain. Charles now thought that the two pillars of Christendom would be able to work in complete harmony and had high expectations. He believed that together they would be able to achieve 'many good and great things, for we shall be as one and act in unanimity.'[4]

It was not to work out like that. Adrian VI left Spain from Barcelona in August 1522, shortly after Charles arrived in Santander. The two were never to meet again. Once in Rome Adrian wished to deal with the numerous abuses that were widespread in the Church and to reform the Roman Curia, but he was in many ways hopelessly out of touch with the realities of life in Rome – he had never visited Italy and spoke no Italian. He disappointed Charles by taking a determinedly impartial line between the Emperor and Francis. He urged Charles to make peace with a generous spirit and criticised all European monarchs for standing by while the Ottoman Turks captured the island of Rhodes at the end of 1522. Charles found it difficult to understand why Adrian had not fully supported him. In May 1522 he wrote to Adrian that: 'the French are rich and generous with wonderful promises and sweet sounding words, but measure friendship according to their own benefit'.[5] In January 1523 he wrote that he believed that it was Francis who caused all the problems in Europe and made it possible for the Turks to take advantage of the situation. Adrian, he believed, should declare that the pope and the emperor would stand together and then, and only then, 'would the King of France show himself ready to accept honourable and reasonable terms'.[6]

Adrian's reformist agenda was very unpopular in Rome. He was met by opposition and obstruction from the more worldly cardinals and priests in Rome, who according to Francisco Guicciardini were 'full of ambition and incredible greed, and almost all dedicated to the most refined, not to say most dishonest, pleasures'.[7] Even the people of Rome, who had previously turned against the excesses of the Church, came to dislike him as an outsider who deprived them of a living because he spent so little money. When he died in September 1523, after little more than a year in Rome, Guicciardini reported that there was 'boundless joy'[8]. The cardinals were not to make the same mistake again. Adrian was to be the last non-Italian Pope for over 450 years, until the election of Karol Wojtyla as John-Paul II in 1978. In Adrian's place, after a divisive and lengthy conclave of seven weeks, they elected Giulio de' Medici, who became Pope Clement VII.

Charles knew that Francis would plan a new invasion of Lombardy but, with his advisers, had already considered how to counter this move. The Treaty of Windsor with Henry VIII had confirmed that in 1523 an English army would invade France from Calais, while Charles attacked from Italy, each with 40,000 troops.

Even better for Charles was the desertion of Duke Charles of Bourbon, Constable of France (the highest military officer under the king), whose relationship with Francis was destroyed by the king's refusal to accept the will of Duke Charles' wife which had been in favour of her husband. Francis and his mother, Louise of Savoy claimed much of her land, which they seized before the conclusion of the legal proceedings. Bourbon began negotiations with Charles, offering to begin a rebellion in France, in return for troops and money, and the possibility of his marriage to Charles' sister, Eleanor, whose husband Manual I of Portugal had died in 1521. When these plots were discovered by Francis, Bourbon fled from France. However, whether through lack of trust or failure of communications, the allies failed to coordinate their campaigns in 1523. The Duke of Suffolk's troops caused much damage in northern France during September and October, advancing to within fifty miles of Paris before withdrawing without a significant military victory. Henry rightly considered that he was not being supported by Charles, now in Spain for more than a year, who had mounted only a relatively minor advance into the French Pyrenees.

In northern Italy the advantage swung to and fro over the next eighteen months. After an abortive French attack into Piedmont in late 1523, Bourbon led an Imperial invasion of Provence in July 1524. His ambitions were encouraged by talk of a new kingdom of Provence being created for him. He took Aix-en-Provence but after sustained attacks failed to capture Marseilles. Neither Charles in the Pyrenees nor Henry VIII in the north supported him with further advances and so when Francis arrived with his army in September, Bourbon was forced to withdraw. Francis now had the initiative. He marched over the Alps through the Argentière pass and advanced on a plague infected Milan. Faced by an army more than double the size of his own, probably 33,000 against 16,000, the commander of Charles' forces in Milan, Charles de Lannoy, the viceroy of Naples, withdrew to Lodi to be joined by Bourbon's wearied troops. Francis failed to take advantage and pursue the retreating troops. Instead he secured Milan, leaving a garrison of nearly 5,000, and moved on to

Pavia, where there was still an imperial garrison of about 9,000 troops under Antonio de Leyva.

These French victories encouraged the new pope, Clement VII, to abandon Charles. While acting the part of peacemaker, urging both sides to come to terms, he came to an understanding with Francis. In this he was joined by Venice, Florence, Siena and others in Italy. Francis sent a further 6,000 troops south to move against Naples, hoping at the same time to draw Lannoy's army with them. The French siege of Pavia looked like succeeding in November when the walls were breached in several places by cannon fire. In expectation of this de Leyva had prepared an earthen rampart inside the walls with a ditch between them covered by light artillery. He was thus able to repel the attackers and inflict substantial losses. The French were further weakened by the withdrawal of 5,000 Swiss mercenaries, while Lannoy, who had remained in Lodi, was joined in January 1525 by 15,000 landskneckts (mainly German mercenaries – pike-men and supporting foot soldiers) commanded by Georg Frundsberg. All eyes were now on Pavia.

# 9
# 'Peace cannot be had without the enemy's consent.' Pavia and Madrid

Charles, unaware of the very latest developments in Italy, was downcast in early February 1525. He recognised that he might be facing defeat and wrote a few notes to help him think through his position.[1] First and last, he wrote, that he wished for peace. This was to be a frequent theme in Charles' statements and letters, but he recognised that 'it cannot be had without the enemy's consent'. He accepted that a successful war would help him, but bemoaned the fact that he had no further resources even to pay for his existing army, let alone an expanded one. He believed that 'friends have forsaken me in my evil hour; all are equally determined to prevent me from growing more powerful and keep me in my present distressed state'. By this he is referring to Pope Clement VII and also Henry VIII, who he claimed 'does not even help me to the extent of his obligations'. He knew that a major battle 'in which I shall either be victorious or wholly defeated cannot be postponed for much longer'. Charles then indulged in some wishful thinking about driving Francis from Italy, but then more realistically accepted that 'my prospects are bad'. He thought that he had done little 'so far to cover myself in glory' and considered that what he should do was to lead an expedition to Italy himself. He realised that there would be problems funding the visit and about the governance of Spain if he were to leave, and considered the possibility of his marriage to Isabella of Portugal as a way to deal with both.

Charles was correct that the battle was imminent. The French army was in secure, entrenched, positions outside Pavia, most encamped at Mirabello, a hunting park to the north of the city, surrounded by almost eight kilometres of walls. A short distance away, having advanced to relieve the town, were Spanish and Italian soldiers under Lannoy, Bourbon and Fernando d'Avalos, marquis of Pescara, together with Frundsberg's German landsknechts. The Imperial commanders no longer had sufficient funds to pay their troops and needed to act before desertions and mutinies destroyed their army. They decided to tempt Francis' army into the open and force a battle or, failing that, achieve some minor success before withdrawing.

Under cover of dark during the night of 23$^{rd}$/24$^{th}$ February engineers moved through heavy rain from their position east of the town to the north of the park. They were followed by the main body of the army. An artillery barrage directed at the French siege lines was maintained to help conceal these movements. The engineers managed to create a major breach in the walls. They had achieved some element of surprise as the Imperial forces advanced through the walls but the French were soon able to direct heavy cannon fire against them. As the advance began to falter Francis, confident of success, ordered a full scale attack. His cavalry, with the king in the vanguard, were initially successful and broke through enemy lines. This put them in direct line of fire from their own artillery which had to cease fire, a significant blow as they had three times as many cannons as the Imperial army. The French, with their remaining Swiss mercenaries, were also exposed to the deadly fire of 3,000 Spanish arquebusiers. These had entered the park before dawn, moved through the woods, and by 6.30 a.m. seized Mirobello castle. The remaining Imperial foot soldiers, now safe from the French artillery, rallied and got the better of their opponents, driving them from the battlefield. With the talented commander, Pescaro, now directing operations, they added to the onslaught on the French cavalry and were joined by Leyva's troops, who had overcome the French troops left in the siege lines and joined the battle from the town.

The battle was over by 9 a.m. and the French army crushed. Many thousands fell on the battlefield or drowned in the River Ticino attempting to escape.[2] The loss of life among the French nobility was immense, comparable with Agincourt over 100 years before. Among the dead were the senior commanders Guillaume Gouffier seigneur de Bonnivet, Louis II Le Tremoille, the newly appointed governor of Milan, Francois de Lorraine and Richard de la Pole, the last Yorkist claimant to the throne of England. Francis suffered the humiliation of seeing his army destroyed. His horse was shot from beneath him and although he continued to fight on foot, he was surrounded and captured along with other generals, Robert de la Mark, seigneur de Flourance, and Anne de Montmorency, Marshal of France. Several knights later claimed the honour of capturing the king, but he always maintained that he surrendered to the viceroy, Lannoy.

How had this victory come about? The tactics of the generals in the field played a significant role, but so too did the changing nature of warfare in the late 15th and early 16th centuries, and how effectively armies and their commanders adapted to these developments. Until the 15th century armies consisted of the infantry (with swords, axes, and various other weapons for cutting and clubbing the enemy) protected by pike-men, bowmen (with crossbow or longbow), and the cavalry who were usually the most highly valued units. The late 15th century saw the increased power of the infantry with the introduction by the Swiss of the mobile pike phalanx. A massed body of foot-soldiers armed with 5 metre pikes had often successfully defended against a cavalry attack, but in the late 15th and early 16th centuries the Swiss made the phalanx manoeuvrable and capable of taking the offensive, under the right conditions. They achieved victories at Morat (June 1476), where they defeated a Burgundian army including 4,000 mounted knights[3], and at Nancy (January 1477), where Charles the Bold, Duke of Burgundy had been killed. The success was repeated at Novara in 1513 where they were able to continue their advance, while under attack from the French cavalry, to defeat the army of Louis XII[4]. The pike phalanx was rapidly adopted by other armies.

Firearms had existed in medieval armies since the 14th century but it was only in the early 16th century that their power began to be fully utilised on the battlefield. The arquebus was a matchlock handgun, about 1.2 metres long, weighing about 5 kgs. It was successfully used by the Spanish troops of Gonzalo Fernandez de Cordoba, the 'Grand Capitan', in the campaign against Granada (1484-92). It took time to reload and often misfired, but despite these problems it added considerably to the killing power of the infantry. An arquebusier could be trained in a few days, much more quickly than a bowman[5]. By adding arquebusiers to the pike-men in the mobile phalanxes Cordoba defeated the much larger French army at Cerignola (1503), and the arquebus was again an important factor in the Imperialist victory at La Bicocca (1522).[6] This combination of pike-men, swordsmen and an increasing number of arquebusiers was to form the basis of the reorganisation of the Spanish infantry into the 'tercios'. At full strength a 'tercios' consisted of ten companies each of 300 men, including two made up of specialist arquebusiers[7] who could cause high casualties and create havoc in the massed ranks of pike-men or cavalry. By mid-century the Imperial armies were increasing the numbers of arquebusiers, in some cases up to 50% of the infantry, though the French and English were rather slower to adapt. The impact of this increased use of firearms was to reduce the incidence of pitched battles and offensive tactics after 1530.

The cavalry was traditionally considered to be the elite of the army, dominated as it was by the nobility and those who could afford the expense of the horses, armour and other equipment required. They were associated with the bravery, virtue and honour of the chivalrous 'Christian knight', and the cavalry charge was much feared on the medieval battlefield. They were not invincible - Bannockburn, Crecy and Agincourt had shown that – but they were valued so highly that one mounted knight was reckoned to be worth ten infantrymen. With the development of the mobile pike phalanx and the increasing use of the arquebus the cavalry charge could be stopped and great casualties inflicted upon them. Cervantes, in Don Quixote, considered firearms to be 'An invention which allows a base and cowardly hand to take the life of a brave knight.'[8] The cavalry still had an important role in scouting, foraging, raiding, skirmishing and following up victory by pursuing fleeing troops, but they were not the strike force that they had been and they were very expensive. The proportion of cavalry in the ever increasing size of armies was reducing. It is estimated that half of the 18,000 soldiers that Charles VIII took into Italy in 1494 were cavalry, whereas at Pavia they made up only 25% of Francis' 24,000 strong army.[9]

Field artillery had a part to play on the 16th century battlefield, but had serious limitations - the slow rate of fire, limited accuracy, and lack of mobility. The cast bronze culverins, weighing over 1,800 kgs., used in the early 16th century were simply too heavy to move around the battlefield at critical moments. They made. an important contribution to French victories at Ravenna (1512), where a ferocious artillery duel occurred at the start of the battle and later the Spanish cavalry were badly damaged by gun fire, and at Marignano (1515) where 72 culverins caused high casualties among the Swiss pike phalanxes.

At Pavia, the characteristics of cavalry, firearms and field artillery all played a significant part in the Imperialist victory. The French, with their king to the fore, placed too high an expectation on the cavalry to drive the opposition from the field of battle. The element of surprise in the Imperial advance, though not total, meant that Francis was unable to coordinate the different units of his army. Although he led his forces with bravery, once they were exposed to the fire of the arquebusiers and abandoned by their infantry, they had little hope of success. The French lacked the much larger number of firearms that the Imperial army could call upon. Their effective use against both cavalry and infantry, made a major contribution to the Imperial victory. Although the French had superiority in field artillery with over fifty cannons, after their initial impact they were unable to use them at a key stage of the battle for fear of cutting down their own troops. Their immobility meant that they could not be redeployed elsewhere in time to have any further influence before they were captured by Lannoy's troops.

News of the victory, achieved on Charles' 25th birthday, reached Spain two weeks later on 10th March. Charles was reported to have at first turned pale, remaining silent and going alone to his room.[10] After months of apprehension and inner turmoil, Charles found release in prayer. Only then did he ask for more details of the battle. He forbade noisy rejoicing, such as bells and fireworks, as was often done on such occasions, instead ordering prayers of thanksgiving and acknowledgement of the victory as the will of God. He announced that 'It is fitting to celebrate victories over infidels, but not those won against Christians', and declared himself pleased 'because the fact that God had aided him so openly seemed to be a sign of being, although undeservedly, in His grace.' He now believed that he had the opportunity to achieve peace in Italy and throughout Europe, and had greater means to do good for his friends and to pardon his enemies.[11] What he found difficult to realise was that a peace based on Habsburg dominance was always going to be challenged. He was now faced with a whole new set of issues and was to learn that a military victory did not always lead to a satisfactory peace settlement.

As a prisoner Francis was treated with all due respect. He was at first held at Pizzighettone, from where he wrote to his mother, Louise of Savoy, that 'all is lost to me except honour and life, which is safe'. Amongst the Imperial generals and Charles' advisers there was much debate as to where he could be most securely held - should it be Naples or the citadel of Milan - and how the negotiations for his release should be carried out. Charles himself was beset by doubts. He was conscious that some blamed him for the death and destruction that the war had caused, yet was convinced that it was Francis who was in the wrong. He believed that God had given him victory and wanted him to now establish a lasting peace, but he was still determined to restore Burgundy to his dynasty, something that Francis was most unlikely to concede.

Charles was given plenty of conflicting advice. His confessor Loaysa, argued that he should be magnanimous in victory and take a lenient approach, the better to bring about a lasting peace and Francis' co-operation in a future crusade against the Turks. 'When I consider to what state Christianity has been reduced, I see nothing more holy and more necessary to God than a universal peace among Christian princes, for it is clear that lacking this, religion, faith, a worthy life for mankind, are all sinking into obvious ruin. On the one side we have the Turks, who have made such progress against Christians because of our discords, and who are now threatening Hungary …… On the other hand, there is the Lutheran heresy, so great an enemy of God, which has already taken such root...'[12] He continued that Charles needed to show faith in Francis. 'For who can doubt that the King of France, if he is treated with such generosity, with such singular liberality, would not as a result of such goodness remain more bound to you in his soul, and more in your power, than he is now in his body?'

The Imperial Chancellor, Gattinara, and the Duke of Alva, a respected Spanish military commander, were much more sceptical of Francis' willingness to come to terms and argued that it was much better to use their present opportunity to the full. Alva recommended that 'one should proceed along those same roads that your fathers and ancestors have always followed, for new and unheard of counsels can at first glance seem perhaps more glorious and more magnanimous, but later undoubtedly they prove to be more dangerous.' He made his case forcefully. 'The will of God principally, and then the valour of your captains and army, have given you the greatest victory that any Christian prince has won for a very long time. But the fruits of victory consist in using it well... And it should be remembered that if the King is freed he can no longer be restrained, but so long as he is in prison, it is always in your power to free him.'[13] Alva had little faith in Francis' virtue, believing that even if treated with great leniency the French king would immediately seek revenge for what he would regard as the disgrace of being captured. If Francis would not agree to Charles' full demands then they should continue to hold him prisoner and renew the war against his country until he did so.

Henry VIII, wishing to take advantage of the situation, sent ambassadors to Spain with orders to advocate the completion of the 'grand project', in effect the partition of France, with the English taking back their old possessions. Charles wished to have what he regarded as his rightful claims accepted, but he recognised that the dismemberment of France was not a realistic outcome. He was torn between the various possibilities and failed to provide decisive leadership. He was rarely, if ever, one to act on the spur of the moment, preferring to listen to the various options and gradually reach a decision. Often taken as a sign of maturity, Charles was to become renowned for his careful consideration of issues, but after Pavia he crossed the fine line into indecision and delay.

It was Lannoy, Charles' viceroy in Naples and commander in Italy, who decided to move Francis to Spain in June 1525, initially without Charles' knowledge. Francis believed that he would be able to negotiate more successfully face to face with the Emperor. Landing in Barcelona, Francis was moved to Xativa in Valencia, and then by late July to Madrid, where he spent the rest of his captivity. Charles, however, left the negotiations to others, showing no interest in making personal contact. He only visited in September when Francis was seriously injured after falling from his horse while hunting. Despite Francis' reputed charm, no friendly relationship developed, and Charles made just one more visit. Francis' mother, Louise of Savoy, acting as regent of France in his absence, sent ambassadors to Toledo. Gattinara found that they were unwilling to surrender any territory at all, an approach fully backed by Francis. With Charles' support the Chancellor was demanding the restoration of the whole of the Burgundian inheritance, as well as Francis' agreement to renounce all claims in Italy, and confirmation of Charles' rights in Flanders and Artois. Francis saw no reason why he should accede to such demands, offering instead a ransom, and suggesting his marriage to Charles' sister, Eleanor, now possible because Francis' wife, Claude, had died a year earlier.

Little was being achieved; an impasse had been reached. Lannoy took over negotiations with a more conciliatory, or in Gattinara's eyes, naive, approach. Francis was increasingly keen to return to France; his ill-health was preventing him from participating in hunting and however comfortable his conditions were in captivity his opportunities for amorous adventures had been curtailed. For his part Charles, too, now wanted a settlement. Events in Italy were not developing in his favour, with the old fear of foreign domination, this time by the Habsburgs, reasserting its influence. The resultant Treaty of Madrid was signed on 14th January 1526. Francis took a solemn oath and assured Lannoy that if he failed to honour the treaty he would return to captivity. By its terms he surrendered suzerainty over Flanders, Artois and Tournai in the Low Countries, agreed to renounce all claims in Italy and the Netherlands, and promised to persuade the Paris 'Parlement'* to agree to the return of Burgundy to the Habsburgs. At the time of his release he would hand over his two eldest sons, Francis and Henry, as a sign of his good faith, and he promised to go on a crusade against the Ottoman Turks. His marriage to Charles' sister, Eleanor, the widow of Manuel of Portugal, previously promised to Charles' ally the Duke of Bourbon, was arranged. Lannoy had developed a good relationship with Eleanor and put to her whether she would rather be Queen of France or married to a military commander who had deserted his native country, however useful he had been to Charles.[14] Charles, however, was concerned about Bourbon's treatment. He was called to Spain, treated with great honour and given control of Milan as compensation.

On paper this was as good a settlement as Charles could have hoped for. Gattinara, however, firmly believed that Charles did not have sufficient guarantees to ensure that the terms of the treaty would be adhered to, and refused to place his seal on it. Perhaps he had in mind Ferdinand of Aragon's earlier claim about needing to force the French to follow the terms of an agreement. He was right to be concerned. Francis had been willing to agree to almost anything, discomforted as he was by his captivity and having secretly vowed, both as early as 16th August 1525 and again the day before the signing, that since he was imprisoned any agreement was

---

* The 'Parlements' were the highest legal bodies in France, of which the Paris Parlement was by far the most important.

achieved by coercion and therefore had no legal standing. He was thus prepared to confirm the treaty with a solemn oath knowing that he had no intention of keeping it. Once the treaty had been signed Charles and Francis met again in February at Illescas, between Madrid and Toledo, exchanging solemn guarantees. Francis promised that he would return to captivity within six weeks if he failed to carry out the terms of the treaty. From there, as Charles travelled south for his marriage, Francis, accompanied by Lannoy as his guard, journeyed north to the French border. He was exchanged for his sons and in response to Lannoy's farewell, 'Your Highness is now free, do not forget your promise', Francis replied 'I shall fail in nothing'.[15]

# 10
## 'Bedrock' – Settling Spain

Since 1522, throughout all these events in Italy and elsewhere, Charles had remained in Spain. During the previous two years, whilst in Germany and the Low Countries, he had been acknowledged as Emperor, attempted to deal with the growing dangers to the church posed by Luther, and seen the start of the conflict with France. There was still much to do there, but whatever his personal wishes, he faced the necessity of returning to Spain in order to fully establish his position. He was Archduke Charles of Ghent, King Carlos I of Spain and Kaiser Karl V in Germany, and as such ruler of almost half of Europe. The responsibilities that went along with these titles would make great demands upon him, and how he used his power would influence the lives of tens of millions, both in his lands, in the rest of Europe and beyond. But for the next seven years he was to remain in his kingdoms in Iberia. This was to be the longest continuous period of time that he ever spent in one of his territories. Although he still exerted an influence on most of the international events which unfolded he could play no active, direct, part in them.

He landed at Santander on 16th July 1522, accompanied by a large entourage of 2,000, made up of advisers, courtiers, administrators, clerks, soldiers, cooks, chambermaids, butlers, tapestry cleaners and many grooms to look after hundreds of horses[1]. Progress for such a company was slow. As he crossed the river Pisuerga into Valladolid in late August 1522, he knew that the revolt of the Comuneros in Castile and the Germanias uprising in Valencia had been defeated, but the atmosphere was still sullen if not openly hostile. Although many tensions had already existed within Spanish society, Charles' actions during his first visit to Spain had done much to provoke the revolts. The population were yet to be convinced that a foreign Burgundian/Habsburg king from the Low Countries, who now had even greater responsibilities elsewhere as Emperor, would either listen to their complaints or respond to their needs. Charles would have to work hard to win them over and now he set about his task with energy. During the early 1520s he learnt Spanish and made a conscious decision to develop a better understanding of the country and its people.

His first task was to deal with the aftermath of the revolts. They had almost brought down his rule in Spain. It was important that his response was one that would both impose his authority and avoid further general discontent and disorder. In Castile there was no widespread bloodbath. In November 1522, at the cortes held in Valladolid, Charles confirmed sentence on the leaders of the Comuneros. He had been urged to act mercifully. Of the thousands that had participated, all but 293 were pardoned, and only 23 were executed, with another 20 dying in prison[2]. The cities were not punished by the loss their privileges. This clemency helped Charles to achieve reconciliation with the people of Castile.

In Valencia the approach was somewhat different. There the challenge to the traditional social order and the position of the nobility had been even greater. They were determined to reassert their authority. The viceroy appointed by Charles in 1523, Germaine de Foix, the widow of Ferdinand of Aragon, and his former lover, dealt harshly with the rebels, with perhaps 800 executions taking place. There was also a more complex religious issue. The 'forced' conversion of Muslims was considered by a group of theologians and lawyers and declared to be valid, because the individuals concerned had been given a choice, conversion or death! This was a problem that Charles would have to revisit in the near future.

Although the traditional powers of the cortes in the different states varied, Charles made clear that his relationship with the representatives had altered. Whereas on his accession he had listened to their demands and grievances before they granted taxes, now, he stated: 'Yesterday I asked for funds; today I want your advice'. He pointed out that: 'You know that the custom had been to grant this (the servicio) first; thus it was under my royal predecessors. Why try to establish an innovation with me? And since many evils have brought me to this necessity, you, like good and loyal subjects, will remedy them by doing your duty as I expect you to do'.[3]

However, Charles was alert to the needs of the time. He was aware that government debts in Castile amounted 'to far more than I receive in revenue'.[4] He wished to secure regular grants from the Cortes without major disputes on each occasion. To do this, demand and coercion were not going to be as successful as effective management of the process and the gradual building up of a good working relationship with the city hierarchies and their representatives. He immediately agreed to restore the traditional system of 'encabezamiento'. City councils would agree with the government what their share of any new tax would be, and organise the collection of their contributions. Charles wished to establish a partnership with the city and town leaders, to give them a stake in the running of the country. They could hope for personal rewards, letters of thanks, remunerative posts and increased status. For the rest of his reign the Cortes of Castile was summoned approximately every three years; half the laws passed had their origin in petitions from the Cortes.[5] He had, in effect, met some of the demands of the Comuneros.

Charles also aimed to improve the effectiveness of the administrative, judicial and financial systems. He needed to show that he could be a just king. In the difficult years experienced in Spain since the death of Queen Isabella, and especially since Charles' accession, many revenues due to the Crown had either been left unpaid or been diverted into the pockets of those in a position to take advantage, be they nobles, administrators or supporters of the Comuneros revolt. Charles' own expenses, for instance on the bribes required for his election as emperor, had added to the financial problems in Castile. It had even been impossible for Charles to award the traditional 'mercedes', rewards for services to the king, to the nobility who had supported his cause because there was no money. Charles first replaced the unpopular, often corrupt, senior officials, particularly in the treasury. The President of the Royal Council was replaced by Juan Pardo de Tavara, Archbishop of Santiago, and three new councillors were appointed. They, like Tavara, had not been involved in dealing with the Comuneros revolt and thus more acceptable to the towns.[6] He had learnt the lesson about the unpopularity of foreign appointments.

He was then encouraged by Gattinara to further develop the system of councils that existed to oversee the administration. The Royal Council, renamed the Council of Castile, was reduced in size, as was the Council of Aragon (which also advised on the Italian territories). Both these bodies acted as the court of highest appeal in their territories. New councils, including a Council of War (established in 1522) and a Council of Finance (1523) were set up, as was a Council of the Indies (1524) to control the administrative, legal and religious issues relating to lands in the Americas. The link between the king and the councils was provided by the royal secretaries, officials loyal to the king[7], who set agendas and oversaw the meetings. The most influential of these was Francisco de los Cobos. Trained as a financial administrator, he had travelled to the Low Countries in 1516 to join Charles' court. He became secretary to the Council of Finance and rose to great influence after the death of Gattinara in 1530, generally travelling with Charles during the 1530's and later remaining as the chief administrator in Spain when Charles was absent, until his death in 1547[8].

The system of councils was also used to administer the lands that had originally belonged to the kingdom of Aragon and then extended to new territories as the empire overseas expanded. By the end of Charles' reign there were nine viceroyalties in the Spanish monarchy - Aragon, Catalonia, Valencia, Navarre, Sardinia, Sicily, Naples, New Spain (Mexico) and Peru. A viceroy, invariably from the high nobility, was appointed to each by the king. They had great powers, but their work was closely supervised by the relevant Council, which received their dispatches, discussed relevant issues, recorded their (sometimes conflicting) views in documents known as the 'consultas' which were passed on to the king before a final decision was made. The decision was then returned to the Council, whose secretary would draft the letters for signature by the king and eventual dispatch to the viceroy[9]. Appropriate checks and balances were thus in place, though the process could be slow, especially given the distances involved and the nature of transport at the time.

The representation of the higher nobility on the councils was reduced. Their support was rewarded with appointment to the viceroyalties and army commands for the most senior, along with backing of their social status and exemption from paying most taxes for the rest. Charles needed their loyalty, as local lords and church leaders, to keep control in the countryside where traditional social roles were largely unaltered. Many from the lesser nobility and landowning classes were later to see opportunities in Charles' other lands, serving as officers in Spanish armed forces sent overseas or as minor officials and administrators, especially in Italy and the New World. Thus what was originally seen as a threatened foreign domination of Spain became an incentive to support the wider dimension of Charles' empire.

Appointments to the councils and legal tribunals were made largely from the lawyers (letrados) educated in the Spanish universities, especially Salamanca, Valladolid and Alcala. Often from the smaller landowners and middle classes, those of ability were able to rise high in royal service. On the positive side this made possible the development of a professional, trained bureaucracy and judiciary. Promotion to the higher posts was increasingly on the basis of ability not family status. On the other hand once a significant post had been achieved, an administrator would train apprentices who could then be appointed to positions within the system. In this way a network of bureaucrats with loyalties to a powerful individual developed. Also the most successful aspired to acceptance by the upper reaches of society and promotion to the nobility. This required money. While a few, like Cobos, might be promoted so highly in royal service that this seemed to come without improper conduct, for the majority pay was low, deliberately so in order to encourage competence that would lead to promotion. Unfortunately this undoubtedly led to corrupt practices. The medieval idea of rewards for services to the king was still widespread and most petitions for such rewards passed through the councils which then made their recommendations to the king. Such were the powers of patronage that in order to secure a swift and favourable response, applicants would approach councillors with inducements that they were unlikely to refuse.[10]

By the mid 1520s Charles was expected to marry soon and produce an heir. It was almost ten years since he had inherited the thrones of Castile and Aragon. In the sixteenth century it was unusual for a monarch not to be married by the age of 25. All Charles' siblings had been married before they were twenty, the younger ones well before. It naturally concerned Charles' advisers, as well as his subjects, that while he was unmarried he could not produce a legitimate heir. All realised that his untimely death would lead to the chaos of a disputed succession and even those who had criticised his rule had no wish for that. The obvious choice to succeed him would be Ferdinand, his brother, but he had now taken on considerable new responsibilities elsewhere. An early death could never be discounted in the sixteenth century. Life expectancy was short and sudden death common. Women had always suffered a high death rate in pregnancy and childbirth, but even men in Charles' position did not escape. Disease, infection and accident all took their toll. He only had to look at his own family. His father, Philip, had died at the age of 28; his mother's brother, Juan, had been only 19.

There was no doubt that he was able to have children. Various liaisons between 1518 and 1523 had resulted in the birth of four daughters, but he needed to have a legitimate child, or ideally several, to calm the worries frequently expressed in Spain. Charles was Europe's most eligible bachelor though the 'pool' of potential brides was limited to royal princesses and the marriage would have to be a good political match. From his early years he had been involved in various 'betrothals', for diplomatic purposes. Initially there was Claude of France (1499 -1524), daughter of King Louis XII, but this was strongly opposed in France and she was later betrothed to and married the future king, Francis, duke of Angouleme, who had become Francis I in 1515. Next, Mary Tudor (1496-1533), daughter of Henry VII and sister of Henry VIII, was advocated by Charles' aunt Margaret. This was called off by Henry VIII in 1514 and she married Louis XII of France and then Charles Brandon, Duke of Suffolk. Other French princesses were considered for Charles including Renee (1510–1574), another daughter of Louis XII, and Louise (born 1515), the first daughter of Francis I, who died in early childhood.

In the early 1520s a serious possibility was Charles' cousin, another Mary Tudor, daughter of Henry VIII and Catherine of Aragon, born in 1516. At the age of two Mary had been betrothed to the Dauphin (the son of Francis I and heir to the French throne who eventually died, aged 18, before his father) but this had been set aside as relations between England and France deteriorated. For Charles this proposed marriage had much going for it. Mary was currently heir to the throne of England, despite Henry's on-going wish for a son, and an alliance with England would help to secure the anti-French position. Charles had come to England and met with Henry VIII in May 1520 and again in 1522. A good impression seems to have been made by all parties and agreement was then reached in the Treaty of Windsor, including the clause that if Henry had no son then the eldest son of Charles and Mary would inherit the English throne. The problem was that Mary was still only six years old and the earliest any marriage could occur was in 1528 when Mary became twelve. The wait for heirs would be considerable.

Much would depend on the political and diplomatic situation that existed at the time as to whether an over powering reason to make a particular match materialised. In the early days of his reign the traditional Castilian friendship with England seemed important. Henry VIII had married Charles' aunt, Catherine of Aragon, and war with France meant that Henry was a useful ally. But in Spain they wished him to marry someone closer to home. The option of Isabella of Portugal, born in 1503, the daughter of King Manuel I of Portugal and Isabella, another of Charles' aunts, had been mooted for some time. There were many benefits to this match. She had a reputation as intelligent, attractive and virtuous, the dowry that she would bring was vast, she was available immediately being only three years younger than Charles, and the close links between Spain and Portugal meant that she would be a popular choice to most Spaniards, making an ideal regent in Spain whenever Charles was absent. Charles himself had mused in early 1525, as he worried about his possible defeat in Italy, that the best way out of some of his difficulties 'would be to hurry on my marriage to the Infanta of Portugal', because she would bring with her 'a very large sum in actual bullion' and he could leave her as regent when he travelled to Italy. He was aware that this marriage might damage relations with England and that it would be a matter of concern if Henry then married his daughter to a French prince.

Victory over Francis at the battle of Pavia in February 1525 meant this was less of a worry. By mid-1525 Charles had decided that Isabella would be the best option. There were already close links between their families. King Manual I had married two of Charles' aunts and then Charles' sister Eleanor. In 1521 he was succeeded by his son John III, Charles' cousin. On 10th February 1525 John married Charles' youngest sister, Catherine. Born shortly after the death of her father when her mother, Juana, was in a state of mental collapse, her early years had been spent with her mother, isolated in Tordesillas. With no freedom and little company other than her unstable mother this must have been a miserable existence. Juana did not wish her to leave and it must have been a relief to Catherine when she was removed from Tordesillas, without her mother being informed in advance, to marry her Portuguese cousin. Of similar age, they seemed to be a well matched couple. Unfortunately of their nine children only two survived childhood. These were later both to marry children of Charles and die themselves before the age of 20, before either of their parents.

John was open to the idea of Charles marrying his sister, Isabella. Negotiations were expedited and an agreement drawn up, including a much needed dowry of one million ducats. Arrangements were made for the marriage to take place in the Andalucían city of Seville in March 1526. With the Treaty of Madrid signed and Francis soon to return to France, Charles was able to set out for Seville believing that he had resolved the conflict with France very much in his favour. This was to be his first and only visit to Andalucía. He came into contact with the history and the physical evidence of the Moorish influence in Spain during the nine months that he spent there. After his meeting with Francis in February, Charles travelled south to Toledo and on through Extremadura. This poor and undeveloped region had already produced many of the individuals that were to go down in history as the conquerors of the New World. Hernan Cortes from Medellin, Francisco Pizarro and Alonso de Sotomajor from Trujillo, Hernando de Soto and Pedro de Alvarado from Badajoz, Vasco Nunez de Balboa from Jerez de los Caballeros were the best known of many who came from the area. Often driven by their relative poverty and hopes of wealth and power, these conquistadores played a leading role in establishing and extending Spain's territories in the Americas. Wealth was beginning to flow back into the towns of Extremadura; large mansions and palaces were being constructed for those who returned from successful expeditions. This, in turn, encouraged more to seek their fortune across the Atlantic.

Charles had no time to linger and travelled rapidly on to Andalucía. Isabella had been greeted in style by Charles' representatives on the Portuguese border early in February and escorted to Seville where she was given a genuinely delighted welcome. The city, captured from the Moors in 1248, with its well-watered gardens and courtyards, had been the favourite residence of many Castilian monarchs. In the early 16th century it was growing rapidly, on its way to become one of the great European cities of the time, its wealth based on the monopoly of trade with the New World. Charles made his entrance to the city on 10th March and his

## Charles V: Duty and Dynasty

marriage to Isabella took place on the same day in the fine setting of the Alcázar Reales, originally a Moorish palace and much remodelled in the mudéjar style of the 13$^{th}$ and 14$^{th}$ century for Castilian kings. The ceremony took place in the 'Salon de Carlos V', with its fine coffered wooden ceiling, constructed for the occasion. Charles recorded the event in his memoirs years later: 'The emperor left Toledo in 1526 for Seville, where he got married, and during the journey he received news that the Queen of Denmark, his sister[*], had died.'[11] At the time he wrote a long letter to his brother Ferdinand, covering the death of their sister, negotiations with Francis I and then mentioned that 'I have now entered upon the state of marriage, which pleases me well'. Perhaps not the most enthusiastic report, but Charles' letters were always restrained and rarely mentioned personal issues. The Portuguese ambassador wrote at the time: 'When the bride and groom are together, though everyone may be present, they have eyes only for one another'.

This was a time of relative calm and happiness for Charles. The marriage had been arranged as a duty, but there is little doubt that he soon came to have a deep love for his wife, charmed and delighted as he was by her beauty and good nature. Isabella, the Andalucían spring, together with the belief that he had successfully dealt with the French king, must have made for a wonderful month or two. During a leisurely journey to Granada the couple stayed briefly in Cordoba, the once great Moorish city. In the 10$^{th}$ century, under Abd al Rahman III and his son Al Hakim II, it was reputed to have had 400,000 volumes in its great library, 27 schools, 50 hospitals, 600 public baths, 1,000 mosques and 213, 000 houses! Although these figures cannot be taken literally, they reveal a city that had no rival in the rest of Europe. For Ash-shakandi, writing in the 13$^{th}$ century, Cordoba had been 'the repository of science, the minaret of piety and devotion, the abode of magnificence, superiority and elegance'. Muslims, Christians and Jews had lived in

---

[*] Born in July 1501, a year and a half younger than Charles, Isabella had been brought up with him in Mechelen.

relative harmony. At the time of its conquest by Christian Castile in 1236, when its Great Mosque (Mesquita) had become the cathedral, its mihrab covered over and its minaret converted to a belfry, the city had been eclipsed by Seville. By 1526 it had already been in gradual decline for nearly 500 years.

Once in Granada Charles and Isabella stayed for six months in the Alhambra palace. If anywhere in Spain was made for romance it was the 14th century Moorish palace, full of delicate plaster work, intricate patterned tiles, superb ceilings, and the surrounding gardens, with their flowing water and magnificent blossoms. The palace had been built during the couple of centuries before the defeat of the last Moorish kingdom in Spain by Ferdinand and Isabella in 1492. This had ended seven centuries of Moorish control in parts of Spain. Charles cannot have failed to respond to the grace and beauty of the buildings that had been constructed during the Moorish period. However, he was very much a Christian Emperor, the grandson of the 'Catholic Monarchs', and he ruled lands that were still threatened by Muslim privateers in the Mediterranean, Naples, Sicily, and the eastern coast of Spain, and challenged by the Ottoman Empire in central Europe.

It is therefore understandable, though some would argue not forgivable, that he would wish to see the imposition of a Christian style and ethos on these Moorish cities. In 1523 he had given permission for the construction of the new capilla mayor (main altar) and coro (choir) in the centre of the cathedral at Cordoba. The construction was not completed until the 18th century, but their Renaissance and Baroque style contrasts sharply with the double arched Islamic columns which surround them. Charles was able to see the early stages of the work on his visit and is said to have remarked that 'You have built what you or others could have built anywhere, but you have destroyed something that was unique in the world'.

During his stay in Granada, Charles commissioned a palace to be built within the grounds of the Alhambra in the new Renaissance style. He wanted it to be an outstanding example of the new ideas in architecture that were coming out of Italy, but of course it would be in complete contrast to the original buildings. This was the only palace that Charles ever planned; it was never fully completed and he certainly never returned to live in it. As events moved on and demands for his presence elsewhere in Europe became irresistible, he was never allowed the luxury of such a home, even if he had thought it desirable. His son Philip did so, with the construction of El Escorial in central Spain, but it is generally thought that this did nothing for Philip's ability to control his other lands and contributed to his failures in the Low Countries where he was always regarded as a foreign monarch. The Renaissance palace in Granada was more about imposing the new order, and while having many features which had gained admiration elsewhere, it remains out of place and generally unloved.

Throughout Charles' reign there remained a significant religious issue in Spain. This was not the challenge of the Protestant Reformation as in northern Europe. This was a problem bequeathed by Spain's history. Under the terms of the surrender of Granada, Muslims were to retain freedom of religion, language, judicial system and dress and to have the right to the Alpujarras area in the mountains to the south of the city. However, these freedoms did not last; intolerance, always present, was increasing. Already in 1492 it had been declared that Jews living in Spain had to convert to Christianity, leave the country or be executed. In Granada there was dissatisfaction with the rate of conversion of Muslims to Christianity. Discrimination and persecution became widespread, provoking a revolt in 1500, first in the Alpujarras, and then in the city of Granada. This in turn provided the pretext for further tightening of the laws and the suspension of the rights granted on the surrender of the city. Henceforth Muslims also had to convert, leave or expect execution.

By the 1520s the many former Jews and Muslims in the south who had converted to Christianity rather than leave Spain or die for their religion, were suspected by many 'old' Christians of secretly adhering to their former beliefs. In addition, despite the earlier decrees and violence directed against them during the Germanias revolt of 1520-22, there were still significant numbers of Muslims, and those who had been forced to convert to Christianity, in Valencia. The consequence was that there was a substantial population that was now nominally Catholic, but who were always going to be suspected of covertly reverting to their old practices. The Spanish Inquisition, originally set up in 1478, would be kept busy investigating, interrogating and reporting on converted Jews (known as Conversos or Marranos) and Muslims (Moriscos). On numerous occasions orders and threats were issued in an effort to prevent the real or imagined failings of the 'moriscos'. They included decrees against: the closing of doors on Fridays and festival days (fear of Muslim services behind closed doors); the 'moriscos' holding weddings, marriages or burials without the presence of an 'Old Christian'; Moorish dances, songs and instruments; books and documents in Arabic; the public bathhouses (associated with ritual cleansing)[12]; traditional Muslim clothing; and the failure to eat pork. Of course there was resistance; there were reports of noise and poor behaviour in church, not giving the sign of the cross, and using Muslim names for children.

Charles took a pragmatic approach to these issues. In January 1526 he accepted an agreement with the landowners of Valencia, who feared losing their workforce, that all anti-Muslim measures would be put on hold for 40 years in return for a payment of 40–50,000 ducats per year[13]. If individuals were brought before the Inquisition punishments were usually lenient - fines, prayers – though this was not always the case. There were floggings and a few were handed over to the civil authorities to be burnt at the stake. In general, however, concessions were made in return for payments throughout Spain[14].

The situation was undoubtedly complex. There were genuine converts; some places seemed to accept more diversity than others; some 'moriscos' accepted their position reluctantly; others encouraged their neighbours to secretly carry out their old ceremonies. How long would assimilation take? Were there sufficient resources put into really teaching the 'new' Christians the basic tenets of the faith? Charles could at least claim that legally Spain was now a country unified by the Catholic religion. This situation was not to last. By the 1550s both external factors (the continued threat of the Ottomans and Muslim corsairs in the Mediterranean) and increasing concern in Spain that assimilation was too slow, resulted in a gradual hardening of attitudes which eventually led to the wholesale expulsion of the 'moriscos' between 1609 and 1614, in the reign of Charles' grandson, Philip III.

By the autumn of 1526 Charles needed to leave Granada in order to be ready to meet the cortes which had been summoned to assemble at Valladolid in February the following year. Isabella had conceived while in Granada and as they made their journey north Charles pushed on while Isabella travelled at a more leisurely pace. Charles was now well on his way to being fully accepted as king and in turn he was increasingly coming to see Spain as the bedrock of his empire, in terms of revenue, soldiers, and religious orthodoxy. Although his Spanish subjects wished him to remain in Spain, a system of government had been established that could function effectively in his absence. The development of support for Charles had undoubtedly been aided by his marriage. This was rewarded with Isabella's pregnancy. On 21st May 1527, in the Palacio de Pimental, opposite the church of San Pablo where Charles had been acclaimed as king of Castile nine years before, Isabella gave birth to a son. Charles was naturally delighted and the festivities at court and across the country were extensive. Congratulatory messages came from across Europe, from monarchs, diplomats and the nobility. At his baptism on 5th July the boy was given the Burgundian name Philip, after Charles' father. His godparents were Inigo Velasquez, constable of Spain, Don Juan de Zuniga and Charles' sister, Eleanor.[15] If it had not been for unwelcome events in the international sphere, Charles would indeed have had plenty to celebrate.

## 11
## 'He should look to his honour' – Renewed War with France

As Charles was celebrating the birth of his son and heir in late May 1527, the first reports, later confirmed, arrived in Valladolid of horrific events in Rome. They were enough to take the shine off any festivity. His informants, including Gonzalo Perez and Francisco de Salazar, left him in no doubt as to the unrestrained and indiscriminate violence that had been inflicted upon the city by the Imperial army. Charles recognised that his reputation was at stake and claimed that such actions had been beyond his knowledge and against his wishes. He wrote that he would 'rather not have won the victory than that this should happen'.

Charles had already learnt that war was unpredictable – battles that should be won could end in disaster, those where defeat seemed likely could become great victories as at Pavia. Unfortunately the same uncertainty applied to achieving a satisfactory and lasting peace settlement. Charles had hoped that the treaty signed in Madrid would achieve stability, but, as Gattinara surmised, it was too much to expect that Francis was willing to end his ambitions in Italy, or indeed that other states would accept a peace based on Habsburg supremacy. Even before Charles had settled in Granada with Isabella it was clear that the French king had little intention of complying with the terms agreed, and was indeed hell bent on overturning the whole basis of the treaty.

At first Francis claimed that the publication of the treaty had made his task of gaining the approval of his subjects far more difficult. Charles instructed his ambassador Louis de Praet to remind Francis of the promises that he had made. To reinforce the message he sent Lannoy to see Francis, then in Cognac. All such efforts failed. On 16th May Lannoy wrote to Charles with the news that Francis had informed him and de Praet that as the treaty had been signed under duress it had no legal standing and that under no circumstances would Burgundy be returned to Charles. It has been suggested that at this time Francis treated Lannoy with the greatest regard, even offering him the lands and honours of the Duke of Bourbon in an attempt to win him over, playing on Lannoy's fears that Charles would be angered by the complete failure of his policy of reconciliation and the treaty that he had agreed with Francis. Lannoy refused such blandishments, remaining faithful to Charles, who in any case treated him with kindness on his return.[1] Charles seems to have been able to gain the loyalty of his senior advisers and commanders; they rarely had to suffer the extreme consequences of an unsuccessful policy imposed by other rulers at the time.

On the 22nd May 1526, less than six weeks after Francis had left Spain, the anti Habsburg League of Cognac was signed, by which the Papacy, Venice, Florence and the Sforza of Milan lined up with France against Charles, with Henry VIII of England showing his goodwill towards the alliance. Another war in Italy was certain since none could accept the dominant position that Charles had achieved. This would leave Francis' sons captive in Spain, but he assumed that he would be able to ransom them back at some point in the future. In the end they were to remain as hostages for three years. The impact of this on the boys, Francis aged 8 (who died in 1536) and Henry aged 7 (later to become king of France) needs little imagination. Henry certainly grew up with an intense hostility to both his father and the Emperor.

Charles was appalled by this betrayal and is reported to have said of Francis that 'he should look to his honour – that is, if he has any left', since he had acted 'dishonourably in not fulfilling the pledge that he gave me in private'. He had learnt the lesson that all leaders need to recognise - that military victory alone does not guarantee a successful peace. He replied to the French ambassador on being informed of the demands of the League: 'Had your king kept his word we should have been spared this. I will take no money from him, not even for his children. He has cheated me; he has acted neither as a knight nor a nobleman, but basely. I demand that if he cannot fulfil his treaty, the Most Christian King should keep his word and become my prisoner again. It would be better for us two to fight out this quarrel hand to hand than to shed so much Christian blood.'[2] This was not the only time he suggested a duel with Francis, something that was never really going to take place, but it was rare for Charles to allow his anger to show quite so clearly.

The other event to disturb Charles' time in Granada was news from Hungary. Here King Louis II, married to Charles' sister, Mary, as part of the double marriage between the Habsburgs and the royal family of Hungary, had been struggling to defend his throne against internal challengers and the Ottoman Empire of Suleiman the Magnificent. The Ottoman Turks had been steadily eroding the defences of central Europe. In 1521 Belgrade had been taken and in the following year the island of Rhodes had been captured from the Knights of St. John after a lengthy siege. In the summer of 1526 Suleiman launched a major offensive towards Budapest. Although many European leaders expressed fear of further Ottoman successes, none were prepared or able to support Louis. Charles' brother, Ferdinand, who might well be expected to provide assistance to his brother-in-law, was occupied in protecting the emperor's worsening diplomatic position in northern Italy. Louis met the vastly superior Ottoman army at Mohacs, south of Budapest, on 29th August 1526 and was crushed. The king, aged only 20, and much of the Hungarian nobility with him, perished. Suleiman's army ransacked the capital before withdrawing in the autumn.

Ferdinand was elected King of Bohemia in October by representatives of the three Estates – lords, knights and towns. Supported by Mary, he also claimed the throne of Hungary, as husband of Louis' sister Anne, on the basis of the earlier marriage treaties. He met determined opposition from John Zapolya of Transylvania, who had himself crowned king in November. Ferdinand was also crowned by his own supporters the following year. Hungary was thus divided between the three competing forces – Ottomans, Habsburgs and Transylvania – and the struggle for control continued for over two hundred years. Ferdinand was to bear the brunt of the work in defending east and central Europe against the Ottomans for 40 years, not always fully supported by those who he believed ought to be more involved. His immediate problems in Hungary prevented him from playing any further part in the unfolding events in Italy

For Charles, as Emperor and thus defender of Christianity across Europe, the defeat at Mohacs was a blow to his reputation and dignity, something that he would wish to put right. His determination to lead Christian Europe in a successful 'crusade' against the Ottomans was sharpened, though he was often to be frustrated by the constraints that his other commitments placed upon him. Thus within a few months of his marriage Charles was directly confronted by two of the three major issues that were to continue to dominate his reign – conflict with France, and the Ottoman threat. The third issue, the continuing growth of religious divisions within Christendom and the related political problems within the Empire, had to be left unresolved. Indeed he was to find that it was impossible to deal with all three challenges simultaneously at any stage in the next thirty years.

Charles had been particularly disturbed by the Papal desertion of his cause, hoping, as he was, to travel to Italy for coronation by the Pope. On his election in 1523 many, including Charles, had high hopes of Pope Clement VII. As Cardinal Giulio de Medici he had showed himself to be an able, conscientious, administrator during the papacy of his cousin, guardian and friend, Leo X. Born in 1475 he was the illegitimate son of Giuliano de' Medici, bought up by his uncle Lorenzo the Magnificent in Florence and placed under the guardianship of his cousin when Lorenzo died in 1492. He was tall, graceful, more serious and intellectual than Leo X. However, unlike Leo, who despite his many considerable faults was often able to achieve his ends by using his natural charm and extravagance, the parsimonious but in many ways more capable Clement was difficult to like. Guicciardini described him in unflattering terms: 'somewhat morose and disagreeable, reputed to be avaricious, far from trustworthy and naturally disinclined to do a kindness'.[3] On his election he was regarded by many as Charles' man, but he soon showed himself to be more concerned with protecting Medici interests in Florence, securing papal secular interests elsewhere, and perhaps, if looked at in a favourable light, working for an Italy free of foreign domination. Caught between the claims and ambitions of Charles and Francis, he was to demonstrate the indecision and lack of resolution that resulted in him being trusted by few. He abandoned Charles' cause before Pavia, encouraging French troops to move against Naples. He then attempted to use the Imperial victory to secure papal territories before organising the Italian states in the name of seeking to reduce Habsburg power in Italy and joining with Francis in 1526.

After the Treaty of Cognac both sides engaged in extensive propaganda to the courts of Europe, while at the same time assembling forces. In Granada Charles received a letter of June 23rd 1526 from Pope Clement. In it Clement claimed that all his actions were motivated by a wish for peace, that the one who disturbed that peace was the Emperor and that he must therefore defend himself. Charles' reply, drafted by Alonso Valdes, firmly challenged this view. The Pope, he argued, had acted purely in his own interests and not that of Christendom. He had no need to defend himself since he was not under attack. He was acting less like a shepherd and more like a wolf. If only he would lay down his arms, others would follow suite and their combined forces could be used against the Ottomans and the heretics. If he would not carry out his duty to defend the Church by convening a general council to consider necessary reforms, then Charles would expect others to do so – a direct challenge to the authority of the Pope. Both sides ensured that their letters were widely published across Europe, seeking to win support for their cause. So much for the 'twin pillars of Christianity'.

In Italy the situation rapidly deteriorated. The Pope and his allies Venice, Florence and Milan raised troops and were expecting additional support from the French. Imperial troops marched into Milan in November 1525 and finally took the citadel, the Castello Sforzesco, in the following July, forcing the surrender of Francesco Sforza, who although he had been installed as duke by Charles in 1521 had joined the League of Cognac. The League suffered the loss of a fine general when Giovanni de Medici (known as Giovanni delle Bande Nere) died of wounds in November 1526. In Rome the Pope experienced a serious threat to his position from Cardinal Pompeio Colonna, leader of one of the most powerful families in the city. A former soldier turned churchman, his troops entered the city in September 1526 emptying the papal palace of its valuables and forcing Clement to take refuge in the Castel Sant'Angelo. Public opinion turned against Colonna and Clement was able to negotiate himself out of his predicament and then deprive Colonna and his family of their privileges and most of their lands.

On the Imperial side, the Duke of Bourbon commanded 6,000 Spanish troops, along with several thousand Italian infantry and cavalry led by Ferrante Gonzaga and Philibert, Prince of Orange. They were joined in February by 14,000 German 'landsknechts' led by the experienced Georg von Frundsberg, who had ably supported the Imperial cause at Pavia. Having removed Sforza from Milan and left de Leyva in command of the garrison there, they marched through Lombardy and into Tuscany. Alarm spread throughout northern Italy. Cities such as Parma and Bologna attempted to improve their defences, but no attack came. The Imperial troops had not been paid and with no sign of new funds arriving they were becoming increasingly difficult to control. Frundsberg and the Prince of Orange, attempted to reason with them but to no avail. Frundsberg suffered a stroke, had to leave and never recovered.

The troops developed the idea that the real cause of their problems was the Pope living amidst the wealth and splendour of Rome. There they would be able to take what they believed they had earned. Marching south, their anger and their various prejudices - loyalty to the Emperor's cause, anti-clericalism, Lutheran hostility to the Roman church - combined with hunger, greed and even guilt at their own lack of discipline, all grew as they approached Rome. Lannoy, Charles' viceroy now back in Naples, negotiated a truce with the Pope to halt the advance. This involved the Pope paying off the Imperial troops, with Lannoy arguing that 200,000 ducats were needed, all forces returning to their original positions before the outbreak of hostilities, and the restoration of Francesco Sforza as duke of Milan[4]. Since this was negotiated without the knowledge of either the Pope's allies or Bourbon, the Imperial commander (who by this deal would lose Milan, given to him after the Treaty of Madrid in 1526), it was ignored. The Pope, still apparently confident that Rome was safe, would not pay up until the Imperial troops had fallen back. Given their mood that was not going to happen.

The Imperial army marched swiftly to Rome, while the forces of the League, now commanded by the Francesco Maria della Rovere, the Duke of Urbino, were slow to respond. The various Italian cities, which provided the troops and their commanders, each had their own priorities, and defence of Rome was not necessarily one of them. The city's physical defences were out-of-date, and troop numbers limited, with only 5,000 militiamen and 500 Swiss Guard, although they did have some effective artillery. However, the Imperial army did not have the resources for a lengthy siege and a direct assault was always difficult. Having arrived outside the walls on 5th May, Bourbon was keen to attack immediately, but was overruled by his officers. Bourbon spoke to encourage his troops, concluding that in order to build upon past victories they must: 'force (themselves) to do all that the present grave situation requires and all that the certainty of future wealth inspires'[5]. Francisco de Salazar later reported to Gattinara that messengers sent into Rome requesting peaceful entry to the city were 'dismissed with very angry words'.[6]

The attack began at dawn on the following day. Bourbon was killed by a shot from an arquebus while scaling the walls (claimed to have been fired by Benvenuto Cellini, the superb sculptor and mendacious self-publicist) and the Prince of Orange took command to prevent panic spreading amongst the troops[7]. The assault, which

## Charles V: Duty and Dynasty

had been in danger of failing, broke through. Of 189 Swiss guards on duty only 42 escaped with their lives. There followed a widespread massacre carried out by troops who made little distinction between combatant and civilian. Few patients in the hospital of Santo Spirito or orphans of the Pieta survived.[8]

There was no chance of any control being exerted as the victorious attackers set about sacking the city. 'Hell itself was a more beautiful sight to behold' wrote Marino Sanuto, an eye witness, as the Spanish and German troops set about helping themselves. Murder and rape were widespread, only easing with the realisation that much could be made from ransoms[9], typically 5,000 ducats for a senior churchman. Churches and monasteries were looted, the palaces of the cardinals and nobility were plundered. Those who did not pay 'were put to the most cruel and strange forms of torture to make them declare what money they had, and where it was hid'[10]. The tortures listed by Liuigi Guiccardini, writing shortly afterwards, included the victims being suspended by the arms for hours, suspended by one foot above the street or over water with the threat of being dropped, led around by ropes tied to their testicles, branded with hot irons, made to eat their noses, ears or testicles, and having their back teeth pulled out[11]. Perhaps 4,000 deaths occurred. The Pope again narrowly escaped capture by fleeing from the Vatican via the covered, raised walkway to the Castel Sant' Angelo, where he remained besieged.

All citizens were in danger, and even pro-Imperial cardinals had to pay to protect their property and lives. Cardinals Catejan and Ponzetti were dragged through the streets and subjected to ridicule and torture. The elderly Ponzetti had to pay a ransom of 20,000 ducats and died of his injuries. Cardinal Aracoeli was forced to admit to 'shameful and bestial things' while being paraded around the city[12]. Some wealthy inhabitants having paid Spanish troops for their safety found that they then had to pay the Germans as well. Giorgio Borassi's experience must have been common when he wrote to his brothers in Venice that he had 'lost everything, though I care little for it. But I do not want to die so young'. Guiccardini reported that 'anyone can imagine' the treatment of girls and women 'in the hands of such a lustful people as the Spanish'[13], and also that the Lutheran Germans delighted in destroying religious relics and revered works of art. Even local inhabitants took the opportunity to wipe clean old debts and act on old vendettas. The palace of Sant' Apostoli, the temporary residence of Isabella Gonzaga, mother of Ferrante Gonzaga, an imperial commander, became the refuge for over 1000 citizens and their valuables, and even they had to negotiate a substantial ransom.

On the third day Philibert ordered the troops to stop the looting, but few obeyed until they had taken all that they could. The idea that there were clear war aims which did not provide the soldiers and commanders of the different factions the chance of enrichment was unrealistic. They had risked their lives and this was their reward. One month later Pope Clement VII surrendered and agreed to pay 400,000 ducats for his life. Having made further concessions he left the city for Orvieto. Meanwhile many papal cities further north were seized by Venice and opportunists from the ducal families in Italy. The Medici family were removed from power in Florence and the republic re-established.

In a letter of 19th March Charles had been made aware of the lack of funds to pay his army. On 13th May he responded: 'We write by this post to the Viceroy telling him what he is to do, and have also sent to Mons. de Bourbon 100,000 ducats for payment of the army under his command'. What Charles did not know was that Rome had already been ransacked and Bourbon killed in the assault a week earlier. The letters of Perez and Salazar, who themselves had to pay to save their lives, arrived later. They referred to the 'atrocious tortures', the mistreatment of 'friars, monks and nuns', the 'pools of blood' and rooms of the Papal Palace being 'turned into stables'. Perez advised the emperor to 'offer some sort of consolation' to cardinals who had been his supporters and yet still threatened and robbed by the looters.

The 'Sack of Rome' has often been seen as a major turning point, the end of an era in which Rome provided at least some stability in the Christian world. In retrospect it was claimed by many that the omens of disaster for Rome had been there for all to see. The plagues of 1524 and 1525; the river Tiber breaking its banks in 1526; a bolt of lightning throwing the baby Jesus from the arms of the Virgin and destroying her crown on a statue in the church of S. Maria in Trastavere; and the ravings of the religious fanatic Brandano in April 1527: 'for thy sins, Rome shall be destroyed'.

These events had a major impact on another issue that was to be of great significance to England, its alignment in international affairs, and its relations with Charles for many years. It was at exactly this moment that Henry VIII petitioned the Pope for a divorce from Catherine of Aragon. Under normal circumstances it would not have been unrealistic for Henry to think that as a reigning monarch his request, however exceptional, would be accepted. After all he had received papal dispensation, wrongly he now argued, to marry Catherine in the first place. In the situation after the sack of Rome it was unlikely in the extreme that Clement would be able to agree to this request. Charles was not likely to approve of Henry's decision to 'put aside' his aunt and his troops controlled Rome and the Papal States. Henry's divorce issue was to continue for nearly six years, but his chances of success had sharply declined and any friendship with Charles soured.

The capture of Rome in this manner left Charles' military position strong in the short term, but his reputation was potentially in tatters. He cannot escape all responsibility, after all it was troops raised in his name, under his commanders, who had carried out the 'sack'; it was the failure of his financial arrangements that had resulted in the non-payment of the soldiers. But Charles was able to persuade himself that others bore a greater weight of guilt. A major propaganda campaign was launched, letting the people of Europe know that Charles had not ordered the attack, and that responsibility lay with those of his enemies who had repeatedly broken their promises and agreements. His ambassador in Genoa, Lope de Soria, wrote to him later in the month that God had 'permitted that the Emperor – who is his most devoted servant and true Catholic Prince – should become the instrument of his vengeance, to teach his Vicar on Earth and the rest of the Christian Princes that their wicked purposes shall be defeated.'[14] It was declared that Charles' most earnest wish was to have peace in Christendom so that it could be defended against its true enemies, heretics and the Ottoman Turks, who after success in Hungary could now threaten Vienna. In his memoirs Charles recorded that 'the detention of the Pope ought to be reproached less to the Emperor than to those who had compelled him to raise for his defence so many soldiers who did not obey him well'[15].

For Charles' enemies this was an opportunity not to be missed. They were reinvigorated, received widespread support, and were once again able to challenge his position in much of Italy. The anti-Imperial forces renewed their aggression believing that they had a just war to fight against an Emperor who had sacked Rome and failed to defend Christianity against infidels and heretics. On 22nd January 1528, at Burgos, heralds from the kings of France and England formally handed over a declaration of war. Charles in reply pointed out that they had unscrupulously been prepared to wage war with no formal declaration for years, that the Pope was now free, and repeated his challenge to Francis for personal combat instead of a war which would cause widespread death and destruction.

Charles' general Antonio de Leyva was able to successfully defend Milan and so the French army, now in the field, moved into southern Italy. Having taken much of Apulia they besieged Naples. By the early summer of 1528 the position of the city was precarious, its limited troops under pressure on land, and the blockade of its harbour by the Genoese navy under Andrea Doria causing food shortages and preventing the arrival of relief forces. It was defended by the young Philibert of Chalons, Prince of Orange. Lannoy had been taken ill and died in late 1527 and his successor as viceroy, Hugo de Moncada was killed in May 1528 attempting to break through the naval blockade. Naples was saved by Doria's growing distrust of Francis I. In July he withdrew his fleet and through the auspices of the Prince of Orange established an understanding with Charles that was to last three decades. The French army, already weakened by disease, hunger and lack of finances, followed by the death of their commander, Lautrec, ended the siege in August. Further north another French army entered Lombardy late in 1528 but the Emperor's forces won a major victory at Landriano on 21st June 1529. Charles was convinced that these victories were the will of God.

Francis needed peace and Charles was not unwilling, but was understandably cautious. The previous year he is reported to have quoted Cicero: 'To let oneself be fooled once is disagreeable, twice is shameful, thrice is stupidity'.[16] The result was the Treaty of Cambrai, often known as the Ladies' Peace as it was mainly negotiated by Charles' aunt Margaret of Austria, still regent in the Low Countries, and her sister-in-law, Francis' mother, Louise of Savoy. It was finally signed on August 3rd 1529, although the likely terms had been known to Charles for several months. This had reasserted the terms of the Treaty of Madrid, effectively removing French influence from Italy, and ending Francis' claims to Flanders and Artois, even though Charles had to abandon any hope of regaining Burgundy for his dynasty. The two French princes, Francis and Henry, held in Spain since Francis' release in 1526, were to be returned on payment of a ransom of one million ducats. It again provided for the marriage of Francis to Charles' eldest sister, Eleanor, first agreed by the Treaty of Madrid, and Francis made fine statements about supporting the Habsburgs in their conflict with the Ottoman Empire[17]. In October Francis received Charles' representative, Charles de Poupet, Lord of La Chaulx, in Paris and spoke in glowing terms of the peace settlement. He would now be Charles' brother and friend, and would happily meet Charles to plan a campaign against the 'Turk'.

Charles V: Duty and Dynasty

# Part Three
# Chasing Ambitions
# 1529-1536

Inscription in Bologna commemorating Charles' coronation by Pope Clement VII in 1530.

Charles V: Duty and Dynasty

# 12
## 'I have come where I have long desired to be' – Coronation

To achieve complete peace Charles also needed to reach a settlement with the pope. Negotiations had been underway for months between Clement's representatives and Charles' advisers, Chancellor Gattinara, de Praet, and the increasingly influential Nicholas Perrenot de Granvelle. It would be easy to fall into the trap of thinking that the Treaty of Barcelona, when signed on June 29th 1529, was the end of all Charles' problems with the Papacy. In the 'high flown diplomatic language of the time' the Pope and Emperor 'joined hands out of grief at the divisions of Christianity, to beat off the Turks and to make way for a general peace'[1]. Both would also act against heretics. In reality the Pope was coming to terms with an Emperor who had gained the upper hand in Italy. Charles now had effective control of Naples and Milan, as well as a close alliance with Genoa.

Clement accepted that he could no longer openly oppose the Emperor: 'I have quite made up my mind to become an Imperialist, and to live and die as such'. Papal support was never certain, but from 1529 onwards Charles was less likely to face a direct challenge to his position. He would get the coronation he so desired, along with promises of future support and forgiveness for those involved in the sack of Rome. In return, several cities (Ravenna, Reggio, Modena) were to be restored to the Papacy, and imperial troops would ensure that Florence was returned to Medici control, with Alessandro de' Medici to marry Charles' natural daughter Margaret when she was 13.

Charles could now undertake the journey for which he had been waiting for since his accession and arrive in Italy with the necessary authority. He believed that many benefits would accrue from the journey and coronation. In his correspondence he is concerned to justify this ambition. To Philibert, Prince of Orange, now Viceroy of Naples and his commander in Italy, he wanted to 'win honour and reputation'; to his sister Mary of Hungary 'to put an end to the war and arrive at a universal peace in Christendom'; to the Castilian Council of State he planned to 'work with the Pope (and) wipe out heresies and bring about the reform of the Church' as well as to 'see my kingdoms and lands and the subjects that dwell within them'; to the Spanish ambassador in Rome (presumably for transmission to the Pope) 'to prepare for defence' against Turkish invasion. Each explanation was clearly tailored to match the expectations of the recipient. Charles wished to show himself as honourable, just, a true champion of Christianity. In retrospect he recorded in his Memoirs that his journey was 'animated by the desire of counteracting as much as possible the errors in Germany which, owing to the wars he had been engaged in, he had only been able to remedy imperfectly'.. 'at the same time to assume the crowns which he had not yet received, and finally to be in a better position to oppose the Turk, who, it was said, was advancing against Christianity'.[2] He denied that he desired further territorial gains or wished to punish his enemies, since that would be left to God.

Nevertheless, Charles' determination to go to Italy was not universally welcomed even by those close to him. Isabella, his wife, was 'pained by the Emperor's departure' but consoled by the fact that 'the absence of her husband whom she so dearly loved, was for the service of God, for the benefit of Christendom and for the faith'[3]. Margaret of Austria, his aunt, wrote to him that 'the dangers to your person and the difficulties of the task cannot but awake ...our apprehension and anxiety'.[4] It was vital, she continued, that he had the money, troops and supplies before he commenced. Many of his Spanish advisers had no wish to see him leave their country, understandably fearing the dangers of an absentee monarch whose main interests lay elsewhere.

Detailed preparations were certainly needed. He had already established a system of government in Spain, with councils and an informal circle of advisers, which coped with the day-to-day business of government without removing his control over policy and appointments. He now had to ensure that it would function in his prolonged absence. Isabella would be regent. The birth of their son and heir, Philip, and of a daughter, Maria, only thirteen months later in June 1528, gave her added authority, but Charles needed to officially establish her as regent and define her relationship with the Councils. The various decrees and instructions that were issued when he left Castile on a visit to Valencia in 1528 could be seen as a trial run. Charles knew by now that in Isabella he had someone on whom he could rely. She was in many ways similar to her husband - pious, dutiful, and someone who could command respect and loyalty from those around her.

Next he appointed a small Council of State, of whom the most influential were Francisco de los Cobos and Juan Tavara, Archbishop of Santiago. Tavara had been President of the Council of Castile since 1524, and was to be created a Cardinal in 1531 and then Archbishop of Toledo and primate of Castile from 1534. They would be given access to all confidential correspondence and were expected to take the lead in policy and executive decisions, while Isabella would perform the official duties of the monarch in government and at court.[5] Charles, though, was careful to restrict their scope for making appointments, recognising the importance of the selection and promotion of officials to his own power. He left Isabella with some confidential advice on the strengths and weaknesses of those who would be around her. He was not always complimentary, but revealed something of his own ability – he was a good judge of men. 'Micer Gualvys', for instance, he describes as 'a nice man; he has no abilities, neither for staying nor for coming along'.[6] Charles also left Isabella expecting their third child.

Shortly before leaving he had audiences with both Hernando Cortes and Francisco Pizarro, meetings that were to influence the future of Central and South America. Cortes, having conquered 'New Spain' (Mexico), was at court to complain about his suspension as governor there. Although not reinstated, he was rewarded for his services, being accepted into the Order of Santiago, raised to the nobility as Marquis of the Oaxaca Valley and appointed military commander in 'New Spain'. Pizarro had already made two unsuccessful expeditions to the Inca Empire in South America, but the governor of Panama refused permission for a third. The purpose of his visit to Spain was to persuade Charles and the Council of the Indies to overturn this decision. In his presentation he emphasised the wealth that he had already seen there and brought gifts including some 'indians', llamas and of course gold. Although no final decision was made Charles was impressed. The following year Isabella signed the document that became known as the 'capitulation of Toledo' giving him permission to proceed with an invasion, naming him as Governor and Captain General of 'New Castile' (Peru).

Charles left Toledo in March 1529, travelling by way of Aranjuez, Siguenza, and Zaragoza to Barcelona, where he arrived at the end of April. There he waited nearly three months. The fleet was readied, the troops gathered, but the money required was still to arrive. He had requested the collection of a 'coronation subsidy' from the States-General of the Low Countries, but the funds that secured the trip came from the sale of the Moluccas in the East Indies[*] to Portugal for 350,000 ducats. As soon as that was delivered to him in late July he set sail, with the crews of many galleys shouting 'Plus ultra'.[7] This was Charles' personal motto, the Latin version of the French 'Plus Oultre' which he had originally adopted while preparing to leave the Low Countries to claim his kingdoms in Spain. Meaning 'further beyond' it was first used by Ferdinand of Aragon after the discovery of the New World and was said to be an encouragement for him to take risks, strive for greater achievements and ignore the ancient myth of the Pillars of Hercules near the Straits of Gibraltar which had the warning 'Non plus ultra', 'nothing farther beyond'. The phrase became popular in Spain and eventually

---

[*] Claimed for Spain by Ferdinand Magellan

## Charles V: Duty and Dynasty

became the national motto. Charles also used the two columns or pillars in the myth as his emblem, again used by modern Spain.*

Sailing via Monaco and Savona, on 12th August he reached Genoa, the home of his new ally Andrea Doria, where he received a grand welcome. 'With cries from 200 small boats, of 'Carlo, Carlo, Impero, Impero, Cesare, Cesare', he landed alongside a specially built pier hung with tapestries and cloth of gold. A great ball appeared with an eagle on top which showered scent, and a boy symbolising Justice handed the emperor the keys of the city.'[8] Besides the dignitaries of the city, led by Doria, whose switch from the French to the emperor's side in 1528 had so helped Charles to gain his position of superiority, there were four cardinals, led by Cardinal Farnese, sent by Pope Clement, and many noblemen, including Alessandro de' Medici, soon to be established as ruler of Florence. He stayed in Genoa for the rest of the month and then travelled slowly, north to Tortona, east to Piacenza, and from there south-east along the old Roman Via Aemilia, through Parma, Reggio, Modena, eventually arriving outside Bologna on 4th November.

After resting for the night at the Carthusian monastery of Certosa de Bologna, Charles entered the city by the Porta San Felice, greeted by twenty cardinals and four hundred Papal guards. Preceded by light cavalry in red, ten pieces of artillery mounted on chariots, and fourteen companies of German foot soldiers, Charles rode in full armour under a gold canopy supported by four lords on foot, with twenty-five pages of honour from Bologna running at his side. Accompanying him were Henry of Nassau and Antonio de Leyva (carried in a chair because of gout). They were followed by Charles' household and Spanish infantry. As the procession took the old Roman road into the heart of the city, standards with the eagle of the House of Habsburg and the Burgundian red cross of St Andrew were prominent.[9]

---

* This had also been used by Ferdinand. It was used on the 'Spanish dollar', worth eight reales, from the late 16th century, and has been suggested as the most likely origin of the U.S. dollar sign.

Pope Clement had travelled to the city the previous month, so that as the person of higher rank he would be there to receive his visitor as custom demanded. Clement greeted Charles on a temporary structure at the top of the steps leading to the portico of the still incomplete basilica of St Petronius[*]. In formal statements Charles declared: 'I have come where I have long desired to be, to the feet of your Holiness, that we may take measures together to relieve the needs of afflicted Christendom'. The Pope replied: 'I thank God that I see you here safe after your long journey by sea and land, and that affairs are in such a state that I need not despair of seeing by means of your authority, peace and order re-established.'[10]

All had been carefully orchestrated. Charles wished to maximise the impact of his time in Italy. The coronation was to be one of many ceremonial events which Charles used to show himself in the most favourable light. Even if today's instant communications did not exist in the sixteenth century, rulers were alert to the value of propaganda. Pamphlets, medallions and prints from woodcuts would be produced and distributed as widely as possible to celebrate and commemorate successes and victories. More expensive and longer lasting were the tapestries, often produced years later based on sketches made at the time, and the formal portraits depicting the 'hero' in his moment of glory.

Charles was lodged in the Palazzo Comunale (also known as the Palazzo d'Accursio), Bologna's seat of government from the 13th century, in rooms directly connected to those of the Pope. In the courtyard the stone plaque commemorating their stay and the coronation still exists. From the Palazzo Charles overlooked the Piazza Maggiore, from where he would have seen the Palazzo del Podesta, the Palazzo Re Enzo, the original Palazzo del Banchi, close to where the money lendérs set up their benches (banchi). A little further away were the Due Torri – the 47m. Torri della Garisenda with its alarming lean and the 97m. Torri degli Asinelli – survivors

---

[*] Named after the 5th century bishop and patron saint of Bologna

## Charles V: Duty and Dynasty

of the hundred towers for which Bologna was famed in the 13th century.

Three and a half months passed before the coronation ceremony. Discussions were held with Pope Clement, often in person, to settle the outstanding areas of contention in Italy. Between the talks Charles spent his time attending splendid public festivities - tournaments, bull baiting in the Piazza Maggiore and horse races through the city streets. He also visited the university, founded in the 11th century, the monastery of San Michele in Bosco, and presided over services for the Knights of the Order of the Golden Fleece and the Knights of Santiago. It was during this time that Charles suffered a second attack of gout. His first had been in 1528 and the ailment was to afflict him for the rest of his life. In his Memoirs scarcely a year goes by without a reference to another attack, initially each lasting up to a week. The fact that he was able to recall when and where each episode occurred two decades later indicates that it had a significant impact on his physical and mental state. Since it was largely untreated, it was always likely that the attacks would not only continue, but become longer, more severe, and also increase the risk of other medical conditions. It was during this time that Charles 'was informed that the Empress had given birth to a second son, Ferdinand'[11], news that must have cheered Charles, even though he knew as well as anyone the precarious nature of a young life.

The protracted nature of the negotiations resulted in the decision to hold the ceremony in Bologna not in Rome as had originally been planned. Charles wanted no further delay having promised to assist his brother against both the Protestant threat in Germany and an Ottoman advance towards Austria. Another, unspoken, reason were the murders and destruction that Charles' unpaid and ill-disciplined troops had unleashed during the 'sack of Rome' two years before; feelings were still too raw for him to be easily welcomed there. This needed to be a celebration unsullied by recriminations. Thus for a short time Bologna housed the nobility, and their retinues, from much of Europe, certainly all the areas that Charles ruled – Spain, the Low Countries and Germany, as well as many from Italy. In a preliminary ceremony on 22nd February Charles was crowned by the Pope with the Iron Crown of Lombardy in the chapel of the Palazzo Comunale.

On the day of the imperial coronation, Charles' 30th birthday, the whole city was decked out with triumphal arches full of imperial references – emperors, generals, victories - from both the Roman and medieval periods. Coins and medals, fruits and sweets were showered on the watching multitude. The processions were to make their way from a window in the Palazzo Comunale along a raised wooden walkway to the top of the steps at the front of the basilica of San Petronio, on the other side of the Piazza Maggiore. It was wide enough for six people to walk abreast, carpeted and draped with blue cloth and tapestries. Faces jostled for position at the windows and on the roofs of the buildings that overlooked the square. The walkway, square and surrounding streets were lined with troops, whose disposition had been checked by Antonio de Leyva, in charge of the military preparations.[12]

At 8 a.m. the papal procession commenced. Pope Clement, wearing his traditional papal triple tiara, started along the walkway in his state chair carried by servants in red livery, with the cardinals and archbishops, chamberlains and secretaries, notaries and judges, patricians and academics, in attendance. There is much debate over the symbolism of the triple tiara. The three sections have been variously interpreted as representing the Pope as the father of princes and kings, ruler of the world on earth, and vicar of Christ, or teacher, lawmaker and judge, or priest, prophet and king. Another compelling suggestion is that as the Holy Roman Emperors were crowned three times as king of Germany, king of Italy and Emperor, then the popes also wished to have a tiara with three crowns. Clement's was a newly created tiara as in 1527 he had ordered the melting down of all existing crowns to contribute to the ransom of 400,000 ducats demanded by the troops of the very man he was about to crown.

After a short pause Charles' procession set out. There were pages, cupbearers, stewards, chamberlains, military officers, councillors, ministers, envoys from across Europe, and then Charles, wearing the crown of Lombardy, a robe of brocade and the royal mantle. The high and mighty from across his lands were there to honour him; the Elector Palatine carried the orb of empire, the Duke of Urbino the sword of honour, the Marquis of Montferrato the golden sceptre and the Duke of Savoy the crown. As Charles reached the steps on the threshold of the Basilica, there was much commotion as part of the walkway behind him collapsed. Soldiers, with their pikes, were pitched into the crowd, some of whom were crushed. Eye witnesses vary as to the extent of the collapse; some said twenty paces, others only two or three. The procession continued, leaving others to attend to the injured and repair the damage. Another incident occurred when the representatives of Genoa and Siena scuffled over an issue of precedence.

Charles was then invested with a cloak which was embroidered with a huge imperial eagle made of pearls and precious stones, with a portrait of the emperor on the collar, flanked by two pillars with his motto 'Plus Ultra'. In scenes now celebrated in the Chapel of St. Abbondio[*] the symbols of office were presented, and Cardinal Farnese (who later became the next pontiff as Paul III) anointed Charles, the whole ceremony being overseen by Pope Clement. Drums, trumpets and cannons sounded. Mass was celebrated and a plenary indulgence (the remission before God of all temporal punishment due to sin whose guilt has already been forgiven through confession) announced. Clement and Charles then walked down the centre of the basilica hand in hand. So packed were the crowds outside that they had to wait half an hour for space to be made for them to descend the steps to their waiting horses. Charles, having dispensed with the orb, sceptre and robes, assisted the Pope onto his horse which he then led for six paces until Clement insisted that he mounted his own. The joint procession, with churchmen on

---

[*] The first chapel of the basilica.

## Charles V: Duty and Dynasty

the right and those of the Imperial court on the left, now headed for the basilica of St Domenico*. The Pope, as planned, left before they arrived. Here, by the tomb† of the founder of the Dominican order, San Domenico, Charles conferred knighthoods on two hundred gentlemen. The ceremonies had taken in total almost nine hours.

Even then the day had some way to go. A banquet was held at the Palazzo Comunale for a select few. Charles sat at a table on his own. Nearby was a table for ten: four cardinals, the Dukes of Savoy, Urbino, and Bavaria, the Marquess of Monferrato, Alessandro de'Medici and Antonio de Leyva. In an adjoining hall there were two more tables, each for thirty guests. Once the feast was over the remaining food was thrown from the windows for the crowds and troops in the square below to add to the loaves already supplied. There, on enormous spits turned by eight soldiers, cooks roasted oxen stuffed with partridges and snipe, suckling pigs and hares, geese and ducks, whose heads protruded from cuts in the sides of the beasts. Two columns representing Charles' symbol, had been erected, topped by a double headed spread eagle, from which fountains with lions mouths supplied wine, both red and white.[13]

The coronation could be seen as the culmination of the work of Mercurino de Gattinara, Charles' Imperial Chancellor and chief adviser for the previous ten years. His vision was of Charles as universal monarch, the unchallenged leader of Europe and all Christianity. Many had sought to prevent this coming together of the two men whose family names have resounded through European history - Habsburg and de'Medici. Charles was now the heir to Charlemagne in a line stretching back to the first imperial coronation in Rome on Christmas Day 800, but what none of those present knew was that this would be the last ever such ceremony, the last time a Pope officiated at the coronation of an Emperor. This ultimate symbol of the unity of church and state, secular and religious authority, was what Charles had worked many years to

---

* Just as in Rome the tradition was to travel from St Peter's to St John Lateran.
† Created by Pisano with later additions by dell'Arca and Michelangelo.

achieve. Now he had reached this apparent position of power, how successful was he to be in using his authority to achieve his religious, political and dynastic aims? Were those aims as wide ranging as his Chancellor's vision? If Charles' experience up to this point had not already given him doubts, he was soon to become aware that this unity was perhaps a chimera, desirable but unobtainable.

## 13
## 'Make the best of things' – Machiavelli, Florence and Warfare

Once the ceremonies and festivities were over Charles remained in Bologna for another four weeks. He was able to take part in some hunting, and sat for the first time before Tiziano Vecelli, better known as Titian, who was later to paint many famous portraits of the Emperor. He produced a life sized portrait of Charles, mounted on the white horse upon which he had first entered the city, who was delighted with it and awarded Titian one thousand gold crowns.[1] But Charles had little time to enjoy the glow of achieving his long held ambition. He needed to move north with some urgency, having pressure from the German princes for his attendance at the forthcoming Imperial Diet. He wished to deal with the long sidelined religious controversy, to arrange for the election of his brother Ferdinand as King of the Romans and hence his successor as Emperor, and to discuss the Ottoman threat. He travelled via Mantua and Trent to Innsbruck, leaving troops under the Prince of Orange, to complete another part of his agreement with the pope, the defeat of the Florentine Republic on behalf of the Medici.

As a member of the League of Cognac, Florence under the Medici, strongly influenced by Pope Clement VII, had sided with the French. In 1527, taking advantage of the pope's weakness immediately after the sack of Rome, enemies of the Medici had removed them from power and a republic had been re-established in the city. The new rulers were faced with a very difficult diplomatic situation. Although it agreed to provide some troops for the Imperial cause, any future agreement between the Pope and the Emperor would make their position very insecure. With the defeat of the French, first in Naples and then at Landriano in Lombardy in

1529, it was clear that Clement had no option but to come to terms with Charles. This left the Florentine Republic isolated. Its former allies were in no position to assist. Despite his promises of help it was too soon for Francis I to yet again defy Charles, and Venice had made a separate peace with the Emperor.

The previous thirty or so years had seen major upheavals in Florence. It was famed for its wealth, sophistication and patronage of the arts, particularly under the leadership of the Medici family since its rise under Cosimo, Piero and then Lorenzo (the Magnificent) through the 15th century. The family had controlled the city without totally removing all representative features of what was still in name a republic. There were always those jealous of them and the death of Lorenzo in 1492, followed by the invasion of Italy by Charles VIII of France in 1494, enabled the radical preacher Savonarola to dominate the city with his brand of hell-fire religion. The Medici had been expelled and a Florentine Republic established, which continued, after Savonarola's execution in 1498, under Piero Soderini. This government lasted until 1512 when the defeat of the French enabled the Medici to return and rule the city until they were ousted again in 1527.

One witness to these events was Niccolo Machiavelli. Born in 1469, the son of a lawyer, he received an education suited to one destined for government service, based on the ideals of ancient Rome, a study of the humane disciplines – Latin, rhetoric, ancient history and moral philosophy.[2] This does not mean that Machiavelli's character was overly academic. All the evidence suggests that he liked to be the life and soul of the party, full of entertaining, if exaggerated, stories of his exploits, with a keen appetite for wine and women. He does not appear to have been overly constrained in his personal life by conventional beliefs and in his later writings, influenced as they were by practical experience, he was able to challenge the widely accepted, though often unrealistic, ideas of the time.

Machiavelli entered the service of the republic around 1500. He was sent on several diplomatic missions, meeting many of the leading figures of the day – Louis XII of France, Cesare Borgia (the son of Pope Alexander IV), and Pope Julius II. Dismissed in 1512 and then temporarily imprisoned and tortured in 1513 when suspected of involvement in a plot against the newly restored Medici, Machiavelli wrote 'The Prince' in an effort to curry favour with the family and regain a position in government. He failed in this attempt. The next fourteen years he spent mainly on his country estate reading and writing. He produced 'The Discourses' (on Livy's history of Rome) investigating how a republic can be established, become and remain powerful, and 'The Art of War'. In the 1520's he was commissioned by the Medici to produce a history of Florence. Ironically this final work made him unacceptable to the new rulers when the republic was restored. He died only two weeks after this rejection in June 1527 at his farm house outside Florence[3] and did not live to see the next stage in the struggle for control of his city.

His exposure to the realities of early 16th century politics during Charles' formative years, enabled Machiavelli to develop ideas and make judgements about the effective exercise of power. His conclusions were based on the evidence apparent to him from his own experiences and observations in Italy and other parts of Europe, put in the framework of classical and Renaissance philosophy. Over the last 500 years Machiavelli has been regarded as advocating an unprincipled approach to power and politics. No one active in domestic politics today can afford to be seen to admire, still less practice, such methods. Yet others believe he was describing the reality of politics, precisely the way rulers (past and present) achieve and maintain power. To refer to someone as 'Machiavellian' is not intended to be a compliment, but it might just have an element of grudging respect or perhaps more likely a fear of the lengths to which an individual is prepared to go in order to achieve an objective.

Machiavelli advocated that it was important for a ruler to act in a courageous, confident and decisive manner. Good laws and an effective army, ideally not one dominated by mercenary soldiers, would provide a sound basis for consolidating power. The ruler should be able to recognise the strengths and weaknesses of an enemy, to know when to fight and when to negotiate; he should not be too trustful of anyone; he should have the appearance of being virtuous even if he was not. Good citizens should be rewarded and honoured, but malefactors must be ruthlessly punished; a few exemplary punishments will discourage others and result in a more peaceful state in the future. It has been written that there are many benefits of absolute power, but a clean pair of hands is not one of them.[4] The rulers of the time must be viewed in this context and if we cannot applaud them, we can at least understand them, in the same way that it is important to understand the motives of our enemies if we are to improve our chances of defeating them. Of the rulers in Machiavelli's time, he most admired Ferdinand of Aragon, Charles' grandfather, because of the great things that he had achieved, not because of the means by which he had achieved them. The fact that Ferdinand, along with others from whom Machiavelli drew his examples, has not always been judged so positively (consider his treatment of Jews, his vast ambition, and the fact that he would never hesitate to break an agreement if it suited him) demonstrates that we are judging him using different criteria.

Machiavelli was making explicit what earlier writers had perhaps been unwilling to accept or dared not publish. All rulers, Charles and Francis included, were aware of these realities. Death was as much feared by most people as now, and was likely to strike at any time. This was a time of widespread political cruelty and executions were common. Heretics were burnt at the stake, torture of prisoners was expected and political assassinations frequent. The professional soldiers of the time looked to augment their unreliable wages by looting, and a town that did not surrender could expect plunder, widespread rape and murder. Their leaders, whether the condottiere who were looking to make a fortune or establish a small state of their own, or crowned monarchs, seemed generally careless of the welfare and livelihood of the population. In such conditions it was admirable that some philosophers and clerics should write about morality, justice and salvation; nor was it surprising that rulers spoke much about these values and how they promoted them. Machiavelli, while acknowledging the worth of these ideals, was writing about the realities of his world.

In 1529, with Charles now committed to the Medici cause, the position of the Florentine republic looked helpless. Some favoured capitulation but after internal disputes Francesco Carducci was appointed as the new gonfaloniere (the leader of the government) and military resistance was planned. The armies of the early 16$^{th}$ century were not national standing armies or mass volunteer armies. While the nobility were expected to fight for their king and others volunteered in the hope of wealth or glory, the majority of soldiers were mercenaries. The time of feudal service to the lord had passed. Machiavelli had argued the case for a trained local militia whose loyalty could be relied upon, but there were several disadvantages. They might be willing to risk their lives in defence of their city, possessions and family, but were unlikely to be ready to do so further afield; if ordered to another country there would be mass desertions. Most rulers had serious reservations about having a well-trained, permanently armed, body of local men too close to home. They could not be relied upon to put down internal unrest and could themselves pose a major threat to the authority of the ruler.

Mercenaries, on the other hand, were trained, professional, well-armed units who were contracted for a specific period or the duration of a campaign, and could usually be relied upon to follow orders, so long as they were paid regularly and had the expectation of plunder when successful. The fact that many units had existed for years meant that there was a comradeship that made them all the more effective on the battlefield. The downside was that if there was no money to pay them, you would not have an army. If they were left unpaid then the commanders could lose control and the consequences were unpredictable, as had been clearly demonstrated in the 1527 'Sack of Rome'.

In Florence they eventually raised a militia of about 8,000 men from the surrounding rural areas and added another 4,000 from the city itself. Money was also raised from the citizens to pay for the employment of mercenary soldiers, and Malatesta Baglioni, the condottiere and ruler of Perugia, was appointed as commander. They reinforced the city defences, at San Miniato for example, and demolished parts of the city outside the main walls in order to make them more defensible[5]. Michelangelo Buonarroti, as 'Governor of Fortifications', was responsible for the improvements and extensions made to the walls of Florence before and during the siege, evidence of the esteem in which he was held in the city, but a far cry from his work on the statue of David or the Pieta, now in St Peter's.

Although field artillery had its limitations, the use of artillery during sieges had become a significant factor by the 16th century. Many different sizes were cast but the 'half cannon' weighing up to 2,000 kgs. (a 'cannon' weighed up to 3600 kgs.), needing 10 or 12 horses to move them, could be manoeuvred into place during a siege, where mobility was less important than on the battlefield. The power of these weapons was such that with continual, well directed fire against the base of the walls they could create breaches through which the attacking soldiers could surge. By this time the traditional isolated medieval castle had lost its significance, but the increasing power of the cannon meant that no city could hold out for long with walls that had been made ever higher to defend against the scaling ladders and towers. In 1519 Machiavelli wrote: 'there is no wall whatever its thickness that artillery will not destroy in only a few days'[6]. For a short time at the start of the century this seemed to be the case. If cities could not be defended he believed that field armies would become larger and that wars would be decided in short campaigns and decisive battles[7].

What Machiavelli had not taken into account were the new defensive constructions, the 'trace Italienne' sometimes known as 'star fortifications', which were being developed during the Italian Wars as a response to the new weapons of attack. Walls were lowered and thickened, from typically 2 metres at the base to 12 metres[8], constructed of earth and rubble faced with brick or stone.

Rather than being vertical they were sloped, the combined effect being to reduce and absorb the impact of the cannonballs. At regular intervals around the defences there were triangular or arrow shaped 'angled bastions' jutting out so that there would be no 'dead ground', where the enemy would be invisible to the defenders. These would also provide positions from which the defenders could return fire with their artillery and fire arms. The whole wall would be surrounded by a widened ditch, sometimes filled with water to prevent mining, with sloping banks of earth in front of them to protect the walls from direct horizontal fire. The surrounding area would be cleared so that there would be little cover for the besieging army. Further refinements could be added when construction was not constrained by time or resources, such as free standing bastions (ravellins), double ramparts and covered infantry walkways. If a breach in the wall was made, attacking soldiers would have to pass through concentrated fire from both sides and once they had crossed the rubble they could expect to be confronted by rapidly raised 'half-moon' earthworks.

These developments swung the advantage back towards defence. It was now much more difficult to capture a city or fortress built in this way. A victory on the battlefield did not mean that the war was won or that territory could be secured. It had been such new defences that had enabled Rhodes to hold out for so long against vastly superior Ottoman forces in 1522. In normal circumstances, the longer a city could hold out the more difficult it became to supply the necessary food and munitions for the offensive forces. However, these defences were extremely expensive to construct. Not every city could afford them or be provided with them. The spread of the 'trace Italienne' was therefore initially restricted to strategically important cities and border fortresses. The Florentines employed as many of these features as the limited time and resources allowed.

The costs and dangers were high on both sides. If the attacking force failed to achieve a breakthrough the only other option was to attempt to starve the city into submission. The walls had to be surrounded with sufficient troops to defend against a relieving force attempting to end the siege and against sorties by the defenders. The longer it continued the greater the cost of maintaining the large numbers of soldiers required. It also meant that those soldiers could not be deployed elsewhere. However, the cost of a siege to the defenders and inhabitants should not be underestimated. Since food was going to run short, commanders often expelled non-combatants before or during a siege so that what supplies there were could be reserved for the troops. Houses and other buildings outside or adjacent to the walls were pulled down, since they would provide cover for the attackers. If the siege was ultimately successful it was usual for the victorious troops to be given three days of looting as a reward, at an enormous cost to the residents in both lives and property.

The imperial army was commanded by Philibert, Prince of Orange, along with Ferrante Gonzaga of Mantua. Spanish troops were added to by companies of both German and Italian soldiers, who, with the end of the main war, were now left without other employment. Recruits from throughout Italy gradually increased their numbers to 40,000, vastly outnumbering the defending forces. However the financial and logistical problems of keeping such a force in the field for a prolonged period of time were immense. Philibert constantly wrote to Charles pointing out the lack of money to pay the troops, his lack of artillery and the shortages of food.

The dangers that all those involved in warfare were exposed to meant that some reward was expected. As armies in the 16th century became larger the costs escalated. The pay of soldiers was increasing. It is difficult to generalise; some troops were valued more than others. An experienced infantryman in 1520 was paid about 3 ducats per month, rather more for arquebusiers, rather less for pike-men. By 1550 the pay was 5.5 ducats per month on campaign and 4.3 ducats on winter garrison duty[9]. The cavalry were paid considerably more, reflecting the additional costs of providing their own equipment. These were not high rates of pay, comparing unfavourably with that of a labourer. It is also doubtful whether the increases even matched the level of inflation that occurred in the same period. What must have tempted many, besides adventure, glory, despair or comradeship, were the hopes of booty from looting or the ransom of important prisoners.

It was not always easy to get the money to the right place at the right time. Most rulers needed to have a secure source of revenue to be able to guarantee payment to the troops. This might be from their ordinary revenue, or subsidies voted for by representative bodies if they believed their own interests were at stake, but more often it was borrowed against future revenues or promised by allies. Charles, and his commanders advancing on Florence in October 1529, had no wish to have a repeat of the sack of Rome; Orange had been an eye witness to those events and Charles seriously embarrassed. Even so the problems of financing the campaign and the resulting difficulties are clearly shown by the details of correspondence between Charles and the Prince of Orange, during the 10 month siege of Florence.[10]

Even before the start of the siege the prince had written to Charles that if the troops were not paid 'the Italians will desert to the enemy who will buy them, which is what they are keen to do. The Germans will mutiny and leave, at the very least. The light and heavy Spanish cavalry will refuse to obey any orders at all.' On October 24th 1529, Orange's troops began the siege with a bombardment of San Miniato. The walls could not be breached and a pattern developed of artillery exchanges and minor skirmishes. By the end of the month Orange wrote: 'relieve me of this command and give it to another who can do what I must do without money, I beg you. At least, spread a rumour that your troops and artillery are on the way from Bologna, with money'. In reply Charles explained that he was constantly putting pressure on Pope Clement VII, who had promised funds since Florence was being besieged for his family's benefit, that Genoa was late with a payment, and that he hoped to raise funds from Flanders, Venice, Milan and Naples. He concluded: 'I beg you cousin, to make the best of things'.

The loyal Orange persevered but shortly after Charles' coronation, he informed the Emperor that: 'it is impossible to keep an army as large as this alive on promises'. Money and food were not only in short supply for the imperial troops. It was increasingly important for the Florentines to secure their lines of supply as food became scarce. In this, control of the city of Volterra to the south-west was vital. Florence still controlled the fortress there, but when the Imperial troops attacked, it was necessary to send soldiers from Empoli[*] under Francesco Ferrucci to assist. Ferrucci was initially successful, but instead of remaining there he marched back to Empoli, which allowed the Imperial army to seize Volterra in a second attack.

Charles may have wished to stay in Italy to see the completion of the task, but it was taking too long and he had urgent business elsewhere. By July 1530 the pressure was building on both sides. Orange told Charles that their Spaniards were demanding six months wages and that he had some sympathy, referring to them as 'poor devils'. He continued that the 'Germans say they want to leave, even if they were paid, because of the plague' that was beginning to take lives amongst the troops. Inside the walls the Florentines, with supplies running dangerously low, ordered Ferrucci to march to the city with a relief army. If only they could have waited longer; it might have been only a matter of weeks before the imperial army started to disintegrate.

At this crucial stage Machiavelli was to be proved correct in his distrust of mercenary soldiers and their leaders. Baglioni, who had already agreed with the opposing Imperial forces that he could return to Perugia at the end of his contract with Florence, opened secret negotiations with the besieging commanders and agreed not to launch a supporting counter attack from Florence. The city had been betrayed. Orange, with no fear of attack from behind, was able to march to meet Ferrucci's forces at Gavinana, near Pistoia on 3rd August 1530. In a decisive conflict the Florentine relief troops were

---

[*] further north between Florence and Pisa

crushed. Both commanders perished. Orange died as a result of two wounds in the chest from arquebus shot and Ferrucci, having been captured, was hacked to death by Fabrizio Maramaldo, the commander of the Imperial reinforcements. Florence, now suffering from starvation and plague, had little option but to surrender nine days later.

There was to be no repeat of the sack of Rome. Pope Clement had made sure that the city to which his family was restored would survive the onslaught. Funds were provided from a number of different sources. Money was borrowed from Italian and German banking houses. Florence had to pay 80,000 ducats towards the dismissal pay of the besieging army[11]. The following year a 600,000 ducat subsidy from Naples 'was, according to comment by Gregorio Rosso, used for the arrears of the Naples-based troops who had fought in the siege of Florence the year before – or for the bankers who had paid their arrears'[12]. Some leading members of the republic, such as Francesco Carducci, were executed; others were exiled.

Leadership of the city passed to Alessandro de' Medici, acknowledged as the illegitimate son of Lorenzo II de' Medici (1492-1519, ruler of Florence 1513-1519 and Duke of Urbino 1516-1519) but believed by many to be the illegitimate son of Pope Clement. The Florentine Republic in effect ceased to exist, a situation formalised in 1532 when Alessandro became Duke of Florence. Negotiations for his marriage to Charles' youthful illegitimate daughter, Margaret, born in December 1522, had begun as early as 1527 and had been finalised by the Treaty of Barcelona. They would marry as soon as she reached an appropriate age. Despite the dissipated reputation of the groom, the marriage took place by proxy when Margaret was just ten and the final marriage ceremony occurred in Florence in 1536. Florence had been secured not only for the Medici but also for Charles' cause.

## 14
## 'Good Viceroys' - Meeting his Family

By the time of his coronation Charles had not met his brother Ferdinand for over eight years. As he left Bologna in the spring of 1530, having received 'the honour and title due', and with Florence soon to capitulate, there still remained the two other motives for his journey as declared on his departure from Spain: to 'achieve a universal peace in Christendom' and 'to protect the Christian faith'. Ferdinand had been acting for him both in the Empire and in resisting Ottoman advances for nearly ten years. He was keen for Charles to provide more help. In a wide ranging letter[1] written to his brother while still in Bologna in January 1530 Charles assured him that once he was crowned by the Pope he would work hard for Ferdinand's election as 'King of the Romans'. He went on to explain that his funds were limited: 'You must realise, brother, that in Spain they abhor all their resources that I have spent for the sake of Italy' suggesting that they would be just as unhappy to see their taxes spent in the Empire, Hungary or Austria. Charles also raised another issue. Since 1527 his power over Pope Clement had successfully blocked Henry VIII's divorce from Catherine of Aragon and he now wrote that the divorce plans would be 'against all justice and reason'. If Henry did divorce Catherine, he wrote, it would 'place us under a great obligation' (to do something about it).

Charles met Ferdinand and their sister, Mary of Hungary, the widow of King Louis of Hungary, at Innsbruck in May and early June 1530. Both were to play a major part in the governance of Charles' realms for the next 25 years. Ferdinand himself already appreciated Mary's qualities, and at Innsbruck she was to impress Charles who had not met her since she left Malines in 1514 at the tender age of eight. He soon recognised that she would be capable of fulfilling a significant role in Habsburg affairs in the future.

It was while at Innsbruck, on 5th June, that Mercurino Gattinara died, less than four months after the coronation that he had worked so hard to bring about. His death effectively marked the end of any notion of a unified, integrated, administrative organisation across Charles' lands. This was, in any case, unworkable and would have involved Charles in on-going internal conflicts throughout his domains. Although the scale of his lands gave him great power, in reality Charles was the ruler of a number of separate territories. Each jealously defended their own identities, insisting on their ancient rights and privileges, and requiring Charles to be 'their' ruler, resisting anything that would make them merely part of 'his' empire. If this emphasised his personal importance, it also placed great demands upon him. He had to deal with the 'local' or 'national' interests as well as maintaining a keen awareness of the wider international consequences of events far and wide.

Charles now emerged more clearly as a mature ruler; he no longer had the advisers from his youthful days. No one in the future was to have such a dominating influence on Charles' thinking as first Chievres and then Gattinara had done. No Imperial Chancellor was appointed to replace Gattinara. Charles' former confessor, Garcia de Loaysa wrote to suggest that 'your Majesty becomes your own Chancellor', recommending that he placed his trust in two individuals who were already well known to Charles, Francisco de los Cobos in Spain and Nicholas Perrenot, lord of Granvelle, in the Holy Roman Empire. Of Cobos he writes: 'you will find Cobos the best repository of your honour and your secrets; his character will make up for any lack in yours and he will be well able to relieve you of burdens... He never complains of his master and he is very popular'. Lord Granvelle, originally from Burgundy, was 'a very skilful lawyer, and a good Latinist, a good Christian, a man who understands affairs.'[2] Charles took this advice.

Loaysa, who had already been master of the Dominican Order, and then created a cardinal in 1530, was to go on to become

Archbishop of Seville in 1539, and serve as President of the Council of the Indies. Charles valued his advice but never recalled him to his personal service. Perhaps he was too forthright in his letters. In 1530 he reminded Charles of his duty to God. 'Your Majesty should be assured that God gives no man a kingdom without laying on him an even greater duty than on ordinary men to love Him and obey His commands.' He also warned Charles that: 'In your royal person, indolence is at war with fame. I pray that God's grace will be on you in Germany and that you will be able to overcome your natural enemies, good living and waste of time.'[3] There is some discordance between this view and the impression that we usually receive of Charles as diligent and hard-working. Charles did enjoy large meals, drank substantial quantities of beer, stayed up late, and in the years before his marriage had an eye for the ladies, but it is rarely recorded that this interfered with the execution of his duties. Charles certainly aimed to be a good ruler though Loasya saw fit to remind Charles again in December 1531 that 'God did not create you so that you could enjoy life but so that you would save the whole of Christendom through your ceaseless efforts'.[4] It could be that Loasya was a particularly hard task master, or that his earlier access to Charles' most intimate thoughts gave him an insight that very few others could share.

If Charles was to take on more direct responsibility for the government of his far flung territories, he had to overcome the problem that he could not be present in most of them for considerable periods of time. One way in which this could be achieved was to make use of family members. They provided loyal substitutes and were seen by his subjects as the next best thing to his presence. They were less likely to be personally involved in local disputes since they had a loyalty to the family which was wider than the concerns of the nobility of each specific territory. It also fitted in with his ideas about dynasty and provided a role for those who were major royal figures in their own right. Their position in the family also meant that they could argue with Charles about policy without any real danger of being thought disloyal. It tells us something about the respect that Charles had as head of the dynasty that his family was willing to serve in this way, just as his advisers and military commanders invariably remained loyal to the end.

This was not always the case in ruling families, in which natural rivalries and jealousies were frequent. The internecine activities of members of the Plantagenets during the Wars of the Roses in 15th century England are well documented. The Habsburgs also provided a significant contrast to the traditional procedure in the Ottoman Empire where it was the custom for the new sultan to execute any remaining brothers, who were regarded as a major threat to the new ruler. Since the Ottomans did not follow the tradition of primogeniture, succession was based on the competition between the sons of the ruling sultan, the survivor being seen as the rightful and most suitable ruler. Suleiman was the only son of Selim I and so had a straightforward succession. But of his sons some were murdered or executed during his reign (Mustafa executed in 1553; Bayazid executed in 1561) easing the way for the succession of his fourth son, Selim II.

There was no such ruthless infighting amongst the Habsburgs at this time. Ferdinand, for instance, had left Spain without complaint or any serious risk of becoming the centre of an opposing faction. This is not to say that they were always in full agreement with, or totally subservient to, Charles. When appointed as regents his relations were publicly given extensive authority, but often the private instructions left by Charles placed significant restrictions upon their power. This was particularly true in relation to appointments, which Charles wished to keep in his own hands. An exchange between Charles and Margaret of Austria in 1527 was concerned with this issue. Some noblemen in the Low Countries who felt that they were not taken into Margaret's confidence complained to Charles. He wrote to his aunt asking her to use her 'great prudence and experience' to deal with the issue.[5] In reply she argued that Charles, by listening to such complaints and by not supporting appointments that she had made, reduced her power to reward or punish, thus undermining her authority. This, she continued, would mean that she would be less effective in gaining support for Charles' policies and in matters such as raising money.

There was a natural conflict in the role of the regents between their duties to the monarch, Charles, and their duties to the subjects of the lands which had been left in their care.[6] If Charles needed money from his subjects, as he frequently did for military campaigns, his regents in the Low Countries, Spain and elsewhere often argued that it was difficult to raise such amounts without great hardship for the people. To a considerable extent Charles became immune to the descriptions of impending disaster from his regents[7]; he was often in no position to respond positively to their requests anyway. As early as 1522 Margaret had wanted Charles to know that: 'to leave great debts behind and few revenues in a country such as this is not conducive to keeping it in such security, obedience and peace as one would wish'.[8] Most such disagreements were kept private. In later years Philip is certainly seen as a dutiful son, and it has been argued that this made him look weak and timid, whereas in reality he was not necessarily overawed by Charles as he gained experience in the late 1540s and early 1550s.[9]

Charles was fortunate in the quality of support that he received from his family. His aunt, Margaret of Austria was able to successfully fulfil her role as Governor of the Low Countries, both during Charles' minority and after he became king in Spain and then Emperor. During his extended journey in Italy, Germany and the Low Countries between 1529 and 1532, and later in the 1530's, Charles' wife Isabella was an effective regent in Spain, working with the council appointed before Charles' departure. That he appreciated this family support is shown in his Political Testament of 1548 where he pointed out to his son that: 'You cannot be everywhere, you must find good viceroys. The best way is to hold your kingdoms together by making use of your children. For this you will need more children and must contract a new marriage'[10]. This had been brought home to Charles while in Augsburg in the autumn of 1530 when he received a communication from Spain announcing the death of his young son Ferdinand.

Charles' greatest family concern had been what to do with his brother. Having been bought up in Spain and then moved to the Low Countries after Charles' arrival, there were no shared youthful experiences that would help to forge a link between them. The lands granted to Ferdinand in Austria and his marriage to Anne of Hungary in 1521 provided him with a fitting role. He would act on Charles' behalf in Germany and the Holy Roman Empire and link with the Christian kingdoms of Hungary and Bohemia in the defence of Europe against Ottoman advances. Now that Charles had been crowned in Bologna, he kept his word and pressed for Ferdinand to be chosen as 'King of the Romans', a position from which he could act for Charles with greater authority. This was not without opposition, especially from the Protestant Elector John of Saxony. In addition the other electors, as usual, took the opportunity to press for payments and favours in return for their support. It is estimated that the election cost the Habsburgs 360,000 florins, much borrowed once again from the Fugger family. Ferdinand was formally elected in Cologne on 5th January 1531 and was crowned six days later in Aachen with all the traditional ceremonies.

Charles had been especially keen to complete this appointment because a month earlier, on 1st December 1530, Margaret of Austria, the last of the key mentors of his youth, had died at the age of 50, as a result of an infection which spread from a poisoned foot. He owed much to her. She had carefully looked after his interests during his youth, and served him with energy and skill as regent during his time in Spain. In 1526 he had written to her that any reward he could give her would be 'insufficient to repay the pain and trouble you take in my affairs'.[11] In her final letter to Charles, dictated from her death bed, she expressed her pride in a job well done. 'My only sorrow is that I shall not see you before I die. You will find (the lands entrusted to me) not only unspoiled but greatly increased, after a government for which I hope to receive God's reward, your contentment and the gratitude of posterity'.[12] She went on to give him a final piece of advice, commending a policy of peace towards both France and England, one which he was unable to follow for much of his reign.

His sister, Mary of Hungary, was still only twenty-six but already had considerable experience. She was intelligent, self-reliant and diligent. Widowed and with no children, she had been available to the dynasty for remarriage after the death of her husband Louis at Mohacs but, like her aunt Margaret twenty years earlier, she made it clear that this was not her wish. Charles did not insist. On Margaret's death he prevailed upon Mary to become regent in her place. It was not something that she had worked towards, indeed she described her appointment to Ferdinand as having a rope put around her neck. While in Hungary she had shown some interest in the new religious ideas that were rife in Europe at the time. Lutherans were always keen to claim royal adherents and some of her close associates had become 'suspect' in the view of Charles' advisers. Charles himself made it clear that although he did not doubt Mary's religious views, any unorthodoxy could not be accepted. He wrote that 'If I had doubts of your religious integrity rest assured that I should neither give you this place nor accord you the love of a brother'.[13] The 'suspects' were to be left behind when she moved to the Low Countries. Although Charles wished her to have advisers only from the Low Countries, Mary had insisted that some trusted staff from her past remained with her. She established her court not at Malines, her childhood home with Margaret of Austria, but in Brussels.

Charles spent a considerable amount of time with her during 1531 discussing the many issues that would undoubtedly confront her, and she was formally granted powers before the States General of the Low Countries in July 1531. To assist her Charles clarified the structure of the councils that she would work with. There would be a Privy Council (or Secret Council) dealing with administration, legal issues and appointments, a Council of State to advise on general policy, especially defence, and a Council of Finance. High nobility were appointed to these councils but Charles ensured that they were effectively run by professional lawyers and administrators.

In January 1532 he added a codicil to his will giving Mary powers of regency and guardianship in the event of his death, indicating that he had future plans for his daughter, Maria, to marry a son of Ferdinand and for the couple to inherit the Low Countries when they became of age. Mary carried out her often onerous responsibilities with commitment and relative success for almost twenty-five years. Both the nobility and the cities were to continue to defend their privileges and the latter regularly make difficulties over taxation. At times Mary was tempted to walk away, but her sense of loyalty and Charles' pleading always prevailed. Later in the reign she was to be an increasingly important figure in the family. She was able to communicate in a forthright manner with the Emperor without giving offence, take the lead when Charles was unable to do so, and help reconcile the brothers when relations became difficult.

Another use to which family members, particularly female ones, could be put was in marriage contracts, often used to cement alliances and secure dynastic ties. It was generally accepted that as head of the family Charles could make decisions over such matters, and over the course of forty years he came up with numerous plans. Frequently younger princesses were not consulted, but this did not always mean that there was no discussion. The views and wishes of other family members had to be heard and sometimes accepted. A few examples give the flavour of these arrangements.

Charles' older sister, Eleanor (born in 1498), had been married to Manuel I, king of Portugal, 29 years her senior, in 1517, and gave birth to a daughter, Maria, who remained in Portugal when Eleanor left after her husband's death in 1521. She was then betrothed to Charles, Duke of Bourbon, a senior French nobleman who had fallen out with Francis I and allied himself to Charles V, becoming his military commander. This marriage plan was set aside when under the Treaty of Madrid (1526), following Francis' defeat and capture by Charles' forces at Pavia in 1525, she was betrothed to Francis I. After further military conflict between the two monarchs, which had resulted in the death of Bourbon, her marriage to Francis eventually took place in 1530. Eleanor was accorded the status and respect due to the queen of France. However no children were produced (Francis had five surviving children from his first marriage) and the king continued to spend considerably more time with his mistresses, especially Anne d'Pisseleu, Duchess of Etampes. Separated from her own daughter and the rest of her family it is hard for us to comprehend Eleanor's feelings, though such circumstances were not unusual at the time. In any case there is no evidence that she held her brother responsible for her plight. She left France only on Francis' death in 1547, when she returned to the Low Countries, her childhood home.

Some marriage alliances did not reap the benefits that were expected. The marriage of Charles' sister Isabella (born 1501) to Christian II of Denmark in 1515, for instance, was intended to create the link between the Habsburgs and the ruling family of Denmark, Sweden and Norway. Even though it had been arranged by his grandfather Maximilian, this marriage brought Charles nothing but problems. Christian, twenty years her senior, refused to give Isabella precedence over his mistress, Dyveke Sigvritsdatter, until the latter's death in 1517. Responsible for the 'Stockholm Bloodbath' in 1520, Christian was deposed in 1523 by his uncle. He lived the next nine years in exile plotting to regain his crown, involving Charles in the politics of northern Europe in ways that could only harm the commercial interests of his subjects in the Low Countries. Charles resisted requests for soldiers and ships. The failure of Christian's invasion plans meant that from July 1532 until his death in 1559 he was a prisoner in his own country. His descendants continued to claim the thrones of the northern countries for centuries, eventually returning when Charles XV became king of Sweden in 1859!

Isabella herself died in January 1526, aged 24, and was buried in St Peter's Abbey, Ghent. Her three surviving children, painted while in mourning for their mother in 1526 by Jan Gossaert [14], were brought up by Margaret of Austria and then Mary of Hungary in the Low Countries. Her son John (born in 1518), of whom Charles became very fond, died in Regensburg while travelling with Charles in August 1532. Charles was uncharacteristically emotional about the death of his nephew. He wrote to Mary that 'He was the nicest child I knew. I feel his death like that of my own son, for I held him as such. It must be God's will but I cannot help regretting that he should be taken from us. I could better have spared his father, God forgive me. Still the little lad will be better off where he is. He died with so little sin to his account... he could not have missed eternal salvation.'[15]

John's two sisters were both married as part of Charles' political manoeuvres. Dorothea, born in 1520, was married in 1535 to Frederick, Count Palatine, aged 53. Frederick was an important figure within the Holy Roman Empire, and had served the Habsburgs well as a military commander, one whom Charles needed on his side. He had already been linked with Charles sisters, Eleanor and Mary, and was disappointed not to have married either. Charles' younger niece, Christina, born in 1521, was married in May 1534, at the age of 12, to Francesco II Sforza, Duke of Milan. The marriage contract, which included an agreement for immediate consummation, was keenly opposed by Mary, who was effectively Christina's guardian. In a lengthy letter to her brother she wrote that although she accepted Charles' right as head of the family to make such decisions 'it is against nature and God's laws to marry off a little girl who cannot yet in any sense be called a woman, and expose her to all the dangers of child-bed'. Charles on this occasion overruled his sister arguing that an element of sacrifice was necessary for the sake of the dynasty, and that the issue of age 'will be a much greater problem for the duke than for our niece'. We will never know quite what Charles meant by this but the Duke died the following year aged 40. Having returned to the Low Countries, Christina soon became the focus of negotiations with Henry VIII, recently widowed by the death of Jane Seymour. This was not welcomed by Christina herself, who is reported to have said 'If I had two heads, one of them would be at the disposal of the king of England'. Henry's reputation had obviously spread throughout

Europe. In 1541 Christina married Francis, Duke of Bar, who became Duke of Lorraine in 1544. She acted as regent in Lorraine after his death during the minority of their son.

Charles' brother Ferdinand and his wife Anne of Hungary had 15 children and later in his reign Charles, aware of the shortage of marriageable princesses elsewhere in the family, was involved in discussions about their marriages. However Ferdinand had his own dynastic interests to consider and also made it clear that he was opposed to the marriage of his children at too young an age. Charles' own children were likewise used in his political manoeuvrings during the 1540s and 1550s, marrying variously into the royal families of Portugal, England and France as well as to cousins in their own Habsburg family.

Charles listened to objections from family members about his plans for marriage contracts and also broader policies. He was able to accept reasoned criticism. One frequent complaint from his regents and commanders was that his communications to them were irregular and that he took too long to respond, whether to requests for instructions and advice or in sending troops or money. His wife, Isabella, complained in September 1530 that 'Your majesty should be advised of the great convenience of his not having responded nor of having ordered information to be sent for such a long period, on matters of great importance'.[16] It seems that Charles was unhurried, even allowing for the slow delivery of letters at the time. At best this could be the result of careful consideration, but more likely the consequence of him concentrating on the immediate problem to the detriment of those in distant lands, or at worst, though generally out of character, it could stem from idleness or indifference.

It was not just his family to whom he would listen. While still in the Low Countries, Charles convened a chapter of the Order of the Golden Fleece, held at Tournai in December 1531. This was the first such chapter held since 1518 and since then twenty members had died. One task was therefore to create new knights. They included Charles' three year old son, Philip, nobility from Germany, Spain, the Low Countries and Italy, notably Ferrante Gonzaga, Alfonso d'Avalor, the Marquis of Vasto and Andrea Doria of Genoa, as well as the Kings of Portugal and Scotland. All members were traditionally subject to the assessment of their colleagues, and the Emperor was no exception. The issues they raised about Charles were substantial. He took too long to make decisions, he concentrated on minor issues to the neglect of more important ones, he consulted too little with his councillors of whom he had too few, he paid ministers too little and too late, and the administration of justice in his lands was poor.[17] Serious criticism indeed; it is not possible to imagine Henry VIII or Francis I listening to such comments with good grace and then seriously responding. Charles answered that he would certainly look into the administration of justice - he had always believed that an efficient and fair system was essential – and that the shortage of councillors was because he lacked sufficient men of quality whom he could trust absolutely. Perhaps this explains the importance that Charles placed on his family in the ruling of his lands, especially after the meeting in Innsbruck in the early summer on 1530.

# 15
## 'Most important is the Religious Issue' – Attempted Reconciliation

Charles' increasing awareness of the religious differences that were shaking Germany had been a major factor in his wish to establish Ferdinand as 'King of the Romans' and to ensure Mary's religious orthodoxy before her appointment as regent in the Low Countries. After the family meeting at Innsbruck he travelled north in June 1530 for the Imperial Diet in Augsburg. This was his first visit to Germany in over eight years. It was unusual for an Emperor to be absent for such a long period and he wanted his arrival, accompanied by Ferdinand, to be memorable.

His entry into the city gives a clear picture of pomp and ceremony attached to such occasions: one thousand infantry, Spanish lords dressed in gold and black, German princes including Duke George of Saxony, Dukes William and Louis of Bavaria, and Margrave George of Brandenburg-Ansbach, more troops, nobles from the Low Countries and Austria, representatives from Turkey, North Africa, England and Poland, the electors, secular and spiritual, all came before Charles 'under a canopy .. in a golden coat' flanked by his brother and the papal legate; they were followed by more Imperial and Spanish nobles, prelates, lords, and finally local soldiers and cannons.[1] The Diet brought large numbers into the city. Balls, tournaments, entertainments and dinners kept them occupied, while the citizens had the opportunity to benefit from supplying them with all their needs, both physical and spiritual.

As the Diet opened Charles wrote to Isabella that they were facing three main issues. 'The first and most important is the religious question. The second deals with Hungary and the Turkish trouble. The third concerns the government of Germany'.[2] Luther's initial protest had appealed to many people already influenced by widespread anti-clericalism and subjected to considerable social and economic upheaval. For many of the princes in the Holy Roman Empire it also presented political and financial opportunities – to end the secular power of the papacy in Germany, to seize church property and to stop the outflow of money to Rome. In the Empire Charles knew that he needed the consent of the princes to rule. He was often to require their assistance, both militarily and financially, against the Ottomans and the French, and needed to tread carefully in order to secure that support. The political and religious issues in Germany had become dangerously interwoven.

In Charles' absence during the 1520s Germany had experienced damaging rebellions. Social tensions had been increasing throughout the Empire for decades, and had come to a head in the Knights' Revolt of 1522-23 and the Peasants' War of 1524-25. The wealth and privileges of the Imperial Knights were in decline. The relative value of the agricultural land they controlled, on which their social status was based, was falling, while the trade and industry-based wealth of the cities had increased. The power of the higher nobility, the princes, had grown, while the knights' raison d'etre, a leading role in armies, had been undermined by recent developments in military tactics and technology. With their influence threatened on all sides, unable to work with either the cities or the princes, a 'Brotherly Convention' of knights was convened by Franz von Sickingen and Ulrich von Hutten.

Both played a major role in formulating a series of possible reforms, including the unification of German-speaking lands, thus abolishing the independent principalities, and the removal of the Church from secular power, hoping to make use of the widespread anti-clericalism in Germany. The knights, true to their origins, decided to defend their position and achieve their demands by force of arms. Their rebellion in the Rhineland, during 1522 and 1523, against their spiritual and temporal princes, was crushed by the forces of Richard, Archbishop of Trier, Louis, Count Palatine and Landgrave Philip of Hesse. Von Sickingen, took refuge in his castle at Landstuhl. He expected to be able to withstand a siege for several months allowing time for relieving forces to arrive, but was overwhelmed within a week by the use of modern siege artillery. He surrendered on 7th May 1523 and died of wounds on the same day. Hutten fled to Switzerland where he died a few months later of syphilis.

Less than two years later many peasants, suffering from the impact of inflation, increasing poverty, with their rights being eroded by the nobility, rebelled. During the harvest of 1524 insurrections started in the south-west and spread across southern Germany (with the exception of Bavaria where a strong government had prevented nobles and monasteries reducing their peasants to serfdom[3]) and into Switzerland and Austria. They received the support of some radical preachers, like Thomas Muntzer, who argued that it was legitimate for the 'righteous' to resist their oppressors. In March 1525 peasant representatives met at Memmingen and agreed the 'Twelve Articles', with the underlying belief that the scriptures, 'godly law', supported their ideas for a fairer society.[4] They demanded the abolition of serfdom, reform of the system of tithes, the use of common land, hunting and fishing rights, the abolition of death duties to their lords and an end to arbitrary justice.

The peasants lacked military experience and organised leadership, and had neither cavalry nor artillery. Peasant armies were defeated at Frankenhausen, Boblingen, and Wurzburg by the armies of the Swabian League, led by the princes of southern Germany. By the end of 1525 the armed rising had ceased. It is estimated that as many as 100,000 peasants perished in the conflicts. Muntzer was tortured and executed for his part in encouraging the rebellion. Luther, a social conservative, argued that the ruling classes were appointed by God to uphold the peace, and supported their right to crush such resistance. He spoke out strongly against the behaviour of the rebels in 'Against the Murderous, Thieving Hordes of Peasants'.

The princes used these successful defences of their rights in the name of the emperor to advance their own position. They recognised Charles' status and were willing to support his policies, so long as there was no conflict with their own interests, whether political or, later, religious. Some of the rulers, such as the Wittelsbach family of Bavaria, had dynastic disputes with the Habsburgs; others sought common ground in the hope of future preferential treatment. A few princes were uniformly hostile to Charles and the Habsburgs. Charles of Egmond, the Duke of Guelders, took every opportunity to make territorial gains from Habsburg lands in the Low Countries; he allied with France, attacked when Charles' troops were committed elsewhere, and undermined efforts to achieve a peaceful settlement. Only later, with the death of the Duke in 1538 and the defeat of his successor, William of Cleves (brother of Henry VIII's fourth wife, Anne of Cleves), was Charles able to take over Guelders and incorporate it into the 17 provinces of the Low Countries. The career of Maurice of Saxony in the 1540s and 1550s reveals how self-interest, in his case territorial gains and becoming elector of Saxony by replacing his cousin, was the major factor in determining which side he would take, and when, in the conflicts of that time. Charles was thus often forced to compromise in Germany so that he would be able to deal with the hostility of France, the advance of Ottoman troops into Hungary and Austria and the incursions of the Ottoman navy in the Mediterranean.

During the 1520s, with Charles absent in Spain, with social upheaval and revolts in Germany, and Ferdinand much taken up with the Ottoman threat and defending his position in Hungary, it had proved impossible to enforce the Edict of Worms and stem the growth of religious dissent. Luther had opened the way for all manner of new ideas and interpretations of the scriptures to flourish. Zwingli, in Zurich, spoke against indulgencies, the cult of saints and clerical celibacy, although there were soon major differences with Luther over the meaning of Christ's words at the Last Supper 'This is my body'. Both, however, criticised the humanist reformer Erasmus for pointing out the faults of the Church yet remaining loyal to the pope. A war of pamphlets and books commenced, involving the various 'reformers' and the papacy. It is estimated that by 1530 as many as 10,000 different pamphlets had been produced. If 1,000 of each were printed that would mean ten million were in circulation[5], available for the increasing number of readers in Germany and further afield. All the major participants initially failed to appreciate that the publication of the New and Old Testaments in the vernacular and the flood of religious literature would enable many more people to join the debate, develop views of their own and form their own religious communities. One such group, the Anabaptists, were vehemently opposed by Catholic and Lutheran alike.

If, at first, Charles and the Catholic princes wished to enforce the Edict of Worms and put an end to all heresies, the chaos caused by the Peasants' War made many realise that control imposed by princes, even if strongly influenced by the new religious ideas, was better than no control at all. Charles, remote in Spain, was slow to appreciate this. Ferdinand, on hand but with many other problems, needed the assistance of the princes and recognised that negotiation and compromise in religion was the price that would have to be paid. But unity was not achieved. The princes divided into a number of loose groupings, determined both by their political and religious positions and the relative importance that they gave to each: loyal to the emperor and the traditions of the Empire or wishing to undermine his power; keen to introduce religious reforms or remain loyal to the Catholic Church.

Many princes thus failed to enforce the Edict of Worms against Lutheran beliefs and made clear their opposition at Nuremberg in 1524. Two years later at the Diet of Speyer, held as the Ottomans advanced into Hungary, the Recess (the closing statement of a Diet) called for a general council of the church to discuss and resolve all religious disputes. Since this was not likely in the short-term given the state of war that existed across much of Europe, a national council should be held. Until this occurred it was agreed that all princes and imperial cities would deal with the issue in a manner that they 'would be ready to answer for, before God and His Imperial Majesty'.[6] This, in effect, gave the German princes and towns control over religion in their own area until a settlement was reached. Once this power had been granted, however temporarily, it was unlikely that it would be willingly relinquished.

When the Diet met in March 1529, again at Speyer, the successes of Charles' armies in Italy had given Ferdinand a stronger position and greater confidence. The previous year a councillor of Philip of Hesse made public what was supposed to be a secret deal amongst Catholic princes to attack their religious opponents. Lutheran forces were mobilized until it became clear that no such agreement existed. Open conflict was avoided but tensions increased. The incident showed the hand of the Lutherans, making Ferdinand and supporters of the papacy more wary of the threat to the Catholic Church and even more determined to defend their position. They were in the majority and the Recess that was voted through reflected this. It declared that some princes had abused the outcome at Speyer and that new doctrines should not be permitted until a settlement by a general council had been reached. In addition, Anabaptists and followers of Zwingli should be persecuted, the Edict of Worms should be reinstated and that those following the old religion should have complete freedom of worship whatever the views of their prince.

Lutherans issued a formal letter of protest in late April 1529 against this attempt to go back on the earlier decision – hence they became known as 'Protestants'. It was signed by Elector John of Saxony, Margrave George of Brandenburg, Landgrave Philip of Hesse, three other princes and the representatives of fourteen cities, including Strasburg, Ulm and Nuremberg. They declared that 'In matters concerning God's honour and the salvation of our souls, each man has the right to stand alone and present his true account before God'.[7] This group had now made a clear public stand against their fellow members of the Diet. Although they had some beliefs in common, there were considerable differences of doctrine amongst them. These divisions were profound and would make the task of anyone seeking to achieve a unification of the church even more difficult.

This was precisely what Charles believed he could do as he arrived in Augsburg for his first personal attendance at an Imperial Diet since Worms in 1521. He wished to enable all to 'come to live again in one Church and one State' and 'unite all opinions into one undivided Christian truth'. In this he was encouraged by Erasmus and a Spanish adviser, Alfonso de Valdes, who argued that settlement could be reached if reasonable men of both sides were brought together by a great prince. It was never going to be easy. Whereas in Worms Charles had faced one dissenter, at Augsburg he was faced by numerous princes and cities who refused to obey Imperial edicts and in whose territories there had been many changes in the forms of worship. Most, though, were willing to participate in a genuine sharing of views. Before the opening of the Diet Charles received from Dr Johannes Eck a paper outlining four hundred and four points of major importance to the Catholic Church. In response Philip Melanchthon prepared a statement of Protestant (specifically Lutheran) beliefs consisting of twenty-one chief articles of faith and seven statements of abuses within the Catholic Church - the 'Augsburg Confession' - outlining their case with moderation. This was read to Charles on 25th June by the Chancellor of the elector of Saxony.

Discussions followed between a selected group of princes and theologians. It was written of Charles (by a supporter) that 'more glorious and marvellous than all his successes was the Emperor's control of his temper'...'he listened to the Lutherans with a calm and judicial' manner. The portrait by Christoph Amberger of Charles at this time shows him seemingly involved in these debates. Charles is plainly dressed, the ever present emblem of the Golden Fleece on his chest, his face pale, hair now cut short in the Italian style in contrast with the long Burgundian style of his youth. Seated, he has an expression of concentration, his large jaw thrust forward, as if ready to counter an argument just made or open the book in his left hand held ready to quote from.

The Catholics clerics, led by Johannes Eck, expressed their opposition to the Lutherans in the 'Augsburg Confutation', which Charles had a hand in redrafting into a more conciliatory tone. Unfortunately it was read out in Charles' name thereby removing any claim that he might have had to impartiality in the settling of the issue. Charles also wrote to Pope Clement to 'beseech and entreat' him to summon a general church council, which only he had the power to do. In this letter he emphasised their joint responsibility for preventing schism, and argued that this was a good time since Europe was at peace. He continued that if there were to be a council then they could gain a great advantage over the heretics, since if the Protestants failed to attend or refused to live by its rulings then they would be seen to be at fault. A council would show that 'Your Holiness and I would have done what we could and others would have to bear the blame'. If, on the other hand, there were no council Charles believed that much of Germany 'would fall into the gravest peril'. In conclusion Charles asked that the pope do all he could to end those abuses of church power that 'can readily be stopped'. Clement's reply was negative. He was wholly opposed to Charles' plan for a council, seeing it as a means of increasing the Emperor's own power at the expense of both the papacy and other European monarchs.[8]

The talks in Augsburg continued through July and August but no agreement could be reached. There were still significant doctrinal difficulties as well as a more political one, the separation of secular and spiritual power demanded by the Protestants. This was a direct attack on the power of the papacy, something that Clement and his representatives could never agree to. As the divisions between the two sides became clearer, the Protestant reply to the 'Confutation', the 'Apologia' drafted by Melanchthon, was less conciliatory than their earlier statements. By September Charles had lost patience. If, at first, he was concerned by the intransigence of the Catholic negotiators, he was now horrified by the beliefs of Protestants and the fact that they were holding their services and listening to sermons in Augsburg as the talks were taking place. Some Protestants, such as Philip of Hesse, had already left, convinced that there would be no agreement while others, such as John of Saxony, soon followed, expressing regret but still maintaining their position. An initial Recess was issued by the Catholic princes but rejected by the Protestants. The final Recess of Augsburg issued in November 1530 was even harsher. It stated that Protestantism 'has given rise to much misleading error among the common people. They have lost all true reverence, all Christian honour, discipline, the fear of God and charity to their neighbour'[9]. All confiscated church property was to be returned. It was, in effect, a restatement of the Edict of Worms and gave the Protestants six months to recant.

What in June had seemed promising discussions eventually failed to bring about the unity Charles so desired. On his arrival in Augsburg he had held too great a belief in his own authority and his years of absence had led him to underestimate the strength of feeling amongst the reformers. A disappointed Charles considered the use of force, but even the Catholic princes would not support such a plan. They had no wish to undermine the precarious social order, and without their support Charles was in no position, politically or financially, to raise an army and enforce his will. Protestant rulers formed an alliance for their own defence – the Schmalkaldic League – in February 1531, motivated partly by their opposition to Ferdinand's election as 'King of the Romans' a month earlier. As a result the status quo remained; the longer the Protestants were able to continue to worship in their own way, the less likely it was that they would ever reach an agreed settlement. Many Catholics too became more intransigent as time went on. Thus when Charles returned to Germany later in his reign with the intention of settling the religious divisions the problem had become even more deep-rooted.

There were many reasons why Charles was unable to prevent the spread of Protestant ideas in Germany and retain the unity of the Church even though this was so important to him. Charles' faith was traditional, but deep. While he did have some sympathy with the need for reform of the administration of the Roman Church, he believed that the best way of achieving this, and thus preserving a universal church, was through a general council of the church. However, the decision to call such a Council was not his to make but the pope's. What Charles did not understand or could not overcome was the fact that the papacy was opposed to such a council as it would inevitably be a major challenge to their own power, as would any reconciliation of the opposing views. As his former confessor, Loaysa, wrote to Charles in 1530: 'I regret to say that the Pope and the cardinals would sooner see this council in Hell than on Earth'. Charles also probably failed to appreciate the depth of the theological arguments that existed and the longer the rift existed the more difficult it would be to heal. He did not believe that it was his role to sort out the doctrinal issues. Erasmus had written to him: 'Caesar is not a doctor of the gospels, he is their champion'. Charles had come to Augsburg in an attempt to heal the religious schism. In this 'most important' task he had failed.

Charles V: Duty and Dynasty

# 16
## 'Trouble, Danger and Expense' – The Habsburgs, Jacob Fugger and 16th century finances

While in Augsburg Charles had stayed at the Fuggerpalast, built between 1512 and 1515, one of the first secular buildings in the Italian Renaissance style in Germany. It was home to Anton Fugger, then head of the banking family. In the early 16th century Augsburg was one of the wealthiest cities in the Holy Roman Empire, a leading city of the German Renaissance, the birthplace of Hans Holbein, court painter to Henry VIII. Of Roman origin, founded by Tiberius and named after his step-father Augustus, the city was located on the river Lech with good access both to the Alpine passes south to Italy and to the east-west trade routes of central Europe. It had flourished in the middle ages, especially after becoming an Imperial free city in 1276. As one of the main financial centres of Germany it was of importance to Charles, beset like so many rulers by constant money problems.

In 1523 Anton's uncle, Jacob, had written to Charles. Having emphasised his loyalty to the House of Austria, and reminded Charles of his services to his 'Grandsire, the late Emperor Maximilian', he continued: 'It is well known that Your Imperial Majesty could not have gained the Roman Crown save with mine aid, and I can prove the same by writings of Your Majesty's agents given by their own hand. In this matter I have not studied mine own profit. For had I left the House of Austria and had been minded to further France, I had obtained much money and property, such as was then offered to me'[1]. He was writing to complain about the failure to repay loans that he had made to the Habsburgs. He must have been either supremely confident of his position or foolhardy in

## Charles V: Duty and Dynasty

the extreme to write in this way to the most powerful man in Europe. How had this situation come about?

Charles had enormous powers over the life and death of his subjects and in matters such as war and peace but when it came to taxation he was severely constrained by his subjects' ability and willingness to pay. During the Renaissance many rulers badly needed money for a range of activities that were becoming increasingly expensive: war, bureaucracy, diplomacy, the administration of justice, and, for many, spending on palaces, works of art and displays of wealth[2]. Charles was by no means the most extravagant in his personal spending but his revenues did not match the rising level of expenditure. Despite all his possessions, he was limited in the amount of money that was readily available for his immediate use. This depended not only on his subjects' wealth but also on their privileges and rights in each territory.

If the traditional tax subsidies and revenues were not sufficient then other means of raising money needed to be used. New demands for taxes could cause serious problems especially if his subjects knew or believed that the money would be spent outside their lands. Family lands might be sold - but only once. Offices in the judiciary or administration could be handed to the highest bidder. More money could be produced from the mint, but this had the obvious danger of currency depreciation, so that in the end more money did not buy more! The rights to certain taxes were sometimes 'farmed out' to individuals or groups who then had the right to collect the taxes for a period of time. Customs duties could be applied to more products and monopolies sold to merchants. 'Forced loans' (i.e. loans where there was no choice about the provision of the money and no security that it would be returned) could be imposed on wealthy sections of the community, though the unpopularity of these 'loans' is easy to imagine.

When all such options failed to meet the pressing needs of the time Charles had to resort to some form of credit. Ready money and credit have always been necessary for commerce to develop and flourish. Without them trade cannot be facilitated and economic development will usually stagnate. Since early times money had often been in the form of metals, although clay tablets were used in the Middle East to promise payment of a specific amount of a certain commodity as early as the 3$^{rd}$ millenium B.C. and paper money existed in China in the 7$^{th}$ century.[3] 'Bills of exchange' started to be used by merchants, promising to pay a particular sum (or an amount of a commodity) to the holder in the future when ready cash was not available. Since these 'bills' could be sold on for cash or other goods they not only oiled the wheels of exchange and commerce, but also provided the merchants/financiers with the opportunity to make a profit from such an exchange.

But if this system was to become fully acceptable it required a change in attitudes to finance. In medieval Europe usury - the lending of money for interest - was condemned. Christian teaching seemed clear. In 1179 the 3$^{rd}$ Lateran Council declared that those engaged in usury would be excommunicated[4]. To Thomas Aquinas (1225-1274), whose thinking was to remain influential for many centuries, money was a measure of value or an intermediary in exchange and any attempt to gain wealth by usury was wrong. Pope Clement V stated in 1311 that the belief in the right to usury was a heresy. Even as late as the 1580s Pope Sixtus V declared interest to be 'detestable to God and man, damned by the sacred canons and contrary to Christian charity'. However the view that usury meant 'unreasonable' interest was gaining ground, implying that moderate interest was admissible. The concept of a just price for commodities - that which is fair and affordable - was still widely supported by both Lutheran and Catholic theologians, although merchants believed that the laws of supply and demand meant that they should charge whatever price that they could get. It was increasingly recognised that money was necessary to facilitate trade, and that using it for a moderate profit was acceptable.

If Christianity had traditionally opposed the lending of money for interest there was no such ban for Jews. The Old Testament (Deuteronomy 23: 20-21) held that lending money for interest to a 'brother' was forbidden, but that it was reasonable to do so to a 'foreigner'[5]; hence the role of the Jews as moneylenders in medieval Europe. For much of the time this practice was tolerated, because it served a useful function to both rulers and citizens, even though Jews had limited rights and were often permitted to live only in specific areas of towns, the ghettos, one of the first being in Venice. However it also left them vulnerable to persecution, especially in times of economic hardship. In late 13th century England Edward I took advantage of widespread resentment against the Jews, using Christian religious belief to outlaw usury and then expel the Jews in 1290. This benefitted royal finances, through the take-over of Jewish properties, and his popularity, by removing the need for many citizens to repay their debts.

Although money lenders were never popular they were often needed. Given the risks of non-payment involved for the lender, most considered that they ought to be compensated. They developed various means to get around the prohibition on usury. Many financiers could not see the problem or could justify their business methods to their consciences. Some ignored the ban and then asked for forgiveness in confession. Lending to princes was sometimes excluded from the ban since the outcome was believed to be for the general good. Loans were sometimes in the form of commodities which were not covered by the ban. Frequently a sum was added to the original capital as repayment for the 'trouble, danger and expense' of the lender.

Centres where the bills of exchange were widely used became known as 'bourse' (after *bursa* the Latin for bag or purse) and grew up in the Low Countries (Bruges, Ghent, Amsterdam and Antwerp), Italy (Venice, Florence, Pisa, Siena, Genoa), France (Lyon, Paris), Spain (Medina del Campo) and Germany (Augsburg, Nuremburg). They had developed from the markets and fairs of medieval Europe where there was a large wholesale trade and a standardisation of goods, so that they could be traded without being seen. Those who transacted many of these exchanges became known as *banchiere* or bankers, after the *banci* or benches on which they sat while negotiating their business. 14th century Italian banking houses such as the Peruzzi and Bardi made, but then lost, fortunes. The losses were largely a result of rulers (e.g. Edward III of England) defaulting on their debts. The most famous such family were the Medici of Florence, who converted economic supremacy into political power, while the Fugger and others from southern Germany became prominent in the late 15th and early 16th centuries.

A ruler's answer to the problem of lack of revenue and the need for immediate funds was to borrow, which Charles did heavily throughout his reign. The level of credit that could be offered would depend upon the belief of the lender that the borrower can, will and must repay the debt.[6] As the belief declines then the level of security required will increase. The sums added for 'trouble, danger and expense' would not always suffice if the likelihood of repayment is low. In such cases it is much better to require solid securities, such as existing assets of the borrower or access to their future revenues. In the case of rulers like Charles, most lenders believed that they 'could' pay – eventually; they had revenues from their territories which could be used. Their 'will' to pay, however, was often overtaken by short term pressures that might divert funds originally intended to repay a loan.

Whether rulers 'must' pay, especially the debts of their predecessors, was more in question. Certainly if they wished to have access to future loans from the same creditors, which they increasingly did, then non-payment was unwise. However in extreme circumstances rulers could declare their state bankrupt. This happened in the second half of the 16th century in Spain and France, a result of the unsustainable expenditure of Charles V and Philip II, Francis I and Henry II. In 1557 both Spanish and French monarchs were bankrupt and this played a major part in bringing about peace in 1559. Cities usually had a better credit rating than rulers, since individual burghers could be made liable for the debts taken on by the city and these burghers, with their increasing wealth, were often able to pay. As a result rulers often used the guarantee of a city to secure loans for themselves or took out loans in the name of a city or a high official.

## Charles V: Duty and Dynasty

Charles' largest creditor was the Fugger family. First recorded as tax-payers in Augsburg in 1367[7], they started as weavers and became involved in the lucrative cloth trade. Within three generations they were in a position to bankroll the Emperor's election and provide loans that enabled Charles to finance his wars. In the 15th century Jacob Fugger the elder (died 1469) became master of the Weavers' Guild, married Barbara Basinger, the daughter of the master of the Augsburg mint, and had seven sons. Initially the eldest, Ulrich, along with Georg and Peter, took over his growing commercial interests, but when Peter died in 1474 the youngest son, fifteen year old Jacob, who had already started training for a career in the church, joined the business[8]. He spent over two years (1477-1479) based in the Fondaco dei Tedeschi, the German business house in Venice on the Grand Canal close to the Rialto bridge, where he learnt double entry book keeping and experienced the Italian methods of business and finance. It was here that he began to develop the drive, the objective view to business deals and the attention to detail that enabled him to thrive.

Augsburg was ideally placed to take advantage of the trade in goods coming in from the east through Venice to northern Europe, such as the spices and silk that the Fugger business was already involved in by the 1470s. In the late 1480s and 1490s they developed access to markets across Europe, from Lisbon to Hungary, from Naples to Antwerp. This, in turn, led to involvement in the growing international financial system. The Fugger family also developed close links with the Habsburgs. In 1473 Ulrich Fugger had provided fine clothes for the Habsburg Emperor Frederick III, his son Maximilian, and their entourage, who were travelling to the betrothal of Maximilian and Mary of Burgundy. Maximilian regularly borrowed large sums, for instance in 1496 (148,600 florins), 1507 (200,000 florins), and 1508 (over 130,000 florins), in return for securities such as property (usually land), trading rights, income from silver and copper mines and anticipated future revenues from taxes. Already by 1500 the family had gained control not only of trade in copper but also its production, with mines in

Hungary (along with the Thurzo family) and Tyrol[9]. This is an example of the monopolistic approach that they were to be accused of as their wealth accumulated.

It was Jacob II, known as Jacob 'the Rich', who is mainly associated with the growth of the Fugger fortune. During the 1490s the brothers (Ulrich, Georg and Jacob) agreed that they and their male descendants should leave their property in the company (while making provision for the dowries of daughters) so that the family business would remain undivided. With the death of Georg in 1506 and Ulrich in 1510, Jacob became head of the family firm but took his nephews, Ulrich and Hieronymous (sons of Ulrich), Raymund and Anton (sons of Georg), into partnership as 'Jacob Fugger and Nephews'. Although at times Jacob resisted Maximilian's requests for further credit, pointing out that earlier loans had not yet been repaid and that the securities of silver and copper had already been pledged for several years to come, he was nevertheless raised to the nobility within the Holy Roman Empire in 1511. His extensive financial network acted as the agent for the transfer of grants from the king of England to the Emperor after 1515[10] and by 1519 he was in a position to lend Charles over 600,000 ducats in order to secure his election as emperor.

Like Maximilian, Charles was frequently in need of ready money, often to pay for armies. Since the use of mercenary troops was normal practice, ready access to substantial funds was essential. The non-payment of mercenaries already engaged would result in desertions or looting and atrocities, thus harming the reputation of the monarch, even though at times they had to collude in order to keep the soldiers loyal. For Charles in particular, given the widespread nature of his territories and commitments, money was not always available in sufficient quantity, at the right time, in the right place, particularly in time of war. The result was that he frequently wished to borrow money and have it paid wherever it was needed, even if eventual repayment was to come from elsewhere. This is precisely what the Fugger family were not only able to offer but become renowned for – at a price. It was not uncommon for this price to be the equivalent of over 10% a year.

Jacob's letter to the Emperor did him no harm at all. When accused of monopolistic practices and usury by those jealous of his position he was able to gain Charles' support. In May 1525 Charles decreed that contracts which placed wholesale trade in ore in the hands of a few merchants should not be regarded as monopolistic. On 25th October 1525 a further decree provided specific protection for the mining interests of the Fugger family. In this statement they are described as 'honest people' and that they have done nothing that 'is condemned by law, or is unseemly or criminal'[11]. In addition their links with Spain (and Naples) were developing in the early 1520's, just at the time when the bullion from the New World was starting to flow into Spain in ever increasing quantities. Charles was able to use this new source of income to secure further loans from the Fugger family and other financial houses.

Jacob had become one of the richest men in Europe. In 1511 his business had a balance of 196,791 florins; by 1526 he had left for his successors a balance of 2,021,202 florins[12]. A financier to monarchs, a devout Catholic, said to be modest with a pleasant manner, he was envied by many. In addition to the near monopoly he had gained over trade in certain commodities, defended by Charles, he was particularly unpopular for his involvement in what some saw as the abuses of the church because of his links with the sale of indulgences. In his own mind he was able to reconcile his business practices with his God. He was responsible for the construction of the Fuggerkapelle in St Anna's church, Augsburg (1508-1518) and he funded an early example of a social housing scheme, the Fuggerei, for 'innocently impoverished' citizens of Augsburg, which by 1523 had 52 houses available. A model of order and organisation, the wide streets, good water supply, church, school and medical facility provided shelter for those Catholic citizens of Augsburg of good character and proven need, in return for a minimal rent and daily prayers for the Fugger family.

Jacob died childless on 30th December 1525, and leadership of the business passed to his nephew Anton who continued the close links with Charles for another three decades. This association was to prove an enormous advantage to Charles, helping him on numerous occasions when his situation became difficult, whether with the Protestant princes in Germany or the king of France. But it would not always work. His lack of funds at other times meant that he was not always able to consolidate victories achieved, or provide the much needed support to Ferdinand in his fight with the Ottoman Empire in Hungary. The impact of the high levels of expenditure on war that was to become a feature of Charles' reign was nearly always negative. If both sides had access to similar levels of credit, then there was no real gain in terms of military success. There was a disruption of financial markets in that if so much credit was being taken by rulers for war, then there would be much less available for commercial credit and thus economic development would be slowed.

The bringing together of political power (Charles V) and financial power (Jacob and Anton Fugger) was criticised on the grounds that resources were used 'not to finance new productive work, but to finance war loans and speculations'[13]. The great demand for credit pushed payments for 'trouble, danger and expense' ever higher and these would eventually have to be paid for by the tax-payers, who were therefore paying for the profits of the wealthy lenders. Little wonder that there was hostility towards them. If on the other hand the loans were not repaid, then the ruler would lose the support of the wealthy elements of the population who had provided the loans in the first place. Links with the house of Fugger and other banking houses were of major importance to Charles if he was to achieve his aims. Charles' reign saw a growing population and developing economic activity in many of his lands, but also increasing taxation levels and often a decline in the real living standards of the people.

# 17
## 'Two Suns in the Sky' - The Ottoman Menace

Events soon presented Charles with an opportunity to accomplish the third of his stated ambitions - to protect Europe and the Christian faith. Since leaving Spain he had achieved his first aim, his coronation, though had failed in the far more challenging one of unifying the church. Ottoman incursions into eastern and central Europe had been a feature of the previous one hundred years, but under Suleiman they had pushed ever further west. In the spring of 1532 the sultan left Istanbul with a vast force which many believed was capable of overwhelming any resistance in Hungary and then taking Vienna. Charles might now be able to play a personal role in the defence of Christian Europe.

It had been an expectation that the Holy Roman Emperor defended Europe against Muslim attacks, but his predecessors, Frederick III (r.1452-1492) and Maximilian I (r.1493-1519) had struggled to carry out this role effectively. With his extensive lands and large potential resources Charles was better placed to lead Christian forces, and others realised that Habsburg power was probably the best defence against the Ottomans. Charles recognised his responsibilities and was keen to fulfil them, after all this was the original purpose of the Order of the Golden Fleece which meant so much to him. As early as 1519, while in Barcelona, Charles spoke of the fight against the Muslims as being 'the thing most desired by us in this world, in which we intend to employ all our realms'. He consistently stated that it was his wish to live in peace with his neighbours and lead a crusade against the Ottomans.

The Ottoman Empire had expanded considerably during the 15th and early 16th centuries. Originating in north-western Anatolia under Osman I around 1300, by 1450 they had expanded to establish a firm base in south-eastern Europe, controlling modern day Bulgaria, Greece and parts of Romania and Albania. Byzantium (Constantinople), unaided by the rest of Europe, then fell to Sultan Mehmet II in 1453. He quickly added Serbia and the remainder of Romania and Albania. The Ottomans also challenged Venetian power in the eastern and central Mediterranean, taking major bases around the Greek coast, such as Coron (now Koroni) and Modon (Methoni), known as the 'eyes of the Republic'. After a peace agreed in 1503 Venice had a major commercial interest in maintaining a peaceful coexistence with the Ottomans[1]. Under Selim I the Ottoman focus was on expansion to the south and east. During his short reign (1512 – 1520) Syria, Palestine and Egypt were over-run.

As Charles had been establishing himself as king in Spain and as Holy Roman Emperor, a new ruler came to the throne in Istanbul. He was to challenge Charles' very right to call himself 'Emperor'. Suleiman became sultan in 1520 on the death of his father and was to rule for 46 years. Now known in the west as 'the Magnificent' and to Turks as 'the Law-maker', Suleiman had ambitions in both east and west. He refused to refer to Charles as anything other than the 'king of Spain'. Charles for his part always wrote about Suleiman and the Ottomans as 'the Turk(s)'. A Venetian ambassador, after expressing the hope of welcoming Suleiman to his city in the future, was told 'Certainly, but only after I have captured Rome'. Fortunately for Christian Europe Suleiman, like Charles, had other commitments and other challenges to deal with. He spent considerable time in each decade of his reign on campaigns against the Safavid dynasty in Persia (Iran) led by Shah Tahmasp. However, whenever his eastern border was secure, he was in a position to lead troops into Europe to seize control of Hungary and threaten Austria, while by sea his fleet posed a challenge throughout the Mediterranean. There were many parts of Europe where the people had good reason to be fearful.

The structure of the Ottoman Empire meant that it could be on a war footing much more readily than Charles was ever able to be. The division of land within the empire was based on the provision of armed horsemen for war. Additionally, in the 'devsirme' (blood tax),

Christian children* from occupied areas were removed from their homes, converted to Islam and trained either for the army, to become the feared janissaries, or for administrative posts. Although officially slaves (kul), the most talented could rise to the highest positions as military commanders or ministers of the sultan. Suleiman therefore had under his command what was effectively a permanent standing army at least for the summer campaigning season. It was traditional for the sultan to lead his troops on campaign each year and return to the capital, Istanbul, as it was coming to be known, each autumn; the army expected the bonuses and plunder that came from a successful expedition and could be troublesome if idle for too long[2]. At sea Suleiman was able to provide increasing numbers of warships and had experienced, ruthless commanders, together with sufficient conscripted or slave man-power for the vessels.

As an absolute ruler the sultan could raise additional funds for campaigns without the need to ask local representative bodies (as Charles had to in his various dominions). By the 16th century the sultan was also the caliph, the religious leader of the Sunni Muslims. Thus Suleiman did not have to deal with a religious hierarchy that could challenge his power, in contrast to the rivalry between Emperor and the Pope. He had a strong grip on power, and this stability enabled him to pursue policies relatively unchallenged for much of the time. As Erasmus wrote in 1521 'The Turk will invade with all his forces, to do battle for the great prize, whether Christian or Turk be monarch of the entire globe, for the world can no longer bear to have two suns in the sky'.

During the 1520s, while Charles had been in Spain, his brother had shouldered most of the responsibility for combating the Ottoman threat. Charles' other problems had already limited his ability to meet this challenge and were to continue to do so through much of his reign. Ferdinand's effectiveness had been hampered by

---

* Ideally aged over 10 years old, of obvious intelligence, physically sound, though not an orphan or an only child.

his relative lack of authority and by divisions within the Empire. Most rulers talked about the need to prevent further Otttoman advances, but few were willing to commit money and troops, preferring to leave that to others. Suleiman had been able to take advantage of these weaknesses. In the early years of Charles' reign he had taken Belgrade, Rhodes and in 1526 sacked Buda. Ferdinand's claim to the Hungarian throne after the death of his brother-in-law was disputed by John Zapolyai, governor of Transylvania, who had the support of many in the country. Although Ferdinand was able to retake much of the country in 1527, this new division further weakened the defences of Christian Europe.

In May 1529 Suleiman, accompanied by his Grand Vizier, a former slave originally from Greece, Ibrahim Pasha*, set out on a campaign with an army estimated to be 120,000 strong. His advance from Bulgaria was delayed by the effects of heavy rain. Having reached Hungary in August he was joined by Zapolyai, who was prepared to accept that Hungary would be a vassal state. They took Buda on 8th September and, moving steadily forward, laid siege to Vienna by the end of the month. Suleiman's army had been weakened by its slow advance; the heavy field guns had been impossible to move along the muddy route and numbers had been reduced by sickness and poor health. Many of the troops who arrived were not equipped for siege warfare. Wilhelm von Roggenhof, the Hofmeister of Austria, had taken charge of the defence of the city. He handed operational command to the vastly experienced, seventy year old mercenary, Nicholas, Count of Salm, whose first taste of battle had been at Morat against Charles the Bold, the Emperor's great-grandfather, in 1476. With about 20,000 troops under his command pitched battle was out of the question. Instead he strengthened the defences by blocking the gates, reinforcing the walls and building more earth ramparts. Once

---

* Often known as 'Frenk' Ibrahim Pasha, meaning the 'European' or 'Westerner' referring to his tastes and manners.

Suleiman's request to surrender had been rejected, the assaults began. The light Ottoman field guns (the heavy ones had yet to arrive) proved insufficient to breach the defences, and attempts to tunnel under the walls were hampered by effective counter attacks. With his army stretched to its limits and disquiet about their failure to make any progress spreading through the ranks, in mid-October Suleiman decided on one final concerted effort. When this also failed, the Ottoman forces withdrew.

These events took place while Charles was travelling to Bologna to prepare for his coronation. It was assumed by most in Europe that Ottoman forces would return within a few years. Charles desired to be seen to take a part in the defence of Vienna and the Christian world. Although it is clear from Isabella's letters that she wished for his return to Spain, there were many reasons why he could not hurry back. In July 1531 Charles wrote to his wife from Ghent declaring that: 'It is my dearest wish to see you again and to be once more in my own home'. He then goes on to explain why his return to Spain would be delayed. Ferdinand urged him to stay. Both the Protestant elector of Saxony and the Catholic Duke of Bavaria were still hostile to Habsburg power. 'All are agreed that I cannot for the moment be spared, and that I must stay and take control of German affairs'. Charles also emphasised the Ottoman danger: 'The Turkish menace has increased so much that I have even considered coming to an agreement with the Lutherans in order to prevent worse disaster'.[3] This became more urgent as Suleiman again led his troops west from Istanbul in the spring of 1532. Charles' opportunity to lead a great expedition against the sultan and fulfil his role as Holy Roman Emperor and master of the Order of the Golden Fleece, to carry out 'great deeds' and win 'honour and reputation', had arrived. His reputation was important to him and he took his duty as leader of Christendom against the Ottoman threat seriously: 'I have decided that if the Turk comes in person, which he can only do at the head of a great force, I will go forth with all the forces I can find to resist him'[4].

On his way to Regensburg for the Imperial Diet, 'whilst out hunting, he had a fall from his horse and hurt his leg; erysipelas having ensued, he suffered from it the whole time that he was in Ratisbon (Regensburg)'[5]. He also experienced his third attack of gout at this time. The Diet ratified a new legal code - the Constitutio Criminalis Carolina - and there were the usual religious arguments. Lengthy negotiations took place, the participants moving to Nuremburg for a time. Many German princes were seeking to take advantage of Charles' problems. As his need for a united front and more troops became ever more pressing, the Catholics seemed to become more intransigent and the Protestants demanded more in return for their support. No final settlement was possible, though a temporary deal was made in early August, so that Charles was able to report to Isabella that all were now acting with equal zeal. Luther had come out in favour of combined action against the Turk, still referring to Charles as 'our dear Emperor Carolus' and writing that he had acted 'so as to win the favour and love of all' at the Diet.[6] The compromise enabled Charles to gather together an army of 80,000 men, the scale that was needed to match the Ottoman forces moving towards Vienna. None too soon, as Suleiman was now in Hungary. Charles moved down the Danube from Regensburg with German troops joined by those from the Low Countries and Italy, along with his most experienced commanders, including Frederick II Count Palatine, Henry of Nassau, Antonio de Leyva and the Marquis del Vasto.

The Ottoman advance was again slow, delayed this time by a three week long siege of Guns (Koszeg), in western Hungary, where they met determined resistance from a defending force of no more than 800 Croatian soldiers. By the time Charles arrived in Vienna on 23rd September 1532, his much stated wish for a decisive confrontation was not to be. Suleiman had already withdrawn his forces, deterred by the slow progress, mindful of the failure of the siege of 1529, aware that maintaining his troops in the field much longer was almost impossible. It has been argued that the campaigns of 1532 were in reality 'a parade of strength' in which a

## Charles V: Duty and Dynasty

major set piece battle was unlikely; instead there had been 'a competition in splendour'.[7] Given the cost of putting together, equipping and supplying the vast armies, neither leader was willing to risk all of this and the enormous loss of prestige if they were defeated. Despite Ferdinand's wishes to take on his rival Zapolya, there was no enthusiasm for pursuing the Ottoman armies back into Hungary; money was short, plague was spreading in the army and winter was coming. The Habsburgs had to accept that they would not control the whole of Hungary, which was effectively divided for much of the century. This aversion to risk was not always the case. On future occasions Charles was prepared to throw enormous resources and his personal leadership into military enterprises where the stakes were high. Some were successful, others were not.[*]

On entering Vienna in 1532 Charles was greeted enthusiastically as the victorious emperor against the infidel invader. Frederick, Count Palatine, had achieved some success against small outlying units of the Ottoman army, demonstrating the effectiveness of the Imperial army; the very fact that Charles had marched to challenge Suleiman was believed to have been a factor in bringing about the Ottoman withdrawal. He had shown that he took the Ottoman threat seriously. He had been prepared to commit resources to the city's defence, unlike most of Europe's rulers, and play a personal part in saving Vienna.

Two main issues are raised by a study of these campaigns. Firstly, did Suleiman really wish to conquer lands in the heart of Europe? It seems more likely that his real aim was to secure gains in Hungary and establish a buffer state under John Zapolya in order to restrict Ferdinand and Charles' capacity to launch counter attacks against the Ottoman Empire in the future. Despite Suleiman's talk of taking Rome, he would have known that this was an unrealistic ambition unless Christian Europe completely collapsed as a result of internal divisions. No-one doubted that such divisions existed and could be

---

[*] Successes – Tunis (1535) and Germany (1547). Failures - Algiers (1541) and Metz (1552)

made use of. The Habsburg–Valois rivalry and the frequent hostility between the Emperor and the Pope were obvious examples. The 1530s saw the first of several alliances between France and the Ottoman Empire, directed against Charles. However these were very unpopular with the rest of Christian Europe and tended to consolidate support for Charles.

Secondly, the campaigns showed the logistical limits of the Ottoman armies. With the tradition of the sultan and his troops returning to Istanbul for the winter months there were no forward bases from which the next advance could be made. As the campaigns started from Istanbul, then the length of the campaigning season (usually April to October) restricted the extent of the possible advance of the army. Suleiman's forces were restrained by the problems experienced by all armies of the time. Forward progress was usually slow. The heavy artillery pieces, required for the destruction of sound defensive walls and ramparts, were difficult to transport. The further they advanced, the harder it was to supply the troops. These were large armies by the standards of the time, as large as any European city, and therefore even living 'off the land' became difficult. By October 1529 during the siege of Vienna, Suleiman's troops were experiencing shortages of food and water; illness was widespread; casualty numbers were rising, as were desertions. Thus the fighting force was considerably reduced. The pressure to withdraw became overwhelming. Similar issues confronted the sultan in 1532. Although they might have caused much damage and loss of life in Vienna, it is unlikely that the Ottoman forces could have advanced much further despite the fears of Europe's leaders and citizens. The main Ottoman challenge to Charles in the future would be in the Mediterranean, linked to his conflicts with France.

With Vienna safe, Charles was now able to contemplate a return to Spain. He had received the honour that he believed was due to him at his coronation, and shown his determination to hold back the Ottoman advance. Reliable family members had been established as his regents in north and central Europe. He was, however, fully aware that he had not resolved the religious schism that was tearing Germany, and even Europe, apart. To achieve this he still believed that a general council of the Church was urgently needed and for this he required, at the very least, the Pope's agreement and to be able to rely on the support of Francis I. Even an optimistic Charles recognised that these two requirements were going to be challenging. He held further talks with Pope Clement as he passed through Italy in late 1532 on his way to Genoa, talks which Charles regarded as disappointing. Sailing from Genoa, he reached Barcelona in April 1533, 'which he had a great desire to do, as he had been absent four years from the Empress, his wife'[8]. If he had known by then that Pope Clement and Francis were already planning a closer alliance, backed by the marriage of the Pope's niece, Catherine, to Francis' son, Henry, he would have been discouraged. Despite pleas to Charles that he was now an imperialist, Clement still had an eye on future accommodation with the French. Charles had misjudged the situation. Apparently he had agreed to Clement proposing this match because he had expected Francis to refuse it![9] Relations with France and the Ottoman menace in the Mediterranean were to take much of Charles' time and energy for the rest of the 1530s and the early 1540s.

# 18
## An Opportunity for 'Great Deeds' - The Struggle for the Mediterranean

Whatever wider issues he had to deal with, by the time Charles returned to Spain he was as secure in most of his possessions as he was ever to be. Spain, with his wife as a respected regent in his absence and a son as heir, was no longer the 'restive and hostile kingdom'[1] that he had returned to in 1522, but a loyal and generally reliable source of support and money. The Low Countries were now governed by his sister, Mary, another loyal and more than capable regent and the Austrian lands under Ferdinand were safe with the Ottoman advances repelled. In Germany the religious schism and political rivalries continued, but compromise had bought some time. Italy was now more settled, with Charles holding sway, having seen off the French challenge, securing Milan, Sicily and Naples, and restoring the Medici to power in Florence.

He was now able to spend two years in Spain with his wife and children, Philip and Maria. During Charles' lengthy absence in Italy and the Empire, his second son, Ferdinand, born after his departure in 1529, had died the following year, in what must have been a difficult time for Isabella. They now hoped to have more children. In his 'Memoirs' Charles refers to the birth of his third son in Valladolid during 1534, but the boy survived but a few days, though the following year, in June 1535, their second daughter, Juana, was born. Even though the court regularly moved, to Monzon (where the Cortes of Aragon met), Barcelona, Valladolid, Segovia, Toledo, Palencia and Madrid, this was a time of relative stability for Charles in comparison to much of his reign.

There were, of course, always difficulties that needed attention. They ranged widely in both location and nature: from the issues surrounding the succession to the throne in Denmark, trading rights in the Baltic, the impact of Henry VIII's divorce from Catherine of Aragon on relations with England, to Anabaptist fervour in Munster. The latter was yet another example of the growing religious heterodoxy that was causing Charles such concern. The lay preacher Melchior Hoffman had travelled widely in northern Europe during the 1520s. He believed that Christ would soon return to establish a 'Heavenly Jerusalem' on earth. While in Strasbourg Hoffman adopted Anabaptist ideas, advocating the need for adult baptism, rejecting infant baptism as invalid. He left Strasbourg in 1530 to spread his ideas in the Low Countries, returning in 1533 only to be imprisoned for his views.

Some of his followers were not prepared to accept such persecution. Jan Matthys of Haarlem rejected Hoffman's pacifist approach and along with 100's of adherents moved to Munster, where they had considerable support, and took over the city in February 1534. Matthys was killed in April 1534 while on a raid against their opponents and leadership passed to John of Leiden (Jan Beukelszoon) who termed himself the king of Munster, which he declared the 'Heavenly Jerusalem'. He introduced widespread sharing of property and goods. Many sources state that he advocated a policy of polygamy, himself taking sixteen wives, although others claim that these accounts originated from the propaganda of his enemies. Many of the practices and teachings of the Anabaptists were abhorrent to both Catholics and Lutherans. Forces were gathered under the ousted prince-bishop of Munster, Franz von Waldeck, and Munster was retaken in June 1535.[2] The Anabaptists were tortured and executed. John of Leiden and two others were secured to a pole by means of a spiked collar, their bodies whipped with red-hot tongs, their tongues pulled out, and a burning dagger thrust into their hearts. Their bodies were then hung in cages from the steeple of St Lambert's church where they remained for fifty years. Many rulers, Charles included, regarded the Anabaptists with horror and initiated further persecution to prevent their spread, though some with more moderate, peaceful beliefs survived under the leadership of Menno Simons in Friesland.

During Charles' time in Spain there was peace with France. He knew as well as anyone that this state of affairs was unlikely to last. The marriage of the pope's niece, Catherine de' Medici, to Henry, second son of Francis I, took place in Marseilles on 27th October 1533 and was a clear indication that challenges to Charles' position in Italy were not over. The death of Pope Clement a year later in September 1534 must have been a relief to Charles. He had reasonable hopes that the new pope, Paul III (Alessandro Farnese), would look more favourably upon the idea of a general council to help to resolve the schism in Germany and bring about much needed reform.

Now that the Ottoman danger to Austria had been reduced, the main focus of the Habsburg-Ottoman conflict had shifted to the Mediterranean. Hostilities here were not new. Ottoman control had already extended around the eastern Mediterranean and, further to the west, bases had been established on the North African coast by Muslim corsairs. The ever present threat to shipping and coastal settlements had increased with the defeat of Muslim controlled Granada in 1492 and the subsequent departure of many thousands of displaced Muslims to northern Africa. This had provided many new recruits for the corsairs who thus gained first-hand knowledge of the coast and its hinterland. Not only was trade seriously disrupted but life was endangered by raids to supply the slave markets. Coastal areas experienced depopulation as the inhabitants moved further inland for safety. Hence Charles' statement in Barcelona about his determination to fight the 'infidel' to the representatives of Aragon in 1519.

One corsair, Aruj (Oruch) Barbarossa, originally from the Aegean island of Lesbos, had helped take Muslim refugees from Spain to North Africa. He later set himself up as ruler in Algiers and the surrounding area, with Ottoman assistance. Not long after his first arrival in Spain, Charles' forces had achieved a victory with the defeat and death of Aruj at Tlemcen (west of Algiers). His body was

## Charles V: Duty and Dynasty

nailed to the city walls and his head was paraded through the area on a lance before being sent as a trophy to Spain[3], practices widely used in both Europe and North Africa at the time. This initial success was not to last long. Aruj's brother, Hizir (later known as Hayrettin Barbarossa), was appointed governor of the area as a province of the Ottoman Empire. This eventually transformed the conflict from a problem of how to deal with local pirates into part of the struggle between two empires. Heyrettin's naval skills and his desire for revenge, when linked to Sultan Suleiman's ambitions, were to make him the scourge of Christians in the Mediterranean for the next 25 years. The raids, destruction and taking of captives continued across the whole area regardless of any formal declaration of war.

Further east, the capture of Rhodes in 1522 had also strengthened Suleiman's hand in the Mediterranean or 'White Sea' as it was known to the Ottomans. The island had been the base for the Knights of St John (the Hospitallers) for over 200 years since their defeat at Acre in 1291 at the end of the Crusades. From Rhodes, which they captured in 1307, they had been a constant threat to Muslim powers in the Middle East. Their attacks on the coastal areas and shipping were regarded as little more than piracy not only by the Ottomans, but also by the Venetians. Indeed Aruj and Hizir Barbarossa had learned much from their tactics; Aruj had been a captive slave of the Knights for three years. However, they did provide a significant hurdle to further Ottoman advances in the Mediterranean. In 1522 Suleiman decided to follow up his success in the Balkans the previous year, when Belgrade was taken.

Despite the overwhelming size of Suleiman's forces which besieged Rhodes town against 500 Knights and perhaps 1,500 mercenaries and local Greeks[4], this had not been easily accomplished. Beginning their attack in July, the Ottomans had still not captured the town by the end of October, usually the end of the campaigning season. Even with skilled siege engineers, miners, and vastly superior numbers no siege could be certain of success against the recently developed defensive methods which had been put in place at Rhodes. The presence of the Sultan, however, meant that failure could not be contemplated and the assault continued. By December 1522, with their numbers seriously reduced, the walls breached and no external help arriving, the Knights were ready to negotiate.[5] They were permitted an honourable withdrawal as the Ottomans took the city.

Now all the Mediterranean islands and much of the Italian and western Spanish coasts were open to raids by the corsairs, and more organised attacks by the Ottoman fleet led by Hayrettin Barbarossa. The Spanish had always attempted to maintain strongholds with castles and harbours on the North African coast in order to restrict the movements of the raiders and if possible pursue and punish them. However during the 1520s many had been lost, including the Penon (fort) of Algiers in 1529. The following year, in an effort to strengthen Christian resistance, Charles gave permission for the Knights of St. John to establish a base in Malta. This was to prove a major obstacle to Ottoman domination in the future, but had only a minor impact in the short term.

An additional concern to Charles was the growing link between the French king and Suleiman. Contact between them had been made as early as 1528, with Francis requesting protection for Christians in the Sultan's lands, but in 1532 renewed efforts were made to reach a formal agreement. Their common interests were obvious. Francis explained to the Venetian ambassador in 1531: "I cannot deny that I wish to see the Turk all-powerful and ready for war, not for himself - for he is an infidel and we are all Christians - but to weaken the power of the emperor, to compel him to make major expenses, and to reassure all the other governments who are opposed to such a formidable enemy"[6]. In 1532 Antonio Rincon was sent on a mission to Suleiman on behalf of Francis I. He reported about life in Ottoman Istanbul: "Astonishing order, no violence. Merchants, women even, coming and going in perfect safety, as in a European town. Life as safe, as large and easy as in Venice. Justice so fairly administered that one is tempted to believe that the Turks are turned Christians now, and that the Christians are turned Turks."[7]

In 1528, however, Charles had gained a vital ally; Andrea Doria of Genoa had abandoned his French alliance and committed his fleet to the Imperial cause. Doria was to act as Charles' naval commander throughout the Mediterranean for the next twenty years, just as Barbarossa did for Suleiman. In September 1532, at the same time as Suleiman was withdrawing from Vienna, Doria's fleet took Coron (now Koroni), the important naval base in southern Greece captured from the Venetians in 1500, and then defeated the Ottoman fleet of 60 galleys sent to recapture the stronghold. Although Ottoman land forces recaptured the castle the following year, Suleiman now decided that he needed to place a greater emphasis on his navy. In order to prepare for this vital naval conflict, Barbarossa returned to Istanbul to oversee the construction of a new fleet of 70 galleys. He was appointed Admiral and governor of all the coastal Mediterranean lands of the Ottoman Empire.

Barbarossa sailed back to raid the western coast of Italy with renewed violence in 1534. Cities were abandoned by terrified citizens, villages destroyed, ships burned and many hundreds of men, women and children taken as slaves. In August, encouraged by the French, he took Tunis from Spain's ally Muley Hassan, who put up no resistance. The loss of Tunis, less than a day's sea journey from Sicily, and with its central position in the Mediterranean, was a major blow to Charles. He immediately began preparations for a campaign to retake the city, which would be followed by a victorious entry to Sicily and Naples, which he had never visited. He hoped that his success would force the king of France to back down from future conflicts and show yet again his determination to meet the Muslim challenge. He now had the chance, denied to him in 1532 at Vienna, to become the victorious warrior fighting to defend his own subjects and Christendom.

Rulers at the time still wished to be directly involved in military campaigns. Charles' upbringing in the Burgundian tradition of chivalry and his leadership of the Order of the Golden Fleece predisposed him to such action. He had been impressed by the aura of victory attached to Henry VIII following his capture of Therouanne and Tournai after the Battle of the Spurs in 1513. He recognised early in his reign that he wished to be responsible for great deeds, to be seen leading his troops, to gain honour and reputation from a great victory. His early years, first as Duke of Burgundy, as king in Spain, and then as Holy Roman Emperor, did not provide these opportunities. He had to secure his own position and was still under the influence of councillors who were all too aware that the dangers were considerable. Many commanders experienced the same risks as their men; Charles de Bourbon was killed at the start of the attack on Rome in May 1527, and the Prince of Orange, Charles' commander at the siege of Florence, died of wounds in August 1530. Royalty was no exception; the capture of Francis I at Pavia in 1525 and the death of Charles' brother-in-law King Louis of Hungary at the battle of Mohacs in 1526 showed this only too well.

Despite warnings and some opposition from his ministers, who either believed that his personal involvement was more fitting to a 'young nobleman' or looked at the adventure only from the point of view of Castile and not Charles' wider concerns and responsibilities, he was not to be deterred. Diplomatic instructions were issued to his ambassadors to minimise the danger of other problems coming to a head at the same time. Military preparations were swiftly underway. Spanish vessels were joined by the Portuguese, led by Prince Luis, Charles' brother-in-law, and the Genoese fleet under Doria. Troops were assembled from Spain, Italy and Germany, many coming together in Cagliari, Sardinia. Altogether they had nearly 100 warships and 300 transports for the 30,000 men and necessary supplies. Charles' intention to lead the expedition in person was kept secret until the last minute, although the size and thoroughness of the preparations led many to suspect his plans. Also accompanying the fleet was Jan Cornelisz Vermeyen, the Dutch artist who was to make sketches that were later to be the basis of a series of 12 tapestries celebrating Charles' campaign.

Having again appointed Isabella as his Regent, on 10th June 1535 they set sail, arriving off the coast of Africa near the ruins of Carthage five days later. Tunis was protected by the fortress of La Goletta, the expedition's first objective. Once the successful disembarkation of men, horses and equipment had been achieved, the siege began. The usual problems of lack of food and fresh water, added to the heat, disease and the counter attacks of Barbarossa's soldiers, meant that it was a testing time for Charles and his troops. After a final assault, which involved a combined artillery bombardment from both land and sea, simultaneous attacks by German, Spanish, Italian troops and the knights of St. John, culminating in the scaling of the walls, they eventually took the fortress on 14th July. They were also able to capture over 80 ships of Barbarossa's fleet and much booty was taken. Many advisers urged Charles to accept this victory and end the campaign, but he was determined to take Tunis itself. As they advanced on the city across an unforgiving landscape, with no shelter from the blazing sun, their horses collapsing from exhaustion, they were harassed by Barbarossa's remaining troops who made access to essential water supplies difficult. The whole campaign was in the balance. Charles led by example, experiencing the same hardships as his troops and being directly involved in skirmishes. Good order was maintained and slow progress was made. Meanwhile the thousands of Christian slaves held inside Tunis, fearing that they would be sacrificed by their captors in any siege, took advantage of Barbarossa's absence, seized arms and captured the city. Barbarossa withdrew his remaining forces, moving along the coast to Bona, where he had kept some galleys, and then on to Algiers.

Charles could only go in pursuit if he went back on his promise to the troops that they could plunder the city once it had been taken. Unwilling to do this, Charles had no choice but to allow Barbarossa to escape his grasp. In Tunis his soldiers killed hundreds, plundered what they could from mosques and the houses of the wealthy, and took thousands to be sold as slaves. The campaign had been fought in the name of 'Our Holy Catholic Faith' but Tunis was handed back to Muley Hassan, an ally, but also a Muslim.[8] Charles' plans to take other ports in North Africa were soon ended by the renewal of war with France.[9] He might have had his military victory but he had not ensured the security of the western Mediterranean. Barbarossa would now rebuild his fleet and renew his aggressive activities. He did so quickly. The population of the Balearics were still in celebratory mood in October when he attacked the town of Mahon in Minorca, taking prisoners and destroying its defences[10].

Nevertheless, Charles could now travel as victor and conqueror to Sicily and from there on to Naples. After two months in Africa he landed at Trapani on 22nd August, spent September in Palermo and Monreale before moving on to Messina. There he was met with great enthusiasm, being seen as the defender of his lands and protector of his people. His triumphal entry is well documented, with temporary wooden and stucco decorations of chariots, angels and winged eagles lining the route, with references to Imperial Rome and Carthage to the fore. Charles' own emblem, the pillars of Hercules, were represented on one city gate with the inscription 'from sunrise to sunset', while the cry of 'long live our victorious Emperor, father of the fatherland, conqueror of Africa, peace-maker in Italy' rung through the streets[11].

Such magnificent entries continued as Charles moved north to the Italian mainland. He wintered in Naples, celebrating Christmas and holding great feasts and tournaments. Here he experienced his 'fifth attack of gout' and also 'received news of the death of the Queen of England'[12] – his aunt Catherine of Aragon. This event, though personally sad for Charles, opened up the possibility of improving relations with Henry VIII, especially after the execution of the English king's 'whore', Anne Boleyn, less than five months later. Charles left Naples in March, moving on to Rome, where he followed the route of the imperial triumphs of old, lined with great canvases of military victories, and then under the arches of Constantine, Titus and Septimus Severus. In late April 1536 he was received in Siena and then Florence, where he rode under arches painted with scenes of recent Imperial victories and classical stories, including Jason with a golden fleece. This was Italy of the Renaissance welcoming the Emperor. Many hundreds of carpenters, painters and other workers were involved in constructing these scenes, as were the best designers and craftsman that money could buy as each city attempted to outdo their neighbours. It was 'ceremonial progress as a political weapon'[13] aimed at consolidating support, 'making concrete the abstract of the Crown in the actual presence of the ruler'[14].

Throughout Italy Charles was securing his position and dealing with issues as they arose – he was after all the final arbiter in any local dispute. In Florence, Alessandro de Medici had been installed as ruler and promised marriage to Charles' natural daughter, Margaret, after the defeat of the republic in 1530. He was created Duke of Florence by the Emperor in 1532, marking the end of the Florentine Republic. In order to dominate the city and consolidate his control he ordered the construction of the massive Fortezza da Basso. Nicknamed 'Il Moro'*, Alessandro had not received the broad classical education of a Renaissance prince or if he had there was little evidence of it. He had a reputation for being uncouth, of wild behaviour, with an unrestrained sexual appetite, though he had two children by his long term mistress Taddea Malaspina. He was also spontaneously generous, often helping those most in need, giving him some popularity in the city. After the death of Clement VII in 1534 any restrain on his actions seems to have been removed. The following year a delegation, led by Cardinal Ippolito de' Medici, was sent from Florence to Charles V about Alessandro's increasingly unacceptable behaviour. The cardinal died en-route to meet Charles, believed by many to have been poisoned on the orders of his cousin, Alessandro. After hearing the charges and listening to a defence of Alessandro by Francesco Guicciardini, Florentine diplomat and later author of the famous history of Italy, Charles ruled in favour of the Duke.

---

* Alessandro's mother was possibly a Moorish servant of the Medici family.

The wedding to Margaret went ahead in January 1536, shortly after her thirteenth birthday, and Charles' visit to the city followed soon after. However in January 1537 Alessandro was murdered while in bed awaiting a lover, in a plan put together by his distant cousin and erstwhile boon companion, Lorenzino de' Medici, who had hoped to replace him as Duke of Florence. This was not to be. The only close family relative was Catherine de Medici, now married to Prince Henry in France, and so senior advisors worked quickly to establish another distant cousin, Cosimo de Medici, as the new Duke. He was the 17 year old son of Giovanni Medici delle Bande Nero who had died defending Florence against the Imperial forces in 1527 as they marched south towards Rome. The choice of Cosimo was backed by Charles and in 1539 the new Duke married Eleanor, the daughter of viceroy of Naples, Don Pedro of Toledo, who brought with her a substantial dowry. Charles now had a reliable ally in power and Cosimo at last brought much needed stability to Florence, remaining in power until his death in 1574, becoming Grand Duke of Tuscany in 1569.

Charles had successfully displayed a zeal for defending Europe from the threat posed by Suleiman's navy and been given a hero's welcome in his lands in Italy. However, as he travelled north, eventually to Genoa and then back to Spain, he was frustrated that he had been unable to follow up his victory at Tunis. War with France had once again broken out and he believed that he had been let down by Pope Paul. He knew that he had only temporarily blunted the effectiveness of Ottoman attacks and despite his best efforts he had not greatly improved the security of those living around the Mediterranean.

Charles V: Duty and Dynasty

# Part Four
# **Confronting Challenges 1539-1545**

A bas-relief of Charles in Ghent – one of the few memorials to the emperor in the city of his birth.

Charles V: Duty and Dynasty

# 19
## 'Anguish and Sorrow' – Conflict and Family Death

In November 1535 Francesco Sforza, the Duke of Milan, married to Charles' niece Christina only eighteen months before, died. With no legitimate heir, it was almost certain that Francis would renew the claim to the dukedom that French kings had long asserted. He made no secret of his wish to control Milan, something that Charles could not countenance. So if Charles had hoped that his victory in Tunis and subsequent triumphal progress through Italy would deter Francis from any further aggressive moves he was rapidly disillusioned. Within months Francis' army invaded Savoy, ruled by Duke Charles III, an ally of the emperor and married to his sister-in-law, Beatrice of Portugal. The French occupied Bourg-en-Bresse in February 1536, moved through the Alpine passes and captured Turin, just as Charles entered Rome, in early April 1536. Charles was furious that so soon after he had defeated Barbarossa, thus giving Christian Europe the chance to remove the menace of 'the Turk' if only they could work together, Francis had acted in a way that divided Europe yet again.

Charles believed that Francis had signed away any claim to Milan in both the Treaty of Madrid and then in the Treaty of Cambrai. In Rome he had lengthy negotiations with Pope Paul in which he emphasised the importance of siding with him against Francis. He believed that this support was due to him, as the Emperor who had defended Christianity. In April 1536 he spoke for over an hour in the Vatican, in Spanish, to the assembled College of Cardinals, ambassadors to the Papacy and his own entourage. He thanked the Pope for working towards a general council and said that his only wish was to gather troops for another campaign against the Ottomans in Africa. He claimed that 'there are those who say I wish to rule the world, but both my thoughts and my deeds demonstrate the contrary'.[1] Charles then outlined the persistent aggression and treachery of Francis over the previous twenty years, despite his own wish to live in peace. He explained that he was prepared to negotiate, that he had even considered offering Milan to the Duke of Angouleme (Francis' third son), in return for reasonable concessions. But failing any agreement, because of his wish to spare the blood of his subjects, he offered to meet Francis in personal combat. If he won he would take Burgundy; if he lost, Francis would take Milan.[2]

In his reply Pope Paul praised Charles' wish for peace but pointed out that Francis too had offered peace. He argued that there was no reason why peace could not be maintained and that the Church must be seen to be neutral so as to be able to act as a trusted mediator in the future. He continued that he would declare against any prince who rejected a reasonable settlement. Paul, like his predecessor, had no wish to antagonise Francis, fearing the secession of France from the Roman church following that of England only three years before, and expressed dissatisfaction with Charles' failure to deal with the Protestant heresy in Germany. He naturally wished to maintain the independence of the papacy and had no desire to become dependent on Charles.

Needless to say, peace was not achieved. Despite his claim that 'my intention is not to war against Christians, but against the infidel', Charles, perhaps encouraged by his recent success, planned an audacious advance into Provence aimed at Marseilles. He intended to use his fleet to supply the army, as at Tunis, and keep French troops occupied by a simultaneous attack from the Low Countries towards Paris. However, the circumstances were different and the challenge greater. The advance, led by Antonio de Leyva, the newly appointed governor of Milan, began on 25th July 1536. The French commander, Montmorency, resorted to the drastic tactic of laying waste the land and setting up well defended positions behind city walls, the main force being at Avignon. He had no intention of being drawn out into a set piece battle. The Imperial army thus advanced into open country with little to sustain them and no battles to fight, except lengthy sieges for which they were ill prepared. The fleet was too far away to supply them. Hunger and illness took their toll and by early September they withdrew, but not before the death of Leyva, one of Charles most experienced and reliable generals. Charles was later to blame this set-back on the lateness of the season but even if the attack had begun months earlier it was doomed to failure.

It was during this time that Francis' eldest son, also Francis, who had been held in Spain along with his brother Henry for over three years after the Treaty of Madrid, died suddenly at Chateau Tournon-sur-Rhone, aged 18. In August 1536 he played a game of tennis[*] and afterwards drunk a cup of water handed to him by his secretary, the Count of Montecuccoli. The count had been brought to the French court by Catherine de Medici, his brother's wife, and was soon accused of being in Charles' pay and of poisoning the prince. A book on toxicology was found amongst his possessions and under torture he confessed to the crime. Although he later retracted the confession, he was condemned and executed on 7th October in Lyons by being attached to four horses and then being torn apart as the horses galloped in different directions. Perhaps he did poison the young Francis, but many at the time and since believe that a more likely cause of death was tuberculosis and that Montecuccoli was a victim of the heightened international tensions of the time, providing the French king with an opportunity to blacken his opponent's name.

Further north it had needed little encouragement from Francis for that long time enemy of the Habsburgs in the Low Countries, Charles of Egmond, Duke of Guelders, to ally with Christian III of Denmark and advance into Overijssel, Groningen and Drenthe. Elsewhere Imperial troops under Nassau made little headway when attacking France from Flanders. Mary needed to use all her military and diplomatic resources to repel the Duke of Guelders and to hold the position in Flanders. A near stalemate was reached but neither

---

[*] The game now known as 'real tennis'.

side was yet willing to make peace. Charles arrived back in Spain from Genoa in December 1536, after a dangerous crossing that involved his ships sheltering from storms off the island of Hyeres, a perilous position close to the coast of Provence. Charles had not wished to find himself a prisoner of Francis in a reversal of the situation eleven years before.

In Spain Charles re-joined his family in Valladolid after a short stay in Barcelona, seeing his young daughter, Juana, for the first time – she had been born just as he was leaving on his Tunis campaign eighteen months before. He remained there for six months, during which time he summoned the cortes of Castile, held numerous tournaments and spent any spare time that he had pondering the wonders of the universe and studying clocks along with other mechanical devices from both Europe and the Arab world. He then had to travel to Monzon for the cortes of Aragon and, after a brief return to Valladolid, to Barcelona. Isabella was once again pregnant and 'consoled herself' that Charles' absences were in 'the service of God'.[3] The birth of another child would have been a cause for great celebration but the boy died almost immediately. This, their third son to die in infancy, was another blow to the couple and Isabella was permanently weakened both physically and emotionally. She was never to fully recover. Charles later recorded that 'The Empress suffered much after her confinement, and since then...was in very bad health'.[4]

Outside Spain the political situation was ever changing. The death of Alessandro de Medici in January 1537 meant that his wife, Charles' natural daughter, Margaret, was unexpectedly available for re-marriage, an important opportunity for Charles given the lack of marriageable females in his family. There were two main possible new husbands for Margaret. The obvious choice was Cosimo de Medici, the new ruler of Florence, though Pope Paul soon let Charles' ambassador in Rome know that he would favour her marriage to his grand-son, Ottavio Farnese. Margaret was another counter that Charles could use on the complex board of diplomatic manoeuvres. Widowed at just fourteen her career was only just beginning.

Also in January 1537, in the Paris Parlement, Charles was accused of breaking the treaties of Madrid and Cambrai and thus giving Francis the right to reclaim Artois, Flanders and Charolais as French territories. The conflict on the border of the Low Countries was renewed with increased vigour, a fresh French offensive resulting in considerable bloodshed. Mary made a successful appeal for additional funds at the States General, though Ghent would not contribute to this new tax, a refusal which was to have major consequences for the city in the future. With both sides fully extended financially and neither making worthwhile gains, Mary was able to negotiate a ten month armistice at Bomy, near Therouanne, in June 1537. Later in the year she met Francis' wife, her sister Eleanor, and then Francis himself, in order to secure the truce.

Francis hoped that by ending hostilities in the north he could gain an advantage in the south. In the Mediterranean sphere he had hopes of his alliance with the Ottomans. Barbarossa's depredations in the Mediterranean continued, especially after the officially sanctioned assassination of the Grand Vizier, Ibrahim Pasha, in 1536, who had usually argued for a pro Venetian policy. In that year Barbarossa, recovered from his setback at Tunis, had attacked Ibiza and the Spanish mainland coast. The following year an Ottoman fleet of 170 galleys landed in southern Italy around Otranto, ravaging the area and taking thousands of people into slavery. They then besieged Corfu, but having failed to take it returned to Istanbul accompanied by a dozen French vessels under Admiral Baron de St-Blancard. The French alliance with the Ottomans clearly put additional pressure on Charles, but at the same time was very unpopular in much of Christian Europe and made it easier for Charles to portray Francis as the real danger and hardly the 'Most Christian Monarch' that he liked to call himself.

On land the war had become one which none could afford or was likely to win. The French had some success in Piedmont, while

Spanish troops advanced slowly into Languedoc. Talks were started, with Charles represented by Cobos and Granvelle and Francis by Montmorency and the Cardinal of Lorraine. A further truce was agreed but neither side were willing to give way to the demands of the other. Francis had good reasons to want peace. Diplomatically his position was weakening. The Italian powers sided with the Emperor, and there was now a marked improvement in relations between Charles and Henry VIII. Pope Paul acted as peacemaker, leaving Rome in March 1538 and travelling to Nice, in Savoy. First Charles and then Francis arrived to negotiate with him. At this time the two kings did not meet, preferring to talk separately with the Pope, but Eleanor did make several visits to her brother, during which she would have delivered Francis' thoughts and listened to Charles' views to report back to her husband. The outcome was an agreement in June 1538 for a truce to last 10 years. Both sides retained all the possessions that they then had, so they could maintain face. The real problems though, such as Milan, remained unresolved. A more positive outcome was a meeting of the two monarchs one month later. Francis invited Charles to Aigues Mortes on the delta of the Rhone. On his arrival Charles was able to welcome Francis on board his galley, and then visit Francis and Eleanor in the town the next day. Isabella was not considered well enough to accompany Charles on this state visit and remained in Valladolid.

Charles was perhaps too optimistic during these meetings in his hopes for a universal Christian peace. He had once again started writing to his brother in enthusiastic terms about gathering forces to attack the Turks and how they could achieve great things in the name of God. His mind was taken up with grandiose plans, joining forces with other powers in the Mediterranean, with the backing of all of Europe, not just to defend coastal areas, but to take the fight to the Ottomans and even launch an attack on Istanbul. Barbarossa's failure to take the Venetian-held island of Corfu in 1537 had brought about a new determination to resist. Venice and the Papacy now looked to Charles for support and the short lived anti-Ottoman Holy

League was created in February 1538, with the Papacy, Venice, the Knights of St John and Charles agreeing to confront Barbarossa. The Genoese admiral, Andrea Doria, was given the overall command. Such an alliance fuelled Charles' more ambitious schemes.

That year Barbarossa, with a fleet of over 120 vessels, captured island after island from the Venetians in the Aegean – Naxos, Paxos, Ios, Syros, Aegina, Tinos – before putting in at Preveza, at the mouth of the Gulf of Arta on the west coast of Greece and taking the fort of Actium*, opposite Preveza, from where they could fire upon any approaching vessels. The rather larger combined fleet of the Holy League blockaded them for three weeks but Doria was unable to take the offensive, deterred by on-shore winds that could drive him onto a hostile coastline. On the night of 27th/28th September Doria moved much of his fleet to the south and was taken by surprise when Barbarossa chose this moment to venture out. In the ensuing conflict the Holy League lost 50 vessels; the Venetians who bore the brunt of the fighting lost most. The Ottoman fleet suffered far less damage. The next day Doria decided to take advantage of favourable winds to withdraw, opting to preserve his ships, despite the wishes of some of his commanders to continue the fight. The lack of co-ordination between the Christian forces was obvious. Doria was accused of holding back and failing to support the Venetians, Genoa's old enemies, and being unwilling to risk his galleys, many of which were his personal property. The chance of preventing Ottoman dominance in the Mediterranean was lost for a generation.†

---

*Opposite Preveza and the site of the famous battle between the fleets of Octavius and Mark Antony and Cleopatra in 31 B.C. Octavius' victory made possible his emergence as 'first citizen' and then Emperor Augustus.
†Despite occasional challenges Ottoman domination was to continue until the Battle of Lepanto in 1571. There Christian forces led by Don John of Austria (Charles' natural son born in 1547) defeated the Ottoman fleet under Ali Pasha in the greatest sea battle of the 16th century, which made the western Mediterranean safe from further Ottoman incursions.

With the failure of the Christian forces and the events that were to unfold after his meetings with Francis, the cold light of reality must have given Charles pause for thought. After the failed treaties of Madrid (1526) and Cambrai (1529) and then the most recent truce, he began to recognise that a permanent peace with France was impossible. The absolute security of his possessions that he wished for, if he was to be able to decisively defeat the Ottomans and reunify the church in Germany, could never come about.[5] He was going to have to work within what was possible, not what was ideal.

Another outcome of the negotiations in Nice was the re-marriage of Charles' natural daughter, Margaret, in November 1538. Charles realised that even if this pope was more open to the idea of a general council to achieve Christian unity than his predecessor, he would still continue the pursuit of papal and family interests as well. Her new husband was Ottavio Farnese, Pope Paul's grandson, later to become Duke of Parma. Farnese was only fourteen at the time, a fact that Margaret, still only fifteen, may well have welcomed, although she had indicated a preference to marry Cosimo de Medici. Francis' son, Henry, had married a Medici pope's niece, Catherine, and now Charles was able to make use of the dynastic ambitions of the current pope. Margaret and Ottavio were never close, often leading separate lives, perhaps made more difficult by the on-going conflict between Charles, the Pope and the rest of the Farnese family over control of Parma. Margaret was later to serve Charles' son, Philip II, as Governor of the Netherlands, as was her son Alexander Farnese, Duke of Parma (born in 1545). He was largely bought up in Spain, developed into a renowned military commander and would have been the commander of the Spanish army to invade England in 1588 had the Armada been successful.

Back in Spain, Isabella, already unwell, was left weakened by the stillbirth of another child in Toledo on 20th April 1539. After a temporary rally her condition deteriorated further and on 1st May she died. Charles expressed his great sorrow in a letter to Ferdinand, praising her 'devout life and her saintly death'[6] and, as usual, put himself in God's hands. He wrote to his sister Mary the following day: 'I feel the anguish and sorrow that you can imagine at so great and extreme a loss... nothing can console me except to reflect on her goodness, her exemplary life as a Catholic.'[7]. He spoke of her 'excellent virtues, prudence and great qualities', and that because of her love for people 'she is as a consequence beloved by them, revered and obeyed'. Charles later wrote in his memoirs: 'It pleased God to call her to Himself, of which we may be certain, seeing His great mercy'. He withdrew for several weeks to the Hieronymite monastery of La Sisla, not far from Toledo.

Isabella had acted as regent for Charles on a number of occasions when he was absent from Spain, and had she survived would no doubt have done so again. For a total of over five years, first when Charles went to Bologna for his coronation and then travelled widely in Italy, Austria, Germany and the Low Countries until 1533, and again in 1535 and 1536 when he led the successful campaign against the Ottoman naval base in Tunis and then visited Italy, Isabella looked after Charles' interests. Historians are divided about how ably and effectively she carried out these duties and the extent to which she relished this role. Charles took care to set up clear structures, with an experienced royal council having access to all papers and extensive powers, giving her every chance of success. Isabella's personality matched Charles'; she was devout, took her responsibilities seriously, controlled her emotions in public and commanded respect. She fulfilled her duties standing in for Charles at court functions admirably. Despite the usual problems of state finances, Charles' frequent requests for more money, and the occasional unrest as a result of taxation, Spain continued to develop as a sound base for Charles, suggesting a job well done.

She personally regretted Charles' absences and although their letters are usually concerned with diplomatic affairs in a rather formal way, at times it is clear that she tries to put pressure on Charles to return home as soon as possible. She had seven pregnancies during the thirteen years of their marriage, though only three children had survived. Charles had been away from Spain for the birth and subsequent death of their son, Ferdinand, and also when his daughter Juana was born. Clearly at these difficult times Isabella would have welcomed the support of her husband, but the demands on Charles and the difficulties of travel in the 16th century made this unlikely. After her death Charles soon made it clear that he did not intent to remarry. This may be surprising given the fact that he was only 39 and had but one male heir, but his attachment to his wife seemed to grow stronger in the years after her death. Perhaps he realised the value of what he had lost, in emotional as well as political terms. He certainly had affairs and one of these resulted in the birth of another son in 1547, but he was deeply moved by his wife's passing. He immediately asked Mary to send to him any portraits that she had of Isabella and it is said that he always carried a miniature of her on his future travels.

# 20
# 'We also come from Ghent' – Imposing his Authority

Charles had only once visited the Low Countries since his departure in 1522. That was to oversee the introduction of Mary as regent in 1531. Even if some of the nobility and a number of lawyers had gained high positions in his service, as military commanders, advisers and ambassadors, the pride that many inhabitants of his homeland might have felt in having their ruler as the premier prince in Europe was wearing thin. There was still a strong personal loyalty to Charles as ruler. In the spring of 1531 the provinces had been generous in their grants to Charles, most agreeing to substantial 'aides' to be paid over a period of six years. Nevertheless the wide responsibilities taken on by Charles, together with the divided nature of the Low Countries, meant that many believed that they were being dragged into wars that did not concern them. There was a growing feeling that he was being ill-advised and that they were over-taxed as a result.

In 1534, with Charles' approval, Mary proposed that all the provinces should join a defensive union, with the cost of a standing army to be met by agreed contributions from all the provinces. While the smaller provinces were generally in favour, Flanders, Brabant and Holland (which as larger provinces would bear most of the costs) opposed the move. Negotiations lasted over a year but no agreement was reached. The idea was dropped. By 1536, as war once again broke out, the need to defend the provinces from attack by the French and the Duke of Guelders made the issue of renewing the 'aides' even more urgent than normal. Mary was clear in her communications to Charles that the situation was difficult and urged him to come from Italy to the Low Countries. Charles, though, had already decided that he should return to Spain. In reply to later requests for his personal support he wrote: 'I am only one and can't be everywhere; and I must be where I ought to be and where I can, and often enough only where I can be and not where I would like to be; for one can't do more than one can do'.[1] This could almost sum up the problems and frustrations that Charles faced throughout his reign. As a result he was more likely to respond to difficulties once they had arisen than to anticipate problems and nip them in the bud – to 'firefight' rather than pre-empt – but he certainly did not concede defeat.

He was well aware of his financial shortfall and urged Mary not to agree to an insubstantial sum. Rather she was to sell land if it became necessary while holding out for a satisfactory grant. In response to Mary's suggestion that the Low Countries should remain neutral, thereby saving expense, Charles pointed out that he could not guarantee peace if the French decided to attack. The talks that Mary's government held with the States-General and with each province were difficult. They did not wish their money spent on anything but their own defence and wanted their issues dealt with before any money was granted – the old argument of which should come first, redress of grievances or agreement to taxes. Mary's negotiators put forward various ideas for raising the money – an excise tax on beer, wine and high quality textiles; a tax on chimneys and smoke holes – but all were rejected. Members of the States-General declared that they were 'not rich enough to finance the Emperor conquering France and Italy'[2] but eventually, with French troops advancing into the Low Countries, an overall sum of 1.2 million gulden was agreed, with each province to raise their allocated amount as they wished.

Flanders was to pay its usual quota of one-third[3] but the city of Ghent refused to contribute, offering armed men, but no money. This had been done before especially when unemployment was high. Mary had assumed that the majority vote would be accepted by all and rejected Ghent's proposal, arguing that war required horses, munitions and wagons as well as men. But Ghent cited the Great Privilege of 1477 as the justification for their refusal to pay.

Even though the Truce of Bomy in July 1537 halted the war with France, the conflict with Ghent over taxation was not settled, even though the city was offered a large 'gracien' – a rebate on the amount that they had to pay, originally used to help towns in times of severe hardship, often caused by fire, war or floods. In January 1538 Charles sent a letter to the administration of the city stating that he had believed that 'in our absence, you would strive to aid, assist and serve us more than any other, because we also come from Ghent and were born in the city', but also pointing out that he would not ignore their refusal to pay if it continued.

Ghent was one of the great cities of medieval Europe. Built near the confluence of the rivers Leie and Scheldt it had developed around the abbeys of St Baaf's (St Bavo's) and St Pieter's (St Peter's), which had been wealthy enough to attract Viking raiders in the 9th century. From the 11th century growth was rapid. It became one of the seats of the Counts of Flanders and around 1180 Count Philip of Alsace constructed the Gravensteen fortress to dominate and intimidate the town. By the end of the 13th century it had a population approaching 50,000, making it second only to Paris in northern Europe. Its wealth was based on the woollen industry; wool was imported, particularly from England, and Ghent became the largest woollen cloth producer of the age. It was here that John of Gaunt (old English for Ghent), son of Edward III and Philippa of Hainault, was born in 1340. John (1340-1399) was founder of the House of Lancaster and his eldest son, Henry of Bolingbroke, became Henry IV (r.1399-1413) after deposing his cousin Richard II, and he was succeeded by his son Henry V (r.1413-1422) and then Henry VI (r.1422-1461; 1470-1471). The Yorkist Edward IV removed Henry VI during the Wars of the Roses, which ended with the victory of Henry VII of the House of Tudor in 1485, descended from John of Gaunt through his third wife, Katherine Swinford and the Beaufort family.

Ruled by the Dukes of Burgundy from early 15th century, Ghent often led resistance to the increase of ducal powers, defending the rights and privileges of the municipalities and resisting taxes imposed upon them. In July 1453 Philip the Good (r.1419-1467) had crushed a rebellion over high taxation by the people of Ghent at the Battle of Gavere, in which it is believed 16,000 inhabitants died. Philip did not totally destroy the city, as some feared he would, saying: 'If I would destroy this city, who is going to build me one like it?' Even though it was troublesome, Ghent was simply too valuable. It did not cease to cause problems for his successors, Charles the Bold (who had to flee from Ghent in 1467 when local inhabitants protested about restrictions on trade with England) and Maximilian. Most recently, Ghent had at first refused to pay towards an 'aide' in 1525. Charles then advised his regent, Margaret, to win them over with sweet words, but to make a note of the ring-leaders and later have them arrested and punished. This 'would be an example to others...and bring them to reason.'[4] This was the kind of action that would be expected from many rulers; it certainly fitted with Machiavelli's analysis of how to maintain power. Yet we have seen that Charles did not always follow such advice; if he gave his word on an issue he wished to keep it if at all possible. On this occasion too Margaret reached an agreement and did not then punish her opponents at a later date. Perhaps by 1538 her successor as regent was wishing that she had done so.

With no agreement over Ghent's taxes likely, Mary wrote to Charles in late 1538, after the truce with France when he was contemplating a major campaign again the 'Turk'. Described as 'the greatest of all her letters', showing her 'sincerity and intelligence'[5], Mary argued that his first duty was to his own subjects. He was the greatest of princes, but he should not begin a campaign on behalf of Christendom unless victory was certain. This would mean having the whole-hearted backing of Francis, the Pope, and Venice, and she questioned how much he could rely on them. The Ottomans could not be defeated in a single year and the resources required for a lengthy campaign would be enormous. If Charles were to be personally involved and take the obvious risks (she had no doubt that he would), he would leave his wife, his family, his lands and Christendom unprotected. Finally she implored him to wait until he had the support of all and had visited the Low Countries, Germany and Italy. A year later, as Mary had predicted, the desired circumstances for Charles' crusade had receded.

The difficulty with Ghent remained unresolved and to add to their offence the city did not join a delegation sent to Charles to offer condolences on the death of his wife, Isabella, in May 1539. Ghent must have been in Charles' mind when he wrote to his son Philip that the Low Countries were 'stubborn, and difficult with riots and mutinies, contempt, scorn and dislike of being governed by anyone whomsoever'[6]. Charles now concluded that his presence was needed there. He had been invited by Francis to travel through France and Charles had no wish to give offence by refusing this offer and going via Italy and the Empire or directly by sea. But with Isabella dead, he needed to make new arrangements for the governance of Spain before he could leave. Although Philip was only 12, Charles decided that he would be regent, with a regency council of trusted advisers to take on most of the responsibilities. Once again Cardinal Tavara was to take a leading role. Charles drew up for Philip the first of several political testaments, which provide us with a wealth of information about his views on government, and a will, in which he went into the many ideas and possibilities of political marriages for his family across Europe, aimed at securing both the Habsburg inheritance and peace with France. These were to be frequently revisited over the next decade. In the event of his death he left a large sum to pay for 30,000 masses for his soul and asked that he should be interred in Granada alongside Isabella, his parents and his Spanish grandparents.

Taking leave of Philip and then his mother, he travelled north from Tordesillas to Burgos, San Sebastian, and crossed into France near Bayonne in October 1539. With a large retinue he continued through Bordeaux and Poitiers, accompanied by Francis' sons, Henry (once Charles' prisoner and now the heir on the death of his older brother Francis in 1536) and Charles, Duke of Orleans. He was met by Francis at Loches on the river Indre, just south of Orleans. Charles had already sought assurances that matters of state would not be discussed, and was pleased that his wishes were acceded to, even though Francis was keen to push for Charles to marry his daughter, the 16 year old Margaret[7]. The emphasis was to be on pleasure and entertainment – hunting and jousts, banquets and balls. First at Orleans, at Fontainebleau for Christmas and then in Paris, Francis and Eleanor played host to the Emperor in grand style. Charles must have enjoyed the time spent with his sister with whom he had spent much of his first eighteen years He was greeted in the French cities with grand formal entries that, unsurprisingly, were more medieval in flavour, with less reference to Imperial glories of the past than those he had experienced in Italy. Here the harmony of princes through personal meetings and the virtues of maintaining peace were stressed. Everywhere there were gun salutes, fanfares and bells; local dignitaries made speeches to which Charles replied; in Poitiers a number of moral and historical mystery plays were performed[8].

Charles entered Paris on 1st January 1540 under a golden canopy, dressed in black with 'his only adornment being the gold chain of the Order of the Golden Fleece'[9], accompanied by Francis. A great crowd turned out to see the Emperor, who until recently had been the subject of so much hostile propaganda as the implacable enemy of France, as he passed under the triumphal arches on his way to the royal palace. The feasts, dances and tournaments continued, but Charles also attended mass with his sister, Eleanor, and gave an audience to those who wished to speak to him. Along with the rest of his company he was impressed by the fine buildings in Paris and by the beauty and elegance of the French court and its ladies. Francis may well have been Charles' lifelong political rival and someone who he had reason to distrust and dislike, but the French king did know how to turn on the charm and style. From Paris Charles progressed through Soissons, St. Quentin, Cambrai and on to Valenciennes where he was joined by his sister, Mary, and Charles in turn entertained his French guests. Peace with France, however, was to be relatively short-lived. The underlying causes of conflict had not been resolved and Francis was soon ready to take advantage

## Charles V: Duty and Dynasty

of Charles' problems elsewhere – in Germany, with the 'Turk', and initially with Ghent, the city of his birth.

Charles had arrived to impose his will on its inhabitants. He could not afford to ignore their refusal to pay taxes; such defiance, if successful, would undermine his authority throughout the Low Countries. The people of Ghent believed that they had a good case. The early sixteenth century had seen a gradual shift in economic and political power from Flanders (with Ghent and Bruges as the major cities) to Brabant (Brussels, Antwerp and Malines). Ghent had initially benefitted when Bruges' outlet to the sea silted up in the early fifteenth century, but itself now suffered from the rapid development of the cities of Brabant, especially the port of Antwerp. Its cloth trade had also experienced competition as English woollen cloth production expanded. These difficulties were felt strongly by the 1530's. Prices had risen sharply since 1500, but wages for most workers had remained the same or even declined. However, the city still had strong social and political traditions and institutions; its constitution allowed wide representation on the council with wealthy burghers, the guilds and the weavers (and now other workers) all electing aldermen.

More radical elements in the guilds demanded that the document relating to Charles' oath on his entry to the city as the new Count of Flanders in 1515, the 'calfvel' (calfskin), be handed over by the aldermen.* It was then ceremonially destroyed on 3rd September 1539, despite warnings from officials that this could have serious consequences. The existing authorities had lost control to the craft guilds, aided by many unskilled workers, the so-called 'creesers' ('shriekers'), who were taking the opportunity to make their voices heard. Aware of the importance of propaganda, the radicals also complained that a document which gave Ghent complete financial independence from its counts had been removed from the city's records. Mary denounced this document as a fiction, but it provided

---

* Many claimed its wording had been changed after the event in order to deny the citizens' rights.

a justification for the radicals to select new aldermen and guild deans, and declare that they would 'not accept the rule of a woman', specifically Mary of Hungary.[10] Some in Ghent who opposed these moves, or who refused to support them, and had not already fled the city, were executed, including Lieven Piet, a seventy-five year old magistrate, who was first put to the rack, accused of betraying the city's privileges. The initial unity of opposition to the taxes had broken down.

As Charles was leaving Spain a royal official arrived in Ghent representing Mary and the Emperor. It was made clear to the inhabitants that Charles was on his way to deal with them. After his arrival in the Low Countries in January 1540 Charles was visited by a deputation from Ghent who still thought that he would be sympathetic once he had heard their case. They were seriously misguided in this belief. After a visit to Brussels he moved on to Ghent, entering in full regal splendour 'accompanied by Mary, by a papal legate, by ambassadors, princes and nobles'[11] and 4,000 troops, in a five hour procession. Even before his arrival the majority had already agreed to pay the taxes, but by then it had become an issue about the right to rule.

Charles established himself in the Prinsenhof and his troops were quartered around the city to ensure that there was no opposition. He showed little sympathy for the city of his birth. On 17th February he called upon the leaders to surrender. The next day arrests took place and rewards offered for those who had slipped away. On Charles' 40th birthday the council was summoned and the accusations read out. The charges of 'breach of allegiance, disobedience, incitement to riot, mutiny' and 'lese-majeste' (offense against the dignity of the sovereign) could not have been more serious. It was made clear that for these crimes they could expect an exemplary punishment. Trials started and around 25 executions took place in the Gravensteen. There was no rush, emphasising who was in charge. A list of those executed shows the wide social range of those involved – from Simon Borluut, a lawyer at the Council of Flanders, to Hans van Kortrijk, a day labourer.

When Charles announced the final verdict on 29th April 1540 it included loss of all rights and privileges, an enormous fine, the confiscation of all weapons and ammunition, a reformed city administration and the ending of the political influence of the guilds, as well as the symbolic removal from the belfry of the city's famous bell, 'Roland', traditionally used to warn of approaching enemies or to celebrate a victory. The abolition of guild representation on the city council was in line with the belief that there was a close link between such representation and votes against tax proposals. Similar action had already been taken under Charles in Mechelen (1519), Tournai (1521) and s'Hertogenbosch (1525).[12] In addition, the old abbey of St. Bavo's was to be demolished and a fortress built on the site, to be paid for by the city, as a base for imperial troops to further intimidate the inhabitants. In a formal submission and humiliation on 3rd May 1540, 30 burghers, 6 representatives of each craft guild, and 50 'creesers' had to go in procession before the emperor, with their heads uncovered, barefoot, in plain white shirts, with nooses around their necks, to beg for mercy. It was granted. The submission of the inhabitants is now remembered in the annual procession of the Stroppendragers (the Guild of Noose Bearers), but it is not difficult to understand why there are so few memorials to Charles in the city of his birth.

## 21
## 'We must thank God for all' – Failure and Defeat

Having imposed his authority over Ghent, Charles was to need all his faith to help him deal with the failures that he was to experience in the following eighteen months. He wished to use the opportunity of peace with France to tackle both the worrying situation in Germany and the continued Ottoman menace in the Mediterranean. To do so he planned to use very different approaches – in Germany painstaking negotiation and in the Mediterranean force of arms. He knew that time was short and that relations with France were unlikely to remain amicable for long. Milan remained an unresolved point of conflict. Charles' decision to invest his son Philip with the fiefdom in October 1540 was the clearest signal yet to Francis that Charles was unlikely to relinquish control, regardless of the discussions of possible marriages between the two royal families, by which the French king hoped to gain either Milan or the Low Countries for a younger son.

Having spent the rest of 1540 in the Low Countries, Charles travelled into Germany with the intention of dealing with the problem that had been growing ever since the failure to bring Martin Luther and his followers back into the Catholic Church after the Diet of Worms in 1521. He had made a determined attempt to end the split in the church in 1530 at the Diet of Augsburg, but the continuing religious and political divisions had been an on-going source of difficulty for both Charles and Ferdinand. Both Protestants and Catholics knew that at some point in this conflict either side might resort to force. In February 1531 the Protestant princes had established the Schmalkaldic League, which they saw as an alliance for their own defence. Many people criticised Charles for not dealing more effectively with the growth of Protestantism. There is no doubt that he would have wished to do so but for most of his reign he had been heavily involved elsewhere. The reality was that if he wished to defend the entirety of his inheritance, which was so important to him, he would struggle to cope with all the other issues that he faced.

The Papacy had never been fully prepared to back Charles' initiatives to resolve the disputes within the church. Successive popes used his failure to do so in their propaganda battles with Charles; they found it useful to claim that the religious divisions in Germany were Charles' problem to deal with, not theirs. His long cherished plan for a general church council was always feared by the pope. Early in his reign, when his former tutor Adrian of Utrecht was elected to the papal throne by the congress of cardinals in January 1522, Charles really believed that they would be able to work together to achieve great things. He had been disappointed, though had not celebrated his death as had most in Rome. Adrian's successor, Clement VII, reverted to type – a Renaissance prince as well as a prelate. He was never going to agree to a council which would limit his scope for religious and secular manoeuvring, even when a virtual prisoner of Charles' forces after the sack of Rome. If necessary Clement made the right noises but that was all. With the election of Paul III in 1534 there seemed to be a better chance for Charles' plans, but for years he had continued to press for such a council, using the pope's dynastic ambitions as a lever, without success.

By 1540 the problems he had confronted in Augsburg ten years earlier had deepened. The 'Religious Peace' of 1532 had only been achieved because Charles needed agreement to deal with the Ottoman advance on Vienna. This permitted Protestant territories to continue with their new forms of worship. The Frankfurt 'interim' of 1539 again allowed this, at least until the holding of the long awaited general church council. Each time that the council looked possible, papal opposition and French influence derailed the plan. Charles' troubles in Germany could, after all, only benefit Francis who, while introducing harsh measures against Protestants in

France, was more than willing to negotiate and ally with those opposed to the Emperor in Germany.

But as Charles travelled to the Diet summoned to meet in Regensburg in early 1541 he had a renewed determination to tackle the dispute that had persisted for over twenty years. He was not at war with France, though relations were strained, and he hoped that the marriage of his natural daughter Margaret to Ottavio Farnese would result in support from Pope Paul. There were also growing divisions amongst the Protestants centred on the bigamous marriage of a leading Protestant ruler, Margrave Philip of Hesse. Back in 1523, shortly before he openly espoused the Lutheran cause, he had married Christine of Saxony. The marriage was without love, certainly on Philip's side, claiming that she disgusted him and he only shared her bed out of duty, even though their union managed to produce ten children! He was habitually unfaithful, gaining a reputation for 'adultery and fornication', and wished to salve his conscience by contracting another marriage within which he might be faithful. After years of requesting and failing to obtain approval for a divorce from Christine, in 1540 he married Margarethe von der Saale. Many of his co-religionists were troubled by his action and turned against him, leading him to seek an accommodation with Charles to secure his political position. Charles hoped to be able to make use of this situation. Against these advantages, Ottoman forces in the Mediterranean were still active and Charles was keen to lead a campaign against Barbarossa's base at Algiers as soon as possible.

Regensburg was in a state of upheaval as preparations for the Diet were made. Originally planned to begin in January, delays meant that Charles did not arrive until 23rd February and many other participants arrived even later. The impact of the arrival of thousands of visitors always required special arrangements. The Emperor, electors, princes, and representatives of the Imperial cities were accompanied by their advisers, servants, coachmen and grooms. Attracted by the possibility of rich pickings hordes of 'players, pedlars, stall-holders, whores, beggars and honest-to-goodness thieves' poured into the city. Armed patrols of up to one hundred men were organised each night. These were to protect law abiding residents and visitors alike. Nevertheless drunkenness and violence were widespread; bodies in the Danube were not an uncommon sight. The inns and lodging houses were packed, large markets were held daily selling food, clothes and everything else that a population on the move might need, and enormous kitchens set up to feed the visitors.[1]

The Diet was formally opened on 5th April 1541 with the Imperial procession following a route from Charles' accommodation in the Golden Cross Inn to the cathedral, for a mass, and from there on to the Alte Rathaus, where they were joined by the Protestants.[2] In the main hall, where the plenary meetings were held, Charles took the throne, with the electors on either side of him on a raised platform at the front. Facing them were the princes, both secular and ecclesiastical, and those from the cities, arranged according to status. Each estate was also provided with private rooms for their separate discussions, the scale of the room again reflecting the status of the estate – electors, princes, cities.* At the opening session Charles outlined the main issues and expressed his hopes for a full settlement of the religious question and agreement on the funding and rapid preparation of a military force to be used in the Mediterranean.

Charles hoped that rational discussion combined with his authority would be sufficient to settle the religious controversy. As a continuation of preliminary discussions that had been held during 1540 and early 1541, a colloquy was arranged so that a free meeting of minds in debate on a series of 23 issues (outlined in the

---

* From 1663 Regensburg became the home of the Permanent Diet. A visit to the Alte Rathaus provides a fascinating insight into the structure of the Holy Roman Empire and shows how meetings of the Diet were organised. The Imperial Hall (Reichsaal), where all estates met together, has the emperor's throne, various seats and benches raised to different levels indicating the relative standing of the three estates. The benches gave rise to the German saying 'to put something on the long bench', that is, to postpone it indefinitely.

Regensburg Book by Johannes Gropper) would produce a set of principles that all could agree to. This would then be presented to the Diet. Charles selected representatives (the collocutors) from Catholic and Protestant theologians, carefully balancing the more extreme – Eck (Catholic) and Melanchthon (Protestant) – with the more moderate – Gropper and Pflug (Catholic), Bucer and Pistorius (Protestant). The balance favoured conciliation if at all possible. Charles and his Chancellor, Granvelle, worked hard to win over moderate opinion.

Using a house on Haidplatz, the largest square in Regensburg, the collocutors approached the talks in a generally cooperative manner when they opened on 27th April. Agreement was reached on Articles I to IV and then also on Article V, on justification, expected to be a major sticking point. However, further discussions, on issues such as transubstantiation and the authority of the Church with regard to interpretation of the scriptures, revealed the depth of the divide. Cardinal Contarini, the Pope's representative, met daily with the Catholic collocutors and while keen for unity, had to protect the basis of papal power. On the other side, if such power was accepted then they would cease to be Protestants! At times Charles intervened, on occasions showing considerable irritation with both Catholic and Protestant zealots. The final debates took place on 22nd May. Much had been achieved, but it was not enough. Both groups now increasingly turned to a defence of their own position and apportioned the blame for the failure to others.

A disappointed Charles had to put before the Diet the amended Regensburg Book together with nine Protestant counter articles. When the Catholic princes could not accept even the 'agreed' articles, and John Frederick, Elector of Saxony, and Luther rejected the agreement over justification, any headway that had been achieved was lost. Charles' great desire for unification had led him to again overestimate the likelihood of success. The final statement by the Emperor on 29th July had to recognise that fact. It seemed to Charles that he alone wanted reconciliation; it had been rejected by the collocutors, the Pope, Luther, and both Catholic and Protestant estates at the Diet. Charles later recorded in his memoirs that 'after many controversies, very few things had been decided upon and still fewer had been executed'.

This was really the last occasion when Catholics and Protestants met together in an attempt to reunite the church with any hope of success. The failure of what had been lengthy and earnest talks persuaded Charles that he might need to take another approach. The differences were by now too great and too established for negotiation. Such was the nature of the splits in Germany that it must be considered unlikely that he could have reunified the church even if this had been his only concern. Indeed it could be argued that as a powerful emperor, with widespread lands elsewhere, he could bring far more pressure and influence to bear than a lesser figure with only the Holy Roman Empire. Charles looked carefully at his situation, positioning himself for a different kind of conflict. At the 1544 Diet in Speyer he again called for a coming together, but in reality he was beginning to think in terms of military action.

The Diet had started late and his five months at Regensburg had been spent with no positive outcome. The delay jeopardised Charles' plans for an attack on Algiers. Peace had not returned to the Mediterranean with his victory at Tunis. The conflict was a combination of piracy and large scale set piece operations by both sides. The seizure of merchant ships and raids on little protected coastal towns and villages right across the Mediterranean increased insecurity in the area. Added to this there were the massive fleets constructed in the arsenal on the Golden Horn in Istanbul and the forces put together by the various alliances struck by the Christian powers, notably Spain, Venice, the papacy, Genoa (allied to Charles) and the Knights of St. John. These fleets also carried out widespread raids, striking fear into all who saw their approach or even read reports of their departure from their harbours. Civilians had every reason to be apprehensive. The Knights of St John would show little mercy to any Muslims captured travelling on the Hajj; the Ottomans would take thousands as slaves and kill all that showed signs of resistance.

## Charles V: Duty and Dynasty

These naval forces played a major role in offensive operations against enemy bases, as had occurred in the Ottoman seizure of Rhodes (1522) and Charles' taking of Tunis (1535).* Logistics and the ability of the combatants to assemble their forces in the right place at the right time was central to their effectiveness. However, there were few major battles at sea. The commanders manoeuvred and threatened, sought to mislead their opponents, but were usually careful to avoid a direct confrontation. Quite simply the risks were too high. The expense of building and equipping the vessels and the need for the constant renewal of the manpower to row in the galleys, meant that a major defeat would be very costly. Perhaps more importantly, defeat would leave major targets exposed to enemy attack, which the very presence of a fleet could deter. The outcome of the only significant purely naval battle in Charles' reign, at Preveza in 1538, had been a psychological blow to Christian Europe.[3]

The key vessel in the Mediterranean in the 16th century was the war galley. Whilst having masts and able to use sail, in raids and battles it was the use of oars that gave them their particular value. The galley was relatively slender and low, with a shallow draught, fast and manoeuvrable, to some extent independent of adverse currents and moderate weather conditions. Galleys could stay close in to the shore and be run up on beaches for raids and for the collection of fresh water. Artillery could be mounted on the bows and be fired directly ahead from close to the waterline. However, it was prone to capsize in stormy weather so its campaigning season was usually limited to between March and October, and it could not travel large distances without collecting fresh water for the rowing crew. It depended on a regular supply of manpower, since mortality rates were high in the galleys even when not in battle.

The men in the Ottoman galleys were often conscripted from their territories, but they, like the Christian fleets, also used prisoners of war, convicts and slaves captured on raids often

---

* Later such campaigns included Charles' assault on Algiers (1541), and Ottoman attacks on Tripoli (1551 - successful), Malta (1565 – unsuccessful), and Cyprus (1570 – successful).

planned for that purpose. There were usually between 100 and 150 rowers in each galley. The large Venetian galleys by the mid-sixteenth century had 24 rowing benches with 3 rowers on each bench, on both sides of the ship – 144 rowers in all. Most were chained to their benches, supplied with minimal food and water, allowed little sleep and when in proximity to the enemy driven with whips. If they survived such treatment they could well succumb to disease which thrived in the insanitary conditions on board. The galley was little better than a sewer. It is said that they could be smelt two miles off and the most effective way to cleanse them and remove the filth and rats was to sink the hull periodically.[4] In battle the galley slaves could expect death from being blasted by cannon fire, drowning if their ship was holed at or below the waterline, or being crushed in collision with an enemy vessel.

The sequence of attacks by both sides brought misery to the inhabitants of Mediterranean islands and coastal areas. The Ottomans were gradually gaining the upper hand and in Istanbul ever larger fleets were built to assist Barbarossa. By 1540 Venice had no choice but to sign a treaty with Suleiman, very much on his terms. It was understandable therefore that in 1541 Charles was determined to aim a significant blow against the 'Turk'. As Mary had pointed out three years earlier, he lacked the resources to fulfil what he claimed was his real wish – a massive land campaign against Suleiman in south-eastern Europe followed by a joint land and sea attack on Istanbul. This was never a realistic prospect. Suleiman was again advancing into central Europe. A German army sent by Ferdinand was defeated and the Ottomans seized Buda in late August 1541. Suleiman then withdrew, perhaps short of resources and supplies just as he had been when advancing on Vienna in 1532.

Charles travelled south from Regensburg, through Munich to Innsbruck, and from there over the Brenner Pass, through Milan to Genoa, issuing orders for a fleet to be assembled and soldiers to be gathered ready for an assault on Algiers. His sister Mary advised him against such an attack, and he received no support from the Pope, who he met at Lucca. It was not until the end of September that Charles, with hundreds of vessels under Admiral Doria, and 24,000 German, Spanish and Italian troops commanded by Ferrante Gonzaga, was ready in the bay of Parma, Majorca. The risks were high. It was now so late in the year that conditions at sea could easily turn treacherous, but Charles ignored all warnings. Having completed his preparations he was unwilling to cancel the expedition.

It was late October before they arrived off the coast of Algiers, hampered continually by poor weather. Disembarkation of the soldiers was impossible on the 21st and 22nd October and so commenced on 23rd. It was still difficult to land provisions and horses; most soldiers had supplies for only two days and there were few tents for shelter from the rain that poured down. The troops rapidly advanced on Algiers, gaining possession of high ground overlooking the city. At this point the chances of success looked to be good. However, on the night of 24th-25th a great storm caused a large number of ships to lose their anchorage and many were destroyed on the rocks. Vessels holding provisions and munitions were scattered. It became impossible to land more troops or supplies. Battle was joined and both sides had limited successes and setbacks, though Charles' forces had to do without the planned bombardment of the city defences from the sea. Within days the lack of supplies made victory for Charles unlikely. He had to re-establish communications with some of his ships. Once this had been achieved, after two days in a difficult rear-guard action, Cortes, the conqueror of Mexico, present on the expedition, argued that Algiers could still be taken. Charles, however, agreed with the majority that withdrawal was the only realistic option. Eventually Doria was able to reassemble the remnants of the fleet and Charles' army marched to meet them under constant attack, though the final withdrawal was delayed by further storms until 23rd November. There were not sufficient vessels to save everyone. Horses were thrown overboard and even then many men were abandoned. The survivors reached Cartagena on the Spanish coast in early December.

Whatever Charles' motivation for this campaign, whether to protect his subjects or to enhance his reputation, its failure was costly. He had refused to take advice to delay the attack until the following year, probably because the mobilisation of his resources had already gone so far. His decision had resulted in extensive losses – perhaps as many as 140 sailing vessels, 15 galleys and 8,000 men, including 300 Spanish aristocrats.[5] There was no way that this could be talked up into a victory. But Charles remained calm. In a letter to his brother Ferdinand, he justified his decision to press ahead with the campaign, and concluded that 'We must thank God for all, and hope that after this disaster He will grant us of His great goodness, some great good fortune'.[6]

## 22
## 'You will be Troubled Enough for Money' – Family and Finances

Charles knew that it was unlikely that he would stay in Spain for long. He had written to Mary five months earlier, in August 1541, that he needed two years to settle matters in his other lands and he would then return to the Low Countries. He was to be true to his word. During his eighteen month sojourn in Spain Charles certainly did not ignore his other responsibilities or stop working to achieve his wider aims, but he had plenty to occupy him in Spain – his family, Spanish finances and developments in the Americas. These issues might have been regarded as specifically Spanish but like so much in Charles' life they had consequences that would impact much more widely.

On his return he met his children – Philip, now 14, Maria, 13, and Juana, 6 – at Ocana and they travelled with his court through Toledo and Madrid to Valladolid. Charles had never developed a close relationship with them in their early years. This was not unusual for monarchs at the time, nor was it surprising. Charles had not experienced an intimate bond with either of his own parents. More than any ruler at the time he was for ever on the move and the children were bought up by trusted personal servants. As they became older Charles found it easier to relate to them. He always found it easier to talk about matters of state than feelings and emotions, and the elder children were now of an age to become involved in such issues. Philip had been regent in Charles' most recent absence, and was soon to be so again. He was to be the recipient of Charles' 'political testaments', documents that provide the clearest insight into the mature Charles' beliefs, thinking and ultimate aims. They also show the care and attention that Charles took in the political education of his son, following Erasmus' advice in 'Education of a Christian Prince'. Maria was now to figure large in his dynastic marriage plans, the means by which he hoped to achieve a permanent settlement throughout Europe. It was the youngest, Juana, who suffered most – losing her mother when she was four, hardly ever seeing her father and then only when she was too young for the reticent, reserved Charles to be able to establish anything like closeness.

If he had any doubts about his own life, the way in which his heavy duties were dealt with seriously and conscientiously at the expense of a lighter and more joyful approach, they did not see the light of day in his plans for his children. They were to be monarch and consorts, to further the destiny of the family as the leading rulers in Christendom. He wished them to have an education that would enable them to take on the responsibilities that being born into this family would entail. Unlike Charles, with his Burgundian background, they were brought up as Spaniards. Philip's development may have been rather limited early on; he was slow to learn to read and write – his writing was never easy to understand. But he gradually developed a love of books, music and tapestries. He certainly acquired his father's love of hunting – Charles had to set a weekly limit on the number of animals that were killed.[1] Philip's behaviour, the development of self-discipline and his physical well-being were entrusted to his god-father, Don Juan de Zuniga, a major figure in the first twenty years of his life. In 1543 Charles wrote to Philip that: 'Every man needs advice, and so I ask you to make Don Juan de Zuniga your watch and alarum in all things. I too have commanded him to do his own part therein and to speak sharply if he must. ...therefore remember that he only acts out of devotion and duty to me, and be grateful to him'.[2]

In the same year Charles also warned Philip: 'You will be troubled enough for money, for you will soon learn how slender are your revenues and how heavily mortgaged'[3]. Charles, hampered by financial worries, wanted to be sure that Philip was aware of the difficulties – fearing that it would be all too easy for someone brought up at court to assume that such problems could easily be dealt with. Philip soon appreciated the problem. Later, in 1543 while regent, he wrote to his father that for 'the common people' the level of taxation was resulting in 'such misery that many of them walk naked'. Such letters from his regents and viceroys complaining of the difficulties caused by high levels of taxation and describing the suffering of his subjects were frequent. But Charles regarded these lands as his personal property and therefore expected them to provide him with what was required for his, and therefore his subjects', dignity and reputation. That they did not readily supply the sums needed caused Charles considerable problems. He was not personally extravagant in terms of dress, buildings, art and other conspicuous expenditure compared with many of his contemporaries. However, travel with a sizeable household was expensive, as was the need to maintain a certain style in keeping with his position – tournaments, balls, hunts, generosity towards those around him – and, of course, his wars had to be paid for.

People across his various lands all claimed that they suffered most, because money was being taken out of their territory to fund Charles' activities elsewhere. There are numerous reasons why it was difficult to determine exactly what revenues were spent on which areas of expenditure: the geographical spread of Charles' territories; the various forms of taxation and other royal income in each territory; the different traditions, rights and privileges in each area; the reality that when money was urgently needed it would be taken from whichever source had money available; and the fact that because subjects in one territory strongly opposed their taxes being spent on campaigns and enterprises elsewhere, there was some deliberate vagueness in the accounts. There were no clear-cut series of account books, with identified sources of income and heads of expenditure for each of his individual territories. It was usually made clear when an army was raised where the responsibility for paying for it, and for how long, rested. However, any calculation of the contribution of a particular territory towards the cost of wider Imperial policies needed to exclude, for instance, the costs of defending that territory which might have occurred anyway. Some costs were paid directly by the territory in which the expenditure incurred and never appeared in the Imperial accounts at all. Certainly the Low Countries, as one of the wealthiest areas of Europe, paid substantial taxes and often complained bitterly about it, but the costs of its defence were also high. The same was true of Milan where the high taxes were spent on the Imperial army based there. Naples also made a considerable contribution to Charles' revenues,[4]* unlike Germany which was without doubt the hardest of his territories to raise money in.[5]† Charles himself recognised that it was Spain that provided him with the greatest financial support. It was certainly not immune from financial and economic difficulties but Charles believed that 'I cannot be sustained except by my realms in Spain'[6].

In Spain itself Charles had to finance the cost of his court, as well as that of Philip and his mother Juana, still in Tordesillas. There were also the expenses associated with the fleet, both the Spanish and a major contribution to Admiral Doria's, the defence of the Mediterranean coast against the privations of Barbarossa and corsairs, and the maintenance of the army to protect northern Spain from incursions from France over the Pyrenees. Revenues also had to cover the cost of debts already incurred, both in Spain and on Charles' military campaigns elsewhere.

A large number of different sources contributed to Charles' Spanish revenues. There were the ordinary incomes from estates and mines owned by the king, from tolls and customs duties, and a range of revenues from the church which included the 'tercias reales' (a proportion of the church tithes that went to the crown),

---

* It has been estimated that probably 40% of the 'donativi', additional subsidies over and above ordinary revenues, was spent on ventures outside the kingdom of Naples.

† An estimated 4.3 million guilders (2.2 million ducats) were collected specifically for Charles' use in over 35 years. If this figure is correct then it represented a tiny fraction of Charles' total revenues and came nowhere near matching what he must have spent in Germany, whether it be on bribes to the electors or military campaigns against Protestant and other rebellious princes.

the 'subsidio' (a tax on clerical incomes), and the 'cruzada' (originally to help fight the Muslims). However the main regular tax in Castile was the 'alcabala', a sales tax at between 5% and 10% for most of Charles' reign (although rates could vary from area to area) which was payable by all subjects whatever their status. As in most states at the time with their restricted administrative capabilities, the 'alcabala' was 'farmed out' to collectors, often a local government or merchant guild, who bought the right to collect the tax within a certain area in return for payment of a fixed sum to the crown. During Charles' reign inflation had the effect of reducing the real value of this fixed sum.[7] Another regular source of income was the revenue from the three orders of ecclesiastical knights, the Santiago, the Calatrava and the Alcantara, of which Charles became head in 1523. The Fugger family first gained the rights to this income in 1524, in return for loans, and held them for most of the time until 1634.

Since these ordinary revenues were never sufficient, Charles also made extensive use of extraordinary income. This could come from the sale of crown lands, government positions, certificates of nobility and monopolies. However the main additional income was from subsidies, known as 'servicios', agreed by regional representative bodies, the Cortes of Castile and Aragon. Originally these were voted to provide additional funds for the monarch in particular times of need, but they became a regular and increasing feature of Charles' income. The average amount provided by Castile, for instance, trebled between 1520 and 1555 to over 400,000 ducats annually.[8] The nobility were exempt from the 'servicio', unlike the 'alcabala', and so were likely to vote for it, supporting Charles in the Cortes, because they did not have to bear the consequences, thus increasing the divisions within Spanish society. Charles' efforts to increase the taxation paid by the nobility came to nought, as in 1538 when a proposed new food tax (the sisa), to be payable by all, was blocked by the nobility. Charles did not continue with the plan; he could not risk losing their loyalty, even though in 1543 he remained convinced that it was the best way 'to get us out of our troubles in peace and war'.⁹

As Charles was still short of money he frequently had to resort to borrowing, using his assets and anticipated revenues as security. The loan agreements were of two main sorts, 'asientos' and 'juros'. The 'asientos' were short term loans made by bankers repayable by a specified date in a certain place (e.g. in Spain, often Medina del Campo; in the Low Countries, Antwerp). There were high rates of interest ('payment for trouble, danger and expense' or a 'handling fee'); 15-20% in a year was not uncommon, rising to even higher rates in the 1550s when the risk of non-payment increased. The 'floating debt' that built up through late payment was damaging to Spain. The 'juros', on the other hand, were longer term loans or annuities, at much lower rates of interest, typically 4-8%, which were funded by specific revenues, such as the 'alcabala', with guaranteed payment at fixed intervals. Once issued these could be bought and sold on the open market. As Spain (especially Castile) became a major source of Charles' revenues, particularly when raising money in other territories became more of a problem, the amounts needed for repayment increased considerably. In the early part of his reign the 'juros' repayments took approximately one-third of normal crown income; by 1550 it had reached two-thirds. Despite this, the 'juros' were preferable to the high interest 'asientos'. Later, in the financial crisis of 1557, Philip II converted the various 'asientos' debts into long term 'juros'.

On occasions Charles' finances benefitted from one off 'windfalls'. During the late 1520s he received several significant sums. His marriage to Isabella of Portugal had generated a dowry of one million ducats. The transfer of the Moluccas to the Portuguese crown by the treaty of Zaragoza in 1529 raised another 350,000 ducats. The ransom paid by Francis I for the release of his sons, again in 1529, was worth one million ducats. Other sources included papal grants for campaigns against the Ottomans and Protestants, and sums from princes in return for confirmation of their powers, for instance the payments by Francisco Sforza of Milan. The gold and silver bullion deliveries from the New World were initially regarded as 'windfall' but the annual convoys provided a regular, if variable, income that was to grow in importance.

By 1542, as the value of the bullion was increasing rapidly, it was a puzzle to many in Spain why these vast riches did not bring widespread prosperity. The 16th century was a period of considerable inflation. The inflow of bullion, by increasing the money supply, may have been the greatest cause of this inflation.[10] At the time it was not widely understood that the value of the silver is relative not absolute – the increase in the supply of silver reduced its value. In 1556 Martin de Azpilcueta Navarro, a lawyer, perceptively wrote: 'We see by experience that in France, where money is scarcer than in Spain, bread, wine, cloth and labour are worth much less. And even in Spain, in times when money was scarcer, saleable goods and labour were given for very much less than after the discovery of the Indies, which flooded the country with gold and silver. The reason for this is that money is worth more where and when it is scarce than where and when it is abundant'[11].

However, the highest inflation rate seems to pre-date the period of greatest bullion deliveries and it is questionable how much of the bullion actually remained in Spain. It was used by Charles to finance overseas wars and to service his debts, while much of the rest was used to pay for foreign goods, since the cost of imported manufactured goods far exceeded the value of Spain's exports. On several occasions during Charles' reign, the Cortes of Castile petitioned that bullion should not be exported from the country, but little changed. That which remained was more often associated with conspicuous expenditure on luxury items rather than being invested for longer term development.

There were also other inflationary pressures. The population was growing, especially in the middle decades of the 16th century, when the population of Castile grew by 50%[12], more in the south than in the north, with the growth in cities usually outstripping that of the surrounding rural areas[13]. Prices rose considerably during Charles reign, more so in Andalucia, less so further north. Grain became more expensive, perhaps doubling in price during the first half of the 16th century, while olive oil prices increased even more. These increases were not matched by comparable wage rises for most people. Thus in Valladolid, while price rises on staple foods ranged from 40% - 60% (1511–1550) and land and house rents rose by perhaps 80%, wages rose by less than 30%.[14]

Taxation was always relatively high for both townspeople and the rural population. Those that had capital – whether nobility or well-off merchants – ultimately aimed to live off rents and unearned income (by lending the money to Charles' government) rather than from wealth creating ventures where the returns were longer term and less certain. Consequently little was invested in manufacturing. The wealthy and influential went into the army, royal service, the law or the church, but not business.[15] Industry and commerce had also been harmed by the earlier expulsion of the Jews and Muslims who had often thrived in business, when other avenues had been close off to them.

Woollen cloth production, which developed particularly around Segovia, might have flourished but much of the raw wool was exported (particularly the highly valued merino wool), processed elsewhere, often in the Low Countries, and then imported as finished products, to the cost of the Spanish economy. The training of the required skilled workers was often poor, resulting in low quality products. The 'mesta', the powerful association of landowners (3% of the population owned 97% of the land in Castile) who used their lands to graze sheep and prevented the incursion of arable farming, had a negative impact on food production. Demand for goods from the rising Spanish population in the New World added to the inflationary pressures. It meant an increase in the production of goods such as wine and olives for export to the Americas at the expense of self-sufficiency in staple food products at home. Shortages of food meant higher prices, disadvantaging the majority of the population. The low paid and those only able to obtain seasonal work suffered most in both town and countryside. Vagrancy became a problem, especially when it threatened the maintenance of law and order. This can be seen in the writings of humanists such as Juan Luis Vives, who advocated a prohibition on begging, and the use of 'hospitals' for the needy to provide both material and spiritual help.[16]

Rising food prices might be expected to have benefitted the rural population. Certainly the large landowners among the nobility and church hierarchy who were able to put up rents increased their income. For the peasants, who farmed the limited amount of communally held land and rented more from the landowners, life was hard. The combination of increased rents, generally low yields resulting from extending the area under cultivation without improving techniques, a restricted amount of good arable land, together with taxation, meant that it was difficult to make ends meet. Such hardships encouraged a general movement from the countryside into the towns, especially in the south, recruitment into the army (Spanish troops were increasingly valued across Europe) and even the hope of seeking a fortune in the New World. It also had a negative effect on Spanish industry. The lack of the growth of the purchasing power of this large sector of the population meant that no internal market developed for the manufactured goods produced[17]. Higher prices of raw materials also meant that Spanish products became more expensive than those of other countries and Spain's external markets began to look elsewhere.

There were areas of success. In the north, wealth was often based on the export of wool to the Low Countries. Burgos in the 1520's was described by the Venetian ambassador Andreas Navagero as having many artisans, some noblemen, 'but the majority of its inhabitants are rich merchants, who travel on business not only throughout Spain but all over the world'. Medina del Campo was a developing financial centre, where families like the Ruiz had made money from the wool trade and broadened their interests into other commercial and financial enterprises, including the provision of credit[18]. In the south, Seville, with its monopoly of trade with the 'Indies', grew rapidly and great fortunes were made by some of those involved, but there is little to suggest that the wider population gained much benefit from this. Trade and finance was often in the hands of foreign merchants from ports such as Genoa and Antwerp, as well as Germany and England. The Genoese in particular benefitted from the removal of restrictions on their activities by Charles as a reward for the loyal support of Admiral Andrea Doria after 1528. Though many vessels used in the trans-Atlantic trade were constructed in northern Spain, the ports there were excluded from participation. In Aragon, Barcelona was already in decline by 1520 as trade gradually shifted away from the Mediterranean, and like other eastern ports it too was not permitted to participate in trade with the New World.[19].

Charles left considerable debts both to his son as his successor in Spain and the Low Countries, and to the people of his territories. He might have won the support of many in Spain for increasing Spanish influence across Europe and opening opportunities for some in military, diplomatic and financial careers, but little was done for the economic well-being of the majority of Spain's inhabitants. By the mid-1550's he had borrowed the equivalent of 28 million ducats and had repayment obligations across his lands of 39 million ducats. This gets to the heart of what is often seen as one of Charles' greatest failing. During the reign of his successors in the late 16th and 17th centuries these financial and economic problems became ever more apparent.

In the early months of 1543, as he made plans to leave Spain, the country which provided him 'the means with which he waged his wars' and where he had 'built the future of his dynasty'[20], Charles took two measures that he hoped would benefit both Spain and his family ambitions. The first was to arrange the marriage of sixteen year old Philip to his double cousin, Maria Manuela of Portugal. Of the same age as Philip, she was the daughter of King John III, brother to Empress Isabella, and Catherine, Charles' sister. Of the Portuguese king's nine children only two were to reach their teens, Maria Manuela and her brother, Joao Manuel, who later married Charles' younger daughter Juana. The Portuguese link was always popular in Spain and this would hopefully secure the dynasty by the production of another heir.

The second measure was to appoint Philip as regent (a prince of blood always had more authority as a regent) and ensure that the Cortes of Castile and the kingdoms of Aragon, Catalonia and Valencia acknowledged him as regent and heir. He again appointed an inner council of his most experienced and trusted advisers – Cardinal Tavera, Francisco de los Cobos and Don Hernando de Valdes. He produced for Philip a full and frank set of instructions and advice, both personal and political, on the role that he would be taking on, to make him aware of the risks and dangers that faced him. As he had done for Isabella he gave Philip information about his advisers at court and urged him to become a student of men so that he too could benefit from the sound judgement which served Charles well. Charles' treatment of his main advisers is in marked contrast to the actions of some of his contemporaries. Henry VIII, for instance, often gave his chief ministers, such as Wolsey and Cromwell, very wide ranging powers, only for them to be removed and often executed when he considered that they had failed him, different policies were needed or new men were able to work their way into his favour. Charles, on the other hand, was remarkably consistent in his use and treatment of his advisers. This was possible because he usually had an accurate gauge of their strengths and weaknesses, their character and their ambitions. He had realistic expectations of these men and what they could do for him.

Charles explained to Philip his reasons for departing Spain on a journey that he considered 'the most dangerous for (my) reputation and honour'.[21] He had therefore 'resolved upon this experiment of leaving you to govern in my stead' even though 'you are still young to bear such a burden'. Philip was to 'be a friend to justice', the administration of which he regarded as second only to duty to God and the Church. He advised Philip that it must be tempered with mercy 'after the manner of our Lord', and that it should not be the 'fruit of passion, prejudice or anger'. He should be 'calm and reserved' and 'easy of approach and pleasant in manner; listen to good advice and take heed of flatterers as you would of fire'.

In government Charles told Philip that he would have plenty of assistance and Charles beseeched him to support the royal council and to follow the instructions that he himself had left regarding the Council of the Indies, finances, the Order of the Golden Fleece, and the Inquisition, but to have 'a special care to finance, which is today the most important department of state'. Charles continued that there must always be two signatures on documents, and although Cobos 'will read everything through carefully before you sign it, you must be ready to take the final responsibility'. After commending 'to your care the Queen (Juana)' and 'your sisters', Charles expressed his wish that Maria and Juana should continue in the retired life to which they are accustomed and not to 'let more gentlemen enter the room (in their presence) than is necessary'. Although well-educated and prepared for their future roles, Charles' daughters had always been rather isolated from the full social activities of the court.

Charles then turned to Philip's personal conduct. The testament gives an insight into what Charles regarded as important for a young ruler, having learnt from his own experiences and mistakes, although this could be seen as the usual plea to a young man to avoid the temptations that would come his way from a man well into his middle years. After pointing out that his 'early marriage and your calling to the regency make a man of you long before your time', he emphasised the importance of study, especially languages, coupled with good company, as being the 'only means by which you will gain honour and reputation'. So far Philip has had 'boys for company' but he now needed to 'seek the company of older men'. 'You must gain the knowledge and judgement which will enable you to do a man's work'. Charles is concerned that Philip will need to learn 'how best to deal with those who try to become your boon companions by splintering lances with you, riding at the ring, jousting and hunting, or who try to tempt you to more unworthy pleasures. You would do wisely to show no pleasure in the company of those who are for ever making unseemly jokes'.

As Philip was about to marry, fatherly advice seemed appropriate. He commended Philip's chastity to this point and warns not to 'give yourself over too much to the pleasures of marriage... as undue indulgence may not only injure your health...(but) even cut short your life as it did of your uncle' (Prince Juan who married Margaret of Austria in 1497 only to die six months later). Charles continued: 'I advise you, shortly after your marriage, to find some excuse for leaving your wife, and do not come back to her very soon, nor stay with her long'. He also urged Philip 'do not let yourself be tempted into any follies (with women)... such things are a sin to God and a scandal in the eyes of your wife and the world'. Charles pointed out that in politics there are 'more exceptions than rules' and that 'even older men than you need someone to keep them constantly alive to their duty and to remind them what has to be done'. Having commended his godfather Don Juan de Zuniga as his most suitable guide in such matters, he later added that 'Zuniga may appear rough and hard, but do not forget that he is a devoted servant who thinks only of your good'.

Charles realised the importance of balancing the influence of various advisers. He urged his son to be impartial: 'Make it clear to everyone that you hold yourself aloof from all parties and quarrels' and avoid 'becoming the instrument of their feuds'. Charles goes on to write about various senior figures at court in Spain, including his closest advisers, and in such a way that it is obvious why he asked Philip to keep the information to himself. 'The Cardinal of Toledo is a good man and in all serious questions you can rely on his honesty. Only do not subject yourself wholly to his influence, lest men should say, on account of your youth, you were but a tool in his hand'. The Duke of Alva 'can be counted on to support whichever party best suits his private interest...He is ambitious (and) will do his best to make himself agreeable to you, probably with the help of female influence. Take heed of him, therefore; yet trust him implicitly in all military matters'.

'Cobos is growing older and easier to manage, but he is true. The danger with him is his ambitious wife. No one knows so much of all my affairs as he, and you will always have reason to be glad of his service.' Charles considered that 'circumstances not he are to blame for the deplorable condition of our finances'. Cobos had achieved great wealth, much of it through bullion from the New World, but Charles advised his son not to allow the privileges that Cobos has built up to become hereditary. Charles wrote that Philip should not bestow major office on the 'Duke of Alva, who will probably ask for it. And do not give it to a son of Cobos or of Zuniga, for...great experience is needed. Cobos has a daughter married to the Viceroy of Aragon, but the Viceroy was only given the place because of all possible candidates, he was the least bad.' Charles explained that Cobos and Zuniga are 'of rather a different social stratum from the others' (less hereditary wealth and therefore a greater need to gain positions for their children) but he recognises that 'each in their own way, will prove your best servants'. Of others Charles again expressed his views succinctly. Granvelle 'will be your best guide in international policy. He too has some private interests in Burgundy and several sons to provide for, yet I think him honest'. However 'the Duke of Orsino is sly and deceitful, but he speaks so little it is hard to see through him. In his office as president of the council of the Golden Fleece he is thought to be masterful and haughty; see to it therefore that he has good advisers to assist him.'

Charles knew that once he had left Spain, such were the demands that would be made upon him, he might not return for a significant period of time. He had done his best to leave the country in good order, with a sound, secure government, and to establish his son as his undisputed heir. Its economy and finances were not particularly healthy but Charles hoped that if the next few years brought about victory against France, a religious settlement in Germany and a reduced threat from the Ottomans, then the consequent fall in his expenditure would improve the position. He was not to know in 1543 that he would not set foot again in Spain for thirteen years by which time his place in the world had completely changed.

## 23
## 'The Greed of Some of Our Subjects' – Faith and Bullion

The additional money brought into Spain by the early convoys from the Americas was very welcome to Charles, who as monarch received one-fifth of the bullion (the *quintus*). The approximate average annual value to Charles of this was a modest 40,000 ducats in the 1520s, rising to 280,000 ducats in the 1540s and 871,000[1] in the early 1550s. He also claimed the right to take more of the silver in return for 'juros' to be repaid from future Spanish revenues – in effect a forced loan. At times he used this to help meet his immediate expenditure and used future bullion shipments as security against loans. While in Italy in 1536 Charles had written to Isabella: 'Rally the people, look for money everywhere, and if God should send money from Peru, lay hands on it even if it is consigned to individuals'[2].

Charles' accession had coincided with the expansion of Spanish territories in the New World. Earlier settlements in the Caribbean, particularly on Hispaniola and Cuba, had been followed by the invasions of the Aztec Empire in Mexico by Hernando Cortes (successful in 1521) and then of the Inca Empire in the Andes by Francisco Pizarro (1532). There were two key motives: to spread Christianity and to gain riches. How such small forces were able to defeat these large empires has been well described and explained by others[3]. With the promise of land and riches there was no shortage of conquistadores and settlers from Spain, many from the lesser nobility who lacked a role in Spain with the completion of the Reconquista[4]. This was less than forty years after the Spanish Pope Alexander VI (Rodrigo Borgia) had issued a papal bull in 1493 which gave Spain rights to newly discovered lands to the west of a pole to pole line 100 leagues west of the Portuguese Cape Verde islands. This line was shifted a further 270 leagues to the west the following year by the Treaty of Tordesillas between Spain and Portugal (who gained the rights to lands to the east of the line). Spanish control of much of central and southern America was thus firmly established.

Charles and his predecessors had given permission for the expeditions in the hope of benefits, but they were not willing or able to share in the costs of opening up these 'new' lands[5]. Charles did not wish to take title 'Emperador de Indies' (Emperor of America), but this reliance on private initiative meant that the crown would have less control[6]. However, he soon became aware of the growing revenues that were being generated, and was naturally keen to share in the profits to be made through trade, which was to be controlled and taxed, and through the ever increasing bullion. Once mined and refined this had to be transported by llama/mule from the mines, often situated high in the Andes, down to the Pacific coast. It was then shipped north to Central America (the 'Spanish Main'), across the isthmus to the Atlantic Ocean and thence by the annual treasure convoys back to Seville. These convoys were to become the target of English and French 'privateers' (pirates as far as the Spanish were concerned) such as Walter Raleigh, Guillaume Le Testu, and Francis Drake in the late 16th century.

Although having no direct role in the colonisation of these lands, once they were part of Castile Charles could not abdicate all responsibility for them. From the early days of settlement, before Charles' time, the powers in Castile wanted the New World to be 'Spanish', closed to any other outside influence. The aim was to achieve the cultural assimilation (Hispanization) of the inhabitants. There would be no foreign trade and no foreign missionaries[7]. Seville experienced rapid growth and gained great wealth based on the monopoly of trade with the New World. From as early as 1493 the settlement and administration of the colonies was under the jurisdiction of Juan Rodriguez de Fonseca, Bishop of Burgos[8]. After his death the Council of the Indies was established in 1524 to oversee the administration of these new territories, always a difficult task given the distances involved, the slowness of communications, delays in responding to petitions, and the independent nature of the conquistadores and settlers.

An important part of the authority given to Spain by the Pope was 'to instruct the aforesaid inhabitants in the Catholic faith, and train them in good morals'. How this was to be achieved and how the native inhabitants should be treated became an issue of on-going concern and debate within Spain and across Europe. The religious, moral and ethical issues that Charles attempted to resolve resonate through the centuries, right up to the present time. The existence of a large population with a completely different culture created practical and moral problems.[9] How were they to be administered and what methods could be used to convert the native inhabitants to the 'true faith'? Had God given America to the Spaniards so that they could save souls or to fully exploit the resources found there?[10]

In 1511 the Dominican priest Antonio de Montesinos had preached to settlers about the exploitation of Hispaniola and its people: 'You are all in mortal sin...on account of the cruelty and tyranny with which you use these innocent people'. This was in reference to the 'encomienda' system which gave settlers control over local native communities, with the responsibilities of converting them to Christianity and 'protecting' them, in return for their use as cheap labour in the exploitation of local resources. This system had been introduced because slavery had been forbidden by Queen Isabella at the time of the first settlements (though with some exceptions)[11], but the reality for the indigenous population was that it was slavery under a different name. Initially intended for one or two years, the 'encomienda' was extended to the life of the recipient and one inheritor on the grounds that this would encourage better treatment of the people because the settlers would then have an interest in their longer term welfare.[12] The 1512 'Laws of Burgos' emphasised that the settlers must diligently instruct their subjects in the Holy Faith. In fact little was done to teach or instruct; the whole system was geared to getting as much work out of the labour force as possible.

Alongside the '1512 Laws' was the 'requerimiento' (Spanish Requirement) of 1513. This was a declaration of Spain's rights to the territories of the New World and was to be read in Castilian to the local inhabitants. It explained that they were privileged to be subjects of the king of Castile. There followed an account of how God had created the world and passed powers on to the popes, who had given the kings of Castile power over their lands. They therefore needed to recognise the Church, the pope, and the king of Castile. The message then asked that 'you take the time that shall be necessary to understand and deliberate upon (what we have said to you), and that you acknowledge the Church as the ruler and superior of the whole world. But if you do not do this...we shall make war against you in all ways that we can; we shall take you, your wives and your children and enslave them, and we shall confiscate your possessions'. How much of this was properly understood is questionable.

At a meeting in 1523 Charles outlined to Hernan Cortes his preferred manner of introducing the native population to Spanish rule. It should be repeatedly explained to them in their own language what the consequences of not submitting would be and only then should force be used. In November 1526, after a meeting of the Council of the Indies in Granada, a Royal Ordinance commented on the 'greed of some of our subjects who go to the Indies', and listed the abuses – great and excessive labour, lack of food and clothing, cruel punishments – that were causing large numbers of deaths.[13] It emphasised to the conquistadores the importance of explaining the virtuous motives of the Spaniards – to give them the true faith and to stop evil practices – and to priests their responsibility to teach Christianity and prevent the abuses.[14] In 1532 Charles was informed that, because of the warlike nature of the people, force was necessary to ensure the safety of settlers and to spread the faith.[15] The papal bull of 1537 issued by Paul III stated that the native people were rational beings, capable of understanding and receiving the faith, and gave Charles and the Spanish monarchy full rights in the Americas.

These statements point to the underlying conflict in the attitude of European rulers generally, in this case specifically the Spanish crown, to colonisation and the treatment of the native inhabitants. On the one hand Charles had a responsibility to care for his subjects (the 'real consciencia'). On the other he had the duty to develop and exploit the new lands for the benefit of the country and the individual settlers who had risked much in the colonisation (the 'real servicio')[16], especially if the crown delegated to the settlers the important role of converting the Indians. The perceived self-interest of the settlers would mean that little attention would be given to humanitarian concerns if left ungoverned. Charles was worried that the settlers who received large areas of land (the 'encomiendores') would challenge royal power. Unsurprisingly there was increasing tension between the appointed royal officials and the 'encomiendores'.

Efforts were made to control the powers of the Spanish settlers. In 1523 further expansion was restricted until there could be greater confidence in the proper treatment of the inhabitants, but such was the pressure for land and labour that the orders were rapidly revoked. The issuing of new 'encomienda' was to be stopped, but this was immediately made irrelevant; Cortes had already started handing them out to reward those who had assisted him in the conquest of Mexico. In 1526 regulations were issued to limit the number of workers in an 'encomienda' to 300. This had little effect; by 1535 the average number in a Mexican 'encomienda' was 6,000[17]. Slavery was again forbidden in 1526, but the exceptions – that people could be enslaved if they refused to accept Spanish rule, refused to accept missionaries, or resisted the discovery and exploitation of mines – opened the way for widespread abuse.[18]

The introduction of a royal 'Audience' (a group of high ranking royal officials), to act as the highest court of appeal, did help to provide some protection for indigenous people who wished to challenge the way they were treated. In theory they could have access to the legal system without having to pay for the cost of litigation.[19] The appointment of members of the highest Spanish nobility as Viceroy of New Spain – Antonio de Mendoza (1535 – 1550) and Luis de Velasco (1550 – 1564) – gave more status to the role; these were people whose decisions had to be taken notice of.[20] There was vacillation on the part of the Spanish government on how best to bring their new subjects into the Spanish culture. Charles' initial belief was to have them living side by side with the Spanish settlers, who would provide an example and a model for them. Mendoza was specifically asked to see if this was useful for encouraging conversions. By the end of Charles' reign it seems likely that ideas had shifted; the massive population decline amongst the pre-colonial population and the continuation of abuses suggested that separation might be more successful, with missionaries and priests taking on the teaching role.[21]

Most closely associated with the cause of the native people was the Dominican priest, Bartolomé de las Casas (c. 1484 – 1566). Born in Seville, he witnessed the return of Columbus from his first voyage and his father and uncles joined expeditions to the Americas during the 1490s. He travelled to the New World in 1502, took part in the conquest of Cuba as a chaplain, was awarded an encomienda, and was both colonist and priest, until he became convinced that he should work to put an end to the evils of the system. He had experienced the massacre of Taino men, women and children in Cuba, the effective enslavement of the survivors to work on the land and in mines, and the start of epidemics of smallpox, influenza and measles from which millions were to die during the 16th century.

He gave up his own encomienda and planned to establish a new settlement on the Venezuelan coast where the local Carib people would be paid wages, provided with a hospital and a church, and encouraged to develop their own farms. The hostility of other local settlers provoked trouble with the Caribs and the scheme ended in failure. In 1523 de las Casas entered the Dominican monastery in Santo Domingo and began work on his 'History of the Indies' as well as working for peaceful conversions to Christianity, for instance in

Guatemala. Such was the hostility to his ideas in the Americas that he had soon realised that if any change was to be achieved he would need to be heard in the Spanish court. He travelled to Spain in the late 1530s, gave public lectures and produced 'A Short Account of the Destruction of the Indies' which documented the murder, expropriation, and exploitation of the existing communities and their lands. He used many of the arguments of the noted Renaissance Roman Catholic philosopher and theologian, Francisco de Vitoria (c.1486 – 1546)[22], founder of the philosophical tradition known as the School of Salamanca, often considered to be the 'father of international law' and an authority consulted on occasions by Charles.

It was the ideas of Vitoria and de las Casas that were circulating when Charles arrived in Spain in December 1541 which encouraged him to support the 'New Laws' of 1542. These laws were aimed to prevent further enslavement and to stop the 'encomienda' system[23] by forbidding its continuation by inheritance, thus ending it within a generation. The reaction of the settlers in the Americas was unsurprising. Protests and riots ensued, especially in Peru, and concessions were made. An 'encomienda' would be able to be passed on once. Thus little was achieved in the short term. In Spain Juan Gines de Sepulveda, a philosopher, humanist and Greek scholar, encouraged by senior church leaders, produced a counter to de las Casas' case for change in 'Democrates Secundus', where he argued that it was legitimate to wage war on the Indians.

With no agreement and increasing pressures for a resolution, the two sides were brought together in the disputation of Valladolid in August 1550, and again in April 1551, at the Dominican monastery 'Colegio de San Gregorio'. Charles ordered the end of further conquests[24] until they could be shown to be 'just', and had summoned a 'junta' (panel) of jurists and theologians to consider the issues and reach conclusions about the proper treatment of the natives. Thus the two conflicting views within Spain would be presented; the two main protagonists were to be Sepulveda and de las Casas. The disputation was a series of theoretical arguments, within the context of the Spanish legal system, using authorities such as Aristotle, the Bible, St John Chrysostom, St Augustine, as well as medieval and Renaissance philosophers.

Sepulveda argued that there was a right to rule over 'inferior' peoples. Using Aristotle's ideas on 'natural slavery', he believed that because they were ruled by 'passion' rather than 'reason' they were inferior barbarians. Since they committed crimes against natural law, such as idolatry and cannibalism, and also themselves killed 'innocents' in human sacrifice, it was Spain's duty to punish and put a stop to these crimes. In addition, they were infidels who needed to be instructed in the 'true faith'. As few would willingly undergo such changes, it was 'just' to carry out a war of conquest in order to pave the way for preaching. The population had to be first subdued and then converted.[25]

De las Casas responded that the people of the Americas were not 'barbarians'. They were certainly non-Christian, but met most of Aristotle's criteria of civilisation – they lived in harmonious societies, had expressive languages, and the 'unnatural crimes' were committed only by a small minority. The people of the Indies were born free, regardless of papal consent for Spain to rule the area, and therefore there was no natural right of conquest in name of higher civilisation or superior faith. He argued that 'punishment' required jurisdiction and that Charles or the Pope had no such jurisdiction over infidels (as opposed to heretics). While he agreed that human sacrifice was evil, he argued that war, with its numerous deaths of even more 'innocents', was a greater evil, and went on to question how God could wish his Church to kill pagans in war in order to save them from their own ignorance. True conversion, he argued, required peace and freedom of choice, and forced conversions had no part to play.

There was no attempt at compromise; both sides claimed that they had 'won' the argument, though there is no evidence of an agreed judgment or proposals for legislation by the panel who heard the debate. The consequences of this were that Charles' 'New Laws', which would see the decline and eventual end of the 'encomienda' system, remained in place, but there was no significant improvement in the treatment of the natives under Spanish control in the New World. The 'encomienda' was replaced by the 'repartimiento de labor'[26] (known as the 'mita' system in Peru) which granted settlers the labour rights of a fixed number of indigenous peoples, in theory under government supervision, for a certain length of time through the year. A slightly different system but not one that improved the lot of those involved.

Most worked on the land; many in mines. It was in the 1540's that the greatest of all silver mines was opened. The Potosi silver mine, in modern day Bolivia, provided some of the worst examples of exploitation and suffering. Potosi is over 4,000 metres (13,000 feet) above sea level. Over a period of 250 years, starting in 1545 in the later years of Charles' reign, it produced 41,000 metric tons of pure silver. Besides long hours of dangerous mining work, forced labourers also worked in the refining process where thousands died of mercury poisoning. The 'patio process' involved the mixing of the crushed silver ore with mercury, salt, copper sulphate and water into an amalgam spread out on a patio (a shallow walled open enclosure) to a depth of between 0.3 and 0.6m.where a combination of sun and mixing creates a chemical reaction. The mixing was done by mule or the forced labour workers treading the ingredients together with their bare feet. The mercury and other impurities are then removed by heating, a process which gives off deadly vapours.

The catalogue of abuses produced by de las Casas was in future used as evidence of Spanish cruelty and inhumanity by other countries whenever they wished to criticise Spanish rule[27], even though those countries were equally culpable of appalling treatment of native inhabitants in their own colonies, but perhaps never so well documented. The indigenous population declined throughout the 16th century, largely the result of 'European' diseases to which they had no natural resistance and the harsh conditions in which they worked. The growing demand for labour was supplied by ever increasing numbers of African slaves brought over on the trans-Atlantic slave trade, thus adding to the ethnic mix of modern Latin

America. The issues of the New World were never particularly high in Charles' priorities. He had too many other concerns closer to home, but he did play a role, by giving consent to further conquest, attempting to establish royal authority over the independent minded settlers, and beginning to grapple with the moral and religious issues of slavery and treatment of the subject peoples.

## 24
## 'The Netherlands were never in so much danger' – The Final conflict with Francis

Charles' failure to take Algiers from Barbarossa and his subsequent return to Spain, had encouraged Francis to continue his pursuit of territorial gains in the Low Countries and in Italy. Nothing had fundamentally altered the relations between the two rulers – certainly not the truce of 1538 or Charles' journey through France the following year. So long as France was surrounded by Habsburg lands Francis would seek to weaken, divide and undermine Charles' position. If France sought to claim territories that Charles believed to be part of his inheritance or strategically important, then he would resist by all necessary means. Charles wished to secure the future of these lands and had certainly displeased Francis by naming his son Philip as Duke of Milan in October 1540. Relations deteriorated rapidly. In June 1541 Francis pushed through the wedding of his twelve year old niece, Jeanne d'Albret, heir to largely Spanish controlled Navarre, to William of Julich-Cleves-Berg.* William had inherited Guelders on the death of his distant relative Charles, Duke of Egmond, in defiance of Charles' own claim. This marriage was a deliberate blow against Charles' position both in the Low Countries, where Guelders would continue to be an anti-Habsburg base, and Navarre, where Francis hoped to encourage anti-Spanish uprisings. Charles was understandably furious, but so was the bride. She had protested passionately against the marriage when it was first proposed the previous year and again at the ceremony itself, where she had to be carried to the altar in her

---

* William was the brother of Anne of Cleves, briefly Henry VIII's 4th wife.

fine gown and jewels by the Constable of France, Anne de Montmorency.

The murder of Antonio Rincon and Cesare Fregoso near Milan in August 1541, while on another mission to the Ottoman court in Istanbul on behalf of France, provided Francis with the excuse to begin a series of aggressive moves. George of Austria, a natural son of the Emperor Maximilian and a loyal supporter of Charles, was seized on a journey across France from Spain to take up a position in the Low Countries. Charles believed that Francis was planning a series of aggressive moves focused on the Low Countries the following year. In addition, it was likely that there would be another attempt to take Perpignan, and the French alliance with the Ottomans would bring the powerful fleet of Barbarossa into the war. No-one was in any doubt that war was coming. Charles urged Mary to strengthen the defences of the Low Countries and asked how important it was that he should travel there himself, and with how many troops. He was fully aware that none of his advisers in Spain would support such an action, writing: 'as you will readily believe, there is not a soul who imagines that I have any intention of leaving the kingdoms. If they knew, they would try to prevent me'.[1] In his memoirs Charles accused Francis of 'going to war when he had assured all that he would not'.[2] He also claimed that he himself was 'as he always had been, inclined to treat for peace, provided that the adverse party was governed by reason, and provided that the peace was sure and suitable to the service of God and to the welfare of Christianity.'[3]

The attacks on the Low Countries, when they came in July 1542, were carefully co-ordinated. To the north, a Danish fleet of 40 ships with thousands of soldiers blocked trading routes and threatened fishing and trading vessels; the French attacked Luxembourg and Artois in the south and west; up to 18,000 troops of the Duke of Julich-Cleves-Berg, led by Maartin van Rossem, invaded Brabant from Guelderland in the east. This was another critical moment for Habsburg control of the Low Countries. Mary recognised the dangers early on. She wrote: 'Since the time of our grandfather, the

Emperor Maximilian, the Netherlands were never in such danger'. She called up the militia, recruited new troops, strengthened defences and arrested then executed those suspected of providing information to the enemy.[4] But by adding to the defensive garrisons of many towns, not knowing which might be attacked next, Mary had weakened her field armies.

This meant that Rossem was able to sweep through Brabant to Antwerp, killing and burning as he went. But the city's defences held firm and Rossem lacked the resources for a long siege. He moved on to Louvain which also resisted, and then into Luxembourg where he joined forces with French troops under the Duke of Orleans. They took the capital by the end of August. This they held, although they were driven out of the rest of Luxembourg by Mary's counter attack. Her commanders then pressed home the advantage by occupying the duchy of Julich, although they were unable to hold it later in the year. What might have been a disaster, with a co-ordinated attack by 50,000 troops, had been repulsed and the Low Countries had suffered less than might have been expected.[5] Elsewhere, in Rousillon, French troops led by Prince Henry, the Dauphin, failed to take Perpignan, which was ably defended by the Duke of Alva, and were forced to withdraw at the end of September.

No major victory had been won and the military campaigns would restart in the spring. Additional resources were needed and Mary was pleased when Charles informed her that he would be coming in person as soon as he could, having secured his diplomatic position. Negotiations with Henry VIII had been underway since June 1542. Charles was put in a difficult position when Henry demanded that his titles of 'Head of the Church of England' and 'Fidei Defensor' (Defender of the Faith) be recognised. Charles would never agree to that but side-stepped the issue by answering that as he had no power to grant such titles he could neither acknowledge them or remove them. The king could call himself what he wanted but Charles would continue to refer to him as 'King of England'. Having renewed trading agreements between the Low Countries and England, and agreed to a joint attack on France, a treaty was signed in February. Philip's forthcoming marriage to his cousin Maria Manuela reinforced the Portuguese alliance and the dowry, 150,000 ducats paid in Spain and the same sum in bills of exchange in Antwerp[6], helped to finance his plans. With Philip established as regent, Charles left Spain in the spring of 1543.

His intention was to once again lead his troops. He believed that his presence could provide a major morale boost to the troops and to the local population. Many of his advisors were concerned and repeated their warnings. Besides the physical dangers of injury, death, and damage to his health, they urged him to consider the problems that his capture would cause, and the harm to his reputation if things went wrong. Mary showed an ambivalence that was probably common among those closest to Charles. She wanted his presence to lead forces and in November 1542 she had reminded him of his promise to fight the French, writing: 'They (the representatives of the provincial assemblies) say you promised them that if we sustained the first shock of combat, you would not fail to come to their aid with all your strength'[7]. On the other hand by October 1543 she was concerned for his personal safety, telling him how much depended on it. In his ambiguous reply he wrote: 'I promise that I will do nothing you would not do, if you were in my place'[8]. Charles had a high opinion of his sister.

Although Charles' presence did not guarantee victory, when he intended to be active in the campaign he and his advisers would not commit themselves without a good chance of success. Wars were often ruinously expensive, and the costs were rising rapidly throughout Charles' reign, with larger armies, higher wages, more expensive equipment and longer campaigns. To pay for these wars additional subsidies were squeezed out of representative assemblies and increasingly Charles had to borrow money, often against future income in Spain. During 'war' years he borrowed more than in years of peace, but in those years of war when he was in the field borrowing was twice as high as in other 'war' years.[*]

---

[*] Tracy has calculated that he borrowed an average of 559,737 ducats in

Charles sailed from Barcelona and had the unnerving experience of encountering some French galleys off the coast near Marseilles. Having disembarked as usual at Genoa, he held meetings with Pope Paul at Busseto, between Piacenza and Parma. Although ending with the usual declarations of ever-lasting friendship, the talks achieved little. This must have been a dis-spiriting time for Charles suffering, as he was, his tenth attack of gout.[9] Paul was displeased by Charles' alliance with Henry VIII and by the recent banning of foreigners holding church offices in Spain. He refused to believe that France had allied with the Ottomans and that their fleets would work together. On the other hand he was keen that his grandson Ottavio should benefit from his marriage to Charles' natural daughter, Margaret, hoping that they would be given power in Milan. This, of course, was in Charles' gift, but he was most unlikely to agree to relinquishing control of such a vital strategic city. The advice that he received from Diego Mendoza, his ambassador to Venice was forceful. Mendoza argued that even the blind could see that the Pope was the cause of all Charles' troubles, both with the French and the Turk. 'Milan', he continued, 'is a fit inheritance for your only son and rightful heir. It is contrary to sense and reason to bestow it on a natural daughter'.[10] No such agreement was made. This failure encouraged the Pope to pursue the idea of a marriage between Ottavio's sister, Vittoria, and the duke of Orleans, the second surviving son of Francis, another doomed plan.

Charles moved north into Germany. Whereas his earlier visits as Emperor had been partly celebratory, newly elected (in 1521) and recently crowned (1530), his arrival now was more combative. Accompanied by his commander-in-chief, Ferrante Gonzaga, viceroy of Sicily, with Spanish and Italian troops, he joined German troops, along with artillery and munitions, at Speyer. His first targets were Julich-Cleves-Berg in the north Rhineland and Guelderland, both ruled by Duke William. With an army of 40,000

---

ordinary 'war' years and 1,154,098 ducats in war years when he was directly involved.

troops he took the well-defended city of Duren in August 1543, causing much damage. Julich then capitulated without resistance. He rapidly moved on to Roermond in Guelderland which immediately surrendered. Duke William, who had received no help from his erstwhile French allies, travelled from Dusseldorf to submit to Charles at Venlo. In return for a pardon and retaining Julich-Cleves-Berg, he had to hand over Guelderland, of which Charles became Duke, desert his allies and return to the Catholic faith. His marriage to Jeanne d'Albret was to be annulled and he later married Maria, daughter of Ferdinand, Charles' brother, thus bringing him into the Habsburg fold. Charles recorded that 'This marriage increased the obligations of the said Duke towards His Majesty, and the love of His Majesty for that Prince'.[11]

The emperor now needed to deal with the greater threat, Francis I. Some progress was made in the autumn of 1543, with imperial troops advancing through Hainault before being halted at Landrecies on the river Sambre in October, where a substantial French army awaited. Charles prepared for battle, but Francis withdrew, preferring a defensive strategy at such a late stage in the campaigning season. Charles was annoyed, later blaming the 'negligence of his scouts' (for not spotting the initial retreat) and the 'dis-order of his match-lock men'.[12] He was, however, able to take control of the bishopric of Cambrai. Having spent several months in military camps, he moved to Speyer for the Diet that opened in February 1544. There he eventually gained promises of military support from the German princes, in the form of 24,000 infantry and 4,000 cavalry. The settlement was much delayed (the 'recess' not being issued until June) by the usual religious divisions and the perennial fear of Charles gaining too much power. The Pope was angered by Charles' compromise with the Protestants detailed in the 'recess', which once again confirmed their rights until 'a general free Christian Council of the German Nation' met. He issued a response that vehemently criticised every aspect of the agreement. Charles refused to give a formal reply to a document that he regarded as insulting, but Luther did not hold back in his attack on the Papacy.

Charles now returned his attention to the military campaign. His troops re-took Luxembourg in June 1544, and then combined with other forces at Metz. Here he met his niece, Christina, now Duchess of Lorraine, before beginning the assault on France. The original plan was that both Charles and Henry VIII should advance on Paris, but both were held up by lengthy sieges, Charles at St. Dizier and Henry at Boulogne. Having taken St. Dizier on 17th August, though with the loss of the Rene of Chalon, Prince of Orange,* Charles marched along the River Marne, through Vitry and Chalons, towards Paris. Both sides now had large armies, perhaps of about 45,000 soldiers each, manoeuvring opposite each other on either side of the river. Charles 'employed every means to bring the King to give battle'.[13] Francis wanted to avoid a pitched battle and Charles was finding it hard to find a way across the Marne. The vanguard of the Imperial troops reached Chateau-Thierry only 50 miles from Paris. In the capital there was panic. Many inhabitants decided it was better to leave than to wait for the chaos and destruction that was certain if enemy soldiers arrived. Though generally popular, Francis struggled to keep control and was under increasing pressure to negotiate. Charles seemed to be in a strong position, and yet behind the scenes informal talks had been going on since late July.

Charles had his own problems maintaining an army in the field for much longer. He knew, more than anyone, the consequences of failing to pay an army. He could not expect any more funds for this campaign. He had already written to Mary pointing out that his finances would not last beyond 25th September. But an army needs more than just pay to survive. It needs weapons, medical care, but most of all food. The larger the army, the greater the logistical problems to be overcome. An army of 45,000 was larger than all but the greatest cities of the day. Even a force of 10,000 was larger than most towns[14] which would have had its established system of supply

---

* According to Charles' memoirs, he was struck by a cannonball and died of his wounds while the Emperor was at his bedside. Rene, who was also Statholder of Holland, Zeeland, Utrecht and Guelders, was the nephew of Philibert, Prince of Orange, who had also died in Charles' service in 1530.

and distribution. Such a system had to be created for an army on the move. Tons of bread, thousands of gallons of beer and hundreds of animals were needed daily. All this, along with other equipment, could only be moved by 1000's of draught animals which in turn required vast amounts of fodder and water. In 'home' territory, administrators could organise large scale contracts with merchants to supply what was needed or a system of compulsory requisitioning of food supplies at a set price was used.

On campaign such methods rarely worked. The campaigning season was generally considered to be from March to October because of the difficulty of feeding an army in winter. Any attempt to extend this usually ended badly. While occupying a town for a short time supplies might be brought from local merchants. For longer periods or while on the move this broke down under the weight of demand. What then took over was foraging, wide scale plundering in which troops took what they could for themselves and their colleagues. This was accepted practice. Francis I had explained in 1521 to the English ambassador that: 'I will march on straight and live upon my enemies' countries, as they have done on mine'[15]. The inhabitants were subjected to the demands of any army which was passing through or, even worse, staying on their land. While there, they would take what they needed or wanted; when leaving, it was not uncommon for the troops to destroy the economic resources of the area, mills, bakeries, crops in the field, in order to deprive the enemy of their future use. On occasions troops carried out the deliberate destruction of resources in their own territory as they withdrew, as the French had done in Provence in 1536, so that the advancing army would eventually run out of supplies.[16] Charles had every reason to think that if he continued the slow and halting progress towards Paris, his army might well fall prey to hunger, disease, and desertion, resulting in a humiliating withdrawal and the waste of the money already spent on the campaign. As he wrote in his 'Memoirs' 'the Emperor, in want of provisions, which it was impossible for him to procure so far in the interior of France...could not remain long enough to attack those places which would have defended themselves...the more so as the soldiers pay was in arrear, and the money requisite to pay them was to be had in the Netherlands'.[17]

Supply problems were probably rather less severe for Francis but the war was still putting exceptional strain on his resources. Another reason for Francis' willingness to negotiate was his increasing discomfort with the Ottoman alliance. After Charles' reversal at Algiers, Barbarossa had continued the pressure on Habsburg lands throughout the Mediterranean. Having attacked settlements in Sicily and southern Italy in June 1543, he joined with a French fleet at Marseilles and together they attacked Nice, ruled by Charles' ally, the Duke of Savoy. The town was taken and plundered, although the citadel held out, before its captors left in September on the advance of a relief force. The Ottoman fleet then wintered in the French port of Toulon. This provided a safe harbour without the need to travel back to Algiers or Istanbul. It must have been seen as a propaganda coup by Suleiman. With over 100 galleys and 30,000 men in the town, the cathedral was converted into a mosque and the faithful were called to prayer.[18] Many throughout Europe were deeply shocked when they later heard of these events, as must have been the inhabitants of Toulon. The alliance was becoming too awkward for Francis' reputation. Relations between the French and the Ottomans deteriorated to such an extent that the next spring Francis had to pay Barbarossa to leave.

From Toulon his fleet, accompanied by five French vessels, made its way back towards Istanbul. His first action was to amass over 200 vessels outside Genoa and demand the release of his colleague Turgut Reis. Born in about 1485 of Greek origin, Turgut had been captured by corsairs as a child and converted to Islam. He was noticed for his military and naval skills and rose to become a commander under Barbarossa, playing a leading role in the battle of Preveza. In 1540, while repairing vessels in Corsica, he was captured by the Genoese who used him as a galley slave before imprisoning him. Having achieved Turgut's freedom Barbarossa unleashed a series of raids down the Italian coast to Sicily. The account of

Jerome Maurand, a priest travelling with the French, leaves little to the imagination. He writes of the sacking of villages and towns; the destruction of churches; the enslavement of thousands; the ransoms paid by the more wealthy inhabitants; the cruel execution of any that resisted. The French ships eventually left and went on to Istanbul ahead, unwilling to witness any more. This wave of violence was to be Barbarossa's last. Arriving in Istanbul in the autumn of 1544, he remained there until his death in 1546, aged eighty, to be replaced as Ottoman commander in the Mediterranean by Turgut Reis.

The tentative negotiations started between envoys sent by Charles and Francis in July increased in urgency by late August when it became clear that both parties were serious in their desire to end the war. Most of the terms had been agreed by 10th September and needed only royal approval. On 7th September Charles had sent the Bishop of Arras to inform Henry VIII that he should march on Paris immediately or else Charles would negotiate a separate peace. No reply was heard until 19th September, even though the previous day news was received that the English had taken Boulogne on the 14th. This certainly concentrated Francis' mind and the Treaty of Crepy, 'written in the vineyards by Soissons but signed at Crepy on 18th September' was confirmed by both rulers the following day.

The Treaty of Crepy in many ways reveals the nature of international politics at the time – sometimes laudable aims, often duplicitous agreements, and then an open disregard for what had been signed. There was both an open treaty and a secret treaty. The open treaty enforced the main terms of the agreement made at Cambrai back in 1529, and stated that all territorial gains made since the truce of Nice in 1538 would be returned. Francis agreed to supply 10,000 foot-soldiers and 600 heavy cavalry to help fight the Ottomans. A more contentious aspect was the understanding about the marriage of Francis' youngest son, Charles, Duke of Orleans and the related territorial settlement. Orleans would marry either Charles' daughter Maria, or niece, Ferdinand's daughter, Anna. If he married Maria, Orleans would inherit the Low Countries on Charles' death; if he married Anna, he would inherit Milan. Charles himself would decide who the bride would be after talks with Ferdinand and his own son Philip. It is often debated why Charles agreed to such a deal. He had control in Italy and the upper hand in the Low Countries. Why did he feel the need to hand over significant lands to the French royal family as part of a marriage contract? He hoped to bring about a lasting settlement of the Habsburg – Valois conflict by using marriages and concessions, thus creating an all-embracing dynastic alliance. This was the latest, but not the last, of Charles' ideas on how this 'permanent peace' could be achieved. He also wished to gain Francis' agreement to fight not just the Ottomans but also the German Protestants if they could not be restored to the church by other means. Such a marriage alliance could help to bring this about.

This becomes clear when the secret part of the treaty is considered. Here Francis agreed to help Charles to bring about a meeting of the general church council that the Emperor had so long desired, to support him in removing the abuses of the church and to bring the German Protestants back into a unified church. What probably needed to remain secret was Francis' agreement to provide troops (10,000 infantry and 600 cavalry – the same as promised against the Ottomans) for use against the heretics if other methods failed, whereas he had previously encouraged German Protestants to make difficulties for Charles. He also promised not to make any agreement with Henry VIII which would be disadvantageous to Charles and would support the Emperor in any future war with Henry.[19] Charles had forced the French to agree to his wishes in both political and religious matters.

Of course we know that, as in the past, rulers did not always regarded treaties as unbreakable, even while they were being negotiated. These marriage and territorial terms were bound to cause problems. In France, the royal family was split. The ambitious twenty-two year old Duke of Orleans, affable and popular at the French court, was undoubtedly his father's favourite. He had been the subject of many marriage plans – into the English royal family, with the Farnese in Italy, with Jeanne d'Albret of Navarre – but was very keen for an independent principality that the treaty provided. The Dauphin, Henry, Francis' heir, married eleven years earlier to Catherine de' Medici, had never been close to his father since his years in Spain as a hostage. He objected to these terms, believing that too much was gained by his younger brother and that this would cause family divisions in the future. A divided French royal family would certainly suit Charles. But Charles would have his own dilemma. How was he to decide which marriage and territorial agreement to choose? His advisers were divided; most of the Spaniards believed that Milan was essential to control in Italy and the links with the Low Countries, while those with a 'Burgundian' background, such as Granvelle, argued that the Low Countries were an invaluable asset. Both had a strong case and Charles was going to be in a difficult position when he came to decide.

In October 1544, while in Brussels, he received a state visit from France, led by his sister Queen Eleanor. With her were Charles, Duke of Orleans, and Anne de Pisselieu, Duchess of Etampes (officially a lady-in-waiting but also King Francis' long-term mistress). With Charles were the regent Mary, his nephews Maximilian and Ferdinand, Ottavio Farnese, together with high officials, and knights of the Golden Fleece. Feasts, tournaments and balls gave these recent enemies the opportunity to display the significance of the newly agreed peace. The festivities gave Charles a chance to over-indulge in the food and drink which he so enjoyed, enormous plates of meat and numerous tankards of ale. Whether this caused yet another re-occurrence of his gout (the eleventh) while in Ghent shortly afterwards it is impossible to be sure. Whatever the cause, 'from December to Easter he suffered from it extremely, although the regime he submitted to for the first time were more severe'.[20] These attacks had become more frequent since 1540 and from this point on it was rare for a year to go by without a period of acute discomfort and pain.

At this time Charles was also struggling to reach a decision as to which marriage option he would support, but by the spring of 1545 he had reluctantly decided that Milan would be sacrificed. As some of his advisers argued, he had won Milan by force and if necessary that could be done again[21], whereas he had deep personal ties to the Low Countries. There is plenty of evidence to suggest that he was regretting the agreement. He was therefore greatly relieved when the need to go ahead with the marriage was removed by the death of Orleans in September 1545. Charles recorded that: 'This death came just in time, and, being a natural one, it could be said that God had sent it to accomplish his secret design'.

In some ways the end of an era had been reached. There were to be no more wars between Charles and Francis. His rival of over 30 years died on 31st March 1547 at the chateau of Rambouillet, aged 52. Henry VIII had died two months earlier, aged 56 at Whitehall Palace. Charles had outlived the two European monarchs most closely associated with him, although the Ottoman sultan, Suleiman, was to live on until 1566, dying in Hungary on yet another military expedition at the age of 71. This did not mean that peace was going to break out over Europe. Francis' successor, Henry II, was as keen as his father for military success and territorial gain. He had no love of Charles; his three years in Spain as a young boy were not to be forgiven. However, the breathing space provided by the Treaty of Crepy and then Francis' death would give Charles the opportunity to deal with the issue that had distressed him for decades – the Protestant heresy in Germany.

# Part Five
# Highs and Lows: Imperial and Dynastic 1546-1556

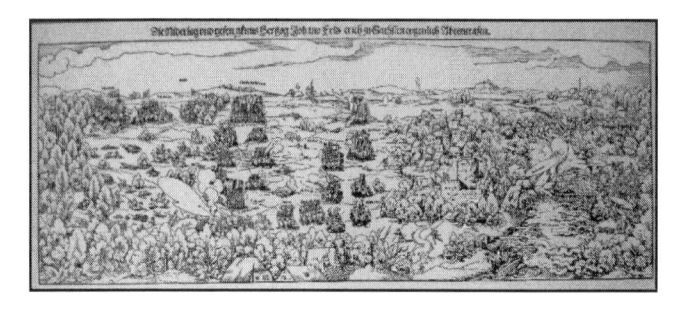

'The Defeat and Detention of John Frederick, Elector of Saxony'.
The earliest illustration of the battle of Muhlberg
– an engraving by Virgil Solis the Elder.

Charles V: Duty and Dynasty

# 25
## 'Arrogance and Obstinacy' - Muhlberg

In his memoirs Charles wrote that he 'had never ceased, whenever he saw either Pope Clement or Pope Paul, and in every journey, and at every Diet in Germany, and at every time and opportunity, continually to solicit, either personally or through ministers, the convocation of a General Council'. In his view a council would be able to deal with 'the evils that had arisen in Germany', 'the errors which were being propagated in Christendom' and 'the abuses of the Church'.[1] In other words, to settle the doctrinal issues and bring about the reforms that he believed were necessary within the Church. When, honouring the terms of the Treaty of Crepy, Francis wrote to Pope Paul removing his objections to a council and permitting the French cardinals to attend, the way was clear. On 19th November 1544 Paul issued instructions for the convening of the council at Trent in northern Italy on 15th March 1545.

Although pleased that the move he had been advocating for at least fifteen years had now been initiated, even Charles must have realised that the chances of its success were slight. The situation in Germany and the attitude of Pope Paul meant that not only was the council much delayed, not opening until December 1545, but also militated against a true coming together of Catholic and Protestant. During the Imperial Diet held at Worms in the first half of 1545 the Protestant princes made it clear that they wished to have nothing to do with the council, instead wishing for another national (German) religious conference. Charles agreed to this conference, to meet at Regensburg in November. Meanwhile the papal legate Cardinal Farnese (Alessandro Farnese, born in 1520, grandson of Pope Paul and brother of Ottavio Farnese, Charles' son-in-law), arrived in

May, bringing with him a subsidy of 100,000 ducats, which was deposited at Augsburg. This was said to be available for use against the Ottomans, but some believed that it might be for more immediate military action in Germany. In any case it gained him a favourable welcome from Charles.

His conversations with Charles rapidly moved on to the possibility of war against the Protestants, and soon after Farnese's return to Rome, in June, Pope Paul decided to support the Emperor. He agreed to a further subsidy, an army of 12,000 infantry and 500 cavalry, and a large grant from church lands in Spain. Paul had good reason to wish for the war now. It would end any chance of the council meeting and keep Charles occupied in Germany, leaving the pope a free hand to pursue his own dynastic ambitions in Italy. Charles must have been tempted. At last a pope was willing to back him. A successful campaign against the Protestant princes of the Schmalkaldic League could force them to accept any decisions that a future council reached and help to restore Imperial authority in the Empire. Charles had believed that these talks were secret, between himself, Ferdinand, Cardinal Farnese and the pope. Much to his anger and inconvenience the plans were soon leaked by the Vatican. Charles had not yet established sufficient political support in Germany for such a move, nor had he made the necessary military arrangements. It was now too late in the year to begin to do so. In July he decided that the moment was not right, sent his reasons to the pope requesting a delay of a year and asked for the negotiation of a formal agreement.[2]

Widespread knowledge of these discussions made eventual war more likely, though Charles always maintained that he was ready to negotiate a peaceful settlement at any time. The Protestant princes stepped up their military preparations and would not be taken by surprise in the future. Charles' position in Germany had deteriorated over the previous few years. Most of the north was now under Protestant control. In 1542 Charles' ally, the Catholic Duke Henry of Brunswick had attempted to expand his territories but was defeated by the forces of the Schmalkaldic League and his lands occupied by its two main leaders, Elector John Frederick of Saxony and Landgrave Philip of Hesse, now reconciled to the Protestant princes. In 1543 the Elector Archbishop of Cologne, Hermann von Wied, had embraced the new faith, and both he and Franz von Waldeck, Prince Bishop of Munster, Minden, Paderborn and Osnabruck, encouraged Protestant preachers and services throughout their sees. In the autumn of 1545, when he attempted to regain some of his lands, Henry of Brunswick was again defeated and captured by the forces of the League. Charles' religious and dynastic interests were under serious threat. The conversion of Frederick, Elector Palatinate*, in January 1546, added to his problems. As Philip of Hesse untactfully pointed out, there were now 'four electors of our faith' (the electors of Saxony, Brandenburg, Palatinate and Cologne) out of a total of seven and 'that if the Emperor and King (Ferdinand) both die, a thoroughly Lutheran Emperor will be elected'[3] – and certainly not a Habsburg.

In Charles' eyes Electoral Saxony had long been a centre of Lutheran heresy. It had provided a safe-haven for Luther in Wittenberg, where the priest had lived ever since his departure from Worms back in 1521, first under Frederick III the Wise, then his brother, John the Steadfast, and since 1532 John's son, John Frederick I. Luther had concentrated on organising the new reformed church in Saxony under the electors, translating the Bible, writing hymns, and been frequently consulted by Protestant theologians on the national discussions that Charles had been so keen to instigate. In 1525 Luther had married Katherina von Bora, a former nun, thereby confirming his approval of clerical marriage. He had opposed a 'Holy War' against 'the Turk', believing that a spiritual battle should be waged through prayer and repentance, but firmly supported a 'just' secular war to defend Europe. At the time of the siege of Vienna he wrote in a prayer 'give our emperor perpetual victory over our enemies'. He also produced anti-semitic tracts, particularly later in his life. His very last sermon, in Eisleben,

---

* Charles old colleague and ally, married to his niece, Dorothea.

referred to the Jews as 'our public enemies'. Luther had suffered from poor health for many years, including kidney and bladder stones, arthritis, and angina. He died in February 1546 and was buried at the foot of the pulpit in the church of Wittenberg Castle. He had played a leading role in bringing about the upheavals that Charles was struggling to control.

Charles realised that unless he took action soon the situation would become irretrievable. He feared the spread of heretical ideas throughout Germany and then to the Low Countries, believing that 'If we do not take a strong line the risk to the faith is enormous'.[4] He had a very difficult hand to play. While he encouraged the religious conference in Regensburg, extending the hope of a compromise to the Protestants, he could not be seen to weaken so much as to lose the backing of Catholic princes or the Papacy. Nor did he wish to show his hand too early. Charles left the Low Countries, where he had spent the autumn and early winter months, holding a chapter of the Order of the Golden Fleece in Utrecht in January. As he travelled through the Rhineland he had almost certainly decided that there would be war but still assured a delegation of electors and princes that his dearest wish was for peace and that he would only resort to arms if forced to do so. His true intentions were revealed in a letter to his son - he hoped to mislead the princes – and later in his 'Memoirs', referring to the 'great arrogance and obstinacy' of the Protestants[5]. In March he met Philip of Hesse at Speyer and although on the surface the meeting was cordial, Charles was deeply offended by Philip's blunt, rigid, approach and by his advice to Charles that he should study the scriptures.[6]

The failure of the general church council at Trent to make headway was hardly unexpected. In the early months of 1546 it was poorly attended with no effective Protestant participation. Pope Paul's determination to settle doctrinal issues before considering reforms ensured that there would be no progress, as he must have known it would. In January 1547 the council decided to make no compromise with Luther's belief in justification by faith. Established Catholic doctrines were reasserted while the abuses of ecclesiastical power that had provoked the initial protests were ignored. Charles' spokesman in Trent commented that 'Together, the council fathers served only Rome, and individually they served only themselves'.[7] It was clear that the Council was not going to achieve any form of reconciliation, a conclusion underlined by its move from the Imperial city of Trent to the papal city of Bologna in March 1547, under the pretext of an outbreak of plague in Trent.

Meanwhile, Charles arrived in Regensburg in April 1546 ready for the coming Diet which eventually opened in June. The religious conference there had already failed and the Protestant representatives had departed. In a two pronged diplomatic initiative Charles now sought to secure his position in the south, while at the same time weaken Protestant unity. The Wittelsbach dukes of Bavaria, while staunchly Catholic, had always been hostile to the growth of Habsburg power. Negotiations were started with the aim of gaining the support of Bavaria, if not for the provision of troops then for the use of Bavaria as a base and for the supply of Charles' army. Duke William IV was keen for dynastic advancement. The marriage of his son and heir, Albert, to Anna, eldest surviving daughter of Ferdinand, would be prestigious and hold out a remote possibility of a future inheritance in Bohemia. An agreement was reached and the marriage took place in Regensburg in July 1546, along with the marriage of Mary, Anna's sister, to Duke William of Julich-Cleves-Berg, which confirmed his continued loyalty to the Habsburgs. A later offer to William of Bavaria that in a war he could take lands off his relation, Frederick, Elector Palatinate, thus dangling the hope of even receiving the electors' hat, pleased William, but also had the effect of neutralising Frederick by drawing him away from the princes of the Schmalkaldic League, who in any case had refused his application to join them, to protect his secular interests.

Meanwhile Granvelle was working hard to divide the Protestant princes and win some to Charles' cause. Charles' dislike of those whom he regarded as being heretics had to be put to one side. Margrave Albert Alcibiades of Brandenburg-Kulmbach had considerable military ability and was usually willing to place his army at the service of anyone who would pay him well – he always needed funds to pay his creditors – was won over. Duke Maurice of Saxony, another accomplished military leader, as well as a skilful negotiator and ambitious prince, was married to Philip of Hesse's daughter. From the junior, Albertine, branch of the house of Wettin*, he had ambitions to replace his cousin, John Frederick, as elector. Religious differences were unlikely to prevent him from taking any advantage that he could. He had supported Charles against France in 1543-44 and his continued support was confirmed by an agreement on 19th June. He could have lands belonging to his cousin if conquered in war and the possibility that he could replace John Frederick as elector, though not promised, was not rejected either. Charles' political position was now much more secure.

He also had some time for relaxation in Regensburg before the electors, princes and representatives of the Imperial cities arrived for the opening of the Diet on 5th June. Having recovered from yet another attack of gout, he spent some time hunting at Straubing. Then, while lodged at the Golden Cross Inn, he joined in the pleasures of court life - the dinners, dances and dalliances - in which many of the local citizens were keen to participate. He had a short affair with Barbara Blomberg, the eighteen year old daughter of a local tradesman, who became pregnant. On 24th February 1547 she gave birth to a son, later known as Don John of Austria, who during his relatively short life was to become one of the heroes of Europe as victor at the battle of Lepanto in 1571. Eighteen months earlier, in August 1545, Charles had become a grandfather – twice. On the 14th Philip's wife, Maria Manuela gave birth to a son, Don Carlos, heir to the Spanish thrones, but Maria died in childbirth. On the 27th Charles' natural daughter, Margaret of Parma, married to Ottavio Farnese, was delivered of twin boys. One, Charles, died in infancy

---

* The Wettin family divided their possessions in Saxony during the 15th century between two sons of Elector Frederick II. The elder brother, Ernest, and his descendants inherited the title of Prince-Elector, while the younger, Albert, and his descendants had inherited the title of Duke.

but his brother Alessandro was to become a leading figure in late 16th century Europe, as Duke of Parma and Governor of the Spanish Netherlands under Philip II.

The Diet of June–July 1546 achieved little, other than to give Charles the opportunity to claim that his opponents, by their refusal to attend, were challenging his authority as Emperor and planning revolt. Their absence could be portrayed as an unwillingness to negotiate and a desire for conflict. This enabled him to disguise the strong religious element in his decision to use force. On 16th June Protestant elements in Regensburg asked him who he was planning to take arms against and he answered that he must deal with disobedient states. But when he wrote to Philip in August his emphasis was different. 'As you know the restoration of the faith is our aim and intention….but it seemed useful to make it known right from the beginning that our concern is to punish those who disobey'.[8]

Events now moved swiftly towards war. Both sides had been recruiting throughout Germany. If Charles hoped that his opponents would find it difficult to raise troops he was mistaken; it was his recruitment agents that faced the greater problems. The peace treaty between France and England signed at Guines on 6th June 1546 meant that more mercenaries might look for employment in Germany. The Schmalkaldic League, warned by the events of the previous year, had already assembled a sizable army. They were also hopeful of assistance from France or England but in the event none materialised. After months of negotiations, Charles and the pope finalised the agreement originally made the previous year whereby the Papacy would raise troops immediately, and provide funds for the campaign, including half the church revenues from the Low Countries. Charles ordered 10,000 troops to march south from the Low Countries under the Count of Buren and for others to move up from Italy. In a letter to Mary he defended his decision to go to war. He wrote that he had done all he could to avoid this but now 'force alone will drive them to accept reasonable terms'. On 20th July Elector John Frederick of Saxony and Landgrave Philip of Hesse were denounced as rebels and traitors. The Diet came to an end on 24th July. For Charles the time was right for a military solution. He had both political and religious motives. France was neutralised by the Peace of Crepy, (but for how long?), there was a truce in Hungary with the Ottomans, the pope was supportive, and the Protestant princes were not fully united.

But Charles still knew that he had a serious fight on his hands. Together, Elector John Frederick and Philip of Hesse had an army of 30,000 infantry and 5,000 cavalry, under the command of Schertlin von Burtenbach. The early stages of the conflict in Bavaria consisted of a series of manoeuvres by both sides along the Danube, around Regensburg, Ingolstadt, Donauworth and Ulm. Initially Charles was playing for time, keen to avoid confrontation until the arrival of reinforcements from Italy and the Low Countries. The papal troops, with Cardinal Farnese, delayed by the League blocking the Fern pass into the Lech valley and thence the Danube, eventually joined Charles at Landshut on 13th August. Those under Buren, who was also bringing money from the Low Countries to pay the army, arrived via the Rhine and Main valleys, on 15th September. The forces were now well matched, with Charles probably having the superior numbers. The League commanders decided not to take Regensburg, which would have necessitated a long siege. The armies came into contact near Ingolstadt and Charles' camp was bombarded on the night of 31st August, an action in which Charles is said to have shown considerable personal bravery, but the League failed to follow this up with an attack until two days later, by which time the Imperial troops were well dug in.

The manoeuvring continued with both sides looking for a tactical advantage but neither prepared to make a decisive move. Of Charles' commanders, Buren favoured taking the offensive, but the Duke of Alva, who Charles always listened to on these matters, urged caution – there was little to gain and everything to lose by rushing into ill-considered action. Minor clashes during October, with neither side gaining an advantage, demoralised both armies. Cardinal Farnese left on 18th October taking with him some Italian troops. Desertions and disease were beginning to take their toll, but it was the army of the Schmalkaldic League that was under most pressure. Their leadership was divided, with Schertlin's judgement frequently challenged by Philip of Hesse and the Elector John Frederick, and their funds running out. Try as they might to get subsidies from France or borrow money from elsewhere they needed to end the campaign.

Their difficulties were magnified by news from Saxony in early November. Duke Maurice of Saxony, having waited until it was clear that the League were not going to defeat Charles, had launched an invasion of John Frederick's lands. Although the Elector did not leave immediately, by the end of November the remaining troops of the League left southern Germany. The major cities – Augsburg, Ulm, Frankfurt, and Strasbourg – surrendered to Charles. Philip of Hesse started overtures to come to terms but with the new turn of events Charles refused to consider anything but abject surrender. He did make his peace with both Frederick, Elector Palatinate, and Duke Ulrich of Wurttemberg, but only after humiliating them. Frederick was only granted an audience after several requests and was then subjected to having his offences read out, followed by a dressing down by Charles. After the Elector had knelt before the Emperor and given his apologies, Charles did not even offer him his hand to kiss. He displayed an anger and bitterness that surprised his household because it was so unusual. He had been appalled by what he saw as Frederick's betrayal. But this did not destroy his political judgement. He extracted a considerable fine from both Frederick and the Duke of Wurttemberg but permitted them to keep their lands and titles, since to do otherwise would have involved military action that would have diverted him from his main objective – to defeat the League.

Charles decided to maintain his armies through the winter - the war had not yet been won. As soon as he had returned north the Elector, rather than attempting to retake his lands over-run by Duke Maurice, launched a counter-attack into Maurice's own lands of Ducal Saxony and besieged Leipzig, Maurice's capital. He then sent troops into Lower Lusatia, an area of Bohemia, increasing Ferdinand's troubles there. Taking advantage of John Frederick's offensive, the Bohemian Diet demanded that Ferdinand, their king, make concessions and threatened revolt unless he granted them. A force under Albert Alcibiades sent to assist Maurice in February 1547 was defeated and its commander captured. Meanwhile, fearful of Charles' success, on 22nd January Pope Paul had ordered the withdrawal of the remaining Papal troops in Germany. Charles was furious, telling Paul's representative that 'the Pope had steered him into this difficult war, and then left him to cope with it'.[9]

After some hesitation Charles had decided by March that he had no alternative but to assist his allies. Racked by gout and carried in a litter he travelled north with his troops. The emperor's arrival quelled the incipient Bohemian revolt and having joined Maurice and Ferdinand the combined army of 50,000 marched along the west side of the River Elbe towards John Frederick's forces. Having abandoned Meissen, the Elector's smaller army was on the opposite bank of the river, keen now to avoid battle and probably heading for Wittenberg, which would be difficult for Charles to besiege successfully. Encamped near Muhlberg, on Sunday 24th April 1547, John Frederick attended church without ordering sufficient guards to be posted or drawing up his men in battle formation. He believed himself safe, as Charles' army would be unable to cross the river. He was mistaken. Charles' scouts found a shallow crossing, and in the mist the Electors' troops were taken by surprise. Their confused retreat, pursued by the Imperial cavalry, meant that this was more a rout than a battle. John Frederick was captured.

The victorious Charles marched on to Wittenberg, which surrendered without resistance. There was little looting, since Maurice wanted his new lands to be intact, and Charles ordered that Luther's tomb should be untouched. John Frederick signed the Capitulation of Wittenberg on 19th May, whereby he formally abdicated the electorate in return for his life, but was permitted to retain some lands for his sons. Maurice became the new elector in his place. John Frederick remained a prisoner and was joined by

Philip of Hesse, who had been persuaded to throw himself upon Charles' mercy by Maurice of Saxony. After a lengthy negotiation Charles had eventually agreed to a document which stated that Philip would not be subject to the death sentence or life imprisonment. Maurice and other electors gave a very positive interpretation of Charles' position to Philip, who then agreed to submit. On 19th June he knelt before Charles and his apology was read out. Charles responded with an arranged speech but refused to give his hand to Philip. After a meal with the Duke of Alva and Maurice, Philip was taken away, much to Maurice's horror. On the 21st Charles announced that only having Philip as a prisoner would ensure the completion of the peace treaty.

Seen as an unworthy act by many, Charles was perhaps motivated by memories of King Francis' release in 1526, the frustration that he must have felt during the years of his inability to deal with the Protestants, by Philip's unreliability in the past, and by his anger at Philip's attitude towards him at Speyer the previous year. In vain Maurice protested about the treatment of his father-in-law and Charles' action put some distance between the new elector and the emperor. Elsewhere the towns of northern Germany submitted to Charles, with the exception of Bremen and Magdeburg. Henry of Brunswick was restored to his lands and the Archbishop of Cologne replaced. Charles believed that he might now be able to achieve a settlement on his terms.

Charles regarded this victory as one of the high points of his reign. Titian's famous portrait of Charles on horseback[10] was produced to celebrate the success at Muhlberg. Painted in 1548 while Charles was residing in the Fuggerhaus at Augsburg, it shows the victorious Emperor after the battle having vanquished his foes. He is in full armour, holding a spear (a Roman symbol of absolute power), with a commander's sash in red (representing the Catholic party), with the insignia of the Golden Fleece clearly displayed – a fine Christian warrior and defender of the Church. The reality was different. He was aging quite rapidly, much hampered by the effects of the gout, with the decades of travel and responsibility beginning to take their toll. A second Titian portrait[11] of the same year is a truer representation. In this he is seated, plainly dressed in black, again with the emblem of the Order of the Golden Fleece prominent against his coat, with a cane by his side. The portrait shows him as serious, thoughtful, self-possessed, his eyes looking directly at the viewer, conveying his authority and determination, but rather weary, looking older than his forty-eight years.

Charles seemed at the height of his power. He had overcome his Protestant enemies and those who challenged Imperial authority in the Holy Roman Empire. There was little to prevent him imposing the settlement that he desired in the Empire or indeed across Europe. His fellow monarchs and rivals of over 30 years, Francis I and Henry VIII had both died. Charles must have thought that at last he would be allowed some rest from the interminable business of government. The fact that he remained for nearly a year in Augsburg suggests that some break from his continual journeying was possible.

# 26
## 'Unfraternal and False' – The Future of the Dynasty

It was to be the usual problems that destroyed any chance of tranquillity - Protestants, the papacy, France and the Ottomans - along with a new one, family disunity. When the Diet of Augsburg opened in September 1547 Charles intended to use his strengthened position to bring about reforms to the Imperial system of justice, the administration of the Empire and to further a religious settlement. If this could not be achieved now, then it would never be possible. The estates of the Diet were willing to agree to most of Charles' plans for the judicial system, if only to reserve their opposition for anything that would weaken their political and religious positions. His high handed treatment of Philip of Hesse and other German princes had once again raised fears amongst the princes and in the cities of an over mighty emperor.

Charles wished to create a greater degree of unity by establishing a 'League' of the whole empire, in the same way that particular areas had created regional leagues, such as the Swabian League between 1487 and 1533. This league would centralize administration and regularize payments for the running and defence of the Empire. Discussions had started in June 1547, and although receiving some backing from smaller states, the larger states were strong in their opposition. No progress was made. The princes, even those who had supported Charles in the recent war, were against any perceived extension of his power. Their authority had grown during the 15th and 16th centuries, in their conflicts with the knights, peasants and towns, and now with the religious divisions, and they were unwilling to agree to anything that would threaten their new found status. It was impossible for Charles to simply impose a settlement.

He had fought the Schmalkaldic League in large part for religious reasons. Within months of victory his hopes for a settlement had taken several knocks. His relations with the Papacy were again at a low ebb. In September 1547 Pier-Luigi Farnese, Duke of Parma, Pope Paul's son, was murdered and Ferrante Gonzaga, Charles' governor in Milan, took Piacenza in the emperor's name. The pope's withdrawal of his troops from Germany in January 1547 and the moving of the council to Bologna had greatly angered Charles. In October Charles demanded that the council returned to Trent and in January 1548 his ambassadors presented a formal 'Protestation' to the council in Bologna and the cardinals in Rome. It stated that 'our Emperor will defy all the attacks to which you and your Pope have exposed the Church: he will take the Church under his own protection'. In the same month he was writing to Philip that: 'You yourself know how unreliable Pope Paul III is in all his treaties, how sadly he lacks all zeal for Christendom, and how ill he has acted in this affair of the council above all. Nevertheless, honour his position. The Pope is old; therefore take careful heed of the instructions which I have given my ambassador in Rome in case of an election'[1] (Paul III died in November 1549).

In Germany, military defeat had done nothing to shake Protestant beliefs. Nor could Charles expect support for a compromise from the papacy. As the negotiations at the Diet dragged on into the spring of 1548, considerable work was put into drawing up a document that was to be released alongside the 'recess'. The Augsburg Interim was yet another holding position as revealed in its full title: 'Declaration of how things are to be managed in the Holy Roman Empire, touching the question of religion, until the general council can be held'. This 'Interim' included some concessions to the Protestants on the marriage of priests and the administration of communion in both kinds (bread and wine) and demanded the protection of Catholic rights within Protestant areas. It gained few supporters. Many Catholic princes refused to agree to the concessions that had been granted and so in effect the 'interim' only applied to Protestant areas. The captive Philip of Hesse accepted it, but his former ally and fellow prisoner, John Frederick, rejected it out of hand. Some Protestant princes and cities agreed because they were under the control of Charles' troops and others hoped for further concessions. Very few had any intention of enforcing it. Many Protestant areas simply ignored the 'Augsburg interim'. The Protestants themselves were divided doctrinally. The 'Leipzig Interim', drawn up for Maurice of Saxony by Philip Melanchthon and agreed by the estates of Saxony and Electoral Brandenburg, permitting observance of Catholic feasts and recognising seven Catholic sacraments, was rejected by many other Protestants, especially in the northern cities such as Bremen, Hamburg, and Magdeburg. Charles also issued an order to Catholics, after consultation with the church representatives at the Diet, requiring them to begin the process of internal reform. He was coming to the conclusion that the Papacy would never willingly undertake the measures that he and many others believed to be necessary.

Early in 1548 Charles wrote another of his political testaments for Philip. In this he gave advice on the political issues of the day and the best interests of the dynasty. He started by wishing Philip to remain on good terms with his uncle, Ferdinand, and asking him to seek his uncle's advice on international matters. Charles had done so with success and he referred to the recent war as an example. Of course Philip is exhorted to 'defend the faith', to put his 'trust in Almighty God' and to try to keep the peace, although Charles admitted that this was not always in one's own hands. He commented on the various rulers in Italy and who could be trusted, particularly the Duke of Florence ('I have done much for him, and he is grateful'), the Duke of Mantua, and Doria of Genoa ('the most important of all to us'). He again warned Philip about the French. 'France has never kept faith and has always sought to do me hurt. The young King seems about to follow in his father's footsteps'. Philip must defend Milan and Naples, Flanders and Artois from the French: 'Never yield to them, not so much as an inch'. He should not try to 'manage without a Spanish army in Italy'.

Charles advised Philip to maintain good relations with Portugal and England, though not to become involved in its perpetual struggle with France, nor to listen to any plans to assist the imprisoned King Christian II of Denmark. He emphasised the importance of maintaining a strong fleet, for defence against pirates in the Mediterranean and to protect Spanish interests in the Indies. He urged him to 'keep yourself well informed of the state of these distant lands for the honour of God and the care of justice. Combat the abuses that have arisen within them'. He wished Mary to continue as governor in the Low Countries since she had done excellent work in both peace and war, but made Philip aware that she had asked to be relieved of the responsibility. On a personal note Charles wished Philip to re-marry, perhaps to a daughter of the French king, or Jeanne d'Albret of Navarre, whom Charles considered attractive and clever.[2]

While in Augsburg, after discussions with Ferdinand, Charles finalised some decisions which were to have an impact on his empire and the history of Europe for several hundred years. He had long considered how he could establish a permanent settlement of Europe and more recently his mind had turned to settling the arrangements for his own lands in the future. In the periods of peace with France there had been discussions as to how best to secure this peace by marriage between the Habsburg and the Valois. The Treaty of Madrid had agreed that Charles' sister Eleanor would marry Francis I and this had come about after the Peace of Cambrai in 1529. It seemed to have done little to cement good relations between the two monarchs, except when other pressures for peace, such as the lack of financial or military resources, came into play. Only then could this personal link be used. Eleanor was a somewhat peripheral figure in Francis' life. She was there for ceremonial purposes and was treated with appropriate courtesy, but was never able to exert as great an influence over his ideas or policies as was his long term mistress, Anne de Pisseleu, Duchess of Etampes. During the late 1530s and early 1540s, Charles had thought at length about the possibility of solving the on-going conflicts over Milan and the Low Countries by marriages between Francis' sons and either his own daughters or those of his brother Ferdinand.

This whole episode of a marriage alliance with the Valois, and who should inherit which lands, was part of Charles' wider concerns about the future of the dynasty. He had begun to grapple with this issue from the time that his son Philip became old enough to take on responsibility as regent in Spain and it became increasingly important to him. The decision to hand over Milan rather than the Low Countries (though this never occurred because of Orleans' death in September 1545) indicated that Charles had concluded that the best solution was that the Low Countries should remain intimately linked with Spain. He seriously considered the possibility of Ferdinand's eldest son, Maximilian, marrying his eldest daughter, Maria, with them inheriting the Low Countries.

As Philip became older, Charles wished him to inherit more of his lands than just Spain. He had already been named Duke of Milan in 1540, though that title could easily have been removed if it fitted in with other diplomatic and dynastic considerations. By the mid/late 1540s Philip, born in May 1527, was of an age to take on a major role, but so was Maximilian, born only two months later. Charles wished to bind together the two branches of the Habsburg family in order to maintain Habsburg supremacy, seemingly achieved by the victory in Germany in 1547. He believed that only by Spain working together with the Empire could the power of the Habsburgs be effectively defended against France, and Christian Europe secured against the Ottoman Empire. Essentially Spanish money and troops were required, but the Spaniards needed a good reason to support this use of their resources.

By 1548 Charles had decided that Philip should inherit the Low Countries in addition to Spain. To that end Charles persuaded the Diet of Augsburg to declare that all 17 provinces were a separate entity, removed from the authority of the Holy Roman Empire. However the provinces would still contribute to the defence of the Empire against foreign enemies, especially the Ottomans, by providing money and troops. On leaving Augsburg, he spent some time hunting in Bavaria before travelling to Brussels, where he was joined by the now widowed Eleanor, who left France and returned

## Charles V: Duty and Dynasty

to her native land. The 'Pragmatic Sanction' of 1549 declared that the laws of succession in each province were altered so that they would remain united under a single ruler, the 'Lord of the Netherlands'. Only Charles and Philip were to ever use this title. Charles now instructed Philip to come to the Low Countries to be introduced as his heir.

These developments did not please Maximilian. He had entertained plans to link the Low Countries (and even Milan) with the Empire, where he eventually expected to succeed his father Ferdinand as emperor. Instead it was decided that he would travel to Spain and marry Charles' daughter, Maria. The union took place in September 1548 and the couple remained in Spain as co-regents while Philip travelled to the Low Countries. Maximilian and Maria were to go on to have fifteen children, but Maximilian's hopes of ruling in Brussels had been dashed.

Responding to his father's order Philip now took his first major journey outside Spain. Leaving Barcelona in October 1548 he crossed the Mediterranean to Genoa, travelled through northern Italy to Trent, and reached Innsbruck in February 1549. He continued north to Munich, then through Heidelberg to the Rhine, finally arriving in Brussels on 1st April. Along the route he was formally greeted in city after city, as if on a triumphal progress. After his welcome to Brussels that involved the usual processions[*], banquets and tournaments, in which Philip took part, he was taken by Charles and Mary to the leading cities of Flanders, Artois, Hainault and Brabant. Everywhere they were received with festivities and the local Estates swore allegiance to Philip as their next ruler. In September a worn out Charles returned to Brussels while Philip continued to the more northerly provinces until the end

---

[*] The 'Ommegang' or medieval pageant held in Brussels each year in early July is a re-enactment of the 1549 pageant dedicated to Charles and celebrating Philip's arrival. 'Ommegang' comes from the Flemish 'omme' ('around') and 'gang' ('march'). The first recorded such event took place in 1359 and they continued until 1810. The tradition was revived in 1930. Details of the 1549 'ommegang' were recorded by Juan Christobel de Estelle.

of October. The rather serious, delicate, aloof and inexperienced Philip did not find it comfortable. Somewhat like his father, he did not have the natural liveliness and ease in company that could win people's affections. From the very start Philip's relationship with the Low Countries was difficult: he was seen as a foreigner, having been brought up exclusively in Spain; unlike Charles he did not speak their language or have an appreciation of the traditional institutions of the provinces; he was regarded as being reserved and haughty. He eventually inherited the lands but he was never able to overcome these initial problems.

The winter was spent instructing Philip in the art of government in general and about the Low Countries in particular. He was also introduced to the palaces, paintings, tapestries and libraries that Margaret of Austria and Mary of Hungary had assembled over the previous fifty years. Charles then left the Low Countries, with Philip, in May 1550 to return to Augsburg. As he travelled for five days down the Rhine he dictated his 'Memoirs' to William van Male, his secretary, covering the period from his accession in the Low Countries in 1515 up to the present time. He intended to have them revised by Granvelle and Philip before having them more widely circulated. Perhaps re-living his past and remembering how much he had desired the Imperial crown increased his ambitions for his son. In an even greater threat to Maximilian's future hopes Charles was now thinking in terms of Philip taking over in the Empire as well. There was no doubt that Ferdinand, as elected and crowned 'King of the Romans' would be the next emperor. Maximilian had always assumed that he would succeed his father but Charles' recent ideas brought this into doubt. Charles was now considering the idea that Philip should succeed Ferdinand and then, perhaps, Maximilian would follow Philip. Since the nephews were the same age, both born in 1527, Maximilian's chances were seriously reduced.

Lengthy and acrimonious negotiations that threatened to tear the family apart began in Brussels and continued in Augsburg where Charles arrived in July. The discussions eventually involved Charles,

Philip, Ferdinand, Maximilian and Mary, who had already been working to avoid a permanent family rift. In 1549 she had assured Ferdinand that Charles would not exclude him from any decision. In May 1550 she expressed her concerns to him that Maximilian could cause serious divisions and reminded Ferdinand that Charles had supported his election as 'King of the Romans' in 1530 to the obvious detriment of his son Philip. In August, the death of Nicholas Perrenot de Granvelle, who had served as Charles' principal adviser since the death of Gattinara in 1530, was a blow. Although Granvelle's son, Antoine, Bishop of Arras, replaced him as secretary of state, he was relatively inexperienced for such delicate talks.

Ferdinand understandably resisted Charles' ideas. He had always respected Charles' position as emperor and head of the family and found it difficult to discuss the issue for fear of offending his brother. When pushed he proposed that Philip become 'Vicar-general' in Italy (effectively the emperor's deputy there). Charles rejected this. Ferdinand became distrustful of Charles, unwilling to give way, and Charles is said to have exclaimed 'we need to establish who is emperor: you or me'.[3] Maximilian travelled from Spain in December to defend his interests. Understandably his attitude towards Charles and Philip was cold and reserved; he avoided Philip altogether. He also had concerns about his father's resolve. He was later to write: 'God grant that His Majesty (Ferdinand) will one day stand up to His Imperial Majesty (Charles) and not always show himself so chicken-hearted as he has hitherto. I am perpetually astonished at the blindness of His Majesty; he will not see how unfraternally and how falsely His Imperial Majesty is treating us'[4]. Relations reached a point when negotiations were being carried out by letter rather than in person.

Ferdinand and Maximilian warned of the serious consequences of pushing Philip's claim to the Imperial crown and of how unpopular it would be with the German princes, given Philip's lack of experience in the affairs of the Empire. It was Mary, arriving from the Low Countries, who played a leading role in developing and pushing the compromise of the 'alternating succession'. Ferdinand would succeed Charles as Emperor and he would then work for Philip to be his successor, so long as Maximilian then became 'King of the Romans'. Philip gave an undertaking to support Ferdinand in the Empire and Hungary and to marry one of his daughters once he was confirmed as Ferdinand's successor. On 9th March 1551, having received various reassurances, Ferdinand signed the agreement but did nothing to ensure that it would be effective[5]. Maximilian was not required to put his signature to it but instead he was asked to give his verbal consent. He did so grudgingly. It was impressive that the content and nature of these discussions were kept strictly confidential, virtually within the family. They might have major differences of opinion but they intended to resolve them without recourse to public displays of animosity, which would have undoubtedly weakened the dynasty as a whole.

Charles' plan was thus reluctantly agreed to, but it would never be implemented. He never appreciated the opposition in Germany to the 'foreign' Philip. In Charles' view, he had been an outsider to Spain, as Ferdinand had been to Germany, and both these moves had been successful 30 years before, so why would Philip not be accepted now? But as Ferdinand had pointed out much had changed in Germany. In any case the choice of emperor would require the majority vote of the electors, and they were most unlikely to support Philip's candidacy. Thus, in reality, Maximilian's position as next King of the Romans and thus future Emperor, while not absolutely secure, was likely. By 1554 the agreement was, in effect, dead; there was little doubt that Ferdinand would succeed Charles and that Maximilian would follow his father.

Such a situation, of course, would finally confirm the separation of the Low Countries from Germany and the Empire and the future permanent division of Charles' territories between the 'Spanish' and the 'Austrian' Habsburgs. Charles had no choice but to recognise this, but was still hopeful that close links of family and marriage between the Spanish and Austrian Habsburgs would be sufficient to uphold their predominance in Europe. As Philip and Maximilian travelled together from Genoa to Barcelona in July 1551 tensions had been reduced to some extent. Philip was returning to take up the reins of power in Spain; Maximilian was travelling to re-join his wife, Charles' daughter Maria (who had been acting as regent in Spain), and their first child, Anne, who years later was to be Philip's fourth wife. Maximilian and Maria then returned to the empire and met Charles in Innsbruck that August.

Intimate ties were indeed maintained, but at the cost of hereditary weakness caused by the regular marriage of close family members. The 'Austrian' Habsburgs continued to rule in Austria–Hungary until 1918, but Charles' descendants in Spain, who ceased to rule there in 1700, are usually regarded as the unfortunate product of generations of inbreeding. Charles had married his cousin, Isabella; his sister Catherine married her cousin, John of Portugal; then the children of these two marriages married! The longest surviving child of these later marriages, the first son of Philip II of Spain, Don Carlos, was unstable and eventually died, locked up by his father, at the age of 23. This did not stop Philip from marrying his niece, Anne of Austria, who was the mother of his successor, Philip III. As Habsburg rulers in the 17th century continued to marry cousins and nieces the negative impact on succeeding generations became increasingly obvious. This culminated in the physical and intellectual problems of Charles II (1661-r.1665-1700). It has been convincingly argued that the empire built on such marriages had within it the seeds of its own destruction.[6]

## 27
### 'No cage big enough' - Innsbruck and Metz

Dynastic considerations meant that Charles had neglected developments in Germany during 1550. Tensions had been building since Charles' victory in the war of 1546-47 and were soon to explode, with his power challenged as never before. He had angered many princes, particularly his Protestant ally Maurice of Saxony, by the continued imprisonment of Philip of Hesse, as well as by his attempts to re-introduce Catholicism into Protestant areas of Germany by the removal of reformist priests. Unless imposed by coercion, the Augsburg Interim was widely ignored and derided. The general church council moved back to Trent in May 1551 and although representatives from Protestant principalities and cities attended, most observers recognised that it was now far too late to achieve any coming together of views.

Events were moving ever more rapidly towards another war. Maurice had received Imperial subsidies to raise an army to capture Lutheran Magdeburg, to which he had laid siege. In February 1550 Duke John Albert of Mecklenburg, Duke Albert of Prussia and Margrave Hans of Kustrin formed a league in Konigsberg, with the intention of relieving the city. In January 1551 Maurice acted swiftly to prevent the formation of their army, winning praise from Charles. But by now Maurice was despised by many Protestants for his support of the emperor and was also distrusted by the Catholics, who had good reason to believe that he had deliberately failed to take Magdeburg in order to draw more funds from Charles so that he could build up his own army. However he shared many of the views of the Protestant princes about Charles' use of foreign, especially Spanish, troops in Germany and by February 1551 had opened talks with his former enemies, while appealing to Charles to release Philip of Hesse. On hearing this Charles refused to free

Philip and instead, as a warning to Maurice, threatened to release the former elector of Saxony, John Frederick. This had the opposite effect to that intended. An angry Maurice came to an agreement with the Protestant princes that they should work together to throw off this 'bestial, intolerable and continual servitude'. In this they were joined by William of Hesse, son of the imprisoned Philip, and the opportunist Margrave Albert Alcibiades of Brandenburg-Kulmbach.

The princes then opened talks with Henry II of France who was naturally tempted to take advantage of Charles' difficulties. His negotiators came to terms with Maurice and the Protestants in October 1551, symbolically signing the agreement in the very hunting lodge on Lochau heath, where John Frederick had surrendered to Charles after the battle of Muhlberg in 1547. Confirmed by the Treaty of Chambord in January 1552, Henry promised to protect German liberties from the threat of the Emperor and agreed to provide significant funds for the Protestant armies in return for control of the cities of Metz, Toul and Verdun. This would sever Charles' access to the Low Countries, and provide a secure position from which his enemies could move against him.

Charles at first refused to believe the seriousness of the situation, despite urgent warnings from Ferdinand and Mary. He was confident of his own position and dismissive of the princes' ability to unite against him. He had some grounds for this belief. Hans of Kustrin disapproved of the French alliance and some of the younger generation of princes would not commit to fighting their emperor. But he had seriously mishandled Maurice. The elector had himself been in a difficult position, discredited in the eyes of both Protestant and Catholics. Had Charles been willing to release Philip of Hesse he might well have prevented Maurice from joining the Protestant alliance. Now Maurice's army became a major threat to Charles. As relations with the rebellious princes deteriorated during February and March 1552 Charles asked Maurice to come to meet him, talks from which Maurice excused himself, claiming that the journey was too dangerous and repeating his demand for Philip's release.

As Henry II fulfilled his part of the Treaty of Chambord moving against the cities of Lorraine - Metz, Toul and Verdun - in the spring of 1552, the princes' army advanced south from Mainz, re-establishing Protestant worship and appointing sympathetic magistrates as they went. While Albert Alcibiades seized Donauworth on the Danube, Maurice took Augsburg on 4th April, and made ready to march south for the Tyrol. Charles, having thought to escape to the Low Countries, realising that his route was blocked both by Maurice's army and the French in Lorraine, retreated to Innsbruck. Militarily he was unprepared. His confidence had been such that much of his army was in Italy attempting to make good his claim to Parma, offered to him by the new pope, Julius III, by removing Ottavio Farnese. The previous year Philip had been sent back to Spain with instructions to raise substantial funds for this venture. Charles had rejected his son's wish to participate in the campaign, arguing that it was not prestigious enough because he was acting as an ally of the pope and that the opposition in Italy was not led by royalty.

Charles needed time to recover his position. He had already initiated talks, sending a trusted councillor and knight of the Order of the Golden Fleece, Joachim de Rye, to Ferdinand, with whom Maurice had always maintained communications. His instructions were clear - to do his utmost to achieve peace. In talks at Linz, Ferdinand was to point out to Maurice and the others that Charles had always been moderate on the religious issue, and had no intention of overthrowing traditional German rights, only to assert his own. De Rye was also asked to watch for any sign that Ferdinand might have some secret understanding with Maurice, and if he had any such suspicions he should immediately remind Ferdinand, and his son Maximilian, of the importance of the dynasty standing together, not only to settle the current crisis but to protect their own future interests. He was to suggest to Maximilian that he could win considerable respect if he were to act as mediator.[1] Charles was clearly worried about his brother's loyalty after the family disagreements, a concern that both Ferdinand's actions at the time and subsequent events revealed to be groundless. However despite the weakness of his position Charles was not yet prepared to concede either the release of Philip, unless Maurice's army was disbanded in advance, or any significant change to the Augsburg 'interim'.

The talks with Maurice and his allies thus failed to achieve a truce, despite Ferdinand's best efforts. Once again, however, Maurice was treading a difficult path. He was aware that his own future might very well depend on future dealings with the Habsburgs and knew that in time Charles would be able to bring together superior forces. But any deal with Charles would be seen by the French as a betrayal; his allies would not be willing to disband their army without some kind of victory. So he made the decision to renew the offensive. Advancing south along the Lech valley to Fussen he defeated an Imperial army near Reutte on the 19th and entered Innsbruck on 23rd May. Charles and his unprotected court narrowly escaped capture and made an ignominious flight over the Brenner Pass and then eastwards, arriving in Villach on 27th May. He had already written to Mary claiming that: 'I can find not a penny, nor anyone who wants to lend me one, nor a man in Germany who seems ready to declare for me'[2]. At the time Maurice probably could have captured the Emperor, but he was aware of the enormity of such an act saying that he had: 'no cage big enough to hold so large a bird'.

In what must have been one of his lowest moments, Charles renewed his efforts and began to summon his resources. Letters requesting funds were sent throughout Europe. Anton Fugger, who was travelling with the court, provided 400,000 ducats; a total of 800,000 ducats was agreed in Naples and the viceroy, don Pedro de Toledo, was able to send 200,000 ducats immediately, and a similar amount soon followed. With Spanish and Italian troops moving north from Italy, the Duke of Alva on his way to lead them, and more forces being raised in the Low Countries, the Protestant leaders knew that their position was weakening rapidly.

Both Ferdinand and Maurice were now keen to achieve a settlement, their aim being a permanent peace in Germany. Ferdinand recognised that he needed assistance against advancing Ottoman forces in Hungary and that Maurice could provide this if only a deal could be reached. For his part Maurice knew that he had already damaged his links with France by holding any talks at all with Charles' representatives and he also wished to protect his position as elector. In further negotiations, at Passau, during June and July, terms were discussed, but neither Charles nor Maurice's allies were yet ready to make the necessary concessions. Ferdinand pleaded with Charles, who would only agree to a religious peace until yet another Diet was held. Maurice could not command the support of all the princes but managed to win over William of Hesse. Despite misgivings on both sides, the truce that was agreed in August 1552 was to pave the way for a more permanent settlement. Philip of Hesse and John Frederick of Saxony were released and Maurice's troops would join Ferdinand against the 'Turk' (although only about half of them did so). In religion the continuation of the toleration of the Protestant faith foreshadowed the Religious Peace of Augsburg in 1555.

The eventual agreement had been influenced by Charles' continued belief that his true enemies were the French and not the German princes. He could now concentrate on that threat. Henry II had stirred up problems for Charles in Italy, urged the Ottoman forces to attack in Hungary and step up their activities in the Mediterranean, and begun military actions in Flanders. In Lorraine his commander, the Duke of Montmorency, had occupied the militarily important city of Metz. Having obtained agreement to his request that the surrounding countryside provide accommodation for his army of 38,000 and that he and his personal entourage could lodge inside the city, Montmorency marched in with 1,500 troops and secured control without resistance. Henry appointed the Duke of Guise as governor who then set about creating formidable defences, destroying the suburbs which would provide cover for an attacking force, and building new inner walls.

Charles, with the encouragement of his commander, the Duke of Alva, was keen to move against Metz as soon as possible. He believed that he needed to restore his reputation, damaged by events earlier in the year, and this blinded him to the realities of the situation.[3] He rejected Philip's expressed wish to go to his father's assistance, claiming that it was too late in the year for Philip to be able to make an honourable entry into European affairs, though Charles' real motive was that he wanted to show that he was still capable of effective action himself. His son's arrival would undermine him, though he was keen to use Spanish funds and troops.[4] Mary, worried that another failure would weaken Charles' position still further, wanted him to wait for the spring and to leave Alva in charge for the time being. Ignoring this cautious advice, Charles marched from Austria, through Munich, Augsburg, Ulm to Strasbourg. To secure his military position he accepted the demands of the remaining Protestant commander, the Margrave Albert Alcibiades of Brandenburg-Kulmbach. Charles had to overcome his conscience by confirming treaties that the Margrave had forced upon Wurzburg and Bamberg, which he had previously rejected. In November 1552 the Margrave joined the Imperial side with 15,000 troops that would otherwise have threatened Charles' advance. Charles wrote to his sister that: 'the only alternative was to disband my army, which would have meant that all my expenses had been in vain... needs must when the devil drives'.[5] By mid-November Metz was under siege. Charles believed that 'if we fail now it will be very serious indeed'.

But fail he did. Despite the size of his army, which now numbered 60,000, the shattering impact of his cannons, and the attempts of his troops to undermine the walls, the defences held. The French had a good supply of food and sound lodgings having expelled many non-combatants to fend for themselves, while the winter cold, snow and lack of adequate shelter weakened the morale of the besieging army. With the cold and damp, Charles' health deteriorated. His chamberlain, van Male, reported that he was overeating and drinking large quantities of iced beer. As the likelihood of failure increased, Charles' anxiety and depression grew. In January 1553 he ended the siege and by early February he was back in Brussels.

With this failure, Charles' health took a further turn for the worse. His sufferings from physical ailments are well documented. From the late 1520s he had been subject to increasingly painful attacks of gout (in his 'memoirs', dictated in 1550, 17 attacks are mentioned). In 1532 there is a description of his experiencing a 'terrible itching' all over his body, with his face swollen and pimply. In 1546 it was reported that at times he had trouble standing and walking. The gout or arthritis limited his mobility. What is certain is that by 1548, the time of Titian's famous equestrian painting, he could scarcely ride a horse, something that must have been of great regret to Charles, given his upbringing and love of hunting.

Charles' mental health was now also threatened. There were perhaps early signs. In 1526 he was said to have been deeply depressed by news of Francis' failure to carry out the terms of the Treaty of Madrid and the subsequent formation of the anti-Habsburg League of Cognac. The English envoy to his court reported that: 'He is full of dumps and solitary musing, sometimes alone three or four hours together. There is no mirth or comfort with him'. By the 1540s he suffered from insomnia, and in 1549 the French ambassador Marillac wrote: 'his face is more that of a dead than a live man'. In November 1552, Antoine Perrenot de Granvelle wrote to Mary that Charles was lethargic and was not willing to give audiences. It might be too easy to remember his mother, Juana, still being held in Tordesillas because of her mental breakdown over 45 years earlier, and conclude that there was a hereditary weakness. But given the pressures of ruling such a vast area for over 30 years, the serious and workmanlike way in which he generally tackled his task, the difficulties that he had faced and the constant strains of almost endless travel, perhaps we should believe that Charles had coped with it all remarkably well until now.

However, what happened in 1553, after his return to Brussels, was of a different order. There are clear indications of a complete physical and psychological collapse. Arthritis 'spread to all the joints, limbs and nerves of his body' (Nicholas Nicolay, a councillor in the Low Countries); he suffered from catarrh and serious haemorrhoids. For lengthy periods he became incapable of the concentration required for the business of government and often refused to see even the most senior advisers, such as Granvelle. At first he blamed his health and later gave no excuse at all. During May and June he had no use of his right hand and in the autumn it was said that he was totally incapacitated. There were genuine fears for his life. Some reports of his melancholy go so far as to suggest that he was a broken man 'Often he weeps for long periods and with such copious shedding of tears as if he were a child'. It was commented that he spent his time alone in deep thought or 'adjusting his clocks of which he has a lot. This is his principle concern'[6]. He suffered a loss of confidence, blaming himself and others for his failures. He believed that he had made more concessions than he should have done at Passau (to Maurice of Saxony) and at Metz (to Albert Alcibiades of Brandenburg-Kulmbach) in both religious and secular fields, and that the princes were deceitful, motivated by self-interest. Charles now left German affairs largely to Ferdinand.

The most powerful monarch in Europe was for the moment 'aging, inept', indecisive, suffering from depression and occasional rages.[7] He depended greatly on his secretary, Francisco de Eraso, and above all on Mary, who showed her skill and abilities in controlling the severely stretched imperial finances and being able to keep knowledge of Charles' true condition from becoming widely known. It was now that Charles began to think more seriously about an idea that he claimed had been in the back of his mind for several years - to abdicate all his powers and authority and to spend the rest of his time on earth preparing for death.

## 28
## 'I can no longer participate' – Relinquishing Power

Given the strength of Charles' wish to become Emperor back in 1519, and the dedication and tenacity he had displayed in carrying out this and his other responsibilities for thirty-five years, the depth of his disillusion must have been profound if he now willingly contemplated relinquishing the role. His frustrations had been enormous. He was never able to rely on the Papacy - they saw German Protestants as Charles' problem and one that reduced their fears of an over powerful Emperor. He had repeatedly had little option but to make temporary religious concessions in order to gain the princes' support against Ottoman advances or French aggression, and these became permanent achievements for the Protestants and princes seeking to weaken Imperial power. It was probably a mistake to link the solution of Germany's problems with a general council of the Church which the Papacy delayed for decades. He had underestimated the strength of belief behind the Reformation and his idea of leading a united Christian world did not sit comfortably with the growth in power of independent rulers. His belief that Europe's best defence was by linking the Empire and Spain had not changed but he now realised that this would not be solely under the leadership of Philip.

This interplay of political and religious factors meant that the vision of a universal monarchy and united Christendom, encouraged in the earlier years of his reign by Gattinara, was now an outdated impossibility. On the other hand it is said that centuries later Napoleon believed that if the Emperor had put himself at the head of German Protestantism in 1520 he would have created a united German nation and solved the 'German question'. Perhaps, but given the nature of Charles' beliefs, his faith, and his other responsibilities, this would have been inconceivable. Although

Charles had shown himself capable of adapting to the particular needs of a specific situation, it was evident that he was increasingly out of tune with many of the broader changes that were occurring as Europe moved away from the medieval world.

In his state of depression through much of 1553 Charles found refuge in thoughts of a simpler world, untroubled by external events. Ten years earlier he had commissioned reports on various places in Spain as to which was best suited to act as a retreat. He had recently sent a trusted aide to inspect the Hieronymite monastery at Yuste and the report had clearly indicated that this could fit his requirements, with its relatively remote location in Extremadura and the close links that existed between the order and the Spanish royal family. He now sent instructions that 'To the side of the monastery at Yuste let a house large enough for me to live as a private person with my most indispensable servants be built'[1]. Plans of this sort were not made public, since they could seriously undermine his position. It was widely known that Charles had suffered illness before but as far as the world was concerned he would almost certainly recover to be able to take decisive action as he had in the past. There would still be a considerable time before Charles made any final decision about retirement, but the foundations had been laid.

Charles' relations with his son were complex in the later years of his reign. Having refused Philip's wish to come from Spain to be involved in the military campaigns either in Italy or at Metz, Charles' inability to take charge in 1553 had left an uncertain situation, especially in the Low Countries now under attack by the French. Mary had, of necessity, taken on many of the key functions of government. In May 1553 the Venetian ambassador reported that 'the queen does almost everything'.[2] As early as 1552 she had negotiated loans in Antwerp on Charles' behalf that were to be repaid from Spanish revenues. When Philip protested that one regent could not impose such debts on the lands of another, Charles over-ruled him. However with Charles' illness, Mary became increasingly convinced that Philip, the acknowledged heir, was needed in the Low Countries if rebellion was to be avoided and royal authority preserved. Having prevented Philip from leaving Spain in 1552, Charles sent instructions in April 1553 telling him to depart for the Low Countries. 'We need someone who can command the loyalty and obedience of these states during the war, in which I can no longer participate'.[3] He was told to bring with him large sums, to cover the cost of the journey, his household expenses and to pay for the following year's military campaign, and to arrive by September 1553.

Such demands put great pressure on Philip. If he arrived without substantial resources he would lose face, especially as expectations were high. On the other hand he did not wish to impoverish his Spanish lands and was bound to face problems raising the sums required on such a tight timescale, especially as many in Spain felt that their own defences against raiding corsairs and a possible attack by an Ottoman fleet were being neglected. Charles, encouraged by Mary, who did not wish more costs to fall upon the Low Countries, mooted the idea of once again using the shipments of bullion from the New World. This involved not making the expected payment of debts and gifts from the royal 'quinto' and the confiscation of other people's bullion in return for government annuities, the 'juros'. Philip objected on the grounds that many people would suffer, from widows and orphans to wealthy bankers, but his arguments were rebuffed. Charles regarded his son's conscience as being too delicate. In response Philip ordered the seizure of the money due to the Schetz merchant bank, which had close links with Mary. In a fury she insisted that Charles demand the return of their money and Charles for his part also made it clear to Philip that he was not to block payments to Anton Fugger either.

Philip was never likely to raise sufficient money and leave Spain as early as September 1553, but there was an alternative source of funds, one which Charles himself had used in the 1520s - marriage. Two years earlier Philip, having returned to Spain, had decided to take his father's advice to re-marry. By mid-1553 he was in the advanced stages of arranging his betrothal to Maria, the daughter of

Charles' sister Eleanor and her first husband, Manuel I of Portugal. This would bring a large dowry and a future regent that would be acceptable in Spain, just as Isabella had been thirty years before. Philip sought and received confirmation that Ferdinand would not enforce the agreement that he should marry one of his uncle's daughters (Ferdinand knew that this would not be popular in Germany) and by August had he agreed terms with Maria's half-brother, King John of Portugal.

Then came news from England. In July 1553 Edward VI died, aged 15, and the accession of Mary Tudor to the English throne opened many possibilities for the Habsburgs. Although Charles was fully aware of the possible benefits of close links with England he was not sufficiently recovered to play a major role in directing the negotiations. Once again it was Mary who took the lead in instructing representatives led by Simon Renard to bring the talks in England to a successful conclusion. Mary Tudor was the daughter of Charles' aunt, Catherine of Aragon; she was a Catholic, and so the country would be returned to the 'true church' which Henry VIII had left; and she was unmarried. Thirty years earlier she had been a possible bride for Charles himself and she still looked favourably upon such a match. Charles would not countenance this, but a marriage between Philip and Mary would fit into Charles' plan for Spain and the Low Countries to be under one ruler, securing the sea route between the two, as well as furthering the trade links across the North Sea. The French would correctly see it as yet a further tightening of its encirclement by the Habsburgs.

Philip also recognised the advantages and was initially enthusiastic. He had to extricate himself from his commitments to Portugal, though he did so slowly in case the English match fell through. However, the negotiations with England, directed by Mary and Grenville from Brussels, were carried out in secret and seemed to further the interests of the Low Countries rather than Spain. A future state covering England and the Low Countries would be ruled by the heirs of Philip and Mary, excluding Philip's first son, Don Carlos, and Philip's power in England was to be severely curtailed.

The formal betrothal took place in London on 30th October 1553. An increasingly concerned Philip did not even see the final treaty before the marriage by proxy had been performed. Indeed he secretly repudiated the terms of the treaty on the grounds that he had not been party to the negotiations and that only filial duty had forced him to accept it. His will in 1557 states that Don Carlos should inherit all his lands, ignoring the marriage treaty, although by then it was unlikely that he and Mary would have any children.

By early 1554 Charles was in better health and was now prepared to resume greater control of affairs. He over-ruled any objections that Philip or Ferdinand, who had thoughts of his second son marrying Mary, might have had. With the marriage arranged and the expectation that he supply one million ducats for the Habsburg cause, Philip decided to get the most out of the situation. Firstly, if Charles himself would not, or could not, return to Spain, a regent needed to be appointed. Don Carlos, under 10 years old, was too young. Charles wished to appoint someone with experience, and was persuaded to send the formal papers to Valladolid with the names of two candidates, one of whom was certainly Charles' preferred choice, Fernando de Valdes, Inquisitor-General and Archbishop of Seville, from whom Philip could choose. Simultaneously, news arrived that Charles' youngest daughter, Juana, had been widowed in Portugal when her husband, Prince John, was killed in a riding accident. Juana gave birth to a son less than three weeks later. Philip went against Charles' clear wishes and persuaded Juana, still only 18, to return to Spain to take up the post of regent. Charles had argued that she was too young and he also believed her to be headstrong. Philip went on to appoint men who had worked closely with him to the regency council and to other administrative and ecclesiastical posts. He would keep control of Spain in his absence.

Secondly, Philip decided to make his mark and increase his prestige by arriving for his marriage in grand style. He raised funds by further plundering of the bullion shipments from the Americas and landed in England on 20th July 1554 accompanied by a fine fleet with an impressively turned out company. The marriage was conducted by Bishop Gardiner, the Lord Chancellor, in Winchester cathedral on 25th July 1554. The reaction of the English to Philip's new position, despite the clear restrictions on his power in the country, was rather like that of the Spanish to Charles' arrival in Spain back in 1517 – hostility to a foreign king, his courtiers and his advisers. His companions, in turn, considered the English to be xenophobic. There were serious rivalries over positions at court, and most of the new arrivals soon wished to leave what they saw as an expensive, uncomfortable and unfriendly country. All this was in spite of Philip's considerable efforts to establish harmonious relations. He came over as courteous and approachable; he 'dined in public and even drank beer, both activities which he intensely disliked'.[4] Mary, who was by now 38, eleven years older than Philip, was very keen for the marriage to work and to have children who would secure the Catholic succession. Philip, keen for a successful political outcome, was chivalrous, ignoring slights to his honour when Mary was given precedence. Charles was surprised when this was reported to him, commenting that he must have changed a lot since he had last seen him. However Philip was unable to reciprocate Mary's affections.[5] The lack of children from the marriage and Mary's death in 1558 marked the start of a breakdown in Anglo-Spanish relations that eventually led to the sending of the Spanish Armada by Philip 30 years later.

While in Brussels during 1553 Charles had prepared a written statement that renounced anything in the agreements made at Passau (with Duke Maurice) and Metz (with Margrave Albert Alcibiades) that was against God, against justice or the laws of the Holy Roman Empire. His conscience was troubling him, but he was persuaded not to publish the document that was sure to incite the various factions involved. In July Maurice of Saxony, having taken arms against the Margrave, who he regarded as the worst type of mercenary commander, defeated his enemy at the battle of Sieverhausen, but died as a result of gunshot wounds. Only thirty-two, Maurice had played a major role in the events of the previous ten years. At Passau, he had pressed Ferdinand and Charles for 'an unconditional and perpetual peace' of the religious issue by allowing rulers to determine the form that religion should take in their own lands. Unwilling to accept a permanent religious division Charles had agreed to this only until the next Imperial Diet.

In June 1554 he announced he would not attend that Diet, to be held in Augsburg the following year. Ferdinand was to take his place, as he had done frequently during the 1520's and 1530's. Charles recognised that the decisions made about religion would be unpalatable to him. He wrote to his brother about his 'unconquerable scruple' regarding the question of religion and drew up a list of all the issues that he thought should be raised at the Diet. Ferdinand responded by asking his brother not to abdicate before the Diet, so that he could have a higher authority to appeal to if needed. The agreement that was reached in Augsburg and eventually signed on 25$^{th}$ September 1555 was therefore in Charles' name, but he wished to have nothing to do with it. The treaty allowed German princes to choose between Catholicism or Lutheranism within the lands that they ruled – 'cuius regio, eius religio' (whose the region, his the religion) - with subjects being given a period of time to migrate to a different region to suit their beliefs. Calvinism and Anabaptism were not included in the treaty. The power of the princes, as opposed to the Emperor, was greatly enhanced. This was very similar to the arrangement proposed by Maurice three years earlier, though Maurice himself had not survived to see it finally put into effect.

Charles' decision to abdicate, like most of his decisions, was not a rapid, spur of the moment one; it had taken over a decade for his first thoughts of retirement to develop into a decision that would soon be put into practice. Had circumstances developed differently Charles may never have gone through with it, but he now concluded that the moment had come. His periods of ill-health meant that at times he could not govern. He was increasingly conscious of his physical limitations. Always aware of a propaganda opportunity Charles wished it to be known that he desired his final years to be dedicated to religious devotion and it suited both Charles' self-image and his public persona to have people believe that he had always intended to retire from the affairs of state. But he now recognised that some of the broader political, social and religious changes of his reign had placed growing constraints upon his power to influence events. This was not a monarch retiring confident that his wider aims had been achieved, rather one who believed that he had done his best over a period of thirty five years and realised that there was little more that he was able to do. He did, however, wish to put a positive gloss on his gradual transfer of power to Philip and Ferdinand.

He knew that in Germany there was no workable alternative to an agreement which would fail to bring about a reunited Catholic church. The war against France was continuing without notable success. After French advances into Hainault and Artois in June 1554, in which Mary's chateau at Binche was destroyed, Charles argued for a new offensive, but his council opposed this, wishing to concentrate on the defence of the Low Countries. Charles' last military involvement was to observe the relief of Renty, south of Calais, in August 1554. Ottoman fleets, allied with the French, were once again causing problems in the Mediterranean. In 1551 Turgut Reis had taken Tripoli. The following year his fleet defeated Doria at the battle of Ponza, off the coast of Naples. Corsica, a Genoese possession, was captured by a joint French-Ottoman invasion in 1553, and Spanish controlled Bougie in North Africa was then lost to Salih Reis of Algiers in 1555. Parts of Sicily and Calabria suffered serious raids and the inhabitants of Andalucía, Valencia and Catalonia feared similar attacks. There were further problems in Italy where Philip, strongly influenced by the Duke of Alva, wished to replace Charles' trusted long time commander Ferrante Gonzaga. Although Philip had always been careful to prevent the growing differences between him and his father from becoming public, Charles recognised that to remain in control would further damage relations with his son.

It was during the first half of 1555 that Charles decided the moment to hand over power had arrived. The exact timing of his formal abdication from his various territories followed by his journey to Spain could not be planned in isolation and delays were almost inevitable. The process had actually begun in July 1554 when he had given Philip the kingdom of Naples on his marriage to Mary Tudor. Charles' mother and co-monarch, Juana, still confined at Tordesillas, died in April 1555, thus clearing any succession issues that might have existed in the Spanish lands. In Italy the French invasion of 1553 in support of Siena had been defeated in 1554 and Siena itself taken in April 1555 by Imperial troops together with those of Cosimo de Medici, Duke of Florence. This, and the stalemate in Artois, made a truce possible. Nonetheless, the new pope, Paul IV, who had succeeded Marcellus II[*] in May 1555, immediately showed himself hostile to what he regarded as Spanish rule in much of Italy and sought a French alliance. It seemed that despite all Charles' efforts over the last forty years very little had changed. It was only when Philip arrived in Brussels in September 1555[†], after over a year in England, and the Peace of Augsburg had been signed in the same month, that he could continue the process of arranging to step down from the many titles that he held.

On the 22$^{nd}$ October 1555 he relinquished his leadership of the Order of the Golden Fleece, which had meant so much to him. Three days later, in the Great Hall of the Coudenburg Palace, a ceremony was held to pass the control of the Low Countries to Philip. Charles entered supported by Prince William of Orange. In attendance were Philip, Charles' sisters Eleanor and Mary, his commander-in-chief Philibert Emanuel of Savoy, the knights of the Golden Fleece, and others of note in the Low Countries. His speech, in French, took his audience back 40 years to his 'coming of age' ceremony in the same hall. He recalled his accession in Spain followed by the Empire, and

---

[*] Pope Julius III (Pope from 1550) had died in March 1555. His successor, Marcellus II, was pope for only 22 days in April-May 1555 before his death
[†] By then it was becoming clear that Mary Tudor was unlikely to conceive, thus disrupting Charles' dynastic plans in northern Europe.

his many journeys to Spain, Italy, the Low Countries, France, Africa and England. He explained that his forces were spent; his health had deserted him. He was disappointed that he could not leave his people in peace, but he had done all that he could and that his wars had been forced upon him by his enemies to defend his lands[6]. He thanked God that He had so often helped him and said that he now only wished to give his own lands to Philip and the Empire to Ferdinand. 'Charles exhorted his son to stand fast in the faith of his fathers, to care for peace and justice. He himself had often erred, out of youth, out of self-will, out of weakness. But he had never wilfully wronged any man. If he had done so unwittingly he asked forgiveness.'[7]

Charles sank to his seat; the audience were in tears, as was Charles himself. Philip knelt before his father and promised to follow his wishes. Having been raised and embraced by his father, Philip introduced the Bishop of Arras, Antoine Perrenot de Granvelle, who was to read his speech because, as Philip explained, he did not speak French sufficiently well. Mary, regent of the Low Countries, spoke next and announced her decision to leave the lands that she had governed for 25 years in order to travel to Spain with her brother and her sister Eleanor. Charles thanked her for her loyal service to him and his lands.

In many ways the Low Countries were the most difficult lands for Philip to rule. He had failed to make a positive impression on his first visit in 1549-50 and even though behind the scenes he had more than stood up to Charles in recent years his public loyalty to his father had convinced many people that he was weak and indecisive. He was not helped by Charles' decision to make numerous military, ecclesiastical administrative and financial appointments, many for life, just as power was transferred. Whether this was to reward those who had served him well or whether it was in revenge for Philip's appointments for the regency in Spain is unclear, but it initially prevented Philip from consolidating his power by placing his own men in many vital posts. Nor was this the end of Charles' attempts to interfere with the future running of his lands. There is considerable evidence to suggest that he wished to retain control of Spanish finances, though if this was the case he was to be prevented from doing so.

On 16th January 1556, in his private apartments, Charles abdicated from Castile, Leon, the Indies, Aragon and Sicily; all his Spanish territories were passed on to Philip, as was the master-ship of the Spanish orders of Santiago, Calatrava and Alcantara. Charles expressed his wish to live in the service of God and to atone for his sins. Back in Spain, Philip was formally declared king in his absence, though the cortes of Aragon at first refused to accept the documentation as adequate and then Juana advised Philip not to publish the proclamation until he returned to Spain. The formal recognition of Ferdinand as Holy Roman Emperor was much delayed. Charles refused to sign the Treaty of Augsburg. Ferdinand took the line that he had negotiated the treaty on Charles' behalf and did not wish to take full responsibility for what he regarded as the result of Charles' policies and mistakes. Philip was concerned that as soon as Ferdinand officially became Emperor he would not be able to call upon German troops without Ferdinand's approval. Although Ferdinand had already become de facto Emperor, the electors did not formally recognise the transfer of power until February 1558, by then with Philip's full backing. Charles retained the title to Franche-Comte until his death, since the neutrality agreement signed by Charles and Henry II excluded their successors.

It was impossible for Charles to make the voyage to Spain during the winter months, and so this would now be made in the spring or summer. It must have been a difficult time for both Charles and Philip, as well as causing much confusion in the Low Countries, with three centres of power - their former lord, their current lord and the new Governor-General, Emmanuel Philibert of Savoy, who had replaced Mary. Charles lived out the last few months of his time there in a handsome, but not grand, house in the park of Coutenberg Palace. Here he greeted the French delegation that had come to ratify the Truce of Vaucelles of February 1556. This break in the fighting made possible a safer voyage along the Channel and across the Bay of Biscay. He received many who wished to take their leave, and was able to say farewell to his daughter Maria, even though her husband Maximilian still harboured some resentment.

# Part Six
# Retreat from the World Stage 1556-1558

Charles' villa at Yuste, attached to the south side of the Monastery.

Charles V: Duty and Dynasty

## 29
## 'We shall not be asked what we have read, but what we have done' - Reflections

The usual lack of funds further delayed Charles' departure, and he eventually left Brussels for the coast on 8th August 1556, accompanied by Philip as far as Ghent. His discomfort when travelling and his wish to see parts of his homeland for the final time meant that progress was slow. Once in Flushing he was joined by Eleanor and Mary, but adverse winds caused yet more delay, giving Philip the opportunity to pay one last visit to his father. In mid-September the fleet eventually set sail. Charles knew that this journey was to be his last. His frequent travelling, his life of responsibility and duty, though not resented nor regretted, had all taken their toll. How long would he have left to study his maps and astronomical charts, to read, to tinker with his clocks, and to prepare for his death? He trusted to God to choose the moment.

Charles would have been familiar with one of the best known devotional books of the time, 'The Imitation of Christ' by Thomas a Kempis[*], and might well have been inspired by it. There had been a number of occasions during his life when he had put trust in God and remained hopeful of eventual victory in the face of defeat, just as Kempis advised. Charles' decision to abdicate could well have been influenced by Kempis' argument that a withdrawal from a life of power, the banishing of temptation and vanity, and valuing the 'inner life', were the best preparation for death. On this final journey to Spain he must have contemplated Kempis' belief that 'At the Day

---

[*] Thomas a Kempis (Thomas of Kempen) is generally acknowledged as the author. The book was written around 1420. It was first printed in 1471, in Augsburg, and by the early 16th century it had been translated from the original Latin into French, German, Italian and Spanish and had more than 100 printed editions.

of Judgement we shall not be asked what we have read, but what we have done'[1], that fervent prayer and holy deeds would be of greater value than feasting and fine words.

It was only natural that Charles would reflect upon his life and consider how his God would judge him. He was less concerned about the verdict of others, even though there would be many keen to voice their opinions. Relations, friends, associates, servants, rivals and opponents – their lives had been determined by his decisions, his needs, his fears. His territories had been so vast and so diverse that each of them would judge him on their own terms, just as they would continue to do into the future.* With his seventy-two different titles by the age of 25, he had ruled twenty-eight million people, 40% of the population of Europe. His empire had no heartland, no capital city, and no common language. His ability to impose his political will or raise taxes varied with the ancient traditions and privileges that existed in each part of his empire.

---

* Scott-Dixon and Fuchs. The subsequent history of each territory has influenced how Charles' reign has been interpreted. It has been suggested that there are four different and conflicting pictures of Charles that express the varying views about him: Charles as a saintly recluse at Yuste; as the exponent of real politic using all means to achieve his aims; as national hero; and as a symbol of European unity (P. Burke in Soly quoted by Scott-Dixon and Fuchs). The lands that he ruled, as well as others that had dealings with him, have had a wide range of views. In the Low Countries Charles is sometimes seen as a hero in his homelands of the south, which remained under Habsburg control until the end of the 18th century. In the northern provinces, with the successful rebellion against Spanish rule in the late 16th and early 17th centuries, he is seen as a relatively minor figure, much less significant in the nation's development than the 17th century age of expansion and trade, art and culture in the Dutch Republic. In Spain he has often been seen as a lesser figure than Isabella and Ferdinand, or his son Philip, though it is recognised that he ruled at a time when Spanish influence overseas grew rapidly. However by his expensive wars elsewhere Charles may be held responsible for sowing the seeds of Spain's decline in the 17th century. In Italy there was a generally positive image of Charles until growing nationalism in the 19th century portrayed him as a conqueror imposing Spanish domination. Religious and political complexities in Germany have meant that there has rarely been any consensus, though he has often been viewed in terms of his impact upon the development of Germany as a nation.

Each territory had its own history, values and beliefs, its own aspirations and therefore its own perceptions of how successful Charles had been.

How would Charles' have judged his forty years in power? There can be little dispute about his central aims; he expressed them on a number of occasions, and demonstrated considerable will power in attempting to achieve them. Dynastically, he wished to pass on the territories that he had inherited, intact and secure, to his successor. In religion he wanted to achieve the unity of the church, to do his duty to God and to defeat the infidel, the Ottoman Turks, who were threatening central Europe and the Mediterranean. Were these still realistic aims in the changing world of the 16th century? Was Charles able to recognise the nature of those changes? Was he able to adapt what was valuable from the past to the realities of a new age? Despite his power and status could he control events or was he merely responding to them?

In terms of the integrity of his complex inheritance Charles would have been pleased that he passed on the lands received from his various ancestors in a generally more secure state than when he inherited them. He had added territories in the Low Countries, though failed to regain Burgundy and lost control of Metz, Toul, and Verdun to France in the later part of his reign. Spain was stable and the lands in the New World had been expanded beyond all recognition. He was undisputedly the dominant force in Italy. In Germany the imperial throne was set to remain in the Habsburg family. Much of this had been achieved through frequent warfare, particularly against France. Even though Charles often claimed that his interest was in peace and that war was forced upon him, he was more than willing to use war as a means of defending and consolidating what he believed to be his by right. His use of dynastic marriages meant that he sometimes bound other families to the Habsburgs, but the frequency of marriage between cousins, when continued for several generations in order to retain the possessions of the dynasty, would have an unfortunate impact on the physical and mental capabilities of his successors.

Despite his efforts, however, he was not handing on a united inheritance. The division of his lands between his son and his brother had effectively been decided way back in 1530 when Ferdinand had been elected as King of the Romans because of Charles' recognition of the need for his support. Charles later came to regret that it was unlikely that Philip would ever become emperor but he was unable to change the reality of the situation which meant that Ferdinand would be succeeded by his son Maximilian and the Habsburg dominions would be split. Charles rightly recognised that individually both might be weaker, but few others in Europe wished to see a united Habsburg inheritance that would dominate the continent.

Charles' belief in the importance of religious unity and loyalty to the Catholic Church was a consistent theme in his letters and speeches. In Germany he had been faced with a major challenge, though it was not of his making. He supported the need for reform of the clergy to put an end to the blatant abuses that harmed the church in the eyes of many. However he could not accept the division of Christianity. Thus in 1521 at Worms he had emphasised his belief that as emperor he regarded himself as the defender and protector of the Catholic Church; in 1530 at Augsburg and again in 1541 at Regensburg he personally urged the Catholic and Lutheran representatives to find common ground for a reunification - in vain. If the issue was so important to him should he have given it more attention earlier in his reign? He was not often in Germany until the 1540s, spending considerably more time in Spain, and when he did attempt to deal with the problem he had repeatedly compromised with the Protestant princes in Germany in order to gain their support for the defence of central Europe from the Ottoman threat. The edicts and decrees against Protestants were almost impossible to enforce without the support of the local rulers. Short term priorities had often taken precedence over his long term, deeply held beliefs.

Charles knew that he had been accused of using religious differences as a cynical cover for crushing opposition and extending his power in Germany. Almost two centuries later Gilbert Burnet (1643-1715), the Scottish theologian who became Bishop of Salisbury under William III, restated this charge. He argued that 'having formed designs of an universal monarchy, (Charles) laid hold on the differences of religion as a good means to cover what he did, with a specious pretence of punishing heresy and protecting the Catholics'.* Charles would certainly have rejected this and indeed levelled much of it at others - German princes who wished to use the religious divisions of the time to undermine the emperor's position, and French monarchs who while persecuting Protestants at home were willing to finance Charles' Protestant opponents in Germany and make an alliance with the 'Turk'. Even when Charles did use force against the Protestant princes, gaining a major victory at Muhlberg in 1547, he was still unable to enforce a religious settlement. This was another example of Charles failing to capitalise on a battlefield victory, as after the capture of Francis I at Pavia in 1525 and the success at Tunis in 1535.

But Charles of all people had learnt that a military victory did not guarantee the implementation of an effective peace on your own terms. This was not just a matter of military might but of faith and belief. It was the combination of religious and political issues that had prevented him imposing in Germany the harsh persecution of heretics that occurred elsewhere in his lands. In Spain there was relatively little growth of Protestant beliefs, and what there was had been rapidly erased. In the Low Countries various Protestant groups had flourished. He had encouraged Mary to take a firm line

---

* The French have usually regarded Charles as a monarch who threatened the security of their country and aimed at European hegemony. British writers have usually seen him as a more distant figure, though while religious tensions were still significant, Charles as guardian of the Catholic Church was bound to be seen as 'on the wrong side', though not as a major threat like Philip. In central and eastern Europe his position has often been seen as positive in his role against the Ottoman Turks but more critical in terms of the development of national identity. Naturally in the Ottoman Empire, as the rival of Suleiman, he was the subject of criticism and regarded as a failure.

against them and he was concerned that they had been unable to stamp out heresy despite the increased penalties later in his reign. He worried that the strict heresy laws were not being fully enforced at the local level, though since some of the more extreme religious groups called for social change and drew their support mainly from the poor, he hoped that the nobility and the wealthier urban classes would deal with them.

Charles perhaps regretted holding out for a solution to the religious schism to come from a general church council which the papacy always found reasons to delay, with the result that by the time the Council of Trent was eventually opened, in 1545, it was too late for any compromise, too late for the reforms that might have helped; both sides had become entrenched. It would have helped if Charles' relations with the papacy had been better, but since most popes were also Renaissance princes not only did they fear that any council would take power away from Rome but their family interests frequently clashed with Charles' dynastic and strategic priorities in Italy. Much to Charles' chagrin the twin pillars of Christianity (Pope and Emperor) had usually failed to work together, but he did not see the fault as his.

Charles' wish for a united Christendom was frequently associated with the idea of the 'universal monarchy'. This was never a realistic objective. Even if Charles did rule 40% of Europe and held the leadership of the Christian world as elected emperor, and even if his early Chancellor, Gattinara, talked in terms of a universal monarchy, the idea faced two very major obstacles. Firstly, the practical issue that Charles could never impose a single coherent administration across the lands that he did rule, let alone extend such a structure further. The fact that Charles never even attempted to put such a concept into effect has been used to criticise him as being lacking in imagination and vision, but could equally be used to praise his common sense; it would have been impossible given the second problem. This was that in 16th Europe the idea of the nation state (and in some areas a national church) as opposed to the medieval ideal of a universal monarchy (and universal church) was taking hold. Not only had this made things more difficult for Charles to rule his already widespread lands, but it meant that an extension was almost inconceivable. Henry VIII suggested the dismemberment of France after Pavia in 1525, with England reclaiming lands lost centuries before, but for Charles this was never a serious option. He even gave up a serious claim to Burgundy, which was dear to his heart, in the second part of his reign in order to achieve security elsewhere. These could be seen as the actions of a weak and unimaginative monarch, but seem to be more the actions of a realist making the most of what was possible.

If Charles was to fulfil his position as secular leader of the Christian world and make good the claim that 'As the sun rules in the sky, so the Emperor rules on Earth' used on coins and medallions at the time[2], then he had to deal effectively with the expanding Ottoman Empire. With Ferdinand taking most of the responsibility in central Europe, with Charles' support (finances permitting), the advances of the Ottomans were contained. The Habsburgs had been unable to take back most of Hungary but Vienna was successfully defended in 1529 and 1532, and further advances were unlikely (although Vienna was to be seriously threatened for the last time in 1683). In the Mediterranean the Ottomans certainly consolidated control of the eastern part during Charles' reign and continued to pose a threat to shipping and coastal settlements in the west. Charles believed that no-one could doubt his commitment, with his personal involvement at Tunis (1535) and Algiers (1541), but it was not until Philip's reign that the defence of Malta (1565) and naval victory at Lepanto (1571) (though neither purely Spanish/Habsburg successes) finally reduced the fear of large scale Ottoman conquests in the western Mediterranean.

Of great significance to Charles was his personal 'honour and reputation'. He believed that this was vitally important to his dynasty and that without it his ability to govern, the inheritance that he would pass on to Philip and the standing of his subjects in the world, would all be diminished. He claimed many of his actions were determined by this principle: his campaigns against the

Ottomans and the French, his need to leave Spain in the hands of a regent, and to be seen throughout Europe as a victorious leader. But this had been portrayed by his opponents as just another cover for imposing his will in Europe, his self-aggrandizement and furthering the interests of the Habsburg dynasty. Certainly Charles saw the preservation of his honour and authority as a more important objective than the immediate welfare of his subjects or the lives of the soldiers in his armies. This, however, could be said of all monarchs of that time (and indeed of most rulers throughout history). He could rarely justify the taxes, the material damage, and the disruption of trade brought about by war in terms of a wider 'national' interest, but instead used the importance of his reputation and the standing of his dynasty.

Were Charles' ambitions and his world view outdated? He lived at a time of great change, a time of movement from the medieval world to a modern one. Alongside the developments of the Renaissance in the artistic and scientific worlds, the old Europe of a single Catholic Church, crusades, chivalry, the world of the Order of the Golden Fleece was disappearing; the one that was emerging was more diverse, one of different creeds, of the nation state. Along with the rest of the population, Charles could not have been aware of these great trends at the time - they are only visible with the benefit of hindsight. Therefore to criticise him for not appreciating the lasting nature of the religious changes or to praise him for leading Spain as a nation state into a 'Golden Age' are equally misleading.[3] He would not have thought in a way that could reach such conclusions. But what did overlap both the medieval and the modern worlds was an idea of great significance to Charles, the dynasty. There can be no doubt that this played a major part in the formulation of his policies and in this respect he was no better or no worse than other contemporary monarchs, other than the fact that he was the head of Europe's most successful and powerful dynasty of the time.

There had been no recent precedent for the amount of territory that he had ruled. Charles and his advisers had no-one to learn from, nothing to base their actions on, and therefore much of his rule had been a matter of improvisation and experimentation, trying to see what worked and what didn't.[4] The distances between many of his territories meant that decisions could not be communicated quickly, a situation not improved by Charles' often painstaking approach to his task. There was no single territory that had dominated his policy decisions or was so important that its needs automatically trumped all others. Rather it was a case of balancing the demands and problems of each. Charles - born in the Low Countries, assertive of his hereditary rights in Spain, keen to become emperor in Germany, willing to fight for control in Italy – knew that he belonged to many lands.

In Spain he had built upon the work of Isabella and Ferdinand. It had developed into a power to be reckoned with, with extensive lands in the Low Countries, Italy and the New World. Such success had been popular, even if there were constant complaints about the cost. After the revolts early in his reign he had established a secure administration and could generally regard the Spanish people as loyal to him. The nobility, who in large part had defeated the rebellions, were given titles, financial privileges and military commands, though a reduced role in government, where Charles now relied more on a growing group of professional administrators. He had visited many cities in person as he (or his regents Isabella and Philip) moved around the country, met their representatives and dealt with their grievances in the cortes. Whether the relative calm was a result of outright enthusiasm for him or more a case of submission to his power could be questioned[5]. The successful resistance of the nobility to attempts to introduce new taxes that they would have to pay, and of the cities to any worthwhile increase in the fixed amounts paid as the alcabala, meant that Charles had to look for finances elsewhere, such as the bullion fleets. In the longer term this reduced the influence of the cortes and had begun to open the way for a more absolute monarchy.

Charles never formally unified the country, but he was able to ensure that he passed on all Spanish lands to Philip,* though he had to cope with regional identities and loyalties which were never lost. Unity was encouraged by the push for religious orthodoxy, based on a widespread conservatism in religion shared by Charles, to the exclusion of others, especially with the hard line taken against Protestants and the discrimination against, and eventual persecution of, the Conversos and Moriscos. Charles had however managed to achieve a balance by the negotiation of concessions to the remaining Muslims (mainly in Valencia) in return for payments, despite the on-going fears of Muslim corsair attacks along the Mediterranean coast. One might have expected the enormous amount of bullion from the New World to result in financial and economic strength. This was far from the case. Much of the country to which he was travelling in 1556 was still poor and life was hard for its impoverished inhabitants. Charles' expenses and the high rates of inflation meant that taxation, for those that paid, was high. The government had become more and more indebted.

In the Low Countries Charles had been able to rely on effective regents in his aunt, Margaret, and his sister, Mary. He had increased the number of provinces to seventeen by northward expansion and consolidated Habsburg control by establishing common laws of succession across all the provinces. Other than this he had very limited success in imposing more centralisation, with each province firmly defending their traditional rights. His attempt to achieve greater collective military and financial obligations in 1534 had been rejected by the States General. He used the nobility as Stadholders in the provinces, gave their leaders status as members of the Order of the Golden Fleece, and did little to challenge their privileges. He had thus retained their loyalty. The cities had caused problems by their resistance to taxation believing that their money was being spent on Charles' ambitions elsewhere. His regents had needed to engage in many local discussions, with offers of favours and privileges, to gain agreement to further

---

* There was always the same monarch across the whole country from his reign onwards.

subsidies. Where this failed Charles had dealt severely with the citizens, taking the opportunity, as elsewhere, to reduce their rights.[6] The example made of Ghent had helped to secure Charles' position; there was now no extensive political opposition.

In Germany and the Empire he had been able to do little to change the traditional structures of government. The power of the princes remained largely unchallenged; he had been unable to establish a permanent system of imperial taxation. Charles had relied on these princes to deal with the rebellions of the Knights and the Peasants in the 1520s, and they had then used religious divisions to full advantage in order to defend their position. Protestant princes asserted power over their own territories, while Charles could not afford to alienate those that remained Catholic. He had realised early on that he needed his brother Ferdinand to act on his behalf in the Empire. He had never achieved a situation where Germany contributed sufficiently to his revenues. Even after his success at Muhlberg, Charles could not set up a permanent army or achieve greater central control, and his true position was revealed in 1552 when the Protestant princes, encouraged as ever by France, forced him to eventually agree to a religious settlement that was very much against his wishes and to which he could never be reconciled.

Despite the strategic and symbolic importance of Italy in the first half of the 16th century, Charles had rarely been there, with visits limited to his coronation (1530), a triumphal progress through Sicily and Naples after Tunis (1535-36), travelling from Spain to Austria and Germany (and back), or negotiations with the Pope. He had successfully secured control of southern Italy and Milan, resisting and defeating persistent French claims and invasions, but most of his reign had been associated with the disruption and destruction of the Italian Wars, the loss of independence, and the sack of Rome. Some spoke of Spanish hegemony and the resultant social, economic and cultural decline. Was Charles' policy dictated by good intentions or territorial ambitions? It was here that Charles' ability to use a calculated combination of force, negotiation and marriage alliances was most apparent. There must have been the realisation that the only likely alternative for Italy was domination by France, which many saw as a worse prospect. Andrea Doria of Genoa, after working with France in the mid-1520s, came to the conclusion that alliance with Charles was the more attractive option, an understanding that served them both well for 30 years. Venice was able to maintain its independence by the use of complex diplomacy as its power declined, although the Florentine Republic was crushed in 1530 as a consequence of his policies.

Though in Spain there was a move towards greater centralisation, he had made no attempt to introduce a unified administration across all his lands. He had ruled each of his territories as a separate entity, using the traditional structures usually respecting the pre-existing privileges of various social groups. Although in each land the economic, social, and political circumstances were different, he needed the support of the nobles. As he moved towards the use of an administrative class he was careful to retain the status of the nobility, whether in Spain, the Low Countries or Germany. His troubles were greatest in Germany when he was unable to retain this support. Charles was not by nature an initiator of grand plans for Europe other than in a dynastic sense. Was this the result of the lack of inclination, the lack of imagination or the lack of power? It was probably because of all three. He was essentially a conservative who wished to pass on what had gone before; he was not a deep thinker about political and administrative processes; and he surely realised that to disrupt the established order would result in serious opposition which would break his control, given the scope of his other problems.

With his vast responsibilities it is hardly surprising that Charles was in most respects driven by events rather than being able to impose his will upon them.[*] He did have clear aims but these invariably had to be tempered by reaction to emergencies and

---

[*] William Stirling-Maxwell (1818-1878) claimed that 'all expeditions and enterprises Charles had undertaken in his life had been prompted more by necessity than by inclination'.

alarms sparked by those that wished to see the Habsburgs reduced in stature. However, in the financial field the constant pressures on his resources resulted in him using the developing 'modern' financial methods, borrowing money on the security of future income, with increasingly serious consequences. Again this was the victory of immediate requirements over long term planning.

If the needs of the time resulted in a change of policy Charles rarely blamed his advisers; he could not be accused of being disloyal to those who served him. He made appointments on the basis of his often perceptive judgements and was usually right, but if they proved unable to perform their duties, he was prepared to remove them, or not give them further responsibility. Thus Henry of Nassau was a close friend of Charles from his early years in the Low Countries, travelled to Spain with him, but was given few military commands later on. Jean Lallemand, originally from Burgundian lands, played a major role in the administration of Spain up to 1528, but was then charged (possibly as a result of court intrigue) with treason and selling influence. After a short time in prison he was cleared of treason, though he never regained favour and eventually returned to the Franche Comte, dying there in 1560.

Most of Charles' appointments were, however, a success. After 1521 the administration was dominated by Gattinara, Cobos and Granvelle. In the military field Charles Lannoy, Philibert of Chalon (the Prince of Orange), Andrea Doria of Genoa, Ferrante Gonzaga, and Fernando Alvarez de Toledo, Duke of Alva all served him loyally, despite frequent shortages of money, resulting in difficulties with mercenaries and lack of supplies. Charles also achieved unswerving allegiance from his ambassadors, using those from Burgundian lands, such as Eustace Chapuys, born in Annecy (ambassador to England 1529–1545), and Louis de Praet, born in Bruges (ambassador to England, 1522–1525, and to France 1525–1526), as well as Spaniards, who were usually sent to Italian courts such as the Vatican, Venice and Genoa. Most went on to serve Charles in other capacities, or had already done so.

It was surely not just chance that enabled Charles to select and promote men of ability to key positions, and perhaps even more important to achieve a degree of loyalty from these men that was unusual for the time. Most worked for him for extended periods, usually until their retirement or death. Yes, they were rewarded with power, with honour and with wealth, but not overmuch, as constant references to Charles' parsimony in this area reveal. We know also that he did not wish these men to automatically place their sons in positions of major responsibility, at least not until they had proved themselves. The hereditary principle was important to Charles in his own family but he was aware that not all were fit for high office. His future comments on his own grandson, Don Carlos, confirm this. Was there something other than self-interest that made these men so loyal?

Charles' character must have played a part. The evidence of his youth has suggested that Charles was in some ways a late developer. He could never have been regarded as a handsome man, or one with unusual intelligence. He was reserved, never fully at ease in the company of others, never leading the way in dance, music, verse, or wit, never the 'life and soul of the party'. But as he matured, and gained more self-knowledge, he was more at ease with himself. Schooled in kingship by some of the best known figures of the age, he developed a strong sense of purpose, and a growing confidence. He had deep religious and political convictions, was clear about his responsibilities, and became conscientious and determined in his approach to them.

From the early 1530s his quest for 'honour and reputation' meant that he involved himself directly on the battlefield. He proved himself courageous, drawing on his Burgundian background in chivalry and honour, though he relied on his commanders to plan the campaigns in detail, recognising that he did not have the knowledge that they had gained from a lifetime of experience. As in international relations, he realised that he needed to learn from others, though increasingly he took the lead in formulating policy. In discussions he showed a quiet dignity and thoughtful authority, questioning without threatening, which impressed those who worked with him and many of those who met him. It was these qualities that engendered loyalty and respect from those around him; they felt that they could trust him and could speak their mind in front of him.

This was the life that would soon be presented on the Day of Judgement. Charles believed that it was one in which he had done his utmost to serve God and do His will on earth. In the testaments that he had prepared over the years for Philip, Charles had made explicit what he regarded as central to his beliefs and to how a ruler should control his lands. Whether he had achieved these standards only the Almighty would decide. He realised that very little would be altered now. In his own mind he had never sought new dominions just for power but as a duty, for the sake of his other lands. Peace in a united Christendom had been his dearest wish, but he had undertaken years of unavoidable war against France. A truly successful crusade against the infidel had been made all but impossible by these wars. As he had expressed in his abdication speech, he knew that he had made mistakes, he knew that he had personal faults, he knew that he had failed in some matters that were important to him. But he also considered that he had done little out of spite or ill-will and had tried to do everything in good faith and that he had never ceased in his efforts. He believed that he had less to fear from the final judgement than many others.

# 30
## 'No other pass shall I cross' – Final Rest

On his last voyage Charles carried with him Titian's portrait of Isabella, ever present on his journeys since it was painted for him in 1548. He had others, and owned them for longer, but this was his favourite. It captured her character and her likeness as he wished it to be. They had been through times of joy and times of great sadness in their years together, cut short by his responsibilities elsewhere and her early death in childbirth. Their children were now settling to their lives' work, as monarch, or as consorts to monarchs, in the Low Countries, in Austria, and in Spain. Now he was accompanied by his sisters. They were travelling not to their birthplace but to a land foreign to them, to be near him. He knew Eleanor, who had also accompanied him on his first voyage thirty-nine years before, wished to be reconciled with her daughter, Maria, left so long ago in Portugal, and Mary desired an end to the unceasing pressures of government after twenty-five years in the Low Countries. Both had suffered for the family - for him - but both were loyal and supportive.

After making landfall at Laredo, east of Santander, on the 28th September 1556 he was annoyed that so little had been organised for his onward progress. Now all the decisions had been made, he was anxious to move on. At first the journey was slow, over the northern mountains onto the plain of Castile. He travelled through Limpias, Ampuero, Rasines, and Ramales, the tracks becoming steeper and narrower as they approached Lanestosa and then over the pass of Los Tornos at 3000 feet (960m.) and down into Medina de Pomar. Yet more passes had to be negotiated before he arrived at Burgos, the city where his father had died aged 28, in the Casa de Cordon, 50 years before. His company was smaller than on earlier journeys; perhaps the courtiers who had flocked to his side in the past preferred to associate with those now in power, not Charles who had left power behind. But as news of his arrival spread, many came out to greet him and to present gifts. He did not wish for great receptions or celebrations and avoided one at Burgos, but as he approached Valladolid he knew that he would have to give in.

The city that he had entered as the new king in 1517 now welcomed him for the final time. He was greeted by his daughter Juana, the nobility, the high clergy, and councillors. Here he would see again the church of San Pablo where he had been acknowledged as king and the nearby Palacio de Pimental where Isabella had given birth to Philip. Earlier, Charles had talked to his eleven year old grandson, Don Carlos, for the first time. He had always been a good judge of character and the meeting had left him with concerns about the boy: 'His manner and humour please me very little, and I do not know what he will be capable of in the future'[1]. Having done with the formalities he wanted to make detailed arrangements for his final destination in Yuste. He met the leaders of the Hieronymite order and the prior of the monastery. He wanted to be sure that as well as his accommodation, designs for which had been sent from Brussels earlier, plans for his spiritual welfare and the organisation of the choir were in hand. He no longer had to go to Tordesillas to meet his mother, Juana, whom he had always made a point of visiting whenever he returned to Spain, but would have recalled his first meeting with Ferdinand in nearby Mojados.

At the end of October Charles, with his entourage of one hundred and fifty, moved on. Undeterred by the rain they passed through Medina del Campo, where his grandmother Isabella the Catholic had died, and close to the imposing Castillo de la Mota. Charles was travelling for the first time in forty years unencumbered by the constant arrival of letters informing him of events elsewhere, raising concerns, requesting money, demanding decisions. By 10th November the company had reached El Barco de Avila, crossing the river Tormes by the old bridge before climbing into the mountains. They took the steep pass of Tornavacas over the Sierra de Gredos, Charles being carried in a chair along the rocky tracks too rough and narrow for his mule-drawn litter[2]. He knew that he would never return: 'no other pass shall I cross, unless it be that unto death'.[3]

He was keen to move into his new accommodation, but had to stay with the Duke of Oropesa[*] in Jarandilla de la Vera until February 1557 when his villa was at last ready. Many had tried to discourage him from making this his place of retirement. They argued that it was bad for his health - cold and damp in winter, too hot in summer, an area known for malaria. But he visited Yuste during the winter to oversee the final arrangements and was pleased by what he saw at the monastery and by the surrounding views. He hoped that he would be granted the time to remain there for longer than he had been able to spend in one place since his coming of age ceremony in Brussels when he was 15.

Charles knew the history of the monastery. It had been founded in the early 14th century with the support of Henry III of Castile. King Henry IV had stayed there and Charles' grandparents, Ferdinand and Isabella, had granted it an annual endowment. In the first decades of the 16th century a new church had been constructed. Under Augustinian rule dedicated to St Jerome, it was a place of solitude, manual labour, prayer and contemplation. This fitted Charles' requirements. His two storey villa attached to the southern side of the church would be more than sufficient for his needs, though he had no intention of living the life of a monk. It consisted of four rooms on each floor, though he was to live mainly on the upper level. A ramp provided him with direct access to the first floor, leading to a shaded terrace from where he could enjoy views of the garden and the ponds.

The rooms were square and opened off a central corridor. He could meet his guests and visitors in the Audience room, which had a door through to his personal study. Opposite that was his bedroom. Lying in his bed he would be able to see the altar in the church through a specially constructed opening in the wall.[†] Above

---

[*] The castle is now a Parador
[†] The stairs that now lead directly into the church were added later by Philip II

the altar he placed Titian's painting 'La Gloria'.* Since its completion in 1554 Charles had always wanted it near him. It represented his new position in the world. He is portrayed with Isabella, Philip and other family members praying, surrounded by figures from the Old and New Testaments. Dressed only in shrouds, his crown lies at his feet, showing his withdrawal from earthly power.

His main concern now was to tend to his spiritual needs. Since this had not been an enforced abdication, Charles must have been relieved that much of his load had been lifted. He was not given to dwelling too much on past events; what was done could not be undone, and he knew that he would be answerable for his actions. If he was to remain calm and retain his self-control he could not allow his thoughts to be dominated by the self-doubt and melancholy that he had sometimes experienced. He hoped to enjoy the time that he had left, spared at least some of the physical pain that his travelling had caused him since early middle age. During much of the spring and summer of 1557 he experienced an improvement in health, raising his spirits after the hardships of the journey to Yuste.

Having at last received funds from his daughter, Juana, he was now able to pay the wages that he owed his servants. Mostly from the Low Countries, they had served him for many years. It was with some regret that he let them go, but they had no role in his new simpler life. The remaining staff of about fifty would see to his future needs in a household directed by Don Luis Mendez de Quijada. These included his secretary Martin de Gaztelu and the secretary-valet van Male; his physician, Dr Mathys and an apothecary from the Low Countries; the clockmaker Gianello Torriano, along with clerks, a barber, cooks and bakers.

Charles developed a daily routine, adjusted in accordance with the season and his health. Breakfast, prayers with his confessor, time spent with his clocks and, after dressing, mass in the church, would take up his mornings. This would be followed by dinner at

---

* Sometimes known as 'The Last Judgement'. The original is now in El Escorial. A copy was installed at Yuste by Philip in 1584.

midday and the reading of a religious text, before a siesta. Later in the afternoon he fished in the ponds, visited his aviary, talked to visitors, or discussed theological and philosophical points from sermons or bible readings, sitting on his first floor veranda or in the garden with its terraces and ornamental flower beds, which he continued to re-design. A light meal came before he retired for the night.[4]

He had never lost his appetite. Now he enjoyed all his favourite Spanish and other dishes to which he had been looking forward since this journey was planned. Of his servants, twenty were cooks, and there were regular deliveries of provisions from far and wide for them to work on, producing roasted wild boar and venison, black hares marinated in wine, bay leaves and onions, stuffed thrushes, casseroled larks, anchovies, grey-mullet, tuna and other fish of all kinds. Despite the best advice of his doctors he had never been able to resist eating to excess. He was aware that others thought this unwise; de Quijada commented: 'Surely kings must think that their stomachs are not like other mens'.[5]

Along with his Titians, rich tapestries lined the walls of the rooms.[*] Surrounded by his clocks and charts, he established a comfortable existence. He ensured that his favourite books on history, philosophy, theology, and astronomy were on his desk - the *Commentaries* of Caesar, Tacitus' *Histories*, Thucydides' *History of the Peloponnesian Wars,* the *Confessions* of St Augustine, and Ptolemy's *Almagest.* On his journey to Yuste he had collected from Valladolid the manuscript of his memoirs which he had dictated to van Male back in 1550. Given the time, he intended to review and finish them[†].

He had no wish to experience unnecessary hardship or cut himself off completely from outside events. He still cared about what was happening in the world where he had been a leading figure for so long. Although he did nothing to encourage visitors,

---

[*] Most of the paintings are now in the Prado, with copies at Yuste
[†] He never completed this task

plenty wished to come. Old associates with whom to reminisce, a few family members, theologians, thinkers and writers. Juan Gines de Sepulveda, former tutor to Philip, and court historiographer, came from his retirement in Cordoba, as did Don Luis de Avila y Zuniga, who was writing a history of Charles' wars in Germany.

Charles communicated regularly with Philip and in return received frequent couriers from the Low Countries carrying news and requests for advice. He was distressed by the failure to follow up advantages in Italy but was delighted when news of victory over the French at St Quentin in August 1557 reached him. He was always prepared to give voice to his concerns when he heard about instances of Lutherism in his former lands. In May 1558 he wrote to Juana: 'Believe me, daughter, this business has upset me and caused so much worry that I cannot adequately express it', and to Philip: 'It is necessary that you root the movement out, as rigorously as possible'.[6] The advantage of retirement is, of course, that problems generally belong to other people. Charles could give advice and voice his opinions but did not usually have to take action on his own account.

In September 1557 Eleanor and Mary came to stay in near-by Jarandilla for several months and made numerous visits. Some family members, however, he refused to see. Philip had expressed a wish that his son, don Carlos, lacking direction and causing increasing problems in Valladolid, should live there with him; Charles rejected the idea, even refusing to allow the boy to visit. He was equally obstinate with Juana, still regent in Philip's name. He sent her constant dispatches about Spain's defences and finances, but most often about the lack of consultation with him and the lack of respect that he received from her regency government. As a result of this it was made clear that her presence was not desired at Yuste. If Charles was finding it difficult to come to terms with the lack of power, others perhaps misinterpreted his interest as a wish to control affairs.

Despite his abdication he could not avoid his duties as head of the family – nor did he wish to - when called upon to adjudicate between the rival claims of his youngest sister, Catherine, and his daughter, Juana, to the regency in Portugal. On the death of King John III in 1557, who was married to Charles' sister Catherine, the new monarch was their grandson, the infant Sebastian, aged 3. He was the posthumous child of John and Catherine's son, John Manual (who had died in 1554, aged 16) and Juana. Juana had only lived in Portugal for two years, having left her son after the death of her husband when recalled to Spain by Philip to act as regent. Catherine, however, had lived there since her marriage in 1525 and would be far more acceptable to the Portuguese. Charles decided in favour of Catherine. He knew that he could never be close to Juana, with whom he had spent so little time.

He also attempted to assist Eleanor in her quest to repair her relationship with her daughter. Back in 1518 Charles had arranged for her marriage to King Manual of Portugal (1469 - r.1495 - 1521). She had given birth to a son who had died aged one and a daughter, the Infanta Maria. After Manuel's death and her later remarriage to Francis I of France, Eleanor had left Portugal and had not seen her daughter, who remained at the Portuguese court, for over 25 years. Returning to Spain with Charles, she passionately desired to be reunited and indeed suggested that her daughter came to live with her. This was rejected by Maria. She had felt abandoned by her mother and had been further estranged from her mother's family when the plan for her to marry Philip had been rapidly jettisoned when dynastic priorities meant that he married Mary of England. Eventually Maria agreed to a meeting with her mother which took place at Badajos, near the Spanish-Portuguese border, at the beginning of 1558. After three weeks, without any meaningful reconciliation, Maria returned to Lisbon. Eleanor's physical and emotional health was fatally weakened. She had paid the price of duty so common in the women of the royal families of Europe: loveless marriages and little contact with her children. Charles cannot have been surprised by Eleanor's death shortly afterwards in February 1558 at Talaveruela de la Vera, a few miles east of Yuste, on her return journey to Jarandilla. Mary, who had accompanied

Eleanor, still close to Charles, stayed with him until 16th March. Philip wished Mary to return to the Low Countries to take up her former position as governor and Charles helped to persuade her to accept the appointment. It was in vain, as her own poor health prevented her from ever travelling back to Brussels.

Another family member who had a role in Charles' final months was his natural son born in Regensburg in February 1547 to Barbara Blomberg. His mother having been married to a court official in Brussels, Jeromin, as the boy was known, was taken to Spain in 1551. From 1554 he was brought up in Villagarcia, near Valladolid, by Magdelena de Ulloa, the wife of Luis de Quijada, now in charge of Charles' household at Yuste. In the spring of 1558, presumably at Charles' request, de Quijada arranged for his wife to bring Jeromin to the village of Cuacos, close to the monastery of Yuste. The village still has streets named after Charles, Luis de Quijada, Magdelena de Ulloa, and the house in which the boy stayed in Plaza Don Juan. Jeromin was taken to meet Charles, though not told that the aging emperor was his father; he must have wondered why he had been chosen. He clearly pleased Charles, who requested further visits, and provided for him in an amendment to his will, in which there was also a legacy to the boy's mother. He left it to Philip to decide Jeromin's eventual status. On Philip's return to Spain in 1559 Jeromin was introduced to the new king. Philip explained to him that they had the same father and thereafter always referred to him as a brother, though was careful to maintain the proper protocol, giving the newly named Don John (of Austria) a position in public ceremonies behind the royal family but ahead of all other grandees. Don John was brought up in the royal household and was quickly at ease with the younger members of the royal family.

In early August 1558 Charles experienced cold-like symptoms, which persisted throughout the month. On 30th August, while sitting on the terrace he was taken ill and it was reported that he was suffering from headaches, heaviness, a great thirst, and fever. There is dispute as to whether these symptoms match most closely pneumonia or malaria. Whichever the sickness, his doctors were unable to provide much relief. After a slight improvement he relapsed and all expected the worse. The last rites of extreme unction, penance and Holy Communion were carried out on the 20th September, with Charles fully conscious in his bed chamber, surrounded by monks, his confessor, Juan de Regla, and the Archbishop of Toledo, Bartolome Carranza. When the end came at about 2.30 a.m. on 21st September 1558, as he looked through to the altar in the church, his prayers were for his eternal soul. In his testament of June 1554 he had requested that he be buried with his wife at Granada, but more recently he had asked that his body be placed in a crypt beneath the high altar of the monastic church at Yuste in a very specific position: 'one half of my body to the breast shall lie beneath said alter, and the other half, from the breast to the head, shall project from it, so that any priest saying mass shall have his feet over my breast and head'[7]. However he left it for Philip to decide his final resting place.

Charles' journeys had not quite finished. He was never interred in the crypt at Yuste. Instead he was placed on the high altar behind an altar-piece. In 1574 Isabella's body was moved from Granada, where she had been placed with Charles' parents and Spanish grandparents, to join her husband at Yuste. They were then both transported to El Escorial, Philip's new palace/monastery to the north-west of Madrid. In 1617, Philip III (r.1598-1621) ordered the construction of the King's Pantheon, beneath El Escorial. This was not completed until 1654, in the reign of Philip IV (r.1621-1665), and it was only then that the earthly remains of Emperor Charles V, King Carlos I, finally came to rest.

Built in Baroque style, with marble (blue from Toledo and red from Tortosa) and gilded bronze, with Corinthian columns, the Pantheon holds the tombs of kings of Spain (both Habsburg and Bourbon) from Charles to Alfonso XIII, who died almost four hundred years later in 1941, with the exception of Philip V (d.1746) and his son Ferdinand VI (d.1759) who wished to be buried in palaces that they had founded. With them are the wives who gave birth to future kings including, of course, Empress Isabella. Other chambers at El Escorial include the Infante's Pantheon, completed in 1888, and a number of rooms where many members of the Spanish royal family are interred. The 9th chamber contains sixteen members of Charles' family (the House of Austria) including his sisters, Eleanor and Mary, Philip's 1st wife, Maria Manuela of Portugal, their son Don Carlos (1545-1568) and Philip's 3rd wife, Elizabeth of Valois, the daughter of Henri II and Catherine de Medici. The tomb of Charles' natural son, Don John of Austria, the victor of Lepanto, is in the 5th Chamber. This is the dynasty writ large – Charles would surely have approved.

# Principal Characters

## *Charles and his immediate family*

**Charles** (1500-1558), Duke of Burgundy, King of Spain and Holy Roman Emperor.

**Eleanor** (1498-1558), Charles' older sister, Queen of Portugal (1518-1521) by marriage to Manuel I, and Queen of France (1530-1547) by marriage to Francis I.

**Isabella** (1501-1526), Charles' sister, Queen of Denmark by her marriage to Christian II.

**Ferdinand** (1503-1564), Charles' brother, elected 'King of the Romans' in 1531, and succeeded Charles as Emperor.

**Mary** (1505-1558), Charles' sister, Queen of Hungary (1521-1526) by her marriage to Louis II, and regent of the Low Countries (1531-1555)

**Catherine** (1507-1578), Charles' youngest sister, Queen of Portugal (1525-1557) by her marriage to John III and regent of Portugal (1557-1562).

**Isabella of Portugal** (1503-1539), wife of Charles from 1526, sister of John III, King of Portugal.

**Philip II** (1527-1598), only son of Charles and Isabella, succeeded Charles as King of Spain and ruler of the Low Countries.

**Don Carlos** (1545-1568), son of Philip, imprisoned on Philip's orders, where he died six months later.

**Maria** (1528-1603), eldest daughter of Charles and Isabella, married Maximilian, son of Ferdinand.

**Juana** (1535-1573), daughter of Charles and Isabella, mother of King Sebastian of Portugal, and regent in Spain (1554-1559).

**Maximilian** (1527-1576), oldest son of Ferdinand and his successor as Holy Roman Emperor (as Maximilian II).

**Margaret of Parma** (1522-1586), natural daughter of Charles, married Alessandro de Medici (1536) and then the Ottavio Farnese, Duke of Parma (1538). Regent of the Low Countries (1559-1567) under Philip II, mother of Alexander Farnese, Duke of Parma.

**Don John of Austria** (1547-1578), natural son of Charles, commander of the fleet at the Battle of Lepanto (1571)

## *Habsburg ancestors*

**Maximilian I** (1459-1519) Holy Roman Emperor. Son of Emperor Frederick III, father of Philip the Handsome of Burgundy and Margaret of Austria. Charles' grandfather.

## *Burgundian ancestors*

**Charles the Rash** (or Bold) (1433-1477), Duke of Burgundy, Charles' great-grandfather, killed in the Battle of Nancy (1477).

**Mary of Burgundy** (the Rich) (1457-1482), daughter of Charles the Rash, married Maximilian I, mother of Philip the Handsome. Charles' grandmother.

**Philip the Handsome** (1478-1506), Charles' father, son of Mary and Emperor Maximilian I. Duke of Burgundy and King of Castile (as Philip I by his marriage to Juana).

**Margaret of Austria** (1480-1530) (sometimes known as Margaret of Savoy because of her marriage to Philibert II of Savoy) Philip's sister and Charles' aunt, a major influence on his early life and later his regent in the Low Countries.

## *Spanish ancestors*

**Isabella** (1451-1504), Queen of Castile, wife of Ferdinand of Aragon and Charles' grandmother.

**Ferdinand** (1452-1516), King of Aragon, wife of Isabella and Charles' grandfather. Together, Ferdinand and Isabella were known as the 'Catholic Monarchs'.

**Juana** (1479-1555), Charles' mother, daughter of Isabella and Ferdinand, and heir to Castile after her mother's death – her brother (Juan) and older sister (Isabella) pre-deceased their mother. Spent over 45 years in a convent at Tordesillas 'for her own safety'. Often referred to as Juana 'la loca' (Juana 'the mad').

**Catherine of Aragon** (1485-1536), Charles' aunt, the youngest daughter of Ferdinand and Isabella. Married Arthur, Prince of Wales and then his younger brother, Henry VIII of England. Divorced by Henry VIII.

## *Charles' advisers and commanders*

**William of Croy, Lord of Chievres** (1458-1521), leading nobleman of the Low Countries, chief tutor and then adviser to Charles from 1509.

**Charles de Lannoy** (1487-1527), soldier and statesman, became a knight in the Order of the Golden Fleece in 1516, viceroy of Naples in 1522 and commander-in-chief of Charles' forces in Italy in 1523.

**Mercurino di Gattinara** (1465-1530), worked for Margaret of Austria in Savoy and then in the Low Countries; became Charles' Chancellor and chief adviser in the 1520's.

**Nicholas Perrenot de Granvelle** (1486-1550), lawyer, Burgundian politician, one of Charles' main advisers in the Holy Roman Empire after 1530.

**Antoine Perrenot de Granvelle** (1517-1586), Nicholas' son, Bishop of Arras, (later created a cardinal) also became one of Charles' ministers.

**Francisco de los Cobos** (1477-1547), Spanish administrator, became secretary to Charles and then the leading figure in the government of Spain for over 20 years.

**Philibert of Chalon, Prince of Orange** (1502-1530), a general in Charles' army in Italy, involved in the 'Sack of Rome', killed in the latter stages of the siege of Florence in 1530.

**Andrea Doria** (1466-1560), major figure in 16th century Genoa. He first served France but dissatisfied with his treatment by Francis I switched sides in 1528 to become Charles' admiral for over two decades.

## *French*

**Louis XII** (1462 - r.1498 - 1515) King of France in Charles' youth.

**Francis I** (1494-1547), King of France from 1515. Charles' greatest rival on the European stage. Married Claude of Brittany (1514-1524) and Eleanor of Austria, Charles' sister, (1530-1547).

**Louise of Savoy** (1476-1531), Francis' mother and sister-in-law of Margaret of Austria.

**Francis, Duke of Brittany** (1518-1536), Francis and Claude's eldest son, predeceased Francis.

**Henry II** (1519-1559), Francis' second son and his successor; held as hostage in Spain with his older brother between 1526 and 1529 when Francis failed to honour the terms of the Treaty of Madrid.

**Charles, Duke of Orleans** (1522-1545), Francis' third son; his father's favourite.

**Charles III, Duke of Bourbon** (1490-1527) Leading French nobleman, Constable of France, became Charles' commander after a major dispute with Francis and Louise of Savoy over his wife's will; killed in the Imperial attack on Rome in May 1527.

## *Italian*

**De Medici family** – leading family of Florence from the 15th century, producing popes (Leo X, Clement VII), dukes of Florence (Alessandro, Cosimo) and the wives of monarchs (Catherine de Medici) in the 16th century.

**Ferrante Gonzaga** (1507-1557) member of the ruling family of Mantua who rose to become one of Charles' leading military commanders. Created a Knight of the Order of the Golden Fleece.

## *Popes*

**Leo X** (b. 1475; Pope: 1513-1521) Giovanni de' Medici, second son of Lorenzo the Magnificent, became pope at the age of 37. Perhaps more suited to be a Renaissance prince.

**Adrian VI** (b. 1459; Pope: 1522-1523) (Adrian of Utrecht) Adrian Florensz Boeyens, a Dutch scholar, tutor to Charles, and his regent in Spain, before his elevation to the papal throne.

**Clement VII** (b. 1478; Pope: 1523-1534) Giulio de'Medici, illegitimate son of Giuliano de'Medici, brother of Lorenzo, legitimised by guardian and friend, Leo X. Elected after a very divisive conclave lasting 50 days.

**Paul III** (b. 1468; Pope: 1534-49) Alessandro Farnese, created a cardinal by Alexander VI (his sister Giulia was Alexander's favourite mistress), and keen to use his influence to advance his family.

## *Ottoman Empire*

**Suleiman** (1494 r. 1520-1566) Ottoman sultan, known as 'the Magnificent' or 'the Lawgiver', whose advances into eastern Europe, North Africa and in the Mediterranean caused Charles great concern and at times demanded much attention.

**Hayreddin Barbarossa** (1478-1546), the commander of Suleiman's Mediterranean fleet.

**Ibrahim Pasha** (1495-1536) known as 'the Frenk' (westerner) and later 'the Maktul' (executed). Taken as a slave by the Ottomans in his youth he rose to become very influential as Suleiman's Grand Vizier until his fall from grace.

# Charles V: Duty and Dynasty

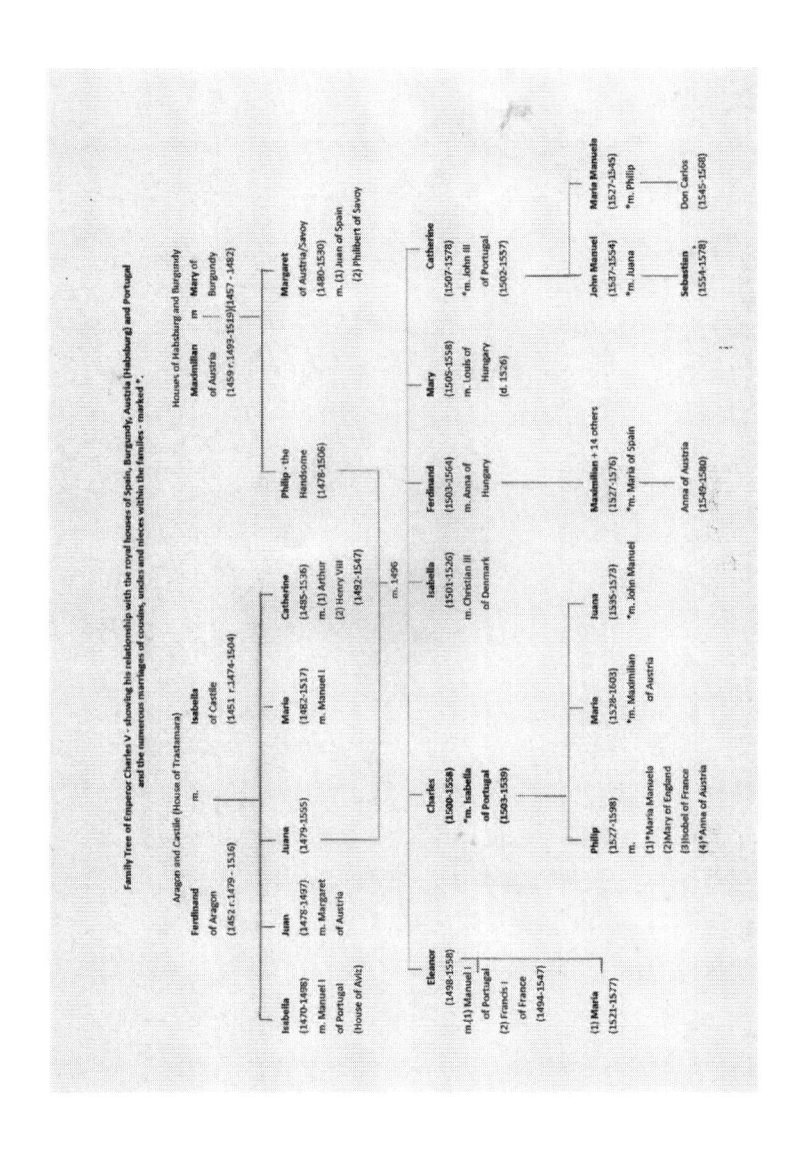

Family Tree of Emperor Charles V - showing his relationship with the royal houses of Spain, Burgundy, Austria (Habsburg) and Portugal and the numerous marriages of cousins, uncles and nieces within the families - marked *.

**Aragon and Castile (House of Trastamara)**

Ferdinand of Aragon (1452 r.1479-1516) m. Isabella of Castile (1451 r.1474-1504)

**Houses of Habsburg and Burgundy**

Maximilian of Austria (1459 r.1493-1519) m. Mary of Burgundy (1457-1482)

Children of Ferdinand and Isabella:
- Isabella (1470-1498) m.(1) Manuel I of Portugal (House of Aviz)
- Juan (1478-1497) m. Margaret of Austria
- Juana (1479-1555)
- Maria (1482-1517) m. Manuel I
- Catherine (1485-1536) m.(1) Arthur m.(2) Henry VIII (1492-1547)

Children of Maximilian and Mary:
- Philip - the Handsome (1478-1506)
- Margaret of Austria/Savoy (1480-1530) m.(1) Juan of Spain (2) Philibert of Savoy

Juana m. Philip (1496)

Children of Juana and Philip:
- Eleanor (1498-1558) m.(1) Manuel I of Portugal (2) Francis I of France (1494-1547)
- Charles (1500-1558) *m. Isabella of Portugal (1503-1539)
- Isabella (1501-1526) m. Christian III of Denmark
- Ferdinand (1503-1564) m. Anna of Hungary
- Mary (1505-1558) m. Louis of Hungary (d. 1526)
- Catherine (1507-1578) *m. John III of Portugal (1502-1557)

Children of Charles and Isabella:
- (1) Maria (1521-1577)
- Philip (1527-1598) m. (1) *Maria Manuela (2) Mary of England (3) Isobel of France (4) *Anna of Austria
- Maria (1528-1603) *m. Maximilian of Austria

Children of Catherine and John III:
- Juana (1535-1573) *m. John Manuel
- John Manuel (1537-1554) *m. Juana

Children of Maria and Maximilian:
- Maximilian + 14 others (1527-1576) *m. Maria of Spain
- Anna of Austria (1549-1580)

Children of John Manuel and Juana:
- Sebastian (1554-1578)

Children of Philip:
- Maria Manuela (1527-1545) *m. Philip
- Don Carlos (1545-1568)

363

Charles V: Duty and Dynasty

# Chronology

*All events refer to Charles unless otherwise stated*

| Year | Date | Charles' location | Events |
|---|---|---|---|
| 1496 | Oct 20 | | Formal marriage of Charles' parents |
| 1498 | Nov 15 | | Birth of elder sister, Eleanor |
| 1500 | Feb 24 | Ghent | **Charles' Birth** |
| 1510 | Nov 18 | | Birth of sister, Isabella in Brussels |
| 1503 | Mar 10 | | Birth of brother, Ferdinand, in Spain |
| 1504 | Nov 26 | | Death of Queen Isabella of Castile |
| 1505 | Sept 15 | | Birth of sister, Mary, in Brussels |
| 1506 | Sept 25 | Malines | Death of Charles' father, Philip, in Burgos Inherits the Low Countries (L.C.) Margaret of Austria regent in L.C. |
| 1507 | Jan 14 | | Birth of sister, Catherine, in Spain |
| 1509 | | | Chievres appointed his Chamberlain Juana confined in Tordesillas |
| | Apr 21 | | Death of Henry VII - accession of Henry VIII |
| 1510 | | | Martin Luther visits Rome |
| 1513 | | | Meets Henry VIII at Tournai |
| 1515 | Jan 1 | | Accession of Francis I to throne of France |
| | Jan 5 | Brussels | Proclaimed ruler of the L.C. |
| | Sept 14 | | Francis regains Milan for France after the battle of Marignano (Italy) |
| 1516 | Jan 23 | L.C. | Death of Ferdinand of Aragon |
| | Feb 18 | | Birth of Mary, daughter of Henry VIII and Catherine of Aragon |
| | Aug 13 | | Treaty of Noyon with Francis I |
| 1517 | Sept 8-18 | Spain | First voyage to Spain |
| | Oct 31 | | Martin Luther issues the 95 theses |
| | Nov | | Visits mother in Tordesillas |
| | Nov | | First meeting with brother, Ferdinand |
| 1518 | Feb | Valladolid | Meets cortes of Castile |
| | April | Zaragoza | Meets cortes of Aragon |
| | Oct | | Gattinara appointed Chancellor |
| 1519 | Jan | Barcelona | Death of Emperor Maximilian in Austria Margaret re-appointed regent in the L.C. |
| | June 28 | Spain | Elected Holy Roman Emperor by electors in Frankfurt |
| 1520 | May 20 | Corunna | Leaves Spain to travel to Germany Adrian of Utrecht appointed regent in Spain |

364

Charles V: Duty and Dynasty

| Year | Date | Charles' location | Events |
|---|---|---|---|
|  | May 26 | England | Visits Henry VIII and Catherine of Aragon |
|  | June |  | Field of the Cloth of Gold – meeting of Francis I and Henry VIII |
|  | June | L.C. | Meets Henry VIII between Calais and Gravelines |
|  | Sept |  | Suleiman becomes Ottoman sultan |
|  | Oct 23 | Aachen | Crowned 'elected Emperor' |
| 1521 | Jan-May | Worms | Diet of Worms – Luther declared a heretic |
|  |  |  | Outbreak of war against Francis I |
|  | Apr 23 |  | Defeat of Comuneros rebels at Villalar |
|  | May | Brussels | Death of adviser, Chievres |
|  | May |  | Marriage of Ferdinand to Anne of Hungary |
|  | June |  | Marriage of Mary to Louis of Hungary |
|  | Aug |  | Capture of Belgrade by the Ottomans |
|  | Dec |  | Milan captured by Imperial troops |
| 1522 | Jan |  | Election of Pope Adrian VI |
|  | June |  | Leaves Flushing for Spain via England |
|  | June 16 | England | Treaty of Windsor with Henry VIII |
|  | July 16 | Spain | Arrives in Spain – where he remains for 7 years |
|  | Dec |  | Birth of illegitimate daughter, Margaret, to Johanna Maria van der Gheyst |
| 1523 |  |  | Revolt of Imperial Knights in Germany |
|  |  |  | Charles III, Duke of Bourbon, defects from Francis I |
|  | Nov |  | Election of Pope Clement VII |
| 1524-1525 |  |  | Peasants' War in Germany |
| 1524 | Oct |  | Francis I retakes Milan |
| 1525 | Feb 24 |  | Major victory at the Battle of Pavia |
|  |  |  | Francis I captured and later moved to Spain |
| 1526 | Jan 16 |  | Treaty of Madrid signed with Francis I |
|  | Jan 19 |  | Death of sister, Isabella, in Low Countries |
|  | Mar 10 | Seville | **Marriage to Isabella of Portugal** |
|  | April |  | Francis I released in exchange for two sons, Francis (8) and Henry (7) |
|  |  | Granada | Charles and Isabella in Alhambra palace |
|  | May 22 |  | Anti-Habsburg League of Cognac formed by Francis I, Papacy, Venice, Florence and Milan |

365

Charles V: Duty and Dynasty

| Year | Date | Charles' location | Events |
|---|---|---|---|
|  | Aug 29 |  | Battle of Mohacs – death of Louis II of Hungary in defeat by Ottomans |
| 1527 | May 6-12 |  | 'Sack of Rome' by Imperial troops |
|  |  |  | Henry VIII petitions Pope Clement for a divorce from Catherine of Aragon |
|  | May 21 |  | Birth of Philip, first child of Charles and Isabella, in Valladolid |
|  | July 31 |  | Birth of Maximilian, first son of Ferdinand and Anne |
| 1528 |  |  | French army besieges Naples |
|  | June 21 |  | Birth of Maria, Charles' second child |
|  | Aug |  | Andrea Doria of Genoa sides with Charles |
|  |  |  | French siege of Naples is broken |
| 1529 | June 21 |  | French defeated at Landriano |
|  | June 29 |  | Treaty of Barcelona with Pope Clement |
|  | July |  | Charles travels across Mediterranean to Italy |
|  | Aug 3 | Italy | Treaty of Cambrai (the 'Ladies Peace') |
|  | Sept-Oct |  | Ottoman advance on Vienna |
|  | Sept |  | Start of siege of Florence |
|  | Nov | Bologna | Arrives for talks with Pope Clement |
|  |  |  | Birth of Charles' second son, Ferdinand |
| 1530 | Feb 24 | Bologna | Charles crowned by Pope Clement |
|  |  | Innsbruck | Meeting with Ferdinand and Mary of Hungary |
|  | May |  | Death of Gattinara |
|  | June | Augsburg | Diet of Augsburg opens – attempt to achieve a religious settlement - fails |
|  | July 4 |  | Marriage of sister, Eleanor, to Francis I |
|  | July |  | Death of second son, Ferdinand |
|  | Dec 01 |  | Death of Margaret of Austria, regent of the Low Countries |
| 1531 | Jan 5 | L.C. | Ferdinand elected 'King of the Romans' |
|  |  |  | Charles appoints Mary of Hungary as regent in L.C. |
|  | Feb 27 |  | Formation of Schmalkaldic League of Protestant princes |
| 1532 | May | Regensburg | Diet of Regensberg – Civil law code |
|  | June-Sept |  | Ottoman advance on Vienna |
|  | Sept | Vienna | Leads army down Danube to Vienna |
|  | Oct | Italy | Negotiations with Pope Clement |
| 1533 | April | Spain | Returns to Spain |

Charles V: Duty and Dynasty

| Year | Date | Charles' location | Events |
|---|---|---|---|
|  | Sept 7 |  | Birth of Elizabeth to Henry VIII and Anne Boleyn |
|  | Oct 28 |  | Marriage of Catherine de' Medici to Henry (2nd son of Francis I) |
| 1534 | May 4 |  | Marriage of Christina of Denmark to Francesco Sforza, Duke of Milan |
|  | Sept 25 |  | Death of Pope Clement VII |
|  | Oct 13 |  | Paul III (Alessandro Farnese) elected pope |
| 1535 | June-Aug | Tunis | Expedition to, and capture of, Tunis |
|  | June 24 |  | Birth of daughter, Juana, in Madrid |
|  | Oct 24 |  | Death of Francesco Sforza of Milan |
|  |  | Sicily | Start of Charles' triumphal journey |
|  |  | Italy | through Sicily and Italy |
| 1536 | Jan 7 |  | Death of aunt, Catherine of Aragon |
|  | Feb |  | French alliance with Ottoman Empire |
|  | April | Rome | Speech to pope and cardinals in Vatican Pope Paul refuses to side with Charles |
|  | May 18 |  | Execution of Anne Boleyn |
|  |  | N. Italy | War with France (1536-1538) |
|  | July-Sept |  | Failure of campaign in Provence |
|  | Nov-Dec |  | Returns to Spain from Genoa |
| 1537 | Oct 19 | Spain | Birth of son, John |
| 1538 | Mar 20 |  | Death of son, John |
|  | June | Nice | Meeting with Pope Paul – peace terms with France agreed |
|  | July | Aigues Mortes | Meeting with Francis I and Eleanor |
|  | Sept 28 | Spain | Naval battle of Preveza against Ottomans |
| 1539 | Apr 21 |  | Birth of still born son to Isabella |
|  | May 1 | Toledo | Death of Isabella |
|  | Oct-Dec | France | Travels through France to Low Countries at invitation of Francis I |
| 1540 | Jan | L.C. | Travels on to Low Countries |
|  | Feb-May | Ghent | Punishment of Ghent |
| 1541 | Apr-Sept | Regensburg | Diet of Regensburg – further attempt to resolve religious divisions – unsuccessful |
|  | Sept | Italy | Meeting with Pope Paul III |
|  | Oct-Nov | Algiers | Failed expedition against Algiers – returns to Spain |
| 1542 |  | Spain | Renewed war with France (1542-1544) French attacks in L.C. and Pyrenees 'New Laws' about treatment of native peoples in the Americas |

Charles V: Duty and Dynasty

| Year | Date | Charles' Location | Events |
|---|---|---|---|
| 1543 | | | Agrees to joint attack on France with Henry VIII |
| 1543 | May | | Charles leaves Spain (until 1556) |
| | Sept | L.C. | Defeats William of Cleves and annexes Guelderland |
| | | | French alliance with Ottomans |
| | | | Barbarossa's fleet winters in Toulon |
| 1544 | Feb | Speyer | Diet of Speyer |
| | July-Aug | France | Invades eastern France |
| | Sept 18 | | Peace of Crepy ends war with France |
| 1545 | July 8 | L.C. | Birth of Don Carlos, son of Philip and Manuela in Spain, followed by the death of Manuela |
| | Sept 9 | | Death of Charles, Duke of Orleans |
| | Dec | Brussels | Opening of General Church Council in Trent |
| 1546 | Feb 18 | | Death of Martin Luther |
| | Apr-Aug | Regensburg | Diet of Regensburg; affair with Barbara Blomberg |
| | Aug | | Start of War of the Schmalkaldic League |
| | Aug-Nov | | Campaign on the upper Danube (Bavaria) |
| 1547 | Jan 28 | | Death of Henry VIII |
| | Jan-Apr | | Campaign in Saxony |
| | Feb 24 | | Birth of illegitimate son, Don John |
| | Mar 31 | | Death of Francis I – accession of Henry II |
| | Apr 24 | Muhlberg | Victory over John Frederick of Saxony who is imprisoned (with Philip of Hesse) |
| 1548 | | Augsburg | Diet of Augsburg |
| | | | Titian's famous portraits of Charles |
| | | | Augsburg 'interim' issued |
| | Sept | | Philip leaves Spain for the L.C. via Italy |
| | | | Maximilian marries Charles' daughter, Maria, and is appointed regent in Spain |
| 1549 | Apr | L.C. | Philip greeted in L.C. by Charles |
| | Nov | | Death of Pope Paul III |
| 1550 | | R. Rhine | Dictates 'Memoirs' to William van Male |
| | | Augsburg | Family rift – discussions about the future control of the Holy Roman Empire |
| 1551 | Oct | | Treaty of Lochau between France and German Protestant princes |
| 1552 | Jan | | confirmed by Treaty of Chambord |
| | Apr | Innsbruck | Revolt of Protestant princes |

Charles V: Duty and Dynasty

| Year | Date | Charles' Location | Events |
|---|---|---|---|
| | May | | Charles flees to Villach |
| | July 31 | Villach | Treaty of Passau – peace with German princes |
| 1552 | | | War with Henry II of France (1552-1559) |
| | | | French capture Metz, Toul and Verdun |
| 1552 | Oct-Dec | Metz | Siege of Metz – fails |
| | | | Marriage of daughter, Juana, to John Manuel of Portugal |
| 1553 | Jan | Brussels | Charles withdraws to L.C. |
| | July 6 | | Death of Edward VI of England – accession of Mary |
| | | | Negotiations for Mary's marriage to Philip |
| 1554 | | | Death of John Manuel of Portugal |
| | | | Birth of Sebastian – son of Juana and John Manuel |
| | July | | Philip leaves Spain for England |
| | | | Juana appointed regent in Spain |
| | | | Philip created King of Naples |
| | July 25 | | Philip marries Mary I of England |
| 1555 | Feb-Sept | | Diet of Augsburg - Charles absent |
| | Apr 12 | | Death of mother, Juana, at Tordesillas |
| | Sept | | Religious Peace of Augsburg |
| | Oct 25 | Brussels | Abdicates as ruler of the Low Countries along with Mary as regent |
| 1556 | Jan 16 | | Abdicates as ruler of Spain |
| | Aug 3 | | Abdicates as Emperor – replaced by Ferdinand (not ratified by Diet until Feb. 1558) |
| | Sept 15-28 | | Voyage from Flushing to Spain, along with sisters Eleanor and Mary |
| | Oct-Nov | Spain | Journey to Jarandilla (near Yuste) |
| 1557 | Feb | Yuste | Moves into villa at the monastery of Yuste |
| 1558 | Feb 25 | | Death of sister, Eleanor |
| | Sept 21 | | **Charles' death at Yuste** |
| | Oct 18 | | Death of sister, Mary |
| | Nov 17 | | Death of Mary I of England – accession of Elizabeth I |
| 1571 | Oct 7 | | Battle of Lepanto – Ottoman navy crushed |
| 1574 | | | Charles' body moved together with Isabella's to El Escorial |
| 1654 | | | Their bodies are laid to rest in the King's Pantheon at El Escorial |

## Acknowledgements

I would like to thank my parents for enabling my interest in history to develop from a young age, especially for our trips to Italy which first introduced me to the Renaissance. The panoramic view of Florence from the terrace of the camp-site accompanied by my father's knowledge of its history gave me a love of the subject that has lasted a lifetime. I was also fortunate to have teachers who encouraged and channelled my enthusiasm. I hope that I was able to do the same for many of my own students.

I owe a debt to those historians whose work on 16th century Europe have both inspired and informed me over the years. V.H.H. Green, John Elliott and Karl Brandi I read studying for 'A' level. Geoffrey Parker's superb recent biography of Philip II, the work of Wim Blockmans, James D. Tracy, Mia J. Rodriquez-Salgado and others, many of whom contributed to 'Charles V 1500-1558 and His Time' edited by Hugo Soly (1999), immediately come to mind. I only wish that I could match the quality of their scholarship and writing.

I have much appreciated the resources available to me at Cambridge University Library and the assistance that the staff have provided. At the many museums, galleries and other buildings that we have visited throughout Europe on Charles' trail I have always found a friendly face. To all of them – thank you.

Most of all I am grateful to Deborah, for her company and perceptive comments on all our visits together. I am glad that that she enjoyed these trips as much as I did. Also for her patience with my demands on her time for reviewing the text and design advice as publication approached. Any errors, of course, remain mine alone.

# References

## Part One – Youthful Endeavours

### Chapter 1 – Birth-right
[1] Blockmans p.13
[2] Parker, (in Soly)
[3] Weighman p.139
[4] Weighman pp.139-142
[5] Weighman pp.124-125
[6] Penn p.216 (For a detailed account of Philip and Juana's stay in England see pp213-225)
[7] Penn p.221
[8] Tremlett pp130
[9] Elliott p.139
[10] Calendar of State Papers, Spain, Supplement to Vols. 1 and 2 Queen Juana 1506
[11] Calendar of State Papers, Spain, Supplement to Vols. 1 and 2 Queen Juana 1506
[12] Calendar of State Papers, Spain, Supplement to Vols. 1 and 2 Queen Juana 1507
[13] Calendar of State Papers, Spain, Supplement to Vols. 1 and 2 Queen Juana 1519 Denia to Charles Oct 1519

### Chapter 2 - Education
[1] De Iongh, Jane: Margaret of Austria: 1941/1954
[2] Thomas p.16
[3] Koenigsberger (2001) pp.93-95. Many in Flanders regarded the English as commercial rivals, while many in Brabant regarded them as trading partners.
[4] Koenigsberger Monarchies, States Generals and Parliaments p.101
[5] Brandi p.52
[6] CharlesV: Memoirs pp4
[7] Calendar of State Papers, Spain, Vol. 2 (1501-1525) pp496
[8] Brandi p.53
[9] Koenigsberger (2001) p.102.

### Chapter 3 - Apprenticeship
[1] Brandi p. 57
[2] Blockmans p.128
[3] Rady p.4
[4] Konigsberger (2001) p.109
[5] Brandi pp.57-59
[6] Calendar of State Papers, Spain. Supplement to Vols. 1 and 2, Queen Juana 1504

[7] Calendar of State Papers, Spain. Supplement to Vols. 1 and 2, Queen Juana 1504
[8] Calendar of State Papers, Spain. Supplement to Vols. 1 and 2, Queen Juana 1516
[9] Quoted in Brandi p.76
[10] Quoted in Parker : Soly(about pp120)
[11] Brandi p.77
[12] Quoted in Koenigsberger (2001) p.105

## Chapter 4 – King in Spain
[1] McKendrick pp.75-88
[2] Elliott (1963) p.135
[3] Elliott (1963) p.144
[4] Calendar of State Papers, Spain. Supplement to Vols. 1 and 2 Queen Juana 1516
[5] Charles' Memoirs p.5
[6] Charles' Memoirs p.5
[7] Frieder p. 25
[8] Frieder p.179
[9] Thomas p.6
[10] Brandi p. 83
[11] Blockmans p.120
[12] Blockmans, W. p.48
[13] Brandi p.93
[14] Elliott p.151
[15] MacDonald p.24
[16] Kamen, Henry, p.74 Spain 1469-1714
[17] Elliott p.145

## Chapter 5 - Emperor
[1] Brandi p.118
[2] Brandi p.124
[3] Fernandez Alvarez
[4] Blockmans p. 34
[5] Parker in Soly p.114
[6] Braudel p.165
[7] Braudel p.207
[8] Maltby p.76

## Part Two – Discovering the Realities of Power

## Chapter 6 – Revolt in Spain
[1] Rady p.31

[2] Elliott p.154
[3] Rady p.31
[4] CSP, Spain Supplement to Vols. 1 and 2, Queen Juana 1518-1520 Adrian to Charles 23rd Sept. 1520
[5] Kamen p.77
[6] Rady p.33
[7] Lynch p.59
[8] Rady p.32
[9] CSP Spain, Supplement to Vols. 1 and 2, Queen Juana 1518-1520 Adrian to Charles 4th Sept. 1520
[10] CSP Spain, Supplement to Vols. 1 and 2, Queen Juana MosenFerrer to Cisneros 6th March 1516
[11] CSP Spain, Supplement to Vols. 1 and 2, Queen Juana 1518-1520 Denia to Charles 30th July 1518
[12] CSP Spain, Supplement to Vols. 1 and 2, Queen Juana 1518-1520 Adrian to Mendoza 4th Sept 1520
[13] CSP Spain, Supplement to Vols. 1 and 2, Queen Juana 1518-1520 Attestation of 1st Sept
[14] CSP Spain, Supplement to Vols. 1 and 2, Queen Juana 1518-1520 Adrian to Charles 1st Sept 1520
[15] CSP Spain, Supplement to Vols. 1 and 2, Queen Juana 1518-1520 Adrian to Charles 14th Sept. 1520
[16] CSP Spain, Supplement to Vols. 1 and 2, Queen Juana 1518-1520 24th Sept 1520
[17] CSP Spain, Supplement to Vols. 1 and 2, Queen Juana 1518-1520 26th Sept 1520
[18] MacDonald p.24
[19] Kamen p.78
[20] CSP Spain, Supplement to Vols. 1 and 2, Queen Juana 1518-1520 Adrian to Charles 23rd Sept 1520
[21] McKendrick p.108

## Chapter 7 - Reformation
[1] Rupp pp.51-52
[2] Blockmans p.81
[3] Lortz
[4] Rady p.23
[5] Maltby pp.22-23
[6] Brandi p.129
[7] Rady p.22
[8] MacGregor Chapter 6 pp91-111
[9] Blockmans p.83
[10] Blockmans p.120
[11] Blockmans p.121
[12] Charles' Memoirs p.9

[13] Charles' Memoirs p.9
[14] Brandi p.177

## Chapter 8 – Conflict with France
[1] Rodriguez-Salgado, M J in Blockmans and Mout
[2] Norwich, J.J. p.285
[3] Norwich, J.J. p.286
[4] Rodriguez-Salgado, M J in Blockmans and Mout
[5] Rodriguez-Salgado, M J in Blockmans and Mout
[6] Brandi pp203-204
[7] Guicciardini, F p.331
[8] Guicciardini, F p.335

## Chapter 9 – Pavia and Madrid
[1] Brandi pp.219-221
[2] Hare, C. p99
[3] Jones p.96
[4] Jones p.97
[5] Jones p.98
[6] Tallett p.24
[7] Tracy (2002) p.31
[8] Jones p.114
[9] Tallett p.29
[10] Hare, C. p.100
[11] Guicciardini, F. pp. 348-349
[12] Guicciardini, F. pp. 349-350
[13] Guicciardini, F. pp. 353-354
[14] Hare p. 102
[15] Brandi p.236

## Chapter 10 – Settling Spain
[1] Thomas p.3
[2] Maltby Ch.4
[3] Kilsby p. 44 Charles to the Cortes of Castile in Valladolid 1523
[4] Kilsby p.45
[5] Maltby p.81
[6] Maltby p.78
[7] Maltby Ch.4
[8] MacDonald p.30
[9] Elliott p.177
[10] Elliott p.180
[11] Charles' Memories p12
[12] Carr p.150
[13] Carr p.103

[14] Carr p.92
[15] Brandi p.255

## Chapter 11 – Renewed War with France
[1] Brandi p.240
[2] Brandi p.242
[3] Norwich p.288
[4] L. Guicciardo p.47
[5] L. Guicciardo p.82
[6] Francisco de Salazar to Gattinara 18th May 1527 - Calendar of state papers , Spain, Vol 3, Part 2
[7] Hook p.164
[8] Norwich p293
[9] Hook p.167
[10] Perez to the Emperor 18th May 1527 - Calendar of state papers , Spain, Vol 3, Part 2
[11] L. Guicciardo p.107
[12] L. Guicciardo p.108
[13] L. Guicciardo p.109
[14] Soria to the emperor 25th May 1527 Calendar of state papers , Spain, Vol 3, Part 2
[15] Charles' memoirs p.14
[16] Dantyszek, Polish ambassador in Spain, quoted in Parker (Soly)
[17] Brandi p.281

## Part Three – Chasing Ambitions

## Chapter 12 - Coronation
[1] Brandi p.276
[2] Charles' Memoirs p.16
[3] Quoted in Thomas p.147
[4] Brandi p.282
[5] Marzahl, In Blockmans and Mout
[6] Marzahl, In Blockmans and Mout
[7] Thomas p.147
[8] Thomas p.147
[9] Strong, Roy: Splendour at Court, p.86. Weidenfeld and Nicholson, London, 1973.
[10] Maxwell, W. S.
[11] Charles' Memoirs p.18
[12] Maxwell, W. S. The account of the coronation celebrations is taken from the introduction by Sir William Stirling Maxwell to a reproduction of the engravings made of the 'Procession of Pope Clement and Emperor Charles V after the Coronation at Bologna' by Nicholas Hogenberg.
[13] Grant p.101

**Chapter 13 – Florence, Machiavelli and Warfare**
[1] Maxwell, W. S.
[2] Skinner p.5
[3] Strathern pp.409-410
[4] Harris p.4
[5] Hibbert Ch.15 Siege and Murder
[6] Machiavelli (in Jones) p.102
[7] Tallett p.51
[8] Jones p.102
[9] Tracy (2002) p.111
[10] Blockmans (in Boone and Demoor) pp.35-46
[11] Tracy (2002) p.123
[12] Tracy (2002) p.285

**Chapter 14 – Meeting his Family**
[1] Used in Parker in Soly p.156
[2] Used in Brandi pp.289-290
[3] Brandi p.290
[4] Quoted in Rodriquez-Salgado in Soly
[5] Koenigsberger, H.G. (2001) p.120
[6] Rodriguez-Salgado (1988) pp.21-22
[7] Rodriguez-Salgado (1988) p.24
[8] Koenigsberger, H.G. (2001) p.117
[9] Rodriguez-Salgado (1988)
[10] Brandi p.585
[11] Used in Rodriquez-Salgado in Soly p.60
[12] Brandi p.320
[13] Brandi p. 321
[14] John, Dorothea and Christina (1526) by Jan Gossaert in the Queen's Collection
[15] Brandi p324
[16] Quoted in Peter Marzahl (in Blockmans and Mout)
[17] Parker (in Soly) pp.160-161

**Chapter 15 – Seeking Unity**
[1] Brady - from L. Von Ranke from R. Aulinger: Bild des Reichstags(1980)
[2] Letter to Isabella July 8th 1530
[3] Tracy, J. Europe's reformations 1450-1650. p.215
[4] Tracy, J. Europe's reformations 1450-1650. p.70
[5] Blockmans p.42
[6] Brandi p. 246
[7] Brandi p. 300

[8] Brandi pp.310-311
[9] Quoted in MacDonald p.89

## Chapter 16 – The Habsburgs, Jacob Fugger and 16th century finances
[1] Ehrenberg p.80
[2] Ehrenberg pp.25-26
[3] Ferguson p.27
[4] Ferguson p.35
[5] Ferguson p.36
[6] Ehrenberg p.32
[7] Ehrenberg p.64
[8] Ehrenberg p.65
[9] Strieder p.105
[10] Ehrenberg p.71
[11] Strieder pp.215-219
[12] Ehrenberg p.85
[13] Hans Wantoch

## Chapter 17 – The Ottoman Menace
[1] Crowley p.366
[2] Imber p.43
[3] Brandi p.325
[4] Charles to Isabella 6 April 1532: Tracy p.37
[5] Memoirs p21   Ratisbon = Regensburg
[6] Brandi p.326
[7] Jardine p.383
[8] Memoirs p.23
[9] Strathern, P

## Chapter 18 – The Struggle for the Mediterranean
[1] De Brake (in Bonne and Demoor) from S. Haliczer
[2] Tracy (1999) p.83
[3] Crowley p.38
[4] Crowley p.16
[5] Crowley p.25
[6] Crowley p.66
[7] Robinson p.158
[8] Rady p.66
[9] Rady p.65
[10] Crowley p.63
[11] Brandi p.368
[12] Memoirs p.28

[13] Strong p.83
[14] Strong p.84


**Part Four – Confronting Challenges**

**Chapter 19 – Conflict and Family Death**
[1] Kilsby p.40
[2] Brandi p.378
[3] Santa Cruz quoted in Brandi p. 383
[4] Memoirs p.32
[5] Brandi p.389
[6] Brandi p.421
[7] Alvarez p.116

**Chapter 20 – Imposing his Authority**
[1] Charles to Mary 5th Oct 1537 quoted in Koenigsberger (2001) p. 123
[2] H. Pirenne 'Histoire de Belgique' (1923) quoted in Rady, M. p.69
[3] Koenigsberger (2001) p.140
[4] 12 October 1525 – quoted in Koenigsberger (2001) p.135
[5] Brandi p.414
[6] Arnade (in Boone and Demoor)
[7] Brandi p.425
[8] Strong p.98
[9] Giron in Alvarez p.118
[10] Maltby p.101
[11] Brandi p. 429
[12] Koenigsberger (2001) pp. 132-135

**Chapter 21 – Failure and Defeat**
[1] Matheson p.62
[2] Matheson pp.79-80
[3] Crowley p.71
[4] Crowley p. 85
[5] Crowley p.73
[6] Charles to Ferdinand quoted in Brandi p.459

**Chapter 22 – Family and Finances**
[1] Parker (Philip II) Ch. 1
[2] Charles' Political Testament to Philip, 1543
[3] Brandi p.488 (from Charles' political Testament 1543)
[4] Tracy p.286
[5] Blockmans p.155
[6] Charles to Ferdinand

[7] Elliott p.202
[8] Elliott p.203
[9] Charles to Philip quoted in Brandi p.490
[10] Hamilton discussed in Elliott pp. 192-196
[11] Quoted in Lynch p.178
[12] Kamen p.98
[13] Lynch p.139
[14] Kamen p.100
[15] Koenigsberger p.40
[16] Kamen p.109
[17] Lynch p.167
[18] Elliott p.197
[19] Maltby p.84
[20] Brandi p. 484
[21] All extracts selected from two main letters which made up Charles' Political Testament to Philip: 1543, quoted at length in Brandi pp. 485-493

## Chapter 23 – Faith and Bullion
[1] Kamen p.88
[2] Alvarez p.71
[3] Most recently by Hugh Thomas in Rivers of Gold (2003) and The Golden Age (2010)
[4] Spanoghe (in Boon and Demoor) p.74
[5] Heer pp.168-169
[6] Spanoghe (in Boon and Demoor) pp.74-75
[7] Heer p.170
[8] Maltby p.87
[9] Maltby p.88
[10] Kamen p.94
[11] Spanoghe (in Boon and Demoor) p.82
[12] Spanoghe (in Boon and Demoor) p.84
[13] Thomas p.114
[14] Blockmans p.108
[15] Blockmans p.107
[16] Heer p.168
[17] Spanoghe (in Boon and Demoor) p.90
[18] Spanoghe (in Boon and Demoor) p.91
[19] Spanoghe (in Boon and Demoor) p.100
[20] Spanoghe (in Boon and Demoor) p.101
[21] Spanoghe (in Boon and Demoor) p.99
[22] Heer p.171
[23] Blockmans p.108
[24] Blockmans p.108
[25] Heer p.172

[26] Maltby  p.89
[27] Heer  pp. 172-173

**Chapter 24 – The Final Conflict with Francis**
[1] Quoted in Brandi p.473
[2] Memoirs p.47
[3] Memoirs p.49
[4] Brandi p.477
[5] Blockmans  p.55
[6] Brandi p.495
[7] Mary to Charles 28 Nov 1542: Tracy p.36
[8] Charles to Mary 30 October 1543: Tracy p.35
[9] Memoirs p.52
[10] Quoted in Brandi p.497
[11] Memoirs p.55
[12] Memoirs p.58
[13] Memoirs p.62
[14] Tallett  p.54
[15] Knecht  pp.110-111
[16] Brandi  p.380
[17] Memoirs pp. 70-71
[18] Crowley  p.74
[19] Brandi  p.521
[20] Memoirs p.72
[21] Rady  p.91

**Part Five – Highs and Lows: Imperial and Dynastic**

**Chapter 25 - Muhlberg**
[1] Memoirs pp. 72-74
[2] Brandi pp.527-529
[3] Philip of Hesse to Strasbourg town council – quoted in Rady p.75
[4] Charles to Mary 9th June 1546
[5] Memoirs p.78
[6] Brandi p.543
[7] Blockmans p.95
[8] Charles to Philip 8 August 1546 – quoted in Blockmans p.94
[9] Quoted in Blockmans p.95
[10] In the Prado, Madrid
[11] In the Alte Pinakothek, Munich

**Chapter 26 – The Future of the Dynasty**
[1] Charles Political Testament of 1548 - Brandi  p.583

[2] Extracts taken from Brandi pp. 582 - 587
[3] Parker p.39
[4] Brandi p.630
[5] Alvarez p.150
[6] Parker (in Soly)

## Chapter 27 – Innsbruck and Metz
[1] Brandi pp. 607-608
[2] Charles to Mary 21 March 1552 quoted in G. Parker (in H.Soly)
[3] Rodriguez-Salgado (1988) p.48
[4] Rodriguez-Salgado (1988) p.49
[5] Brandi p.620
[6] Details of Charles' health: Parker (in Soly), especially pages 148,161,192,203,207,217 and 218
[7] Rodriguez-Salgado (1988) p.2

## Chapter 28 – Relinquishing Power
[1] 17th December 1553 to Philip, quoted in Prieto
[2] Quoted in Rodriguez-Salgado (1988) p. 75
[3] Charles to Philip, quoted in Rodriguez-Salgado (1988) pp. 49-50
[4] Rodriguez-Salgado (1988) p.89
[5] Rodriguez-Salgado (1988) p.90
[6] Blockmans p.9
[7] Brandi p.634

## Part Six – Retreat from the World Stage

## Chapter 29 - Reflections
[1] Book 1, Chapter 3
[2] von Habsburg p.221
[3] Rady p.97
[4] Parker (in Soly) p.113
[5] Macdonald p.32
[6] Macdonald p.19

## Chapter 30 – Final Rest
[1] Alvarez p.175
[2] Brother Jose de Siguenza: History of the Order of St Jerome
[3] Prieto p.14
[4] Alvarez p.181
[5] MacDonald p.9
[6] Alvarez pp.183-184
[7] Prieto p. 26

# Bibliography

**Alvarez**, Manuel Fernandez: Charles V: Elected Emperor and Hereditary Ruler. Thames and Hudson, London, 1975. Translated from the Spanish by J.A. Lalaguna

**Arnade**, Peter: Privileges and the Political Imagination in the Ghent Revolt of 1539 - in **Boone**, Marc and **Demoor**, Marysa (eds.): Charles V in Context: The Making of a European Identity. Ghent University and Brussels University Press, 2003

**Blockmans**, Wim: Emperor Charles V (1500 – 1558). Arnold, London, 2002 Translated by Isola van den Hoven-Vardon

**Blockmans**, Wim: Logistics of warfare in Central Italy 1527-1530, in **Blockmans**, Wim and **Mout**, Nicolette (eds.): The World of Emperor Charles V (proceedings of the Colloquium, Amsterdam, 4-6 October 2000), Royal Netherlands Academy of Arts and Sciences, Amsterdam 2004

**Blockmans**, Wim and **Mout**, Nicolette (eds.): The World of Emperor Charles V (proceedings of the Colloquium, Amsterdam, 4-6 October 2000), Royal Netherlands Academy of Arts and Sciences, Amsterdam 2004

**Boone**, Marc and **Demoor**, Marysa (eds.): Charles V in Context: The Making of a European Identity. Ghent University and Brussels University Press, 2003

**Brady**, Thomas: German Histories of the Age of Reformations. Cambridge University Press, Cambridge, 2009

**Brandi**, Karl: The Emperor Charles V, The Growth and Destiny of a Man and of a world-Empire.   Transl:  C.V. Wedgewood.  First published in 1939. Humanities Press, N.J. 1980

**Braudel**, Fernand: The Mediterranean and the Mediterranean World in the Age of Philip II. 1949, Abridged version Harper Collins 1992

**Burke,** Peter: Presenting and Re-presenting Charles V in 'Charles V 1500-1558 and his Time' ed. H. Soly, Mercatorfonds, Antwerp, 1999

**Burckhardt**, Titus: Moorish Culture in Spain. Translated by Alisa Jaffa. Unwin and Allen, London, 1972.

**Carolus**. Sociedad Estatal para le Conmemoracion de los Centenarios de Felipe II y Carlos V. Published in connection with the 'Carolus' exhibition – Museo de Santa Cruz, Toledo (October 2000 – January 2001)

**Carr**, Matthew: Blood and Faith: The Purging of Muslim Spain. Hurst, London, 2009

**Crowley**, Roger: Empires of the Sea: The Final Battle for the Mediterranean 1521 – 1580. Faber and Faber, London, 2008

**Dixon**, C. Scott and **Fuchs**, Martina (eds.): The Histories of Charles V. Aschendorff, Munster, 2005

**Dixon**, C Scott: Charles V and his reign in British Historical Thought in **Dixon**, C. Scott and **Fuchs**, Martina (eds.): The Histories of Charles V, Aschendorff, Munster, 2005

**Ehrenberg,** Richard: Capital and Finance in the Age of the Renaissance – A Study of the Fugger and their Connections. Translated by H.M.Lucas. Jonathan Cape, London, 1928

**Elliott**, John H: Imperial Spain. Penguin books, London, 2002. (First published- Edward Arnold, 1963)

**Espinosa**, Aurelio: The Empire of the Cities – Emperor Charles V, the Comunero Revolt, and the Transformation of the Spanish System. Brill, Leiden and Boston, 2009

**Fagel**, Raymond: A Broken Portrait of the emperor: Charles V in Holland and Belgium 1558 – 2000 in **Dixon**, C. Scott and **Fuchs**, Martina (eds.): The Histories of Charles V, Aschendorff, Munster, 2005

**Ferguson,** Niall: The Ascent of Money – A Financial History of the World. Allen Lane, London, 2008

**Frieder,** Braden: Chivalry and the Prefect Prince – Tournaments, Art and Armor at the Spanish Habsburg Court. Truman State University Press, 2008

**Garcia-Frias,** Carmen and **Sancho** Jose Luis: Real Monasterio de San Lorenzo de El Escorial. Patrimonio Nacional, 2003

**Grant,** Neil: Charles V, Holy Roman Emperor. Franklin Watts, London, 1970

**Guicciardini,** Francisco: The History of Italy (Storia d'Italia) translated and edited by Alexander Sidney. Collier, New York, 1972

**Guicciardini,**Luigi: The Sack of Rome, translated and edited from the 1867 Italian edition by James MacGregor, Italica Press, N.Y. 1993

**Habsburg,** Otto von: Charles V. Translated from the French by Michael Ross, Weidenfeld and Nicolson, London, 1970

**Haliczer,** Stephen: Comuneros of Castile – The forging of a revolution 1472-1521. Univ. of Wisconsin Press, Madison and London, 1981

**Harris,** Robert: Imperium. Hutchinson, London, 2006

**Headley,** John M.: The Emperor and his Chancellor. A study of the imperial chancellery under Gattinara. Cambridge University Press, Cambridge, Cambridge University Press, 1982

**Heer,** Friedrich: The Holy Roman Empire. Transl. by Janet Sondheimer. Weidenfeld and Nicolson, London, 1968

**Hibbert,** Christopher: Florence – The Biography of a city. Viking, London, 1993

**Hook,** Judith: The Sack of Rome 1527. MacMillan, London, 1972

**Imber,** Colin: Ottoman Empire 1300-1650: the structure of power. Palgrave, MacMillan, Basingstoke, 2002

**Iongh,** Jane de: Margaret of Austria, Regent of the Netherlands, Jonathan Cape, London, 1954, translated from the Dutch by

M.D.Herter Norton. First published in Holland in 1941

**Iongh**, Jane de: Mary of Hungary, Second Regent of the Netherlands, Faber &Faber, London, 1958, translated from the Dutch by M.D.Herter Norton

**Jardine,** Lisa: Worldly Goods, A new history of the Renaissance. Macmillan, London, 1996

**Kamen**, Henry: Spain's road to Empire: the making of a world power, 1492-1763. Allen Lane, London, 2002

**Kamen**, Henry: Spain 1469-1714. A Society of Conflict. Longman, London , 1983, 2nd edition 1991

**Kilsby**, Jill: Spain: rise and decline 1474-1643. Edward Arnold, London, 1987

**Koenigsberger**, H: The Habsburgs and Europe 1516-1660. Cornell Univ. Press, Ithica, N.Y., 1971

**Koenigsberger**, H. and **Mosse**, George L.: Europe in the 16th Century. Longmans, London, 1968

**Lortz,** Joseph: The Reformation in Germany (2 vols.)(1939-1949) Translated from the German by Ronald Walls. London 1968

**Lynch**, John: Spain 1516 – 1598 From Nation State to World Empire. Blackwell, Oxford, 1991

**MacDonald**, Steward: Charles V: Ruler, Dynast and Defender of the Faith, 1500-1558. (Access to History) Hodder and Stoughton, 1992

**MacGregor**, Neil: Germany: Memories of a Nation, Penguin, London, 2014

**Maltby**, William**:** The Reign of Charles V, Palgrave, Basingstoke, 2002

**Marzahl**, Peter: Communication and Control in the Political System of Charles V: The First Regency of Empress Isabella, in **Blockmans**, Wim and **Mout**, Nicolette (eds.): The World of

Emperor Charles V (proceedings of the Colloquium, Amsterdam, 4-6 October 2000)

**Matheson,** Peter: Contarini at Regensburg. Clarendon Press, Oxford, 1972

**McKendrick**, Melveena: A Concise History of Spain. Cassell, London, 1972

**Moreno**, Ana Martin: Charles V. Aldeasa, 1999. Translated by Nigel Williams

**Norwich**, John Julius: The Popes, Chatto and Windus, London, 2011

**Parker**, Geoffrey: 'The Political World of Charles V' in 'Charles V 1500-1558 and his Time' ed. H. Soly, Mercatorfonds, Antwerp, 1999

**Penn**, Thomas: Winter King: The Dawn of Tudor England. Allen Lane, London, 2011

**Potter**, David: Emperor Charles V in the French Historical Tradition in **Dixon**, C. Scott and **Fuchs**, Martina (eds.): The Histories of Charles V

**Prieto,** Maria Teresa Rodriguez: Yuste: Monastery of St Jerome. Patrimonio Nacional 2008

**Rady**, Martin: The Emperor Charles V. (Seminar Studies in History) Longman, London and New York, 1988

**Robinson**, A. Mary F: Margaret of Angouleme, Queen of Navarre. W.H. Allen and Co., London, 1886

**Rodriguez-Salgado**, Mia J: Charles V and his Dynasty, in **Soly,** Hugo (ed): Charles V 1500-1558 and his Time, Mercatorfonds, Antwerp, 1999

**Rodriguez-Salgado**, Mia J: Obeying the Ten Commandments: the First War between Charles V and Francis I 1520-1529, in **Blockmans**, Wim and **Mout**, Nicolette (eds.): The World of Emperor Charles V (proceedings of the Colloquium, Amsterdam, 4-6 October 2000), Royal Netherlands Academy of Arts and Sciences,

Amsterdam 2004

**Rodriguez-Salgado**, Mia J: The Changing Face of Empire. Charles V, Philip II and Habsburg Authority 1551 – 1559. Cambridge University Press, Cambridge, UK, 1988

**Rupp**, George: Luther's Progress to the Diet of Worms, 1521. SCM Press, London, 1951

**Shaw**, Christine: Charles V and Italy in **Dixon**, C. Scott and **Fuchs**, Martina (eds.): The Histories of Charles V. Aschendorff, Munster, 2005

**Soly,** Hugo (ed): Charles V 1500-1558 and his Time. Mercatorfonds, Antwerp, 1999

**Skinner,** Quentin: Machiavelli – a very short introduction. OUP, Oxford, 2000

**Spanoghe**, S.: Imperialising the Amerindian Other: Between forced Integration and Dual Citizenship, in **Boone**, Marc and **Demoor**, Marysa (eds.): Charles V in Context: The Making of a European Identity. Ghent University and Brussels University Press, 2003

**Strathern**, Paul: The Artist, the Philosopher and the Warrior – Leonardo, Machiavelli and Borgia – a fateful collusion. Jonathan Cape, London, 2009.

**Strieder**, Jacob: Jacob Fugger the rich, merchant and banker of Augsburg 1459-1525. Translated from the German by Mildred L Hartsough (ed. N.S.B.Gras). The Adelphi Company, New York, 1931.

**Strong**, Roy: Splendour at Court, Weidenfeld and Nicolson, London, 1973

**Te Brake**, Wayne: Charles V and his Contentious Subjects in **Boone**, Marc and **Demoor**, Marysa (eds.): Charles V in Context: The Making of a European Identity, Ghent University and Brussels University Press, 2003

**Thomas**, Hugh: The Golden Age: the Spanish Empire of Charles V. Allen Lane, London, 2010

**Thomas**, Hugh: Rivers of Gold: the rise of the Spanish Empire. Weidenfeld and Nicolson, London, 2003

**Tracy**, James D.: Emperor Charles V, Impresario of War: Campaign Strategy, International Finance and Domestic Politics. Cambridge University Press, 2002

**Tracy**, James D.: Holland and Habsburg Rule, 1506-1566. Univ. Of California Press, Berkeley and Oxford, 1990

**Tracy**, James D.: War finance and Fiscal devolution in Charles V's realms, in **Blockmans**, Wim and **Mout**, Nicolette (eds.): The World of Emperor Charles V (proceedings of the Colloquium, Amsterdam, 4-6 October 2000, Royal Netherlands Academy of Arts and Sciences, Amsterdam 2004

**Tracy**, James D.: Europe's Reformations, 1450-1650. Rowman and Littlefield, Oxford, 1999

**Tremlett**, Giles: Catherine of Aragon: Henry's Spanish Queen. Faber and Faber, London, 2010

**Wantoch,** Hans: Magnificent Money Makers. Translated by J.S.H.Moore. 1932

**Weightman**, Christine: Margaret of York, Duchess of Burgundy (1446-1503). Alan Sutton, Gloucester, 1989

# Index

Aachen(Aix-la Chapelle) 55, 65
Acuna, Antonio de, Bishop of Zamora 81-82
Adrian of Utrecht, Pope Adrian VI 25, 33, 40, 48, 56, 75-76, 78-81, 87, 89, 103-104, 241, 362
Africa 2
Aigues Mortes 226
Albania 199
Albert, Archbishop of Mainz 84-85
Albert Alcibiades, Margrave 292, 297, 313, 316, 318, 324
Albret, Henry d' 102
Albret, Jeanne d' 274, 279, 285, 304
Alcazar Real (Seville) 126
Aleander, Hieronymous 87,89-90
Alexander VI (Pope) (Rodrigo Borgia) 101, 264
Algiers 242, 245-248, 274, 339
Alhambra 127-128
Alpujarras 128
Alva, Duke of 113, 262, 299, 314, 326, 345
Anabaptists 184, 208-209, 325
Anatolia 198
Anna (daughter of Ferdinand) 283
Anne of Brittany 11, 39
Anne of Hungary 93, 177
Antwerp 9, 36, 61, 237, 255, 259, 276, 320
Aquinas, Thomas 191
Aragon 13, 16, 40, 42, 47-48, 50, 54, 73
Aristotle 271
Armada (1588) 2, 228, 324
Arras, Treaty of (1435) 35
Arthur, Prince of Wales 16, 20
Artillery, 16th Century 111, 161-162, 210-202, 205
Artois 34-35, 114-115, 142, 275, 306, 326
Asientos 255
Atlantic Ocean 9
Augsburg 61, 86, 179, 185, 189, 194, 196, 240, 290, 297, 299, 304
   Augsburg interim 302, 311, 313
   Religious Peace of 325, 327
Austria 13, 93, 151
Avila 75, 78

Baglione, Malatesta 161, 165

Baltic Sea  9
Barbarossa, Aruj  209
Barbarossa, Hayrettin  210-214, 221, 226-227, 242, 247, 274, 282-283, 362
Barcelona  54-55, 114, 145, 148-154, 198, 278
Bay of Biscay  46, 330
Belgrade  133
Binche  326
Blomberg, Barbara  294, 355
Bohemia  293, 297-298
Boleyn, Anne  215
Bolivia  272
Bologna  1, 95, 149-154, 301
Bora, Katharina von  291
Borgia, Cesare  99-101, 158
Borluut, Simon  238
Boulogne  280, 283
Bourbon, Charles III, Duke of  105, 115, 132, 136-137, 139, 174, 362
Bourg-en-Bresse  21, 221
Brabant  10, 231, 237, 276, 306
Brandon, Charles, Duke of Suffolk  30, 105, 125
Bravo, Juan  77, 82
Brenner Pass  314
Brittany  97
Brou, Royal monastery of  21
Bruges  9-10, 96
Brussels  30, 36, 38, 40, 64-65, 173, 285, 305, 317, 324
   Brussels, Treaty of (1516)  43
Bullion (from the Americas)  256, 264
Buren, Count  295-296
Burgos  18, 47, 56, 76, 81, 141, 235, 258, 348-349
   Laws of  266
Burgundian dynasty  39, 97
Burgundy  7-9, 12, 21-22, 34, 115, 142, 233
Burnet, Gilbert  337

Cadzand, Treaty of (1492)  10
Cajetan, Cardinal  86-87, 138
Calais  104
Calfvel  237
Calvinists  325
Cambrai  35, 279
   Treaty of (1529)  142, 221
Carducci, Francesco  160
Carlos, Don (son of Philip II)  294, 323, 346, 349, 358
Casas, Bartolome de las  269-273

Castel Sant' Angelo (Rome) 138
Castile 13-19, 40, 47-50, 53-54, 75-82, 118, 256-257, 265, 267, 348
Catalonia 54
Catherine de Medici 206, 208, 216, 285
Catherine of Aragon (1st wife of Henry VIII) 16, 28, 64, 140, 208, 217, 322, 360
Catherine of Portugal(Charles' youngest sister) 18, 20, 50, 77, 124, 259, 358
Cellini, Benvenuto 137
Cerignola, battle of (1503) 42, 110
Chambord, Treaty of (1552) 312
Charles II of Spain 310
Charles V
  *Family*
  ancestry 7-8
  baptism in Ghent 7
  relations with parents 13
  first meeting with Juana in Spain 49
  first meeting with brother 50
  marriage plans 16, 30, 40, 42, 65, 96, 101, 122-124
  marriage 125-126
  birth of son, Philip 130
  birth of daughter, Maria 147
  birth of daughter, Juana 228
  relations with children 250
  family as regents 167-174
  planning marriage alliances 174-177, 235, 283-286, 304
  family rift 307-310
  impact of marriages within the family 310
  *Personal*
  education and upbringing 20-31
  interests 23, 352
  physical features 24
  hunting 24
  character 26, 31, 169
  accepting criticism 177-178
  judgement of character 260
  health issues 317-318
  abdication speech 327-328
  diet in later years 352
  *Coming to Power*
  inheritance 13, 19, 40-41, 55
  arrival and accession in Spain 46-52
  coming of age ceremony 30, 38
  coronation (Aachen) 65
  election as Emperor 60-62

coronation (Bologna) 145-146, 148-155
*Beliefs/Ideas*
chivalry 24, 212, 340
Christian unity 2, 338
crusade against the Ottomans 52, 134, 198, 212, 221, 226, 234-235, 284
speech at Diet of Worms 90-91
reputation 202
working for a religious
settlement 179-180, 185-188, 240-245
meeting Philip of Hesse 292
political testaments 171, 225, 250-251, 260-263, 303-304, 347
passing on his inheritance 304-310
*Military action*
wars with Francis I 101-110, 141-142, 221-226, 275-286
Pavia, battle of (1525) 107-109
defence of Vienna (1532) 202-205
capture of Tunis (1535) 21-215
attack on Algiers (1541) 247-248
leading troops - costs 277
and Schmalkaldic League 290-299
victory at Muhlberg 298
flight from Innsbruck 314
failure at Metz 316
*Other*
rule in the Low Countries 32-39, 231-235, 237-239
revolt in Spain – causes 56
revolt in Spain 73-83
administration of Spain 120-1
visits to England 64-65, 96
communicating with regents 177
finances 189-197, 251-259
meeting with Francis I (1538) 226
travelling through France 235-236
speech at the Vatican (1536) 221-222
and the New World 264-272
Charles VIII of France 11, 13, 20, 39, 98, 100
Charles of Egmond, Duke of Guelders 35, 38, 102, 182, 223, 274
Charles 'the Bold' ('the Rash'), Duke of Burgundy 7, 9, 22, 39, 234, 359
Charles, Duke of Orleans (youngest son of Francis I) 235, 283-286, 361
Chievres, William of Croy, Lord of 26-31, 33, 38, 42, 55-57, 73, 95, 102, 360
Christian II of Denmark 29, 175, 223
Christina of Denmark 176, 221, 280
Church Council 184, 186, 188, 206, 209, 221, 228, 241, 289, 319
Cisneros, Cardinal Archbishop of Toledo 17-18, 40-42, 48-49, 53

Claude, 1st wife of Francis I  16, 38, 114, 123
Clement VII, Pope  1, 99, 104-107, 134-140, 149-153, 156, 164-167, 185-186, 206, 216, 241, 361
Cobos, Francisco  120-121, 147, 168, 226, 260, 262-263, 345, 360
Cognac, League of  132
Communications in the 16th Century  67-69
Comunidades de Castilla, Guerra de las  75-82
Contarini, Cardinal  244
Conversos  129, 341
Cordoba  47, 76, 126-127
Corfu  225
Coron  179, 212
Coronation of Charles V  152-154
Cortes, Hernan  1, 94, 96, 125, 147-148, 248, 264, 267
Corunna  16, 55-56
Coudenberg Palace, Brussels  30, 327
Council of the Indies  120, 169, 261, 265, 267
Court of Savoy (also see Margaret of Austria and Mechelen)  22
Cranach, Lucas  21
Credit  190-193, 254-255, 259
Creesers  237
Crepy, Treaty of (1544)  283-286, 289, 295
Cuba  264, 269


Denia, Marquis of (guardian of Juana)  19, 49, 77
Doria, Andrea  141, 149, 178, 212, 227, 248, 253, 259, 303, 344-345, 360
Dorothea of Denmark  176
Dover  96
Drake, Francis  265
Durer, Albrecht  23, 87, 96

Eck, Johannes  186, 244
Edward IV of England  9, 15, 233
Edward VI of England  322
El Escorial  128, 356-357
Eleanor, sister of Charles  50, 130, 358
  birth  13
  youth in the Low Countries  20, 32
  journey to Spain (1517)  44
  improves condition of sister, Catherine  50
  godmother to Philip
  marriages  44, 105, 114-115, 142, 174-175
  relations with Francis I  175, 304-305
  meets Charles in Paris  236

393

    visit to Charles in Brussels 285
    journey to Spain (1556) 333, 348
    attempted reconciliation with daughter 354
    death 354-355
    tomb 357
Electors (in the Holy Roman empire) 59
Emmanuel Philibert of Savoy 329
Encabezamiento 119
Encomienda 268-270, 272
Encomiendores 268
Enriquez, Admiral Fadrique 79
Epidemics (in the New World) 269
Erasmus 1, 23, 25-26, 37, 44, 188, 200
Extremadura 320

Farnese family 94, 99, 103, 149, 224, 228, 242, 285, 296, 302, 362
    Ottavio, Duke of Parma 278, 289, 294-295
Ferdinand II of Aragon 8, 12-13, 16-17, 39-43, 48, 99, 101-102, 159, 341, 350, 359
Ferdinand, Charles' brother, later Holy Roman Emperor 358
    birth 14
    upbringing in Spain 20
    first meeting with Charles 50
    possible candidate in Imperial election 60
    in the Low Countries 60, 92- 93
    betrothal and marriage 92-93
    inheritance in Austria 93
    king of Bohemia 133-134
    election as King of the Romans 156, 172, 179, 336
    meeting with Charles and Mary in Innsbruck 167
    marriage of his children 177, 283
    in Hungary vs. Ottomans 167, 172, 200, 204, 339
    against Schmalkaldic League 290
    discussion re.future of the dynasty 304, 306-310
    negotiations with Maurice of Saxony 313-315
    Religious Peace of Augsburg 325
Ferdinand (Charles' second son) 151, 171
Ferrucci, Francesco 165-166
Field of the Cloth of Gold (1520) 64-65
Finances in the 16th Century 189-194
Flanders (province) 10, 34-35, 306 37, 73, 114-115, 142, 231-232, 237
Florence 98-100, 132, 135, 155-157, 160-162, 164-166, 216
Flushing (Vlissingen) 46, 333
Fonseca, Juan Rodriquez de (Bishop of Burgos) 265
Franche Comte 8-9, 97

Francis I 361
  marriages 16, 174
  reputation in youth 24
  inheritance 38-39
  early successes 42
  and the Imperial election 61-62
  Field of the Cloth of Gold 64-65
  animosity to Charles 95, 97, 274
  wars with Charles 101-106, 141-142, 221-226, 275-286,
  at battle of Pavia 108-109
  Charles' prisoner 112-116
  alliances with Suleiman 205, 211, 225, 275, 282-283
  marriage of son, Henry, to
  Catherine de Medici 209
  invasion of Italy 1536 234
  death of son, Francis 223
  host to Charles 226, 235-236
  death 300
Francis (son of Francis I) 132, 142, 223, 361
Francis, Duke of Lorraine 177, 280
Frankfurt 62
Frederick III (Holy Roman Emperor) 10, 194, 198
Frederick the Wise of Saxony 61, 84-85, 89, 91
Frederick, Count Palatine 23, 33, 44, 153, 176, 203, 291-293, 297
Friesland (province) 102
Frundsberg, Georg 106, 108, 136
Fugger family 61, 85-86, 172, 194
  Anton 189, 197, 314, 321
  Jacob 189, 194-197
Fuggerei 196
Fussen 314

Galley 246-247
Gandia, battle of (1521) 74
Gardiner, Stephen 324
Garigliano, battle of (1503) 42, 100
Gattinara, Mercurino 54, 63, 95, 103, 113-115, 120, 131, 145, 154, 168, 319, 335, 345, 360
Gaztelu, Martin de 351
Genoa 98, 145, 149, 206, 259, 278
George of Austria 275
Germaine de Foix 17, 19, 40, 52, 118
Germanias, Revolt of the 74, 129
Ghent 3, 9-10, 36, 175, 225, 231-239, 285, 333
Gheyst, Johanna Maria van der 94

Giron, Don Pedro 81
Golden Fleece, the Order of 7, 15, 21, 23, 29, 32-33, 38, 42-43, 51, 151, 177, 212, 261, 263, 292, 300, 313, 327, 340, 342
Golden Horn (Istanbul) 245
Gonzaga, Ferrante 99, 136, 139, 163, 178, 248, 278-279, 302, 326, 345, 361
Gout 317
Granada 12, 47, 56, 76, 127-128, 235
Granvelle, Antoine Perrenot de 317, 328, 360
Granvelle, Nicholas Perrenot de 145, 168, 226, 244, 263, 360
Gravelines 65
Gravensteen 9
Great Privilege of 1477 10, 232
Greece 199
Guelders (province) 35, 38, 43, 94, 102, 182, 223, 231, 274-275, 278
Guicciardini, Francesco (Florentine diplomat and historian) 61-62, 104, 135, 138
Guilds 36
Guines, Treaty of (1546) 295
Gustinian, Antonio 62

Habsburg family 1, 7-8, 11, 50, 55, 59, 92-93, 99, 170, 205, 310, 322, 336
Haidplatz (Regensburg) 244
Hainaut (province) 10, 34-35, 279, 306
Haller, Wolff 61
Henry II of France (son of Francis I) 24, 132, 142, 189, 206, 235, 285-286, 313-314, 361
Henry III of Castile 350
Henry IV of Castile 350
Henry VII of England 12, 15-16, 21
Henry VIII of England
  meets Philip of Burgundy 15
  jousting injuries 23
  Imperial election 61-62, 64
  discussions with Charles 94-96
  divorce from Catherine of
  Aragon 98, 140, 167, 208
  Treaty of Windsor (1522) 101, 103
  English campaigns in France 105, 280
  plan to partition France 113, 339
  and League of Cognac 132
  character 178
  improved relations with Charles 226, 276, 278
  treatment of ministers 260
  death 300

Henry of Brunswick 290-291
Henry of Nassau 23, 32, 39-40, 52, 61, 102, 149, 203
Hispaniola 264
Hispanization 265
Hoffman, Melchior 208
Holbein, Hans 189
Holland (province) 10, 35, 40, 231
Holy League (1511) 28
Holy Roman Empire 58-63, 84
Hungary 133, 201, 314
Hyeres 224

Ibiza 225
Ibrahim Pasha 201, 225, 362
Imperial Diet 59
Indulgencies 84-85
Inflation 256-258
Ingolstadt 296
Innsbruck 92, 156, 167-168, 313-314
Inquisition 129-130, 261
Isabella, sister of Charles 13, 20, 29, 175, 358
Isabella of Castile 8, 12, 14, 16, 40-41, 48-49, 341, 349, 359
Isabella of Portugal, Charles' wife 358
   and Charles' travels 3, 202
   betrothal and marriage to Charles 79, 107, 124-126
   regent in Spain 146-147, 171, 214, 229
   letters from Charles 179, 202, 264
   family life 207, 223-224
   ill-health and death 235
   Titian's portraits 348, 351
Istanbul 199-200, 205, 226
Italy, in the early 16th Century 98-101

Jarandilla de la Vera 350, 354
Jews in Spain 128
John of Austria, Don 294, 355-357, 359
John of Denmark 175-176
John of Gaunt 233
John of Leiden 208
John III of Portugal 124, 259, 322
John of Saxony 172, 185-186, 291
John Frederick of Saxony 241, 290-291, 294-299, 302, 312
Jousting 23, 236
Juan, Prince of the Asturias 8, 12, 20
Juana (la Loca) 7, 12-19, 41, 49-50, 53, 76-81, 327, 359

Juana (daughter of Charles V) 228, 251, 261, 323, 349, 353-354, 358
Julius II (Pope) 59, 85, 87, 100-101, 158
Julius III (Pope) 313
Junta (of the Comunidades de Castilla)
Juros 255, 321

Keizerstraat (Mechelen) 11
Kempis, Thomas a 333
Knights of St. John 210-211, 214, 226, 245
Knights' Revolt (1522-1523) 180-181
Kortrijk, Hans van 235
Koszeg 203

Landriano, battle of (1529) 142, 156
Landuedoc 225
Lannoy, Charles de 23, 33, 57, 105-106, 114-116, 131-132, 141, 360
Leipzig 297
Leipzig 'interim' 303
Leo X (Pope) 42, 61, 65, 87, 101-102, 361
Leonardo de Vinci 99
Lepanto, battle of 294, 339
Letters, delivery time 67
Leyva, Antonio de 105, 108, 136, 141, 149, 152, 203, 222
Lieven, Piet 238
Llorenc, Juan 74
Loasysa, Garcia de 168-169, 188
London 96
Louis XI of France 10
Louis XII of France 16-17, 20, 27, 30, 38-40, 42, 98, 100, 123, 158, 361
Louis II of Hungary 60, 92, 133
Louise (daughter of Francis I) 42, 101
Louise of Savoy (mother of Francis I) 105, 114, 142, 361
Low Countries 8, 13-15, 19, 28, 30, 32-40, 45, 92, 97, 151, 225, 231-240, 274-276, 304-307, 321-322, 326, 341-342
Luther, Martin 1, 45, 84-92, 179, 181-182, 203, 240, 244, 279, 291-292
Lutherans 183-187, 202, 208, 242, 291, 325, 336
Luxembourg 34-35, 102, 275-276, 280

Machiavelli, Niccolo 17, 99-100, 157-162
Madrid 50, 114, 250
   Treaty of Madrid (1526) 115-116, 125, 221
Magdeburg 85, 299, 311
Mahon (in Minorca) 215
Mainz 85
Male, William van 307, 316, 351

Malines – see Mechelen
Malta  211, 339
Manuel I of Portugal  13, 44, 105, 322
Maramaldo, Fabrizio  166
Marche, Olivier de la  24
Margaret of Austria (Charles' aunt)  359
   at Charles' baptism  7
   early betrothals and marriage  10-12, 15
   influence on Charles' upbringing  20-31
   relations with Chievres  33
   Regency Council in Low Countries  45
   and Charles' election as Emperor  60-61, 93
   upbringing of Margaret of Parma  94
   Ladies Peace (1529)  142
   advice and warning to Charles  146, 170-171, 179-171,
   death  172-173
Margaret of Parma  (natural daughter of Charles V)  94, 145, 166, 217, 224, 228, 242, 278, 294, 359
Margaret of York  7, 9-12, 22, 25
Maria (daughter of Charles V)  147, 173-174, 207, 250-251, 261, 283, 306, 310, 330, 358
Maria of Portugal (daughter of Eleanor)  321, 348, 354
Maria Manuela of Portugal  259, 277, 294
Marignano, battle of (1515)  42, 101
Mary of Burgundy  7, 9-10, 194, 359
Mary of Hungary, Charles' sister
   birth  14
   in Low Countries  20
   betrothal and marriage to
   Louis of Hungary  29, 92
   upbringing of Margaret of
   Parma  94
   death of husband  133
   regent of the Low Countries  173-175, 285
   skills – diplomatic and military  223, 316, 318-321
   role in healing family rift  307-308
   opposition in Ghent  238
   recognition of dangers of war  275-277
   abdication as regent  327-328
   travels with Charles to Spain  333, 348
   visits Charles at Yuste  353, 355
   tomb  357
Mary I of England (daughter of Henry VIII)  65, 96, 321, 324
Mary (sister of Henry VIII)  16, 29-30, 64
Matthys, Jan  208

Maurice of Saxony  182, 294, 297-299, 311-315, 318, 324
Maximilian I, Holy Roman Emperor  7, 10-13, 20, 22, 24, 27, 30, 39, 42-43, 55, 59-61, 92, 99, 194-195, 198, 275, 359
Maximilian (son of Ferdinand and later Holy Roman Emperor)  306-310, 330, 335, 358
Mechelen (Malines)  9, 11-12, 22-23, 37, 240
Medici family  94, 100, 103, 156-158, 193, 361, 362
   Alessandro  145, 149, 154, 166, 216-217, 224
   Cosimo  217, 228, 303
Medina del Campo  76, 255, 258, 349
Mediterranean Sea  2, 9, 46, 199, 209-211
Melanchthon, Philip  90, 185-186
Mendoza, Antonio de  269
Mercenary soldiers  99-100, 106, 108, 160
Metz  280, 312-313, 315-316, 318, 320, 324-325
Mexico  264, 268
Michelangelo  99, 161
Milan  42, 97-98, 101, 103, 105, 135, 141, 145, 221-222, 239, 275, 278, 283-284, 286, 304-305
Mirabello park (Pavia)  107-108
Mita system  271
Modon (Methoni)  199
Mohacs, battle of (1526)  133
Mojados  50
Moluccas (East Indies)  148, 255
Monaco  149
Montesinas, Antonio de  266
Montmorency, Anne de (Constable of France)  222, 226, 275, 315
More, Thomas  44
Moriscos  129, 342
Muhlberg, battle of (1547)  298, 312
Munster  208
Muslims in Spain  74, 128-130, 342

Naples  8, 42, 97, 100, 105, 141, 145, 156, 196, 215, 314
Navarre  39, 53, 82, 102, 274
New Laws (1542)  270-271
New World  8, 121, 256-257, 341
Nice  226, 282
Nicholas, Count of Salm  201
Ninety-five theses  84-86
Nobility
   Germany  180-182
   Low Countries  36-37, 43, 51
   Spain  47-48, 51, 74, 83, 119, 121

Novara, battle of (1513) 101
Noyon, Treaty of (1516) 42, 65, 101

Ommegang 306
Orange, Philibert, Prince of 136-138, 141-142, 146, 156, 163-165, 345, 360
Orley, Bernard van 21
Oropesa, Duke of 350
Ottoman Empire
  accession of sultans 170
  expansion 1, 198-199
  capture of Rhodes 104, 133
  in Hungary 133-134, 315
  structure of the Ottoman Empire 199-200
  siege of Vienna (1529) 201
  advance on Vienna (1532) 202-204
  limitations 204-205
  naval threat in the Mediterranean 209-212, 225, 245-249
  defeat at Tunis 212-215
  alliances with France 205, 211, 225, 275, 282-283
  gains in the Mediterranean in the 1550's 326

Pacheco, Maria 83
Padilla, Juan de 77, 82
Palazzo Comunale (d'Accursio) (Bologna) 150, 152, 154
Paris 236, 280
Parma 278
Papacy 98, 132, 145, 241, 301, 319
Papal States 97
Passau 315, 318, 324-325
Paul III (Pope) 153, 217, 222, 226, 241, 267, 278, 288-289, 298, 302, 362
Pavia, battle of (1525) 106-109, 337
Peasants' War 180-181
Pena, Orsolina de la 94
Peris, Vicenc 74-7
Peru 271
Philip the Good, Duke of Burgundy 21, 233
Philip the Handsome, Duke of Burgundy (Charles' father) 7, 10-19, 37, 359
Philip II (Charles' son)
  birth 130, 147
  relations with Charles 171, 207, 203
  bankruptcy in 1557 193
  advice from Charles 250-252, 302-304
  created Duke of Milan 274, 305
  in the Low Countries 306-307
  discussions re. the future of the dynasty 305-310

regent in Spain 277, 323, 341
  marriage to Mary of England 321, 324
Philip of Hesse 184, 186, 242, 291-292, 294-302, 311-312
Philibert II of Savoy 20-21
Pisseleu, Anne de, Duchess of Etampes 175, 304
Pizarro, Francisco 1, 94, 125, 147-148, 264
Political Testaments 171, 250, 303-304
Potosi (silver mine) 272
Pragmatic Sanction 306
Preveza, battle of (1538) 234
Prinsenhof Palace, Ghent 7, 9, 238
Printing 86, 183
Protestants 184-187, 203, 222, 240-244, 255, 289-292, 299, 301, 311-315, 336-337, 342-343
Provence 97, 105, 222, 224

Quijada, Don Luis Mendez de 351, 355
Quintus 264, 321

Raleigh, Walter 265
Real Consciencia 268
Real Servicio 268
Regensburg 203, 242-245, 293, 296
Rene of Chalon, Prince of Orange 280
Repartimiento de labor 271
Requerimento 267
Reutte 314
Rhodes 104, 133, 162, 201, 210-211
Richard III of Engfland 9, 12, 233
Rincon, Antonio 211, 275-276
Romania 199
Rome 85-86, 100, 160, 166
   sack of 1, 131, 137-139, 215
Rossem, Maartin 275
Rovere, Francesco Maria della, Duke of Urbino 137

St. Anna's church, Augsburg 196
St. Augustine 271
St Dizier 280
St Quentin, battle of 353
Safavid dynasty (Persia) 199
Salamanca 75, 121, 270
San Sebastian 235
Santa Domingo 269
Santander 46, 117

Santiago de Compostela 55
Sauvage, Jean de 33, 53, 57, 102
Savona 149
Savoy 98
Schmalkaldic League 187, 240, 290-293, 295, 301
Segovia 75
Senlis, Treaty of (1493) 10-11
Servicio 53, 119, 254
Seville 47, 56, 75-76, 125-127
Sforza family 20, 42, 100, 103, 132, 136-137, 176, 221, 255
Sicily 18, 215, 282, 326
Sickengen, Franz von 62
Siena 215
Simancas 83,
Slavery 266, 272
Soderini, Piero 157
Spain, revolt in 73-83
Spanish economy 253-258
Spanish Main 265
Speyer Diet of 1524: 183
    Diet of 1529: 184
    Diet of 1544: 245, 279
Stadholder 38, 342
States-General (of the Low Countries) 34, 36, 225, 232, 342
Stockholm bloodbath (1520) 175
Stroppendragers 239
Suleiman (the Magnificent) 2, 198-202, 210, 286, 362
Swabian League 181, 301
Swiss Guard 137-138
Syphilis 100, 181

Tavara, Juan 120, 147, 260
Taxation
  General 190-194, 197
  Germany 343
  Low Countries 36-37, 231-234, 342
  Spain 53-54, 119, 233-235, 252-253
Tetzel, Johann 85
Therouanne 35, 213, 225
Titian 1, 156, 299-300, 348, 351
Tlemcen (battle of) 209
Toledo 75, 83, 114, 148, 228-229, 250
Tordesillas 19, 47, 49, 78-81, 235, 327
  Treaty of (1494) 265
Torriano, Gianello 351

Toulon  282
Tournai  29, 35, 102, 115, 177, 213, 239
Trace Italienne  161
Transport in the 16th Century
   Land  68-69
   Sea  67-68
Trent, Council of  289, 292-293, 302, 312-313
Tunis  212-214, 221-222, 245
Turgut Reis  282-283, 326
Turin  221

Ulloa, Magdelena de  355
Ulm  296-297
Universal monarchy  63-64
Usery  191-192
Utrecht  35, 292

Valencia  52, 73-75, 114, 118, 129, 326, 342
Valladolid  51, 55, 80, 117-118, 121, 250, 323,
   disputation of 270-271
   San Pablo  52, 130, 349
   Colegio de San Gregorio  270
Valois (royal family of France)  1, 7, 205, 284
   family divisions  284-285
Vatican  138, 221, 290
Vaucelles, truce of (1556)  329
Velasco, Inigo Fernandez (Constable of Castile)  79, 82, 130
Venice  101, 132, 135, 194, 199, 234, 247
Verdun  314
Vermeyen, Jan Cornelisz  213
Viceroys  120, 269
Vienna  92, 201-204
Villach  314
Villalar, battle of (1521)  82
Villaviciosa  46
Vitoria, Francisco de  270
Vives, Juan Luis  257
Volterra  164-165

Waldeck, Franz von, Bishop of Munster  208, 291
Warfare in the 16th Century  109-111, 160-164, 205, 280-281
   naval warfare  245-247
Wied, Hermann von, Archbishop of Cologne  291
William of Cleves  182, 274-275, 278-279, 293
William of Croy  53

Winchester 15, 324
Windsor 15-16
  Treaty of (1522) 96, 103-104
Wittelsbach, Duke William of Bavaria 293
Wittenberg 84, 292, 298
Wolsey, Cardinal 64, 95-96
Worms, Diet of (1521) 31, 88-91, 94-95, 185
  Edict of Worms (1521) 91, 182-183, 187
  Diet (1545) 289

Xativa 75, 114

Yuste 320, 349-356
Ypres 10

Zapolya, John 133, 201, 204
Zaragoza 54
Zeeland (province) 34, 40
Zuniga, Don Juan de 130, 251, 262-263

Printed in Great Britain
by Amazon